Corporate Govern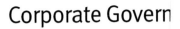

**KEY TEXT
REFERENCE**

Corporate Governance

Principles, Policies, and Practices

Bob Tricker

OXFORD
UNIVERSITY PRESS

Great Clarendon Street, Oxford OX2 6DP

Oxford University Press is a department of the University of Oxford.
It furthers the University's objective of excellence in research, scholarship,
and education by publishing worldwide in

Oxford New York

Auckland Cape Town Dar es Salaam Hong Kong Karachi
Kuala Lumpur Madrid Melbourne Mexico City Nairobi
New Delhi Shanghai Taipei Toronto

With offices in

Argentina Austria Brazil Chile Czech Republic France Greece
Guatemala Hungary Italy Japan Poland Portugal Singapore
South Korea Switzerland Thailand Turkey Ukraine Vietnam

Oxford is a registered trade mark of Oxford University Press
in the UK and in certain other countries

Published in the United States
by Oxford University Press Inc., New York

British Library Cataloguing in Publication Data

Data available

Library of Congress Cataloging in Publication Data

Data available

Typeset by Macmillan Publishing Solutions
Printed in Great Britain
by Ashford Colour Press Ltd,
Gosport, Hampshire

ISBN 978–0–19–955270–2

5 7 9 10 8 6 4

Dedicated to Sir Adrian Cadbury and to the directors and partners of:

Imperial Chemical Industries Ltd
Imperial Group Ltd
British National Oil Corporation
Deloitte Haskins and Sells
British Petroleum Co. Ltd
The Delta Group Ltd
Donald Macpherson Group Ltd
Ocean Transport and Trading Ltd
Reed International Ltd
John Swire and Sons Ltd

who supported the work of the Corporate Policy Group trust that led to the publication in 1984 of the first book to use the title *Corporate Governance*

Acknowledgements

....

I owe a considerable debt to the many who, over the years, have contributed to my knowledge and understanding of corporate governance. Gratitude is clearly owed to the directors of the ten organizations who supported my original research in the Corporate Policy Group at Nuffield College, Oxford, from 1979 to 1983, which led to the publication of *Corporate Governance* in 1984. Since then a long and fascinating road has led me to the present work.

Sir Adrian Cadbury has made a special contribution. His internationally influential report *The Financial Aspects of Corporate Governance* was published in 1992. Subsequently, he graciously commented that '*your 1984 book introduced me to the words* corporate governance'.

Colleagues who have been influential include Alan Au, Raymond Chan, Thomas Clarke, Lex Donaldson, Robert Gibson, Jim Gillies, Fred Hilmer, Simon Ho, Bill Judge, Gregg Li, Jay Lorsch, Chris Mallin, Bob Monks, Fred Neubauer, Bernard Taylor, Shann Turnbull, and many, many more. My students, directors of client companies, and contributors to *Corporate Governance: An International Review* both during my editorship and subsequently, have added much to my understanding. The anonymous reviewers for the Oxford University Press also made suggestions that have significantly improved the book. I am grateful to them all.

The helpful advice received from the CSRC in Beijing and Martin Wheatley of the Securities and Futures Commission in Hong Kong is acknowledged. Responsibility for the interpretation of their advice, however, is solely mine.

The opportunity to draw material from the websites of companies, regulators, and other institutions is also much appreciated.

Chapter 1 has been adapted from Bob Tricker's editor's introduction to the following collection of papers: *Corporate Governance*, seminal readings in the History of Management Thought series, R. I. Tricker (editor), Ashgate, Aldershot, UK, and Dartmouth, USA, 2000.

Figures (2.1–2.7 and 10.1) and Cases (Tyco, Drexell Burnham Lambert, HIH Insurance, Robert Maxwell, Independent Insurance, Enron) are based on material which first appeared in *The Economist Essential Director*, by Bob Tricker, Profile Books, 2003. Reproduced with kind permission.

Finally, thanks to my wife, Gretchen, not only, as so many authors say, for her support during the writing, but for her direct contribution. Being an editor and a writer herself, among other things she wrote the centennial history of the Hong Kong Stock Exchange, she has strived to make this script more readable.

Bob Tricker, Oxford, 2008

Contents

LIST OF CASE STUDIES   xiii

LIST OF BOXED ILLUSTRATIONS   XV

Introduction   1
    What the Book is About   1
    Who the Book is For   2
    The Basis of the Book   2
    Why the Book was Written: A Personal Note from the Author   2
    A Pedagogic Note   4

PART 1   Principles

1. Corporate Governance: A Subject Whose Time Has Come   7
    Corporate Governance As Old As Corporate Entities   8
    The Separation of Management from Ownership   9
    Significant Developments in the 1970s   10
    Developments in the 1980s   12
    Developments in the 1990s: In Practice and Conventional Wisdom   13
    Developments for Listed Companies in the 21st Century   15
    Developments for Other Corporate Entities in the 21st Century   17
    New Frontiers for Corporate Governance   17

2. Governance and Management   25
    The Significance of Constitutions for Corporate Entities   25
    The Distinction Between Governance and Management   35
    The Performance and Conformance Aspects of Governance   37
    Definitions of Corporate Governance   38
    The Scope of Corporate Governance   39
    Drivers of Good Corporate Governance   46

3. Directors and Board Architecture   50
    Different Types of 'Director' and Director Appointment   50
    The Appointment of Directors   55
    The Chairman and Chief Executive Roles   57
    Board Structures   61
    Board Committees   67

4. **Complex Corporate Structures**   **75**
    Ownership Patterns in Modern Companies   75
    The Governance of Complex Corporate Structures   76
    Cross-holdings of Shares: *Keiretsu* and *Chaebols*   90
    Block-holders and Universal Ownership   91
    Dual Listed Companies   92
    Dual Class Shares   94
    Listings on Alternative Stock Markets   94

5. **The Governance of Private Companies and Other Corporate Entities** **98**
    The Governance of Subsidiary and Associated Companies   98
    The Governance of Family Controlled Companies   101
    The Governance of Hedge Funds, Private Equity Firms,
    and Sovereign Wealth Funds   103
    The Governance of Joint Ventures   111
    The Governance of NGOs and Non-profit Corporate Entities   113
    The Governance of Partnerships and Limited Liability Partnerships   116

6. **Functions of the Board**   **120**
    The Functions of the Board   120
    Corporate Transparency   132
    The Delegation of Board Functions to Management   134
    Balancing the Board's Performance and Conformance Roles   139

PART 2   Policies

7. **Corporate Governance Codes**   **145**
    From Cadbury to the Combined Code: United Kingdom   146
    Codes in Other Countries   151
    The Sarbanes-Oxley Act: United States of America   155
    Principles or Prescription: The Governance Debate   158
    Codes from International Agencies   159
    Codes from Institutional Investors   161
    Company Codes   163
    Codes for the Public and Voluntary Sectors   165
    Codes for Individual Directors   166
    Compliance with Corporate Governance Codes   166
    Appendix: Corporate Governance Codes around the World   169

8. **Models of Corporate Governance**   **181**
    How Context and Culture Affect Corporate Governance   181
    The American Rule Based Model   183
    The United Kingdom/Commonwealth Principles Based Model   184
    The Continental European Two-tier Model   186
    The Japanese Business Network Model   187
    The Asian Family Based Model   189
    Corporate Governance in Mainland China   192
    Corporate Governance in Russia   200
    Corporate Governance in India   205
    Corporate Governance in the Middle East   207
    Corporate Governance: Convergence or Differentiation?   208
    Institutions Necessary for Successful Corporate Governance   210

9. **Theories and Philosophies of Corporate Governance**   **217**
    The Agency Dilemma   217
    Agency Theory   219
    Transaction Cost Economics   223
    Stewardship Theory   223
    Resource Dependency Theory   226
    Managerial and Class Hegemony   226
    Psychological and Organizational Perspectives   227
    The Societal Perspective: Stakeholder Philosophies   229
    Differing Boundaries and Levels: Systems Theory   231
    A Subject in Search of its Paradigm   233

PART 3 Practices

10. **The Reality of the Boardroom**   **241**
    How People, Power, and Politics Affect Practice   241
    Sources of Governance Power   242
    Games Directors Play and the Manipulation of Meetings   244
    Board Styles   250
    The Significance of the Chairman   255
    Implementing Corporate Governance Below Board Level   259

11. **Directors' Capabilities and Responsibilities**   **263**
    Desirable Attributes in a Director   263
    The Core Competencies a Director Needs   267

Roles Directors Play 268

The Legal Duties of a Director 272

Shareholder Rights Differ Between Jurisdictions 275

The US Sarbanes-Oxley Act 2002 276

UK Companies Act 2006 278

12. **Board Effectiveness** **282**

Managing Board Committees 282

Managing Meetings, Agenda, and Minutes 285

Board Information 288

The Role of Company Secretary 292

Director Induction, Training, and Development 294

Director Remuneration 296

Director and Officer Insurance 299

Appendix: Director's Induction Checklist 306

13. **Assessment of Directors, Boards, and Companies** **311**

Reviewing Individual Directors' Performance 311

Reviewing Board Performance 313

Corporate Governance Rating Systems for Companies 321

Corporate Governance Assessment Systems for Countries 325

14. **Corporate Risk Assessment** **328**

Responsibility for Risk Profiling, Risk Strategy, Risk Policy,
and Risk Supervision 328

Levels and Types of Risk 331

Risk Analysis 335

Risk Recognition and Assessment 337

Risk Evaluation 340

Risk Management Information Systems 342

Risk Transfer 343

15. **Corporate Social Responsibility and Sustainability** **349**

New Expectations in the Governance of Organizations 349

Corporate Social Responsibility: Strategies and Policies 351

Corporate Social Responsibility Reporting 358

Sustainability Reporting 363

Balancing Corporate Responsibilities 370

16. The Future of Corporate Governance   **374**

Some Remaining Questions   374

Driving Forces for Change   381

What Might the Future Look Like?   386

APPENDIX 1 ENRON   395

APPENDIX 2 NEW YORK STOCK EXCHANGE: CORPORATE GOVERNANCE RULES   398

APPENDIX 3 ANSWERS TO SELF-TEST QUESTIONS   410

INDEX   421

List of Case Studies

1.1	Robert Maxwell	16
2.1	Momcastle Museum Ltd	26
2.2	The American Red Cross	33
2.3	Network Rail	34
2.4	Great Western Railway Company	40
2.5	The Australian Stock Exchange (ASX)	41
2.6	Companies House: The UK Company Registration Service	43
2.7	The History of the US Securities and Exchange Commission	44
2.8	The Role of the Hong Kong Securities and Futures Commission	45
3.1	The International Finance Corporation (IFC)	51
3.2	Finance House Appoints Nominee Director	54
3.3	Cross-directorships in Saint-Gobain SA	56
3.4	The Removal of Directors: Trans-Tec	57
3.5	Marks and Spencer: Combining the Roles of Chairman and CEO	58
3.6	Vodafone	60
3.7	Board Architecture at Arcelor Mittal	63
3.8	Volkswagen's Supervisory Board	65
3.9	Vodafone/Mannesmann	66
3.10	The Collapse of Arthur Andersen	69
3.11	BP and the Retirement of the Chief Executive	71
4.1	The ARE Group: Governed for a Country/Customer Based Strategy	78
4.2	Incorporation in a Tax-haven: The Example of BVI	79
4.3	Union Carbide and the Bhopal Tragedy	80
4.4	Hutchison Whampoa Ltd (HWL)	81
4.5	General Electric (GE)	83
4.6	The Agnelli Family Chain of Companies	85
4.7	The Overseas Trust Bank	86
4.8	The Jardine Matheson Group	87
4.9	The Elders IXL Shareholding Network	89
4.10	Carnival Corporation and Plc: A Dual Listed Group	93
4.11	The Wallenberg Group	95

5.1	Singapore Airlines	100
5.2	Long Term Capital Management (LTCM)	104
5.3	The Man Group Plc	105
5.4	The Blackstone Group	108
5.5	Teletronic Riches Ltd	112
5.6	More on the Collapse of the Andersen Partnership	117
6.1	IBM's Failure to Appreciate Microsoft Strategy	125
6.2	South American Resources Ltd: Board Policy on Reserved Powers	127
6.3	Examples of Sub-optimization	130
7.1	Marconi	154
7.2	General Electric (GE)	157
7.3	The Hermes Principles	162
8.1	TYCO	185
8.2	Siemens AG	187
8.3	China Sinopec	199
8.4	Gazprom	202
8.5	Yukos	203
9.1	Drexel Burnham Lambert	235
10.1	Independent Insurance	251
10.2	Iceland	258
11.1	Lord Black	264
11.2	Sunbeam Corporation	269
11.3	ChinaUnicom and SOX	277
11.4	Waste Management	279
12.1	The Walt Disney Company	301
13.1	HIH Insurance	321
14.1	The Sage Group Plc: An Approach to Corporate Risk	329
14.2	The University of Sussex (US): Risk Profiling	341
14.3	Northern Rock	344
15.1	A Manufacturing Company's CSR Policy	353
15.2	Exxon Europe CSR Policy	356
15.3	HSBC Holdings Plc: Corporate Responsibility Report	358
15.4	Li & Fung Ltd	360
15.5	CLP Group: Social and Environmental Report	361
15.6	General Motors: CSR Key Performance Indicators	364
15.7	Swire Pacific's Sustainable Development Policy	366
16.1	The Governance of the University of Oxford	386

List of Boxed Illustrations

2.1	Example of the Contents of Articles of Association	29
2.2	Example of Contents of a Prospectus: British Energy Group Plc	30
2.3	*Corporate Governance: An International Review*	39
2.4	The Listing Rules of the Australian Stock Exchange	42
3.1	Shadow Directors Identified	53
3.2	Associate Directors	55
5.1	Sir David Walker's Voluntary Code for UK Private Equity Firms	109
5.2	New York Stock Exchange (NYSE)	116
6.1	Examples of Mission Statements	122
6.2	SWOT Analysis for a Long Established Realtor (Estate Agent)	123
6.3	A Multiple Measure Management Control System	129
6.4	Examples of the Interplay Between the Board and Top Management	134
6.5	Guidelines for a Board Strategy Seminar or Workshop	138
7.1	Corporate Governance Codes in the United Kingdom	146
10.1	A Few Thoughts on Boardroom Communication	250
11.1	Microsoft Corporate Mission and Values	266
11.2	Disclosure of Personal Interests	272
11.3	The Seven Principles of Public Life	273
11.4	Lord Caldecote's Advice to Executive Directors	275
12.1	Lord Caldecote on Building an Agenda	286
12.2	An Opinion on Drafting Agenda and Minutes	287
12.3	Sir Campbell Adamson's Experience of Board Briefing	290
12.4	Harvey Jones on the Role of the Company Secretary	293
12.5	Lord Denning on the Evolution of the Company Secretary's Role	294
12.6	Legal Costs Paid by D&O Insurance	300
13.1	Director and Self-assessment by Chairman of a UK Company	312
13.2	Director Development by Chairman of an NYSE Company	313
13.3	Highest and Lowest Corporate Governance Ratings in Developed Countries	326

14.1   Risk Management Manual: Contents Page   333
14.2   Risk Assessment in a Pharmaceutical Company   334

15.1   A Comment on CSR from the British Chancellor of the Exchequer
       (Who Later Became Britain's Prime Minister)   351
15.2   CSR Resisted in Exxon   357

16.1   Classical Phraseology of Corporate Governance   380

Introduction

- In which we see:
  - what the book is about
  - who the book is for
  - the basis of the book
  - why the book was written: a personal note from the author
  - a pedagogic note

What the Book is About

This book will enable readers to:

- Appreciate the nature, functions, and realities of boards of directors and other governing bodies
- Analyse board structures, systems, and procedures, including board committees, chairmen, and chief executives, board remuneration, board leadership, and board effectiveness
- Understand major aspects of corporate governance
  - corporate governance principles and codes of practice
  - board's performance roles: strategy formulation and policy making
  - board's conformance roles: executive supervision and accountability
  - board's responsibility for handling corporate risk
  - assessment of board and director performance
  - corporate governance rating systems
- Understand various theories of corporate governance
- Appreciate corporate governance processes around the world
  - adopt an international and comparative perspective on the subject
  - contrast corporate governance regimes around the world
  - understand the cultural aspects of different approaches to governance
- Recognize the issues that are influencing corporate governance and board thinking, including strategic risk management, corporate social responsibility, sustainability, and business ethics

Who the Book is For

The book will be useful for:

- Master's level students of corporate governance, strategy, and business policy
- Directors of companies
- Members of the governing bodies of other corporate entities
- Senior managers working with members of boards and governing bodies
- Auditors, lawyers, company secretaries, and corporate governance consultants advising boards and directors
- Academics teaching and researching corporate governance

The book recognizes that the subject of corporate governance is changing and expanding all the time. Consequently, readers are encouraged to explore developments through the many references to relevant websites. The book also combines detailed text and explanations with vignette case examples. A dedicated website reflects the latest developments.

The Basis of the Book

The book is based on material that the author has developed over the years for directors' courses at the Institutes of Directors in London and Sydney, the MBA programme at the Australian Graduate School of Management, executive MBA courses at Hong Kong University, Melbourne University, Hong Kong Baptist University, and corporate governance courses for Russian university teachers sponsored by the Canadian Government at the Schulich School of Business in Toronto. My thanks to the very many faculty and students who have contributed to the development of these ideas.

Some of the material has been adapted from previous publications with the approval of the copyright holders, including:

- *Corporate Governance: An International Review*, Blackwells, Oxford
- *Corporate Governance*, seminal readings in the History of Management Thought series, R. I. Tricker (editor), Ashgate, Aldershot, UK, and Dartmouth USA, 2000
- *The Economist Essential Director*, Profile Books, 2003
- *Governance*, InfoAustralia

Why the Book was Written: A Personal Note from the Author

My initial work in the field was sponsored by Deloittes, the international accountancy firm, in the 1970s. The aim of the project was to examine the growing use of audit committees in the United States and to explore the possibility of introducing them into British companies. Audit committees were standing sub-committees of the main board, made up mainly of outside independent directors, acting as a bridge between external audit firm and board. Unfortunately, it quickly became clear that the concept of the audit committee would not work in British listed companies, because there were not enough independent directors to staff them. Worse, whilst the concept of non-executive directors was understood, the notion of director independence was not. Power on British boards at that time was the prerogative of executive directors. The conventional wisdom in the UK was that non-executives could be useful in board deliberations; about a third of the board was probably a good balance, but never as many as half. The notion that non-executive directors should be independent of the company was not part of the conventional wisdom. The resultant book explained that audit committees without independent directors would be ineffective and was entitled *The Independent Director.*[1]

My interest in boards and their behaviour was really kindled, however, in the 1970s, when I was head of the Oxford Centre for Management Studies, subsequently to become Templeton College, Oxford. The Management Centre was incorporated as a company limited by guarantee and its large board comprised Heads of Oxford colleges and leaders of major British companies, in equal numbers. At one stage the Council outnumbered the academic staff. Their divisive cliques, political power plays, and unpredictable interpersonal relations astounded me. This was not the behaviour of the classical organization theories, analytical decision making, and basic management concepts that we were teaching in the Management Centre.

It occurred to me that governance was different from management. Throughout the 20th century the focus had been on management. But where was the board on the management organization chart? Clearly the governance of corporate entities and the processes of their governing bodies was a subject that deserved study. The subsequent opportunity to research at Nuffield College, Oxford, then led to a paper, 'Perspectives on Corporate Governance: Intellectual Influences in the Exercise of Corporate Governance' that was published in 1983 in a collection of essays.[2]

Nearly 25 years later, that paper's first sentence, which linked John Maynard Keynes, John Stuart Mill, and Karl Marx, seems unbearably pretentious. But the paper did manage to introduce the subject and the phrase 'corporate governance'. It identified some issues that remain pertinent to this day: the structure of boards, the role of non-executive directors, the governance of complex groups, the board's supervision of management, accountability, corporate regulation, and corporate social responsibility. In those days board level participation by employees was also an important topic.

The ideas in my paper in the Earl collection were developed in the book *Corporate Governance*, published in 1984.[3] I remember agonizing over the term 'corporate governance' in the title. Though 'governance' was an ancient concept, *corporate* governance was not then in use. Indeed, I had named the trust that funded my research at Nuffield College the Corporate *Policy* Group, not the Corporate *Governance* Group.

---

[1]Tricker, R. I. (1978) *The Independent Director.* London: Tolley.

[2]Earl, M. (ed.) (1983) *Perspectives on Management: A Multidisciplinary Analysis.* Oxford: Oxford University Press.

[3]Tricker, R. I. (1984) *Corporate Governance: Practices, Procedures and Powers in British Companies and their Boards of Directors.* Aldershot, UK: Gower Publishing.

Subsequently, of course, the subject has come centre stage. Indeed, it may well be that the social historian sees the 21st century as the era of corporate governance, just as the 20th had been that of management.

A Pedagogic Note

This book has been derived from material produced over the years for courses involving post-experience master's degree students and corporate governance practitioners (company directors, company secretaries, auditors, corporate lawyers, and so on). The sequence of the chapters—from diverse group ownership, through alternative board structures and processes, then corporate governance codes, before covering theories of corporate governance—responds to their experiences and expectations. Some teachers, particularly those working with students without a lot of business experience, might prefer to build their courses from theory to practice. This is quite feasible, not least since to date the theories of corporate governance, other than a broad concept of agency, have not contributed significantly to its development. The underlying paradigms have been derived from company law and the codes of good practice have emerged as responses to corporate catastrophe and collapse.

To assist the learning process each chapter has a set of self-test questions and answers, which enable readers to see what knowledge they have gained. For teachers wanting exercises that develop a critical analytical perspective, most of the boxed cases offer questions for discussion, and there are some possible projects suggested at the end of each chapter. More information, case studies, and supportive material can be found on the supporting website.

Part 1

Principles

1 Corporate Governance: A Subject Whose Time Has Come

....

- In which we see how corporate governance has evolved:
  - corporate governance as old as corporate entities
  - the separation of management from ownership
  - significant developments in the 1970s
  - developments in the 1980s
  - developments in the 1990s: in practice and conventional wisdom
  - developments for listed companies in the 21st century
  - developments for other corporate entities in the 21st century
  - new frontiers for corporate governance

Corporate governance has been practised for as long as there have been corporate entities. Yet the study of the subject is less than half a century old. Indeed, the phrase '*corporate governance*' was scarcely used until the 1980s.

The 20th century saw massive growth in serious management thought. Organization theories took great strides, but the board did not appear on the organization chart. Strategic management acquired new significance, although the contribution of the board seldom received a mention. Important theories and practices were developed for the management of finance, marketing, and operations, but little concern was shown for the role of the directors.

Yet the board of directors of a company, indeed the governing body of every corporate entity, is ultimately responsible for that organization's decisions and its performance. It is the board that is accountable to the owners, members, and other legitimate stakeholders. The directors should be providing direction and supervising the work of executive management.

Corporate governance is about the exercise of power over corporate entities. It has become one of the central issues in the running and the regulating of modern enterprise today. However, the underlying ideas and concepts of corporate governance have been surprisingly slow to evolve. The underpinning frameworks still owe more to mid-19th century thinking than they do to the realities of complex modern business.

The 19th century saw the foundations laid for modern corporations: this was the century of the entrepreneur. The 20th century was the century of management: the phenomenal growth of management theories, management consultants, management gurus and management teaching, which all reflected a preoccupation with management. Now the 21st century promises to be the century of governance—as the focus swings to the legitimacy and the effectiveness of the wielding of power over corporate entities worldwide.

In this chapter we review the corporate concept, trace the evolution of the idea, and see how often changes have been responses to critical situations not theoretical concepts.

Corporate Governance As Old As Corporate Entities

Although the theoretical exploration of the subject is relatively new, the practice of corporate governance is ancient. Governance issues arise whenever a corporate entity acquires a life of its own, and the ownership of an enterprise is separated from its management. The Merchant of Venice, in Shakespeare's play (Act 1 Scene 1), feared for the safety of his argosies sailing out of sight on the high seas. How were the owners' interests to be protected; how was oversight to be exercised over those delegated the task of running the venture? Who set the direction of the enterprise and ensured accountability?

The great trading companies of the British and Dutch empires of the 18th century, established with the patronage of the monarchs, operated under rules set by the state. How was power over the enterprise exercised and legitimized? To whom was a company accountable and, ultimately, responsible? Such questions will always be crucial when rights and duties attached to investment and ownership cannot be applied directly. Corporate governance is about the exercise of such power.

A much quoted comment by Adam Smith shows that he understood the issue of corporate governance, even though he did not know the phrase: '*The directors of companies, being managers of other people's money than their own, it cannot well be expected that they should watch over it with the same anxious vigilance with which the partners in a private copartnery frequently watch over their own*' (Smith 1776).

At the start of the 19th century there were basically three ways to engage in business (other than through corporations created by the crown or state): as a sole trader, in a partnership, or as an unincorporated body in which some were managing partners running the firm and others sleeping partners just providing finance. In each case, if the business became insolvent, the creditors could pursue their debts with any and all of those involved until ultimately they became bankrupt and were sent to debtors' prison, while their families went to the workhouse. This was quite a disincentive to investment by those not directly involved in management activities. By the end of the century the situation had changed totally.

The classical concept of the company stems from legislation developed in the mid-19th century. It has proved to be one of the finest systems man has ever designed. The key concept was the incorporation of a legal entity, separate from the owners, which nevertheless had many of the legal property rights of a real person—to contract, to sue and be sued, to own property, and to employ. The company had a life of its own, giving continuity beyond the life of its founders, who could transfer their shares in the company. Crucially, the owners' liability for the company's debts was limited to their equity investment. Yet ownership remained the basis of power. Shareholders elected their directors, who reported to them. Company law was the original underpinning of corporate governance.

The notion was elegantly simple and superbly successful, enabling the subsequent creation of untold industrial growth, employment, and wealth around the world. Superb—but unfortunately the mid-19th century model now bears about as much relationship to reality as a hang-glider to a jumbo-jet. But the original corporate concept remains the essential basis of contemporary company law.

Initially, all joint stock, limited liability companies were public companies. Their *raison d'être* was to raise capital from the public, whose liability for the corporate debts was limited. By the early 20th century business people saw that the model could be used to give limited liability to family firms and other private businesses, even though they did not need access to capital from outside investors. Such private companies, incorporated in jurisdictions around the world, now far outnumber public companies, which are able under company law to offer their shares to the public.

By company law we mean that body of statutes and supporting rules and regulations, and in the common law countries case law, that regulates corporate activities. Company law varies by jursidiction, providing one of the factors that differentiates governance around the world. As we shall see the law provides a fundamental underpinning to the subject.

However, commenting in 1972 on British company law, Hadden wrote: '*company law is not unworkable. But it is tied to a conception of capitalism which has been discarded by all but the most ardent free-market economists. It has also ceased to reflect the realities of the commercial and industrial world.*'

Since then company law in Britain and many other countries has developed significantly, as we shall see.

The Separation of Management from Ownership

The early years of the 20th century saw another significant development. In the United States, the United Kingdom, and other economically advancing countries, shares in many public companies were now listed on stock exchanges. Shareholders had become more numerous and were geographically spread. Their links with management in their companies had become remote.

Using data from companies in the United States, Berle and Means (1932) drew attention to the growing separation of power between the executive management of major public companies and their increasingly diverse and remote shareholders. They realized the significance of corporate power. They observed that:

The rise of the modern corporation has brought a concentration of economic power which can compete on equal terms with the modern state—economic power versus political power, each strong in its own field. The state seeks in some aspects to regulate the corporation, while the corporation, steadily becoming more powerful, makes every effort to avoid such regulation . . . The future may see the economic organism, now typified by the corporation, not only on an equal plane with the state, but possibly even superseding it as the dominant form of social organization. ([1932] 1967)

This was the first seminal work of corporate governance (though that was not a phrase Berle and Means used), and is one of the most frequently cited works in corporate governance writing today. The recognition of issues raised by this work was instrumental in the creation of the US Securities and Exchange Commission. Berle and Means left a vital intellectual inheritance for the subject. It is surprising that it was so long before it was taken up.

For the next forty years, the work of directors and boards remained the province of jurisprudence, enlivened by anecdote and exhortation. In 1971 a pioneering work by Mace, based on research in US companies, sought to discover what directors really did and in the process challenged the conventional wisdom:

In most companies boards of directors serve as a source of advice and counsel, serve as some sort of discipline, and act in crisis situations if the president dies suddenly or is asked to resign because of unsatisfactory management performance.

The business literature describing the classical functions of boards of directors typically includes three important roles: (1) establishing basic objectives, corporate strategies, and board policies: (2) asking discerning questions; and (3) selecting the president.

[Instead] I found that boards of directors of most large and medium-sized companies do not establish objectives, strategies, and policies however defined. These roles are performed by company management. Presidents and outside directors generally agreed that only management can and should have these responsibilities.

A second classical role assigned to boards of directors is that of asking discerning questions—inside and outside the board meetings. Again it was found that directors do not, in fact, do this. Board meetings are not regarded as proper forums for discussions arising out of questions asked by board members.

A third classical role usually regarded as a responsibility of the board of directors is the selection of the president. Yet it was found that in most companies directors do not in fact select the president, except in . . . crisis situations . . . (Mace 1971)

Significant Developments in the 1970s

Three significant developments occurred in corporate governance thinking in the 1970s. In the United States the significance of independent outside directors was recognized and audit committees were introduced. In Europe two-tier boards were promoted, and on both sides of the Atlantic debates arose around board duties towards other stakeholders.

An increasingly litigious climate in the United States, with shareholders of failed companies seeking recompense from directors, boards and, in particular, auditors (whose indemnity insurance was seen to provide a 'deep pocket' to be emptied for their benefit) led to more emphasis on checks and balances at board level. In 1972 Pfeffer drew attention to the importance of the link between organization, environment, and board power. Auerbach (1973) wrote of the audit committee as a new corporate institution. Mautz and Neumann (1970, 1977) discussed audit committees of the board. The Securities and Exchange Commission (1972) called for standing audit committees composed of outside directors. Moreover, outside directors were to be independent—with no relationship with the company, other than the directorship and, perhaps, an inconsequential shareholding that could affect the exercise of independent and objective judgement. Such emphasis led to commentators such as Estes (1973) suggesting that outside directors were more vulnerable than ever. In the UK, Tricker (1978) undertook a study of British board structures, membership, and processes, intending to advocate audit committees in the UK but concluding that, first, there had to be independent directors on the boards of British companies. Sir Brandon Rhys-Williams, a British Member of Parliament, also called for non-executive directors and audit committees in the UK, a proposal that led to a green paper 'The Conduct of Company Directors' (1977) and a parliamentary bill calling for audit committees, which ultimately failed.

The European Economic Commission issued a series of draft directives on company law harmonization throughout the member states. The EEC draft fifth directive (1972) proposed that unitary boards, in which both executive and outside directors were responsible for seeing that the business was being well run and run in the right direction, be replaced by the two-tier board form of governance practised in Germany and Holland. In this form of governance, companies have two distinct boards, with no common membership. The upper, supervisory board monitors and oversees the work of the executive or management board which runs the business. The supervisory board has the power to hire and fire the members of the executive board.

The idea of the two-tier board was not well received in Britain, partly because it would replace what was seen, at least by directors, as a viable system of governance, but also because, in addition to the separation of powers, the directive included co-determination ideas then practised in Germany, in which the company was seen as a partnership between capital and labour with the supervisory board made up of equal numbers of shareholder and employee representatives. The UK's response was the report of the Committee chaired by Lord Bullock. *The Report of the Committee of Inquiry on Industrial Democracy* (1977) and the research papers (1976) associated with it, reflected the first serious corporate governance study in Britain. The Committee's proposal, for a continuation of the unitary board, but with worker representative directors, was not well received in Britain's boardrooms either.

Meanwhile, a number of corporate governance problems featured in the reports of inspectors appointed by the UK government Department of Trade. Pergamon Press (1971) in which the inspectors concluded that Robert Maxwell should not again run a public company (advice that was ignored, enabling him to build a media empire which collapsed dramatically twenty years later), Rolls Royce (1973), London and County Securities (1976), Lonrho Ltd (1976) and others all added to the interest in the governance of companies.

The 1970s also saw a questioning of the role of the major corporation in society. Broadly, the argument was made that public companies have responsibilities beyond their legal prime duty to their shareholders. Given the scale and significance of such companies, boards should report to and, some argued, be accountable to a range of stakeholders who could be affected by board decisions—customers, suppliers and others in the added-value chain, employees, the local community, and the state. In the United States there was an important dialogue between the American Bar Association, looking for an alternative basis of power over companies, and the Corporate Roundtable representing directors' conviction of the value of the existing model. Consumer advocate Ralph Nader offered a specification for a model corporation rooted in stakeholder thinking. Jensen and

Meckling (1976), whose work was subsequently to become key in the development of agency theory, asked whether the concept of the company could survive.

The debate was picked up in the United Kingdom. A committee of the Confederation of British Industries, chaired by Lord Watkinson (1973), reported on the wider responsibilities of the British public company. A report by Fogarty (1975) discussed companies' responsibilities and stakeholder participation. The Accounting Standards Steering Committee produced *The Corporate Report* (1975), a seminal paper which called for all economic entities to report publicly and accept accountability to all those whose interests were affected by the directors' decisions. The political implications of these proposals for the widening of accountability and control over companies, and the related erosion of managerial power, soon consigned this report to the top shelf.

Developments in the 1980s

In the 1980s broader stakeholder concerns became overshadowed by the market-driven, growth-orientated attitudes of Reaganite and Thatcher economics. Directors' responsibility to increase shareholder-value was reinforced. The profit performance model became the basis for the privatization of state run entities—rail, coal, electricity, gas, water enterprises were all privatized in the UK and, gradually, around the world. The threat of predators (the so-called market for control) was presented in Anglo-American circles as an essential incentive for strong board level performance. Hostile bids, at this time, were often financed through newly available high risk, high rate 'junk' bonds.

By the late 1980s the down-side of such thinking was becoming apparent. In the United States, the names of Ivan Boesky, Michael Levine, and Michael Milken were to go down in the annals of corporate governance through the massive junk bond financed, insider-dealing deals through Drexel Burnham Lambert. In Australia, the names of Alan Bond, Laurie Connell of Rothwells, and the Girvan Corporation were being associated with questionable governance practices. In Japan, Nomura Securities and The Recruit Corporation were accused of dubious corporate governance. In the UK, it was the Guinness case and, subsequently, the collapse of Robert Maxwell's companies. Boards dominated by powerful executive directors were seen to need checks and balances, particularly where the posts of chief executive and chairman of the board were combined and the outside directors were weak.

Now the concepts of corporate governance were at last about to become the focus of attention. Indeed the phrase itself was about to appear.

'Governance' is actually an ancient word, used since the time of Chaucer (he spelt it in two different ways—'*To han the* gouernance *of hous and lond.*' '*In him is bountee, wisdom,* governaunce'). But the phrase 'corporate governance' was new. In 1983 it appeared as the title of a paper in *Perspectives on Management*, Earl (1983) and in 1984 as the title of a report of the American Law Institute on the *Principles of Corporate Governance* and also as the title of a book *Corporate Governance: Practices, Procedures and Powers in British Companies and their Boards of Directors*.

In the mid-80s research into corporate governance expanded, for example Baysinger and Butler (1985), using the phrase 'corporate governance', looked at the effects on corporate performance of changes in board composition and Mintzberg (1984) posed the question '*who should control the corporation?*' But the subject came centre stage, less as the result of academic, research based deliberations, more as a result of official inquiries set up in response to the corporate collapses, perceived board level excesses and apparently dominant chief executives of the later part of the 1980s.

Developments in the 1990s: In Practice and Conventional Wisdom

In the 1990s, led by developments in the United States, boards and their directors were coming under pressure from various sources—not least, institutional investors, investigative media, and the threat of litigation.

Major institutional investors rediscovered investor power and became pro-active in corporate governance. Drucker (1991) was one of the first to draw attention to the potential governance power in shareholders' proxy votes. Companies needed to influence their share price and to tap the ever-increasing pension funding and savings around the world. Expectations of institutional investors for performance improvement grew, along with pressure to end corporate governance practices that benefited incumbent boards and reduced the probability of the company being subjected to hostile bid. In the United States, the directors of American Express, General Motors, and IBM all had cause to regret the power of institutional fund managers to vote their shares against incumbent members of boards they considered to be performing badly.

The first report on corporate governance was on the financial aspects of corporate governance in the UK, produced by a committee chaired by Sir Adrian Cadbury (1992) set up in response to various company collapses. The report's proposals and its code of best practice emphasized the importance of independent non-executive directors, with independence defined as '*independent of management and free from any business or other relationship which could materially interfere with the exercise of independent judgement, apart from their fees and share-holding*'. Audit committees were advocated. Some critics of the report argued that the report went too far—the emphasis on the importance of non-executive directors would introduce the controls of the European two-tier supervisory board by the back door, they said. Others felt that the report did not go far enough—it lacked teeth by proposing de-listing rather than legally enforceable sanctions. Subsequently seven more reports on aspects of corporate governance have been produced in Britain, together with a combined corporate governance code. In chapter 7 we will explore Cadbury and the other reports in detail.

The Cadbury Report became significant in influencing thinking around the world. Other countries followed with their own reports on corporate governance. These included the Viénot Report (1995) from France, the King Report (1995) from South Africa, the Toronto Stock Exchange recommendations on Canadian Board practices (1995), the Netherlands Report (1997), and a report on corporate governance from the Hong Kong Society of Accountants (1996). As with the Cadbury Committee Report (1992), these reports were particularly concerned about the potential for abuse of corporate power. Similarly they called for greater conformance and compliance at board level, recommending the use of audit committees as a bridge between board and external auditor, the wider use of independent outside, non-executive directors, and the separation of the role of chairman of the board from chief executive. More checks and balances to avoid executive domination of decision making and protect the rights of shareholders, particularly minority shareholders, was the theme.

An Australian Committee on corporate governance (1993), chaired by Professor Fred Hilmer of the Australian Graduate School of Management, however, advanced a view that added a new dimension to the conformance and compliance emphasis of the Cadbury and the other reports. Governance is about performance as well as conformance, the report argued: '*the board's key role is to ensure that corporate management is continuously and effectively striving for above-average performance, taking account of risk*'. Adding, almost as an afterthought '*this is not to deny the board's additional role with respect to shareholder protection*'.

They gave their report the splendid title *Strictly Boardroom*—after the film *Strictly Ballroom*, which portrays the world of competitive ballroom dancing, in which originality, creativity and innovation had been sacrificed to inflexible and inhibiting rules and regulations. This is the danger facing current governance practices, argued Hilmer, with conformance and compliance overshadowing improved corporate performance.

An issue that generated many corporate governance debates in the 1990s was director remuneration. In the US institutional investors took a stand against allegedly excess directors' rewards. In the UK a group of City of London institutions commissioned Sir Richard Greenbury to look into directors' remuneration. His report, Greenbury (1995), recommended full disclosure, a code of best practice and, particularly, the use of remuneration committees composed of independent outside directors to advise on director remuneration issues.

In 1998 the OECD (the Organisation for Economic Co-operation and Development) proposed the development of global guidelines on corporate governance. The report, usefully, emphasized the contrast between the strong external investment and firm corporate governance practices in America and Britain and those in Japan, France, and Germany, which had less demanding governance requirements. In these countries other constituencies, such as employees, receive more deference, the regulatory structures are less obtrusive, directors are seldom truly independent, and investors seem prepared to take a longer term view. The report encouraged states to introduce corporate governance guidelines along these lines. Some dismissed the proposals as '*pointless*'; others saw merit in establishing some core principles of good corporate governance. Then the Commonwealth countries also produced a code of principles of good corporate governance, which makes recommendations on good corporate governance practice at the level of the company.

In the US organizations, such as Institutional Shareholder Services and the Investor Responsibility Research Centre, emerged to inform institutional fund managers on governance issues. In the UK the Association of British Insurers and the National Association of Pension Funds actively advised their members on proxy voting issues. In Australia it was the Australian Investment Managers' Association. The Californian State Employees pension fund (CalPers) was particularly active, producing Global Principles for Corporate Governance, intended to benchmark corporate governance practices in companies in their portfolio around the world. Other organizations published corporate governance codes. In response some companies, such as General Motors (1996) published their own board governance guidelines on significant governance issues.

However, probably the most telling driver of change in corporate governance in the 1990s was the dynamic, flexible new corporate structures, often global, that were now replacing the stable, often regional, corporate groups of the post-war years—massively complex networks of subsidiary companies and strategic alliances with cross-holdings of shares, cross-directorships, chains of leveraged (and often public) funding, dynamic and ever changing operational and financial linkages throughout the added-value chain. Networks that operated in multiple jurisdictions, cultures, and currencies; groupings with voracious appetites for growth. Top management of major corporations around the world was now wielding enormous power. Whilst claiming to reflect owners' interests, directors were seen to be pursuing their own agendas and expecting huge rewards—privileges reserved in earlier generations for kings and courtiers.

Developments for Listed Companies in the 21st Century

As the 21st century dawned corporate governance seemed to be developing well around the world. Codes of principles or best practice in corporate governance for listed companies, those with shares quoted on a stock market, were in place in most countries. The importance of good corporate governance was well recognized. As we will see later, many of the corporate governance codes called for director appraisal, training, and development and for board level performance reviews. Many felt that markets were offering a premium for shares in well-governed companies. This was particularly the case in the United States. Indeed, there was a widespread expectation in the States that the rest of the world would gradually converge with the American approach to corporate governance and US generally accepted accounting principles (GAAP), not least because the world, it was felt, needed access to American funds.

But the new century had scarcely begun when disaster struck. Enron, one of the largest companies in America, collapsed on the back of heavy, unreported indebtedness and dubious corporate governance attitudes among the executive directors. Governance problems appeared in companies in other parts of the world—Enron,[1] Waste Management, Worldcom, and Tyco in the United States, Marconi, British Rail, Independent Insurance, and Tomkins in the UK, HIH Insurance in Australia, Parmalat in Italy, and Vodaphone Mannesmann in Germany, for example. Arthur Andersen, one of the big five global accounting firms, who were the auditors of Enron, Worldcom, and Waste Management, collapsed as clients changed auditors and partners changed firms.

American accounting standards (GAAP) were now pilloried as being based on rules that could be manipulated, rather than on the principles of overall fairness required in international accounting standards. The financial transparency, the governance processes and, most significantly, the corporate governance attitudes in other companies were questioned. Confidence in the financial markets was shaken. Suddenly, from being the leaders of economic success, entrepreneurial risk-taking, and sound corporate governance, directors were depicted as greedy, short-sighted and more interested in their personal share options than creating sustainable wealth for the benefit of the shareholders.

[1] See Appendix 1.

The response in the United States was more legislation. As we will explore in detail later, the Sarbanes-Oxley Act, which was rushed through in 2002, placed new stringent demands for the governance of all companies listed in the United States. This act, now nicknamed 'SOX' or 'Sarbox', significantly raised the requirements and the costs of corporate governance. The New York Stock Exchange and Nasdaq changed their listing rules. Only

---

Case Study 1.1 Robert Maxwell

Robert Maxwell was born in Slovakia in 1923, grew up in poverty, fought with the Free Czech army and received the British Military Cross. He became an international publishing baron. In the early 1970s, inspectors appointed by the UK government led an inquiry into his company Pergamon Press and concluded that he was not *'a person who can be relied on to exercise stewardship of a publicly-quoted company'*. Nevertheless, he subsequently succeeded in building a media empire including two public companies—Maxwell Communication Corporation and Mirror Group Newspapers. Following his death in 1991, in mysterious circumstances at sea, it was alleged that he had used his dominant position as chairman of the trustees of the group's pension funds to siphon off funds to support his other interests and that he had been involved in an illegal scheme to bolster the price of companies in the group. Eventually, the lead companies were declared insolvent and the group collapsed. Investigators estimated that £763 million had been plundered from the two public companies and their pension funds to prop up Maxwell's private interests.

There are many lessons for directors in the Maxwell affair. Maxwell's leadership style was dominant: he reserved considerable power for himself and kept his top executives in the dark. An impressive set of non-executive directors, who added respectability to the public company boards, were ill informed. Maxwell threatened litigation to prevent criticism of his corporate affairs: many investigative journalists and one doctoral student received writs. The complexity of the group's organizational network, which included private companies incorporated in tax havens with limited disclosure requirements, made it difficult to obtain a comprehensive overview of group affairs. The auditors were criticized. In a revealing internal memo (discovered by Avinash D Persaud and John Plender: *'All you need to know about ethics and finance'*, 2006) the senior partner of CoopersLybrandDeloittes wrote: *'The first requirement is to continue to be at the beck and call of Robert Maxwell, his sons and his staff, appear when wanted and provide whatever is required.'* The failings of the auditors, the trustees of the Maxwell group pension fund, and the regulatory bodies were all recognized.

Discussion Questions

1. Research for information on Robert Maxwell (for a start try googling his name).

2. Born in extreme poverty in the Carpathian mountains in Czechoslovakia, Jan Ludvik Hoch—as he was then—succeeded in twice building a publishing empire that spanned the world, despite two corporate failures which led to government inquiries. What accounts for his enormous success and subsequent failure?

independent directors could now serve on audit and remuneration committees, share-holders must approve plans for directors' stock options, subsidized loans to directors were forbidden. A new institution was created to oversee audit firms, which must rotate their audit partners, to prevent an over familiarity between auditor and the client's finance staff. Auditors were also forbidden to sell some non-audit services to audit clients, and audit staff must serve a cooling off period before joining the staff of an audit client—all of which had happened in Enron (see Appendix 1).

Developments for Other Corporate Entities in the 21st Century

Although up to the end of the 20th century the main emphasis had been on the governance of listed companies, a parallel development occurred during the 1990s, accelerating into the 2000s: the concepts and principles of corporate governance developed for listed companies were also seen to be relevant to private companies that were not listed and to many other corporate entities.

Corporate governance policies and procedures were developed for charities, educational, sports, and medical bodies, professional institutions, government corporations, and QUANGOs (Quasi-Autonomous Non-Governmental Organizations). In some cases corporate governance codes and best governance practices were published. As this book unfolds the relevance of corporate governance principles and practice to all corporate entities, in which there is a separation between members or owners and executive management, will become apparent.

New Frontiers for Corporate Governance

Today corporate governance is changing rapidly on many fronts. We will be exploring these new frontiers throughout this book, but for now let us consider some of the more significant.

Society's Changing Expectations of Directors and Boards

Once upon a time a directorship was a sinecure—an occasional meeting between friends, maybe a few supportive questions, then a fee and probably lunch. Not now. Today more is expected of company directors, indeed of the members of all governing bodies, than ever before. The work of governing corporate entities has become demanding, often difficult, and open to challenge. Nevertheless, the work and responsibility is often crucial and can be rewarding, both financially and personally.

In listed companies, shareholders are no longer compliant. They expect their directors to increase shareholder value, but not at the price of accounting distortions and misleading financial disclosure. Institutional investors in these companies—the insurance companies, pension funds, and financial institutions—put pressure on poorly performing boards, complain publicly about allegedly excessive directors' remuneration, and demand high standards of corporate governance. The requirements on listed companies and their directors, from financial regulators, stock exchanges, and an increasingly investigative media around the world have also increased. The threat of litigation against companies, boards, and individual directors has introduced the risk of serious financial exposure as well as the potential for public derision.

But directors of private companies, that is those without public investors, including entrepreneurial businesses, subsidiary companies, joint venture entities, and family firms, cannot escape the corporate governance spotlight. The interests of minority shareholders must be protected. In certain circumstances directors can find themselves personally responsible for their company's debts. They can also be fined heavily if the company fails to meet its statutory obligations. Moreover, like their public company counterparts, shareholders in private companies now expect their directors to set high standards of governance and deliver improving corporate performance.

Members of the governing bodies of not-for-profit institutions, such as hospital trusts, arts and sports organizations, professional bodies, cooperatives, and colleges also face demands for good governance. Whether their governing body is called a committee, council, senate, or whatever, its members are required to act professionally and their activities are increasingly expected to be transparent.

Changes in Ownership Patterns

In the early days of the corporate concept the shareholding owners of the company were just one removed from the board of directors they elected to run their company. This can still be the case in small and start-up companies. But otherwise the situation has become strikingly different. Between the investors and the company in which they are ultimately investing can be a long chain of intermediaries acting as agents. For example, an individual might invest in a pension fund, which invests in a highly geared hedge fund, which invests in an index tracking fund, which invests in the shares on a given stock market index. Moreover, shares in the chain could be lent to cover other transactions of the financial institution involved. Consequently, it can be difficult for the ultimate owner to exercise any influence over the governance of the company in which his funds have been invested, which was the original intention of the corporate concept.

Further, the recent growth of private equity deals in which financial institutions take listed companies private, often with highly leveraged financial positions has added to issues of corporate governance, particularly accountability and transparency.

Growing Corporate Complexity

As we will see in chapter 4, in the early day's companies stood alone. If they merged a new company was formed and the original companies were wound up. Then it was realized that one company could own another company and by the 1970s vast pyramids of group companies had been formed. This created a number of corporate governance issues, as we shall see. But more significantly, in some jurisdictions such as Italy and Hong Kong, chains of listed companies were formed enabling the head of the chain to control vast corporate resources, with a relatively small investment, using the leverage of other shareholders' funds in the chain.

Further complexity arose from companies linking through joint ventures, from take-overs, as well as attempts to protect specific activities from liability, which produced complicated networks of cross-holdings. Now the corporate governance implications had become complex. Some companies had dual-listings in different corporate governance regimes. Others had different classes of shares with unequal voting rights. A few even attempted cross-holdings that enabled them to own themselves. The governance of part-nerships and, newly-created, limited liability partnerships added to the corporate govern-ance complexity. No longer did the simple 19th century concept of the joint stock limited liability company mirror reality.

Business Continuity and Enterprise Risk Management are Board Responsibilities

Running a business, indeed running any enterprise, involves risk. Risk can only be avoided by choosing to do nothing; and even then unexpected events can occur. In many business situations the greater the risk, the greater the potential return to the enterprise. The chal-lenge to boards is to balance risk with acceptable reward. In other words to understand the exposure of their company to risk, to determine how those risks are faced, and to ensure that they are handled appropriately. Corporate governance involves creating business value whilst managing risk.

Some corporate governance codes and companies' law now call for boards to give assur-ances, in their regular corporate governance reports to shareholders, that systems are in place to handle corporate risk. The 1999 Turnbull Report added this responsibility in the UK, which is now enshrined in the UK combined code. The Sarbanes-Oxley (SOX) Act in the United States made similar demands. The Basel II agreement on risk management in the financial world also calls for professional risk assessment.

Directors need to understand where value is added within their business, at which points the company is critically exposed to risk, and what policies are in place to manage those risks. These responsibilities call for a formal system to ensure that risk is properly assessed at board level and professionally managed throughout the company. But, as we will see in chapter 6, the ways that these board responsibilities are carried out are still evolving.

Rule Based or Principles Based Corporate Governance

Many commentators on corporate governance used to contrast what they called the Anglo-American (or Anglo-Saxon) approach to corporate governance with the continen-tal European approach. In effect they distinguished the case-law based company law in the US and the UK, from the rule based European law. However, when the US responded to the Enron saga with stringent new corporate governance law (the SOX Act), it became appar-ent that American and British corporate governance no longer shared similar foundations. Indeed, it is now apparent that they are based on fundamentally different philosophies. One is built on a prescriptive rule based legal approach to governance, the other on a non-prescriptive, principles based, more self-regulatory approach.

In the United States and China, which have adopted a similar approach, corporate gov-ernance regulation is essentially through the law. Companies, boards, and directors are expected to obey the law, and follow the regulations of regulatory authorities and stock exchanges, or face penalties including in some cases unlimited fines and jail.

By contrast in the United Kingdom and Hong Kong, indeed in all those commonwealth countries whose company law has been influenced over the years by UK law, including Australia, Canada, India, Singapore, South Africa, and other smaller nations, corporate governance regulation is based on compliance with codes of principles and good practice. Companies, boards, and directors are expected to follow the relevant code or explain the corporate circumstances which have led the board to choose not to conform.

This frontier is really a fundamental philosophical debate of massive significance for the future of the subject.

The Assessment of Individual Director's Performance

Not many years ago most directors would have baulked at a review of individual director's performance. Appointment to the board itself, they argued, proved that a director had the requisite experience and skills. Moreover, how could director-level performance be assessed, when boardroom activity is a collective team effort and directors inevitably make quite different contributions and, moreover, those contributions change as circumstances facing the company change? Such attitudes have had to change quickly as corporate governance codes and stock exchange listing rules called for an annual assessment of the performance of individual directors. Further listed companies in most jurisdictions now have to report that they have complied. Most directors now recognize that, just as they accept management appraisal systems, they need to have a well-run director appraisal programme that works effectively.

How does one go about assessing a director's performance? Who conducts the review? What is the outcome? These are issues we will explore in chapter 13.

The Evaluation of Corporate Governance at the Company and the Country Level

Just as many corporate governance codes now call for an annual assessment of the performance of individual directors, most now also expect an annual evaluation of the performance of the main board and its committees. Some directors faced this imposition with trepidation. But experience is showing that a board with strong and respected leadership, with directors who trust each other, and which is directing a successful enterprise, find the exercise worthwhile and the experience rewarding. Unfortunately, on the other hand, experience also suggests that a poorly led board, with directors in disagreement, leading an organization that is failing to meet its goals, finds the process antagonistic and the outcome potentially catastrophic.

Later in the book we will discuss the planning and preparation that is essential before a board review takes place. The approach we shall advocate analyses the board and committee structures and processes, studies the strengths and weaknesses of the directors, and reviews the processes of the board and its committee, and ensures that appropriate disclosure and accountability is being provided. The outcome is a strategy for board development and corporate governance improvement. Just as an enterprise has longer term strategies for developing its operations, technologies, markets, finances, and people, the board review project leads towards an agreed strategy for board and governance development. In other words, the strategy for board development becomes part of the overall corporate strategy.

There are a number of schemes for evaluating and grading the corporate governance standing of companies. Others provide evaluations of the overall level of corporate governance by country. We will study each of these approaches later.

Cultural Considerations

As we saw in exploring the evolution of corporate governance, earlier in this chapter, significant driving forces have come from the unitary board countries, principally the United States and the United Kingdom, whilst continental European countries provide a counterpoint with their two-tier boards. But subsequently the importance of unique aspects in other countries in affecting the way that corporate governance develops has become apparent. For example, the way business is done, the extent to which legal contracts or interpersonal trust form the basis for business decisions, the sources of capital, the legal traditions, the state of company law, the reliability of the courts, the existence of relevant institutions, the standing of the accountancy, audit, and legal professions, the standing and powers of the regulatory authorities, overall the traditions of the country and the expectations of its people, all influence the way that corporate governance develops.

In Japan, the *keiretsu* groupings of companies have wielded major power and influence over the years. Their traditional approach to governance with large boards consisting almost entirely of the upper echelons of management, doubts about the use of independent outside directors, and the practice of board level auditors have come under pressure in recent years. But the importance that the cultural aspects of business in Japan play need to be appreciated.

In China, the recent development of corporate governance has been remarkable. The State authorities have laid down within a decade what took over a century in the US and the UK.

China's form of corporate governance structure is unique. A board of supervisors and a board of directors combines elements of the German-style two-tier board model with China's traditional concept of employees as masters of enterprises, although unlike the German model the numbers of shareholder and employee representatives do not have to be equal. Directors with board-level audit responsibilities reflects the Japanese model. Whilst the requirement for independent outside directors on the main board adopts ideas from the US and UK models. In practice, the leaders of companies' political party committees have tended to take the chair and vice chair of their companies' boards of supervisors, which are often not as powerful as the main board. Other problems have been the need to change attitudes from those of the old state enterprises which have been partially privatized, the lack of suitable directors, corruption, and the political nature of the courts.

In chapter 8 we will explore the relevance of culture to corporate governance, reviewing governance in China, India, Japan, and those countries in which the traditional Chinese-led family business dominate.

Social Responsibility and Sustainability

Societies' expectations of companies, boards, and directors are changing, too. The movement we saw in the 1970s, expecting more of companies than just making a profit for their shareholders whilst remaining within the law, has reappeared with new rationales and new force. In a world affected by global finance, trading, and services, the need for socially responsible behaviour by companies has acquired new momentum. Corporate social responsibility (or CSR as it is now widely known) has brought a new dimension to corporate governance. Further, the concern for ecology, global warming, and conserving the planet's resources has added the notion of sustainable development, taking corporate decisions that do not deplete the world's resources to the detriment of future generations, to corporate governance agenda. We will study both CSR and corporate sustainability in chapter 15.

The 2008 Financial Crisis

The financial crisis prompted by the securitization of sub-prime mortgage loans in the United States, which led to the collapse, takeover and, in some cases, nationalization of banks and other financial institutions around the world raised some fundamental corporate governance issues. Where were the directors of these failed institutions, particularly the independent directors who were supposed to provide checks on overenthusiastic executives? Did the boards understand their firm's exposure to strategic risk? Did the auditors ensure that their clients' exposure to risk was reported? Will those who designed and encouraged the derivative products and securitization systems be held to account? Were any of the companies' activities illegal? To what extent did top management bonuses influence the outcome? These and other questions will be explored in chapters 14 and 16, with the Northern Rock case, and on the Online Resource Centre associated with this book.

New Concepts of Corporate Governance

Overall, corporate governance continues to evolve. The metamorphosis that will determine the bounds and the structure of the subject has yet to occur. Present practice is still rooted in a 19th century legal concept of the corporation that is totally inadequate in the emerging global business environment. Present theory is even less capable of explaining coherently the way that modern organizations are governed. What is needed is a vibrant alternative way to ensure that power is exercised, over every type and form of corporate entity and strategic alliance around the world, in a way that ensures both effective performance and appropriate social accountability and responsibility. It would be good for such concepts to be rooted in rigorous and replicable research. Unfortunately, the driver of further changes in corporate governance is most likely to be the exposure of further board level excesses and corporate collapses.

As the book now unfolds each of these frontiers will be explored in depth.

REFERENCES AND FURTHER READING

Accounting Standards Steering Committee (1975) *The Corporate Report: A Discussion Paper.* London: Accounting Standards Steering Committee.

American Law Institute (1984) *Principles of Corporate Governance: In Three Parts.* Philadelphia, PA: American Law Institute.

Auerbach, Norman E. (1973) 'Audit Committees: New Corporate Institution', *Financial Executive*, September, pp. 96–7, 102, 104.

Baysinger, Barry D. and Henry N. Butler (1985) 'Corporate Governance and the Board of Directors: Performance Effects of Changes in Board Composition', *Journal of Law, Economics and Organization*, 1: 101–24.

Berle, Adolf A. and Gardiner C. Means ([1932] 1967) *The Modern Corporation and Private Property*. London: Macmillan (revised edn. by Adolf Berle, Columbia University, 1967; Harcourt, Brace and World, New York 1967).

Bullock, Lord (1977) *Industrial Democracy: A Report of the Committee of Inquiry on Industrial Democracy*, Cmnd. 6706 (with European Experience—reports prepared for the Industrial Democracy Committee, Eric Batstone and P. L. Davies). London: HMSO.

Cadbury, Sir Adrian (1992) *The Financial Aspects of Corporate Governance: A Report of the Committee on Corporate Governance*. London: Gee and Co.

Drucker, Peter F. (1991) 'Reckoning with the Pension Fund Revolution', *Harvard Business Review*, March–April, pp. 106–14.

Earl, Michael J. (ed.) (1983) *Perspectives on Management*. Oxford: Oxford University Press.

Estes, Robert M. (1973) 'Outside Directors: More Vulnerable than Ever', *Harvard Business Review*, January/February, pp. 107–14.

European Economic Community (1972) *Proposal for a Fifth Directive on the Structure of Companies*. Strasbourg: European Economic Community.

Fogarty, Michael P. (1975) 'Company Responsibility and Participation: A New Agenda', *PEP Broadsheet*, August, XLI(554).

Greenbury, Sir Richard (1995) *Directors' Remuneration: The Report of a Study Group*. London: Gee and Co.

Hadden, Tom (1972) *Company Law and Capitalism*. London: Weidenfeld and Nicolson.

Hampel, Sir Ronald (1998) *Committee on Corporate Governance: Final Report*. London: Gee and Co.

HMSO (1977) *The Conduct of Company Directors*. White Paper, Cmnd. 7037.

Hilmer, Frederick G. (1993) *Strictly Boardroom: Improving Governance to Enhance Company Performance*. Melbourne: Information Australia.

Jensen, Michael C. and William H. Meckling (1976) *Can the Corporation Survive?* Rochester, MN: Centre for Research in Government Policy and Business, University of Rochester, May.

Mace, Myles L. (1971) *Directors: Myth and Reality*. Boston, MA: Graduate School of Business Administration, Harvard University.

Mautz, R. K. and F. L. Neumann (1970) 'The Effective Corporate Audit Committee', *Harvard Business Review*, November/December.

——(1977) *Corporate Audit Committees: Policies and Practices*. New York: Ernst and Ernst.

Mintzberg, Henry (1984) 'Who Should Control the Corporation?', *California Management Review*, XXVII: 90–115.

RSA (Royal Society for the encouragement of Arts, Manufactures and Commerce) (1995) *Tomorrow's Company: The Role of Business in a Changing World*. London: RSA.

Securities and Exchange Commission (1972) 'Standing Audit Committees Composed of Outside Directors', *SEC Accounting Rules*, Release No. 123, March.

Smith, Adam ([1776] 1976) *The Wealth of Nations* (revised edn., George J. Stigler (ed.), University of Chicago Press, Chicago).

Tricker, R. I. (1978) *The Independent Director: A Study of the Non-executive Director and of the Audit Committee*. London: Tolley with Deloitte, Haskins and Sells.

——(1984) *Corporate Governance*. Aldershot, UK: Gower Publishing.

Watkinson, Lord (1973) 'Responsibilities of the British Public Company'. Report of the Company Affairs Committee of the Confederation of British Industry, London, September.

USEFUL WEBSITES

www.corpgov.net
A valuable site, full of vital corporate governance information by company, country, and topic; reviews, updates, and library plus vital links to other relevant corporate governance sites.

www.thecorporatelibrary.com
An independent research firm providing corporate governance data, analysis, board effectiveness rating, risk assessment tools, plus regular corporate governance reading and reviews.

PROJECTS AND EXERCISES

1. Prepare a report on why the underlying ideas and concepts of corporate governance were slow to evolve. Why was the phrase '*corporate governance*' not used until the 1980s and the subject scarcely studied during the later half of the 20th century when the study of management was at its height?

2. Research one or more of the cases of early corporate collapses mentioned in the text: in Australia, Alan Bond, Laurie Connell of Rothwells, and the Girvan Corporation; in Japan, Nomura Securities and the Recruit Corporation; in the United States, Ivan Boesky, Michael Levine, Michael Milken, and Drexel Burnham Lambert; in the UK, Guinness and the Robert Maxwell companies. Prepare a report or class presentation outlining the case(s). What was the underlying reason for the failure? Would today's corporate governance codes, rules, and regulations have prevented these outcomes?

3. Study the cases of recent corporate collapse mentioned in the text (Enron, Waste Management, Worldcom, and Tyco in the United States; Marconi, British Rail, Independent Insurance, and Tomkins in the UK; HIH Insurance in Australia, Parmalat in Italy, and Vodaphone Mannesmann in Germany. Is there an underlying explanation for their failure?

SELF-TEST QUESTIONS

To confirm your grasp of the key points in this chapter try answering the following questions. Answers are at the end of the book.

1. Define corporate governance.

2. What are the main attributes of the limited liability company?

3. What is the basis of corporate power?

4. What did the classical Berle and Means (1932) study emphasize?

5. What was the response of the UK Bullock (1977) Committee Report?

6. What did the Corporate Report (1975) from the UK Accounting Standards Committee propose?

7. Name some corporate collapses in the 1980s that led to the first studies of corporate governance.

8. What was the first official report on corporate governance and why was it commissioned?

9. What were the major recommendations of the Cadbury Report?

10. What additional dimension did the Australian Hilmer report add to the conformance and compliance concepts of corporate governance?

2   Governance and Management

- In which we recognize:
  - the significance of constitutions for corporate entities
  - the distinction between governance and management
  - the performance and conformance aspects of governance
  - definitions of corporate governance
  - the scope of corporate governance
  - drivers of good corporate governance

The Significance of Constitutions for Corporate Entities

Every Corporate Entity Needs a Constitution

A corporate entity is formed whenever a group of members organizes a company, institution, society, association, or other entity to serve their purpose. Being artificial, corporate entities have to be created. For that they need some form of constitution, which may be formal under the law, for example under company law or the law registering cooperatives, or it can be informal, consisting of little more than a name, a purpose, and a set of rules. As the name indicates, corporate governance is about the way these corporate entities are governed.

In each case the entity has an existence separate from its members, runs activities, and needs to keep separate financial accounts. Its constitution defines the rights and duties of its members, and lays down the rules about the way it is to be governed. Typically, the constitution will define the nature of the governing body, its rights and duties and how its members are elected or chosen.

Table 2.1 provides some comparisons of corporate entities, showing the separation between corporate entities and their members, with examples of different constitutions and governing bodies.

The governing body usually wields governance power over a corporate entity. However, in the case of companies, particularly public companies other drivers of governance power can include shareholder activists, institutional investors, corporate raiders, holders of blocks of shares, as well as threats of hostile takeover bids. We will discuss these later in this chapter.

Table 2.1 **Examples of the governance arrangements in different corporate entities**

Corporate entity	Members	Constitution	Governing body
Limited liability company	Shareholders	Memorandum and articles of association	Board of directors
Professional organization	Qualified members of the profession	Charter and membership rules	Council
Local football club	Club members	Rules	Committee
Trades Union	Registered members	Constitution and branch rule books	General Executive Council
Oxford College	Fellows of the College	Founding statute or charter	Governing body

Whether the constitution is formal, as required under the respective law, or an informal set of rules, it is a fundamental underpinning of the corporate entity and, hence, its governance. Yet, amazingly, many people, appointed as directors of limited companies or elected to councils or committees of other bodies, have never read that entity's constitution. An important part of the induction of every director should be to study and understand the memorandum and articles of their company.

Case Study 2.1 Momcastle Museum Ltd

Momcastle Museum Ltd was incorporated to run a heritage museum in one of England's ancient towns. It had forty members with one share each. To avoid domination and to keep the membership local, the founding members included terms in the articles which restricted members to one share each and required anyone wanting to sell their share to seek the directors' approval of the new member.

Unfortunately one shareholder was unaware of these conditions and sold her share to a business colleague in another town, who turned out to be unacceptable to the board of directors. The sale of the share was not accepted by the company. The problem would not have arisen had she appreciated the significance of the company's articles of association.

Discussion Questions

1. Was it reasonable for a shareholder to be expected to know what was in the company's articles of association?

2. Are most shareholders aware of the contents of the articles or the memorandum of companies in which they invest (consider both private and public companies)? How can a shareholder obtain a copy of a company's articles of association?

3. Would your answers be different if the shareholder was also a director of the company?

Incorporating a Joint Stock Limited Liability Company

The incorporation of a limited liability company involves the registration of formal documents, in line with the company laws of the jurisdiction in which the company is to be incorporated. Typically, the founding members (shareholders) of the company have to prepare and submit the memorandum and articles of association for the proposed company to the company's registrar. Alternatively, the promoters of the company may buy a company 'off the shelf' from a business that specializes in setting up companies, and simply change the name of the company to the one they want.

The companies' registrar will check the proposed company name to ensure that there is no duplication and that the name is not undesirable (for example, in the UK names that suggest a connection with the royal family or involvement with unacceptable activities are not allowed). On incorporation, the company's name is entered on the companies' register and the memorandum and articles become public documents, available for scrutiny by anyone. Other statutory documents, such as an annual return with the details of the shareholders, officers, and directors, changes to company details and changes to the capital structure have to be filed along with, in some jurisdictions, financial accounts.

In the United States of America companies are incorporated under the laws of one or other of the states. Many public companies, with shares listed on a United States stock market, are incorporated in the state of Delaware, where corporate laws allow more flexibility in conducting business than in many other states. Delaware also has a highly respected business court known as the Delaware Court of Chancery, which is considered by some to be sympathetic to boards of directors. Unlike most other countries, there is no provision for the formation of a company at the federal level in the United States, although the Securities and Exchange Commission provides federal level oversight of public companies listed on United States stock markets.

In Europe, however, it is now possible to incorporate a company at the European level. The European Company, known by the Latin term 'Societas Europaea' (SE), enables companies incorporated in different member states of the European Union to merge or to form a holding company at the European level. In other words it provides firms with the option of incorporating in other member states. Formation of a SE holding company is available to both public and private companies with registered offices or branches in different member states. One-tier or two-tier boards are permitted (which we will explore in the next chapter). Provisions also call for the participation of employees in company matters.

During the 19th and early 20th centuries, with the spread of the British Empire, British company law became the basis of company law in many other countries—Australia, Canada, India, many African countries, New Zealand, Singapore, Malaysia, and Hong Kong, for example. Of course over the years company laws have diverged as these countries have developed, but linkages still remain through the commonwealth.

Typically, companies can be divided into three main types:

(1) Public limited company, where the company's shares may be offered for sale to the general public. Members' liability is limited to any amount unpaid on their shares. In the UK, public limited companies must add the designation 'PLC' to their name, elsewhere they are required to add the word 'Limited' or 'Ltd' to their name, so that those contracting with them understand that the shareholders liability is limited. Not all public companies are listed on a stock exchange, but all listed companies must be public companies.

(2)   Private company limited by shares, where members' liability is limited to the amount unpaid on shares they hold. This is by far the most common form of incorporation. Again private limited companies are required to add 'Limited' or 'Ltd' to their name.

(3)   Private company limited by guarantee, where guarantor members' liability is limited to the amount they have agreed to contribute to the company's assets if it is wound up. This is often only a nominal amount. This form of incorporation is often used by charities and other not-for-profit entities and in many jurisdictions the word 'Limited' need not appear in the company name.

The recently developed Community Interest Companies (CICs) in the UK, to facilitate participative ventures between the public and private sectors, may be private companies limited by shares, companies limited by guarantee, or public limited companies.

We will study subsidiary and associated companies, and complex groups of companies (the result of one company owning another) in chapter 4.

The Memorandum and Articles of Association

A company's memorandum is usually a short document that states a company's name, outlines the purposes for which it has been created, gives the address of its registered office, lists the nominal amount and classes of shares with which it is being formed, and states that the liability of its members is limited to the equity capital subscribed. In most jurisdictions, details of the initial subscribing members are also included. A registered office is needed because the company is not a person and anyone dealing with the company needs to know where to find it. The objects clause in a memorandum defines its purposes. In the early days this was, in effect, a constraint imposed by the community for allowing the company to trade with limited liability. Action taken by a company outside its objects would be invalid. Subsequently this clause has often been drawn very widely, so that the company is free to carry on a wide range of activities. Because of the breadth of activities now included some company laws no longer require an objects clause.

The articles of association are, in effect, the rules by which the company is governed. Companies Acts in many jurisdictions contain a draft memorandum for guidance.

In most jurisdictions the number of members of a private company is limited and the requirements for filing documents with the registrar are not as demanding as those for public companies, those which may offer shares to the public.

By contrast, private companies may not offer their shares to the public. As we saw in the last chapter, in the original 19th century concept of the corporation all companies were public, being incorporated to obtain funds from the public. Subsequently companies were incorporated to obtain the benefit of limited liability for a business, without seeking funds from the public. Today private company registrations far outnumber public companies.

To obtain a listing on a stock exchange a company must meet the listing requirements of that exchange. In some jurisdictions the company also has to pass the scrutiny of the securities regulatory authority. Typically, a listing requires the preparation of a prospectus.

Box 2.2 provides an example of the typical contents of a prospectus to raise shares. This is a prospectus issued by the British Energy Group PLC seeking an introduction on the official list of the London Stock Exchange.

Box 2.1 Example of the Contents of Articles of Association

A typical set of articles might contain detailed rules on the following:

Share Capital

Details of the share capital, including any class of shares with special rights such as voting rights or being preferential in dividends, also the means of varying such rights. If the shares are not fully paid up on issue, the way that calls may be made. The way shares may be transferred from one shareholder to another. The type of meeting and resolution of the members required to alter the company's capital.

General Meetings of the Company

The requirement to hold an annual meeting of the shareholder members. The rules governing special or extraordinary meetings of members. The notice required for meetings. Proceedings at general meetings, including the necessary quorum, the appointment of the chairman, and voting on resolutions by a show of hands of those present or by a poll based shareholdings.

Directors

The number of directors, any shareholding qualification for directors, the determination of the remuneration of directors. The powers and duties of directors. The disqualification of directors, for example by becoming bankrupt, being of unsound mind, missing meetings, or being prohibited by the courts or companies registrar from acting as a director. The length of service and the rotation of directors, for example with one-third retiring every year. The proceedings at directors' meetings, including notice of meetings, quorum, election of chairman, delegation of powers to committees of the board.

Officers of the Company

The board's power to appoint a managing director or chief executive officer, a company secretary, and other officers such as a chief finance officer.

Dividend Policy and Reserves

The powers of the members in general meeting to agree policies on reserves and the payment of dividends. Typically, on such matters the general meeting will follow the proposals put before it by the board.

Requirements for Accounts and Audit

The requirement for the directors to keep proper financial records for the company and to provide regular accounts, including a profit and loss account and balance sheet to the members periodically. The appointment of auditors in line with the Companies Acts.

Provisions for Winding up the Company

The procedures for winding up the company with the members' agreement or on enforced liquidation.

Box 2.2 Example of Contents of a Prospectus: British Energy Group Plc

CONTENTS

		Page
Indicative timetable of principal events		3
Directors, secretary and advisers		4
Key Information		6
Part I	Description of the New British Energy Group	39
	Introduction	39
	The electricity industry	41
	The nuclear generation industry	46
	Coal-fired generation	62
	Electricity sales	66
	Regulation	69
	Property, plant and equipment	82
	Insurance	83
	Employee share incentive plans	86
	Pensions	86
	Directors, senior management and employees	89
	Corporate governance	93
Part II	Risk factors	101
	A. Operating, industry, environmental and regulatory risk	101
	B. Risks related to ownership of New Shares, New Bonds and Warrants	123
Part III	Operating and financial review and prospects	128
	Section 1: Current trading and prospects	128
	Trading at the time of the announcement of the Restructuring	128
	Current, financial and trading prospects	128
	Business strategy	132
	Trading	133
	Eggborough power station	134
	Relationship with Government	135
	Dividend and financial policy	136
	Section 2: Operating and financial review	138
	Overview of the Group	138
	The Restructuring	138
	Financial reporting requirements and format of the New British Energy Group	140
	Critical accounting policies	140
	Fixed assets	145
	Factors affecting our results of operations	146
	Exceptional operating and financing items	152
	Results of operations for the year ended 31 March 2004 compared with the year ended 31 March 2003	154
	Operating profit/(loss)	157
	Results of operations for the year ended 31 March 2003 compared with the year ended 31 March 2002	159
	Review of our balance sheet items as at 31 March 2004	164
	Liquidity and capital resources	167
	Post balance sheet events	169
	Contingent liabilities	169
	Financial instruments and risk management	170
Part IV	Financial information	173
	Section 1: Financial information on British Energy plc	173
	Section 2: Results for British Energy plc for the three months ended 30 June 2004	239

		Page
	Section 3: Financial information on British Energy Group plc	287
	Section 4: Financial information on British Energy Holdings plc	290
	Section 5: Summary of differences between UK and US GAAP of British Energy	293
	Section 6: Implications to the New British Energy Group under US GAAP	312
	Section 7: Implications to the New British Energy Group of International Financial Reporting Standards	314
Part V	Unaudited pro forma financial information	316
Part VI	Further information relating to the Restructuring	328
	Overview	328
	Other material contracts relating to the Restructuring	334
	Restructuring conditions and termination	348
	State Aid	353
	The restructured group	358
	Admission and dealings	362
	ADRs	363
Part VII	Terms and conditions of the New Bonds	365
Part VIII	Conditions of the Warrants	432
Part IX	Description of American Depositary Receipts	451
Part X	Additional information	458
	Incorporation and registered office	458
	Share capital	458
	Memorandum and articles of association	462
	Convertible shares and special share and limitations on Shareholders	471
	Directors and senior management	478
	Directors' and other interests	481
	Directors' service agreements and letters of appointment	482
	Employee share incentive plans	486
	Pensions	504
	Principal subsidiaries and associated undertakings	509
	Principal establishments	511
	Taxation	512
	Working capital	525
	Significant change	526
	Historic insurance arrangements	527
	Litigation	530
	Material contracts	533
	Electricity generation and supply licences	655
	General	659
	Listing and settlement	660
	Documents for inspection	660
	Use of proceeds	661
Definitions		662
Glossary		690

Other Forms of Incorporation

We have looked at the incorporation of limited liability companies (private company limited by shares, private company limited by guarantee, and public company limited by shares), under the Companies Acts of the jurisdiction in which the companies are registered. But there are other ways that corporate entities can be formally created, as we saw in table 2.1.

Some sectors, for example savings and loan associations in the United States, building societies in the UK and Commonwealth countries, farmers and other suppliers cooperatives in Canada, consumer cooperatives in the UK, are incorporated under legislation designed to facilitate and regulate that specific sector.

Incorporation of specific corporate entities by the state is also common in many countries. The legislature provides the new organization with its own facilitating legislation, which defines and creates the entity and determines its governance processes, including its mission and accountability, the form of its governing body and how the directors are appointed, which is often by the government or state agencies. For example, the Federal National Mortgage Association (Fannie Mae) was created by the US government to provide government backing for financial products and services that make it possible for low and middle-income families to buy homes of their own. Such entities are sometimes referred to as quangos, which is an acronym for quasi-autonomous non-governmental organization, because, although they have a life and mission separate from the state, the state maintains an arm's length interest in them.

To add a degree of confusion, quango is also used, particularly in the United Kingdom and Australia, as an acronym for a quasi-autonomous *national* governmental organization to describe organizations to which governments have devolved power, but in which they retain a direct influence. Examples include the Adult Learning Inspectorate of the UK Department of Education and Skills, the Vehicle Certification Agency of the Department of Transport, the Agricultural Wages Board of the Department of the Environment, Food and Rural Affairs, and the Job Centres of the Department of Work and Pensions.

Charities are often set up as not-for-profit, incorporated bodies and registered under the charities law in the relevant jurisdiction. Most of the principles and practices discussed in this book apply to the governance of such entities, although those serving on their governing bodies may also be trustees and subject to additional requirements of trust law.

Professional bodies provide some interesting cases of alternative approaches to incorporation and governance. In some countries professional bodies are incorporated under their own statute by state authorities. In the UK and some other Commonwealth countries many professional bodies are created under a Royal Charter. Such chartered professional bodies have sovereignty over their own affairs, including the examination and admission to membership, the maintaining of standards and the disciplining of members.

The engineering profession in both the United States and Britain has developed with constitutionally separate professional bodies to represent the interests of the various branches—electrical, civil, and mechanical and so on. Subsequently, in Britain, the Engineering Council was created by Royal Charter to oversee an effective federation of the separate bodies. Unlike the engineers, the UK accountancy profession has not managed to agree a federation and has a number of separate professional bodies. Criticisms following the collapse of Enron and its auditors, Andersens, led to the creation of the

---

Case Study 2.2 The American Red Cross

The American Red Cross was established in 1881, and subsequently set up by Congress as a chartered organization, which established its mandate with governance by a Board of Governors with fifty members. In recent years there has been media criticism of the Red Cross and questions whether the way it was run was appropriate to the new demands that it had to face. In late 2005, the Senate Finance Committee initiated a Congressional inquiry into several aspects of the organization's governance. Subsequently, in February 2006, the Chairman of the Senate Finance Committee expressed concerns about the mission and organizational culture of the Red Cross, the size of its Board of Governors, the participation of board members and whether they were sufficiently independent to exercise proper governance. As a result the Board of Governors set up a comprehensive assessment of its governance model to identify concrete reforms and streamline the organization's ability to meet the growing demands of its mission.

Discussion Questions

1. The constitutions of corporate entities set up with charitable objectives often call for members of board members to be representatives of various stakeholders. If you were designing such a constitution, what interest groups would you require to be represented? (Consider employees, benefactors, the state, regulators, societal interests, and any others.) Should the board include representatives of the beneficiaries?

2. Should the chief executive and top executives of such organizations be board members?

Public Company Accounting Oversight Board (PCAOB) in the United States, as we will explore later. In the UK standards and oversight of the accounting profession are maintained by a number of independent bodies. In Canada, by contrast, there are provincial institutes of chartered accountants with a Co-ordinating Council of Institutes of Chartered Accountants of Canada. The governance of professional bodies, many of which have relatively large governing bodies (often called councils) can be intriguing. As we shall see, many of the political aspects of corporate governance can come into play.

Finally, we should note that a vast number of small corporate entities are created simply by agreement between interested parties. Sports clubs, drama groups, arts societies, religious organizations, all provide examples. Nevertheless, all such entities need governing as well as managing, and, consequently, need some form of constitution, which should be written if unnecessary disputes are to be avoided.

In this chapter we have distinguished many different forms of incorporation. The principles and practices of corporate governance apply to them all, although obviously they need adapting to the circumstances. To avoid unnecessary repetition, however, from now on we shall focus on the governance of companies, recognizing that all other corporate entities need corporate governance and the methods of governing companies can be adapted to the not-for-profit and other non-company sectors.

Case Study 2.3 Network Rail

The railways in Britain had long been nationalized and run by the state enterprise British Railways. In 1994, the then Conservative Government privatized the railway system. Companies were granted the rights to run train services over various routes. Meanwhile, Railtrack PLC was incorporated to control the entire railway infrastructure (tracks, signals, bridges, tunnels, and some stations) as a public company listed on the London Stock market.

Over the following few years Railtrack was criticized for its poor performance in maintaining and developing the rail infrastructure, the spiralling costs of new projects, including extensions to the Euro Tunnel route, and particularly on its poor safety record. Fatal crashes occurred. Railtrack's use of contractors on maintenance work with alleged loss of control and reduced safety were alleged; so was the original strategy of having a single company run the rail network, which was used by all the train operators.

Following the second of these crashes the Railtrack board of directors was said to have been near panic. Maintenance and safety routines were examined, emergency tests showed major faults on many lines, and speed restrictions were imposed around the system causing major problems to the train operators and the passengers.

By 2001, Railtrack had reached a level of indebtedness, which left it no longer financially viable without repeated subsidy from the taxpayer. Controversially it used this government funding to pay a dividend to its shareholders. But by now the Government had changed. In October 2001 the New Labour Secretary of State for Transport, Stephen Byers, called for Railtrack to be put into administration on the grounds of its insolvency.

Critics accused the government of deliberately bankrupting the company to partially re-nationalize the railway system, bringing the infrastructure back under state control. The Government offered no compensation to the shareholders, arguing that the company was insolvent and that in such a case administration was covered in the original privatization legislation.

Then in October 2002, the Government created a new company to run Britain's rail infrastructure: Network Rail, which was incorporated as a private company limited by guarantee. Governance was expected to meet the standards required of a PLC. The company had over a hundred guarantor 'members' (not shareholders), who represented the rail industry, the Department of Transport, and the public. The company explained that it was a '*not for dividend company*', that it operated as a commercial business directly accountable to its members, who received the annual report and accounts, attended the AGM and approved the appointment of directors and auditors. The members could remove top executives.

Some of the weaknesses of this approach to governance were seen in 2008 when significant overruns on maintenance work left hundreds of thousands of travellers stranded over the New Year holidays. Some of the governing members complained that management was not really accountable to anyone. '*There is a democratic deficit*' wrote Lord Berkeley a member representing the rail freight industry, calling for a new board with fewer 'governors' who would have wider powers to supervise management.

Discussion Questions

1. Was it a sound strategy for the government to franchise different companies to run train services over various routes, whilst incorporating Railtrack PLC to control the entire railway infrastructure (tracks, signals, bridges, tunnels, and some stations) as a public company listed on the London stock market?

2. Was the Government right to offer no compensation to the shareholders of Railtrack PLC, arguing that the company was insolvent?

3. Evaluate the new 'not for dividend' private company limited by guarantee called Network Rail, with guarantor members not shareholders, representing the rail industry, the Department of Transport, and the public. What problems might be expected in its governance?

The Distinction Between Governance and Management

As we saw in the first chapter, professional management was the major focus in business throughout the 20th century. Today the way companies are governed has become more important than the way they are managed. Yet some people fail to make the distinction between governance and management.

The notion of management as a hierarchy is commonplace—as in the classical pyramid of figure 2.1.

A chief executive has overall responsibility, with other managers reporting to him or her and so on down the management hierarchy. Authority and responsibility is delegated downwards with matching accountability expected upwards in return. The classical theory enables functional departments to be depicted and line and staff management responsibilities to be defined. We understand that this is an inadequate picture of the realities of management, but we generally accept that management operates through hierarchies. We know who reports to whom in the organization.

But where is the board? Boards seldom appear on organization charts. The board is not part of the management structure. Neither is it a hierarchy. Every director has equal responsibility and similar duties and powers under the law. There is no 'boss' of a board. The work of the board, the governing body of the entity, is depicted in figure 2.2 as a circle, superimposed on the management.

In a unitary board, that is a board with both executive and non-executive, or outside directors, the executive directors hold a managerial role in addition to their responsibilities as a member of the board of directors. Shown □ in figure 2.2, they sit in both the board

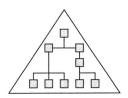

Figure 2.1 Classical depiction of management

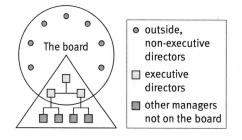

Figure 2.2 The board and management

circle and the management triangle. As executives they are employees of the company and covered by employment law. Directors, as such, are not employees and are subject to company law. The other directors, shown ⊙ in the figure, are the non-executive or outside directors—members of the board circle but not part of the management hierarchy. Other managers, who are not on the board, are shown ▣.

A further important distinction can be drawn between outside, non-executive directors who are independent of the entity, and outside non-executive directors who, although they are not executives of the company, have some link with it. Independent non-executive directors have no relationship with the company that could affect the exercise of independent judgement. Those who are not independent have some link with the company, such as close family ties to the chairman, being a representative of a dominant shareholder, having previously served as an executive of that company, having links with major trading partners of the company and so on. Such connections raise questions about these directors' independence. There may be good reasons for having them on the board, but we shall refer to them as connected non-executive directors. These issues will be explored further in chapter 3. In the United States the common practice is to refer to non-executive directors as outside directors. For consistency we will use the acronyms INED (independent non-executive director) and CNED (connected non-executive director). Some authorities refer to a CNED as an affiliated non-executive director.

We now have a model which enables us to distinguish governance from management. (See figure 2.3.)

In other words—management runs the business; the board ensures that it is being well run and run in the right direction.

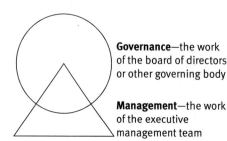

Governance—the work of the board of directors or other governing body

Management—the work of the executive management team

Figure 2.3 Governance distinguished from management

The Performance and Conformance Aspects of Governance

Board Responsibilities

We can now explore what the board does. Overall, the board's task is to direct the company, which is why directors are so called. This activity can be seen to involve four basic elements—strategy formulation and policy making, supervision of executive management, and accountability to shareholders and others. In fulfilling their duties, directors have to consider the future of the company as well as its present position and recent results, also take a view looking inward at the company and its component parts as well as externally at the company in its competitive market context and the broader economic, political, and social context in which it operates. These basic board perspectives and processes are shown in figure 2.4.

In formulating strategy the board works with top management, looking ahead in time and outside the firm, seeing it in its strategic environment. Strategies then need to be translated into policies to guide top management action and provide plans for subsequent control. The board also needs to monitor and supervise the activities of executive management, looking inwards at the current managerial situation and at recent performance. Accountability involves looking outwards and reflecting corporate activities and performance to the shareholders and other stakeholders with legitimate claims to accountability.

Boards vary in the extent to which the board as a whole engages in these functions or delegates work to the CEO and the management team, whilst ensuring that the necessary monitoring and control processes are in place.

Of course, a simple 2 × 2 matrix necessarily presents a simplified view of board processes; but at least by looking forwards and backwards in time and internally and externally in space it is all embracing!

An extension of the basic quadrant of board processes introduces a central cell recognizing that boards work with and act through management, working with and through their chief executive or managing director.[1] Figure 2.5 depicts this process. Boards can choose the extent of their delegation of functions to the management. In some cases, for example, boards play a major part in the formulation of the company's strategy, in others this is

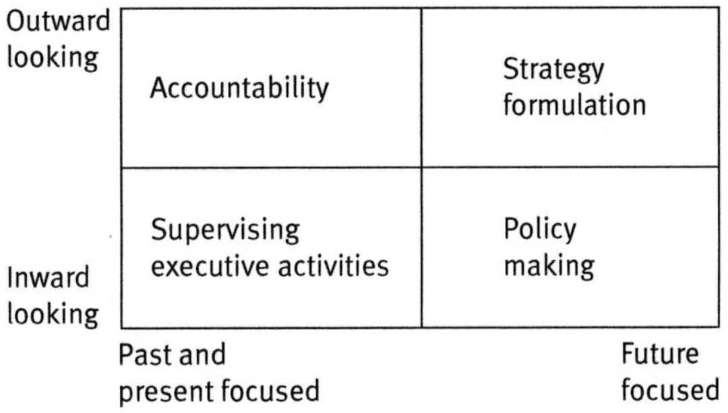

Figure 2.4 The basic board perspectives and processes

[1]Hilmer, Frederick G. (1993) *Strictly Boardroom.* Sydney: Information Australia.

Figure 2.5 Framework for analysing board activities

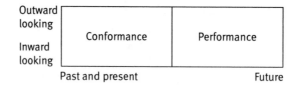

Figure 2.6 The conformance and performance aspects of a board's work

delegated to top management with the board receiving, questioning, and finally approving management's strategic proposals.

Figure 2.5 can also highlight a potential dilemma for the unitary board. The roles in the right hand column—strategy formulation and policy making—are performance roles, concerned with the board's contribution to corporate direction. Those on the left—executive supervision and accountability—are essentially concerned with ensuring conformance. Figure 2.6 shows this important distinction.

As Lord Caldecote, a very experienced board chairman, once commented 'a problem with the unitary board is that directors are marking their own examination papers'. In a two-tier board, as we shall see later, the roles are separated with the executive board responsible for performance and the supervisory board responsible for conformance.

Definitions of Corporate Governance

There have been many attempts to define corporate governance, many of them more penetrating than the, perhaps, over-simple distinction between governance and management drawn earlier: '*management runs the business; the board ensures that it is being well run and in the right direction*'.

In chapter 1, we were offered the broad views that: '*corporate governance is about the way corporate entities are governed*' and '*corporate governance is about the exercise of power over corporate entities*'. This view, which is reinforced by Clarke (2004), is the perspective adopted in this book.

> **Box 2.3** *Corporate Governance: An International Review*
>
> *Corporate Governance: An International Review*, an academic journal founded in 1992, defines corporate governance broadly as 'the exercise of power over corporate entities so as to increase the value provided to the organization's various stakeholders'.
>
> Now in its 18th year this journal is published by Blackwell Publishing, Oxford and New York and is now edited by Dr William Judge, Old Dominion University, Norfolk, VA, USA.

Both the Cadbury Report (1992) and a subsequent report from the OECD—the Organization for Economic Co-operation and Development (1999) offered: '*corporate governance is the process by which companies are directed and controlled*'. This definition, of course, mirrors the performance and conformance dichotomy we mentioned earlier.

By 2001, the OECD had broadened their definition:

corporate governance refers to the private and public institutions, including laws, regulations and public institutions, which together govern the relationship, in a market economy, between corporate managers and entrepreneurs, on the one hand, and those who invest resources in corporations on the other.

Also in 2001 two influential American practitioners Bob Monks and Nel Minow offered: '*corporate governance is the relationship among various participants in determining the direction and performance of corporations. The primary participants are the shareholders, the management and the board of directors.*'

We have already noted the opinion of Hilmer (1993) that: '*the board's key role is to ensure that corporate management is continuously and effectively striving for above average performance, taking account of risk, [which] is not to deny the board's additional role with respect to shareholder protection*'.

The variations between the definitions illuminate the different perspectives taken by the authors. Those who see corporate governance as principally concerning the activities of the shareholders, the board, and management (Monks and Minow) have taken a relatively sharp focus. Other contributors recognize the context in which corporate governance is practised and include the regulators, auditors, and market institutions involved in the provision of capital (OECD 2001). With the widest focus are those who recognize that an understanding of corporate governance needs to involve all and every element that can affect the exercise of power over corporations (Clarke 2004 and this book).

The Scope of Corporate Governance

Obviously, the structure, the membership, and the processes of the governing body are central to corporate governance. But relations with shareholders and other sources of finance, the link with the independent external auditors, and (in listed companies) the influence of the stock market and the financial institutions, are fundamental. So are the effects of the company law, the legal institutions, and the regulatory mechanisms of the country concerned. The company's relationships with contractual stakeholders—employees, suppliers, customers, for example—have also become vital in understanding the governance of corporations. Corporate social responsibility and the interests of other,

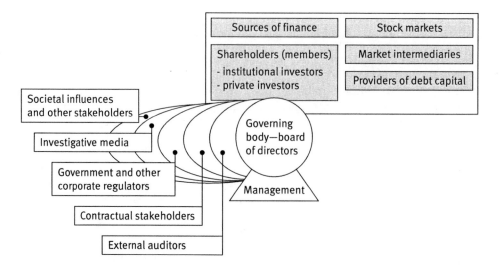

Figure 2.7 The scope of corporate governance

non-contractual stakeholders and society at large are also now wielding significant influences in corporate governance, as we will see in the second part of this book.

The schematic of figure 2.7 attempts to provide an overview of the scope of corporate governance.

Central to the study of corporate governance are, of course, the members of the entity (shareholder in a limited company), the governing body (the board of directors in a company), and the management of the enterprise. We shall be focusing on the structures, relationships, and realities of these groups throughout this book.

Auditors play a crucial role in corporate governance, though they are not often presented as central to its study. In the original 19th century concept of the corporation the shareholders appointed some of their own members to act as auditors, to check on the reports presented to them by their directors. Subsequently they were replaced by professional auditors, as the accounting profession developed in the later years of that century.

Case Study 2.4 Great Western Railway Company

Report of the Audit Committee

The auditors and Mr Deloitte attended the committee and explained the various matters concerned with the finances and other departments of the railway, which explanations were highly satisfactory.

The committee considered the auditors had performed their arduous duties with great care and intelligence and therefore confidently recommend that they be continued in office.

(Paddington Station, Benjamin Lancaster, 22 February 1872)

Discussion Question

1. How does the audit committee in the old GWR differ from its modern counterpart?

Later we shall consider the implications of audit in the modern, global world, with just four massive, international firms of accountants, following the demise of the fifth, Arthur Andersen, after the Enron debacle. The importance of audit committees, standing committees of the main board, which are now required by all the codes of good practice in corporate governance, will also be studied in depth.

The contractual stakeholders are all those firms and individuals who have a contractual relationship with the company and whose interests are increasingly recognized as part of corporate governance interests, as we shall see when comparing the codes of good corporate governance practice around the world. The contractual stakeholders include the employees of the company, all those firms and individuals in the company's added-value chain, from suppliers of original goods and services, through supply firms, distributors, wholesalers, retailers to the final customer, as well as the suppliers of finance (other than the equity share capital), including banks and other financial institutions for loans and other debt capital.

For public, listed companies the stock markets and their listing rules are, clearly, vitally significant to corporate governance. The rules that govern the stock market, on which the company's shares are listed, and in particular the requirements laid down for listing are fundamental to the effective governance of listed companies. Stock markets around the world are also playing an important role in the creation and policing of corporate governance codes.

Case Study 2.5 The Australian Stock Exchange (ASX)

ASX has two basic functions:

1. To operate Australia's primary national stock exchange for equities, derivatives, and fixed interest securities, including settlement facilities. It also provides comprehensive information on the Australian stock market, including share prices. Under the Australian Corporations Act ASX is required to operate markets that are fair, orderly, and transparent.

2. To supervise the market, including monitoring participants' conduct and enforcing compliance with the rules. To protect the integrity of the market, ASX sets standards for the behaviour of listed companies through its Listing Rules.

In 2006, to overcome concerns about conflict between its regulatory and commercial functions, and to provide greater transparency and accountability ASX placed its supervisory function in a separate subsidiary called ASX Markets Supervision, with its own board. ASX Market Supervision processes applications for listing on the ASX, monitors compliance with the Listing Rules, and reviews proposals from listed entities for significant restructures, re-organizations, and new issues.

The ASX Corporate Governance Council has developed a set of guidelines, Principles of Good Corporate Governance and Best Practice Recommendations.

(For more information see www.asx.com.au)

Discussion Questions

1. Evaluate the ASX policy of putting its supervisory function into a separate subsidiary called ASX Markets Supervision. Is this a sound policy?

2. How does this ASX policy compare with those of another stock exchange with which you are familiar?

Box 2.4 The Listing Rules of the Australian Stock Exchange

To protect the integrity of the market, ASX sets standards for the behaviour of listed companies through its Listing Rules. These Listing Rules cover the following matters:

- Admission of companies to the ASX Official List
- Market quotation
- Continuous disclosure of relevant information
- Periodic disclosure of specific information
- Additional reporting for mining and exploration firms
- Securities trading
- Changes in capital and new issues of shares
- Transfers and registration of share transactions
- Restricted securities
- Transactions with persons in a position of influence
- Significant transactions
- On-going requirements
- Additional requirements for trusts
- Meetings required
- Documents required
- Fees
- The halting of trading, suspension and removal of companies
- Application of the listing rules

(The ASX Listing Rules, Appendices, and Guidance Notes are available in electronic format)

(For more information see www.asx.com.au)

Market intermediaries play an increasingly important role in modern corporate governance. In the original model of the corporation, shares were held by individual shareholders who interacted directly with their company. Today, although individual investors do have a significant share in some markets, institutional investors play a very significant part in most. The institutional investors may include an array of financial institutions such as pension funds, investment funds, life assurance funds, unit trusts, hedge funds, and other investment houses. There can be a raft of intermediary institutions between the company and the ultimate investor in its shares. Investment bankers may act as underwriters in launching shares in an IPO, an initial public offering of shares. Brokers, merchant bankers, and other institutions can hold shares on behalf of others. A further complication can arise if the financial institution holding shares lends them as security for another transaction. This situation can make it difficult for companies to know who their voting shareholders are and for those shareholders to exercise their proxy votes and take part in the governance of the company.

Governments obviously provide the underpinning to corporate governance by enacting the legislation that facilitates, regulates, and constrains the activities of corporate entities registered in their jurisdiction. The creation and updating of Companies Acts are obvious examples.

The registration of companies and the filing and access to corporate documents is also a function of the relevant government department. The relationship between government, which in effect allows the corporate entity to be created and operate in its jurisdiction, and companies is an important element of corporate governance.

Case Study 2.6 Companies House: The UK Company Registration Service

In the United Kingdom, Companies House is the central registry for all companies registered in the UK—private, public, and limited by guarantee. All companies in the UK have to be formally incorporated through Companies House, and must file the required documents and financial accounts, annually or whenever changes occur. These documents are then available for public scrutiny.

Companies House WebFiling Service allows companies to file required forms on line. XBRL (eXtensible Business Reporting Language) is a standard system which describes financial data and facilitates the creation, distribution, and use of business reports.

Companies House provides a free searchable index of company names and addresses on over two million companies registered in the UK. Companies House Direct is an on-line search tool, for accessing and downloading company information from over 250 million company documents including company accounts. Copies of a company's latest accounts and annual return and some company reports can be bought on-line.

(For more information see www.companieshouse.gov.uk)

Discussion Question
1. Check out the information available on a sample of companies in the UK. How does this compare with that available in other countries?

Corporate regulators play an ever increasing role in corporate governance. Many company jurisdictions now have a separate regulatory authority, which monitors stock market activity, determines and requires compliance with corporate governance codes, and has the power to ensure compliance.

In the United States the US Securities and Exchange Commission (SEC) exists to protect investors, maintain fair, orderly, and efficient markets, and facilitate capital formation. The SEC oversees the key participants in the securities world, including securities exchanges, securities brokers and dealers, investment advisors, and mutual funds. Crucial to the SEC's effectiveness in each of these areas is its enforcement authority, being able to take legal action against insider trading, accounting fraud, and the provision of false information.

Case Study 2.7 The History of the US Securities and Exchange Commission

The SEC was created following the great crash of 1929. Previously there was little support for federal involvement. During the 1920s over twenty million shareholders set out to make their fortunes on the stock market. Of around US$50 million in new securities issued, half became worthless. Countless fortunes were lost. Many banks failed. Depression followed and confidence in the markets collapsed.

Congress passed the 1933 Securities Act to restore investor confidence. The Securities and Exchange Commission was set up to enforce the new laws designed to promote security in the market by requiring public companies to tell the truth about their business, their securities, and the risks involved, and requiring security dealers to treat investors fairly and honestly.

The mission of the US Securities and Exchange Commission is to protect investors, maintain fair, orderly, and efficient markets, and facilitate capital formation. Unlike the banking world, where deposits are guaranteed by the federal government, stocks, bonds, and other securities can lose value. The laws and rules that govern the securities industry in the United States derive from a simple and straightforward concept: all investors, whether large institutions or private individuals, should have access to certain basic facts about an investment prior to buying it, and so long as they hold it. To achieve this, the SEC requires public companies to disclose meaningful financial and other information to the public. This provides a common pool of knowledge for all investors to use to judge for themselves whether to buy, sell, or hold a particular security.

The SEC oversees the key participants in the securities world, including securities exchanges, securities brokers and dealers, investment advisors, and mutual funds. Crucial to the SEC's effectiveness in each of these areas is its enforcement authority. Each year the SEC brings hundreds of civil enforcement actions against individuals and companies for violation of the securities laws. Typical infractions include insider trading, accounting fraud, and providing false or misleading information about securities and the companies that issue them.

To help support investor education, the SEC provides a mass of information, including the EDGAR database of disclosure documents that public companies are required to file with the Commission.

Though it is the primary overseer and regulator of the US securities markets, the SEC works closely with many other institutions, including Congress, other federal departments and agencies, the self-regulatory organizations (e.g. the stock exchanges), state securities regulators, and various private sector organizations. In particular, the Chairman of the SEC, together with the Chairman of the Federal Reserve, the Secretary of the Treasury, and the Chairman of the Commodities Futures Trading Commission, serves as a member of the President's Working Group on Financial Markets.

(For more information see www.sec.gov)

Discussion Questions

1. Explore the SEC website. What is your impression of the EDGAR database?

2. What are the key issues the SEC is pursuing at the moment?

Case Study 2.8 The Role of the Hong Kong Securities and Futures Commission

The Securities and Futures Commission (SFC) is an independent non-governmental statutory body outside the civil service, responsible for regulating the securities and futures markets in Hong Kong, responsible for administering the laws governing the securities and futures markets in Hong Kong, and facilitating and encouraging the development of these markets.

The statutory duties of the SFC are:

- To maintain and promote the fairness, efficiency, competitiveness, transparency, and orderliness of the securities and futures industry

- To promote understanding by the public of the operation and functioning of the securities and futures industry

- To provide protection for members of the public investing in or holding financial products

- To minimize crime and misconduct in the securities and futures industry; to reduce systemic risks in the securities and futures industry and to assist the Financial Secretary in maintaining the financial stability of Hong Kong by taking appropriate steps in relation to the securities and futures industry.

As the statutory regulator of the securities and futures markets in Hong Kong, the Commission places great importance on corporate governance. '*We always strive to enhance our accountability to the public and the transparency of our work. We adopt and implement corporate governance practices commensurate with the best standards applicable to public bodies.*' All important policies and decisions are discussed and approved by the board, which meets regularly every month and holds additional meetings as necessary. Divisional staff attend board meetings to explain policy proposals, report on important operational matters and regulatory issues. Members are also briefed on the financial positions of the Commission and provided with monthly financial statements.

(For more information see www.sfc.hk)

Discussion Questions

1. The SFC won the platinum award in the 2007 Best Corporate Governance Disclosure Awards, run by the Hong Kong Institute of Certified Public Accountants. (www.hkicpa.org.hk) Do you agree with their judgement?

2. Evaluate the board structure of the SFC. Should senior executives be members of the board?

Previously the press showed little interest in business affairs unless there were major catastrophes. But in recent years the media has shone a spotlight on corporate activities, and the investigative media now play a useful role in the corporate governance process and have to be considered by practitioners.

Finally, the growing importance of societal influences and other stakeholders in corporate governance needs emphasis. In earlier days companies tended to be left alone to carry on their activities in the pursuit of profit without interference, provided that they abided by the laws of the jurisdictions in which they operated. No longer. Today many people expect companies to adopt a socially responsible attitude to their activities, for example by not doing objectionable things, such as polluting the environment, exploiting workers, or killing animals.

Corporate social responsibility (CSR) reflects what some commentators see as companies' obligations to everyone who might be affected by the company's activities (the stakeholders). Not only contractual stakeholders, such as employees, suppliers, and customers, but local neighbourhoods who could be affected by a plant closure, cities and states affected by the loss of jobs and tax revenues by a company's strategy to move activities elsewhere, even larger international society for company's employment policies, environmental impacts, or marketing polices around the world. We shall explore these issues later.

Drivers of Good Corporate Governance

In this chapter we have seen that the board is the major driving force of governance in a company. Primarily, the board determines whether a company's governance is sound. But there are other drivers of good governance in a company.

In the original model of the company, shareholders were individuals and met together periodically to receive the report and accounts of their directors, to elect or re-elect them, and to approve significant changes, such as an alteration in the share capital, as required by company law or the company's articles.

But today the potential for individual shareholder activism in a company with large numbers of diverse shareholders is low. The one share, one vote principle of, so-called, shareholder democracy no longer leads to shareholder power. In America shareholders can only run a campaign to nominate or remove directors at their own expense, whereas the company pays for the board's campaign. Under the proxy voting rules only 'for' votes count, votes cast against a candidate are ignored. Moreover, incumbent boards frequently refuse to put shareholder resolutions on the proxy ballot and, even if a resolution succeeds, the board may choose to treat the resolution as advisory and ignore it. In Britain shareholders do have the right to have resolutions put on the ballot and, if successful, they are usually binding on the directors.

For major companies, particularly those listed in the liquid markets of the United States or the United Kingdom, a significant proportion of their shareholders will now be institutional investors—banks, insurance companies, pension funds, hedge funds, sovereign funds (all of which we will discuss later). Many of these institutions hold between one and five percent of the equity and in America now account for around two-thirds of the investment in major companies.

Some of these institutional investors have become drivers of corporate governance change, wielding governance power particularly if they act in concert through an independent association. Dissatisfaction with boards has increased in recent years with concerns over poor corporate performance, allegedly excessive directors' rewards, loss of investor confidence following down turn in markets, and company collapses. A few hedge fund managers have become active shareholders. Interestingly, they can sometimes afford the advice of leading lawyers and investment bankers, who previously might have felt a loyalty to their corporate clients but now recognize the fee potential of activist adventurers.

Some commentators have depicted the situation as an irresistible rise of shareholder power and an inevitable struggle between shareholders and top management. Others take the opposite position, arguing that the separation between shareholders and top management is at the heart of the governance system. Boards need freedom, they argue, to take business decisions in good faith without interference from interventionist institutions. Otherwise boards might respond to investor pressure by focusing on the short term, failing to make crucial long term investments. Moreover, they add, institutional investors are in effect intermediaries in the chain between ultimate individual owners and companies. Such institutions have governance problems of their own in recognizing and responding to the different aims of their investors.

Corporate raiders are a special case of institutional investor and obviously can exert considerable governance power. By acquiring a sufficiently large holding in a company these investors can directly influence its activities. For example, investor Kirk Kerkorian was able to place his nominee on the board of General Motors in 2006. On the other hand, Carl Icahn and some hedge funds failed to gain control of the board of TimeWarner.

In 1989, the Supreme Court of Delaware ruled that directors of the Time publishing company could turn down a US$220m. hostile bid from Paramount and accept a lower bid from the friendly Warner company creating TimeWarner, despite the effect on shareholders. Since then, boards of the many major US companies incorporated in Delaware became entrenched, and felt safe from pressure from their shareholders. Then they adopted anti-takeover poison pills, staggered board elections (thus making it impossible to replace a board at one time), and ignored shareholders' pressure to change board membership.

The market for corporate control, that is the ever-present threat of a hostile takeover bid from a predator company, is supposed to provide an incentive for board performance and is another potential driver of governance power. In liquid markets (such as the US and the UK), the potential of the market for control is significant and boards need to be constantly vigilant on corporate performance and their share price. As we will see in a subsequent chapter this is a significant feature that distinguishes corporate governance systems and practices in these countries from those where the stock markets are relatively illiquid and reliance is placed more on debt capital (such as Germany and Japan). In such markets driven by debt rather than equity, the banks and other sources of finance become a driving force for good governance.

In passing we should also note that giving directors and top management incentives in the form of stock options also provides a driver for better governance.

In some countries controlling block-holders of shares, often founders and their families, also provide a significant driver of governance power by being able to influence decisions in the boardroom over and above the power of the shareholder vote. However, the deepening of the stock markets in countries such as Italy and Spain is beginning to reduce some of the significance of such block-holders.

Finally, in reviewing drivers of governance we should note the effective driver of governance that a holding company has over the subsidiary and associated companies in its group, that family members have over the board of a family company, and that the joint venture partners have, through the joint venture agreement, over their jointly-held joint venture company. We will explore the nature and governance of such entities in a future chapter.

REFERENCES AND FURTHER READING

Clarke, T. (2004) *Theories of Corporate Governance*. London and New York: Routledge.

—— (2007) *International Corporate Governance: A Comparative Approach*. London and New York: Routledge.

Colley, John L. et al. (2003) *Corporate Governance?* New York: McGraw Hill.

—— (2005) *What is Corporate Governance?* New York: McGraw Hill.

Davies, Adrian (1999) *A Strategic Approach to Corporate Governance*. London: Gower.

Hilmer, Frederick G. (1993) *Strictly Boardroom: Improving Governance to Enhance Company Performance*. Sydney and Melbourne: The Sydney Institute and Information Australia.

Mallin, Chris (2006) *International Handbook on Corporate Governance*. London: Edward Elgar Publishing.

Monks, Robert A. G. and Nell Minow (2007) *Corporate Governance*, 4th edn. Chichester, UK: Wiley.

USEFUL WEBSITES

www.governance.co.uk
Governance, an international monthly newsletter on issues of corporate governance, boardroom performance, and shareholder activism.

www.icgn.org
International Corporate Governance Network—exchanging corporate governance information internationally and raising standards.

www.oecd.org
(follow links by topic or country to corporate governance) Organisation for Economic Co-operation and Development—corporate governance principles and discussion of corporate governance topics.

www.sec.gov
US Securities and Exchange Commission—their role, latest regulations, filing requirements including a tutorial on the 'EDGAR' filing system

PROJECTS AND EXERCISES

1. The European Union has passed legislation permitting the incorporation of a 'European Company' transcending the borders of its member states. Would it be a good idea if companies could be incorporated in the United States at the federal level?

2. Chart the governance and management structure of a corporate entity with which you are familiar using the circle and triangle schematic. Academic, sporting, or professional bodies could be covered as well as public or private companies. Does the diagram help to depict the potential to exercise power in that organization?

3. Consider the scope of corporate governance outlined in figure 2.8. In your opinion does this adequately cover the extent of the subject? What would you change to give a better perspective?

SELF-TEST QUESTIONS

To confirm your grasp of the key points in this chapter try answering the following questions. Answers are at the end of the book.

1. Why does a corporate entity need a constitution?

2. What is the principal difference between a private and a public company?

3. Explain the difference between governance and management.

4. What are the two aspects of the board's work that can provide a paradox for the unitary board?

5. Describe the scope of corporate governance.

6. Where can one inspect company accounts, annual returns, and other documents filed under the UK Companies Acts?

7. What led to the creation of the US Securities and Exchange Commission? When?

8. What is the mission of the US Securities and Exchange Commission?

9. What does the SEC enforcement authority do?

10. What is CSR? Is this part of the scope of corporate governance?

3   Directors and Board Architecture

- In which we consider:
  - different types of 'director' and director appointment
  - the appointment of directors
  - the chairman and chief executive roles
  - board structures
  - board committees

Different Types of 'Director' and Director Appointment

The architecture of corporate governance is concerned with the design and style of governance and the way its structures match form with function. But before we proceed, we should note that the title 'director' needs to be used with care.

Firstly, consider the legal title *director*. Company law in most jurisdictions does not distinguish between different types of director. In these laws directors all have similar roles and responsibilities. Moreover, any person occupying the position of director may be treated as a director in law, though given another title (for example 'governor'). Now let us distinguish some further uses of the title 'director'.

An *executive director* is a member of the board of directors who is also an executive manager of the company, as noted in the previous chapter. In the wording of our governance/management model, an executive director is a member of both the board circle and the management triangle. The chief executive officer, often known as the *managing director* in commonwealth law jurisdictions, is likely to be a member of the board, but does not have to be. Similarly, the chief finance officer, the chief operating officer and other members of what is sometimes called the 'C' suite of top executive officers may or may not also be executive directors.

By contrast a *non-executive director* is a member of the board who does not hold any executive management position in the company. In recent years, a further distinction has crystallized between those non-executive directors who are independent of the company and those who, though not executives, have other connections with it.

The *independent non-executive director* (INED) is a director with no affiliation or other relationship with the company, other than the directorship, that could affect, or be seen to affect, the exercise of objective, independent judgement. The definition of independence in a director is clarified in the codes of good practice in corporate governance, as we shall see in chapter 7. The definitions of independence used by the International Finance Corporation (see below) lists the criteria that are typically used. In reality, however, independence is a state of mind. As well as meeting the independence criteria, the successful INED needs to be capable of thinking independently, making a stand and, if necessary, being tough-minded.

However, the affiliated or *connected non-executive director* (CNED) is a director who, though not a member of management, does have some relationship with the company. The connection might be that the director is a retired executive of that company; is a close relative of the chairman or the chief executive; was nominated by a large shareholder; is linked with an important supplier, distributor, or customer; is a representative of a major financial partner; or is even a retired partner of the firm's external audit firm. Of course, there may be good reasons for appointing a person with such experience or connections to the board, but they should be recognized as connected not independent. The significance of the distinction between INED and CNED will become clear when we study the requirements in most codes of good corporate governance practice for independent directors to serve on various board committees.

A question that is often raised about the classification of an INED is whether an INED can ever be, genuinely, independent? Some question the nomination process. A potential director's name may well be suggested by existing directors, particularly the chairman or chief executive. Such a nomination may be influenced more by personal relationship than the reputation, experience, and ability of the new member and their potential to contribute productively to board deliberations. On the other hand, the new member does have to work with the board and be acceptable in its unique culture, so the reactions of the existing directors, particularly the chairman are not unimportant. We will shortly discuss the use of a board nominating committee to help to resolve this dilemma. Other commentators express concern about INEDs who serve for long periods. The longer the length of service, the more a director learns about that board and the company the greater the contribution to board decisions. But the more a director becomes part of the board culture, being involved in the long term evolution of the company, the less that director is able to exercise, and be seen to exercise, really objective, independent judgement.

Case Study 3.1 The International Finance Corporation (IFC)

A Definition of Independent Director

IFC is an international body at governmental level, which suggests that:

> The purpose of identifying and appointing independent directors is to ensure that the board includes directors who can effectively exercise their best judgment for the exclusive benefit of the Company, judgment that is not clouded by real or perceived conflicts of interest. IFC expects that in each case where a director is identified as 'independent' the board of directors will affirmatively determine that such director meets the requirements established by the board and is otherwise free of material relations with the Company's management, controllers, or others that might reasonably be expected to interfere with the independent exercise of his/her best judgment for the exclusive interest of the Company.

'Independent Director' means a director who is a person who:

1. Has not been employed by the Company or its Related Parties in the past five years.

2. Is not, and is not affiliated with a company that is, an advisor or consultant to the Company or its Related Parties.

3. Is not affiliated with a significant customer or supplier of the Company or its Related Parties.

4. Has no personal service contracts with the Company, its Related Parties, or its senior management.

5. Is not affiliated with a non-profit organization that receives significant funding from the Company or its Related Parties.

6. Is not employed as an executive of another company where any of the Company's executives serve on that company's board of directors.

7. Is not a member of the immediate family of an individual who is, or has been during the past five years, employed by the Company or its Related Parties as an executive officer.

8. Is not, nor in the past five years has been, affiliated with or employed by a present or former auditor of the Company or of a Related Party.

9. Or is not a controlling person of the Company (or member of a group of individuals and/or entities that collectively exercise effective control over the Company) or such person's brother, sister, parent, grandparent, child, cousin, aunt, uncle, nephew or niece, or a spouse, widow, in-law, heir, legatee and successor of any of the foregoing (or any trust or similar arrangement of which any such persons or a combination thereof are the sole beneficiaries) or the executor, administrator or personal representative of any Person described in this sub-paragraph who is deceased or legally incompetent, and for the purposes of this definition, a person shall be deemed to be 'affiliated' with a party if such person (i) has a direct or indirect ownership interest in; or (ii) is employed by such party; 'Related Party' shall mean, with respect to the Company, any person or entity that controls, is controlled by or is under common control with the Company.

(See www.ifc.org)

Discussion Questions

1. Is the definition of independence really so important? Why?

2. What sort of individual or organization might constitute 'related party'?

3. Are there any other relationships, not mentioned in the IFC definition that might compromise independence?

The term *outside director* is widely used in the United States and jurisdictions influenced by US practices to refer to a non-executive director, as previously noted. Unless there is evidence to the contrary, outside directors are typically perceived to be independent. Under the US federal law[1] independence requires a director not to accept any consulting, advisory, or other compensatory fee from the company or be an affiliated person of the company or any of its subsidiaries.

A s*hadow director* is a person who, though not formally a member of a board, is able to exert pressure on the decisions of that board. In many jurisdictions a shadow director can be held liable as though a legally appointed director of the company.

Box 3.1 Shadow Directors Identified

When the company law in Hong Kong was changed to require the regular publication of individual directors' remuneration, a number of prominent directors resigned. Many of them held major shareholdings in successful family businesses, which had been listed, and wanted to preserve the secrecy of their personal finances. However, where it was apparent that the board continued to be strongly influenced by their thinking, they were recognized as shadow directors, and held responsible as though they were directors.

The constitutions of some companies allow for the appointment of an *alternate director*, a person who can take the place of another director when that director cannot attend meetings. Alternate directors are often named for directors who live in different countries and cannot attend every board meeting. When acting as a director, the alternate has all the rights and duties of any other director under company law.

A *nominee director* is a director who has been nominated to the board by a major shareholder or other contractual stakeholder, such as a significant lender, to represent their interests. Nominee directors can find themselves in tricky situations because of their inevitable dual loyalties. As a director they owe a duty to the company—that is to all the shareholders equally. In board deliberations they should be representing the interests of all shareholders and contractual stakeholders equally, not representing one set of interests alone. Moreover, they may not divulge sensitive information to an outside party. Yet that is precisely why the nominator had the director appointed in the first place. We will consider this issue further in chapter 11 on directors' responsibilities.

A *governing director* is a title used mainly in Australia to describe a director with dominant powers in a private company. Although the Australian legislation requires such companies to have two directors, the statutes do not prevent companies from framing their articles of association to give virtually all powers to one person: the governing director.

A phrase that is sometimes heard, particularly in Europe, is *worker director* or *employee director*. Proponents of industrial democracy argue that, since governing a major company requires an informal partnership between labour and capital, employees should participate in corporate governance. In the German supervisory board one half of the members are

---

[1]Sarbanes-Oxley Act 2002 sec 301.

Case Study 3.2 Finance House Appoints Nominee Director

An electronics company was incorporated in Palo Alto California to develop, launch, and market a new satellite tracking device. A New York based financial institution provided the initial working capital under an agreement to turn the loan into equity when the company was listed. The terms of the agreement provided for the finance house to nominate a director to the board of the start-up company.

All went well for the first two years, when the 'rate of burn' (the level of initial expenditure) was within budget. Unfortunately, the expected technological breakthrough did not occur and by year three the finance house was getting concerned. The director they had nominated to the board found himself being frozen out of technical discussions by the executive directors and unable to obtain satisfactory answers to his questions. The matter had eventually to be resolved formally between the finance house and the company, based on the original agreement.

Discussion Questions

1. How should the nominee director in this case react to the situation described?

2. What role should the nominee director play in board meetings of the electronics company?

---

chosen under the co-determination laws through the employees' trades union processes. In the 1970s, the draft fifth directive of the European Community (now the European Union) proposed supervisory boards with employee representation for all large companies in member states. The British Bullock Report, written in response to the EEC directive, proposed unitary boards but with some worker directors. Neither proposal became law. Since then the company law harmonization process in the EC has been overtaken by social legislation, including the requirement that all major firms should have a works council through which employees can participate in significant strategic developments and changes in corporate policy.

Finally, we come to the person who has the title of director but who is not legally a member of the board at all. Many companies create titles including the word 'director' for senior executives who are not, in fact, members of either the main board or, indeed, the board of a subsidiary company. Such people are sometimes referred to as a*ssociate directors.*

Associate directors do not have the rights or responsibilities of a director, unless those dealing with them could reasonably believe that they were dealing with a member of the board with the authority to speak for the company, in which case the associate director might be held to have bound the company and accept personal responsibility.

Why do companies give executives an associate director title? There seem to be three basic reasons—prestige, reward, and status. The title 'director' tends to convey a level of standing and respect, which some clients, customers, or other authorities dealing with the company expect. Other companies use the title 'director' as a form of reward, in other words recognition for success. Finally, in some communities the title 'director' is a mark of distinction, with important social implications.

Box 3.2 Associate Directors

An international insurance broker based in London has a group devoted to writing airline insurance policies. Every member of the senior staff of that group has the title 'executive director'. None of them are members of the board of directors. The reason for their title is that their airline clients expect to be dealing with a person at director level.

An Australian commodities firm had a long serving security officer. He began his career as a uniformed guard at the gates. He had been promoted to sergeant, with a smarter uniform, then security officer, with a gold-braided cap, and finally was created 'Security Director'.

Sceptics in the company said that all this promotion was in lieu of pay increases. The man himself was well pleased. But he was not, legally, a director of the company.

In a major French organization the title 'directeur' was much sought after, even though directors were not members of the board and the title did not bestow any financial benefit. But directeurs were entitled to use the directors' dining room which boasted superb cuisine, and gave convivial access to members of top management.

Whilst discussing the concept of directorship, we should mention *cross-directorships*, which are directorships held by a set of directors in various companies. In the simplest form director A of company A is made a director of company B, whilst director B of company B joins the board of company A. Plotting common directors within a network of companies and identifying the key nodes—the directors who wield real power—can be interesting. In some countries the network of cross-directorships highlights surprising concentrations of power within a relatively small circle of people. The arguments for cross-directorships are, obviously, that the network of linkages brings economic benefits to the companies concerned, and enables the rare talents of experienced and well-connected directors to be more widely available. The counter-argument is that such concentration of power is undesirable because it is not readily transparent and not the focus for accountability. Cross-directorships are typically legal, provided that there is nothing in a company's constitution preventing them and that the companies are not competing, in which case anti-monopoly rules might come into play. The Saint-Gobain case that follows provides an example of cross-directorships.

The Appointment of Directors

There are three situations that lead to the appointment of a director: re-appointment on the expiry of a director's term of office, appointment to fill a vacancy arising on a resignation, death, or when a director is unable to serve, and on the creation of an additional directorship.

How are directors appointed? In the original 19th century model of the limited liability company the shareholder members met and decided. The founder, chairman, or

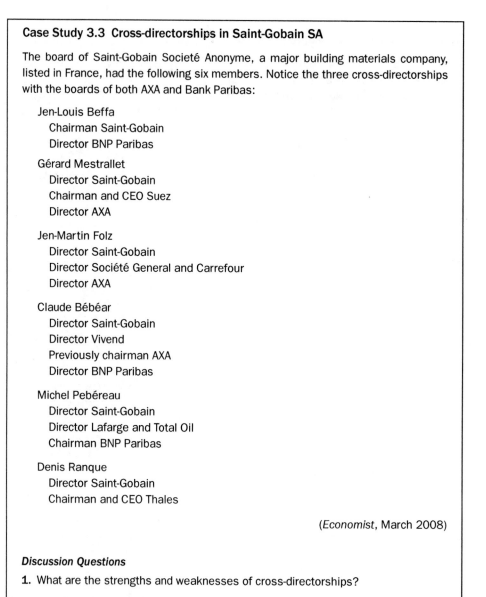

Case Study 3.3 Cross-directorships in Saint-Gobain SA

The board of Saint-Gobain Societé Anonyme, a major building materials company, listed in France, had the following six members. Notice the three cross-directorships with the boards of both AXA and Bank Paribas:

Jen-Louis Beffa
  Chairman Saint-Gobain
  Director BNP Paribas

Gérard Mestrallet
  Director Saint-Gobain
  Chairman and CEO Suez
  Director AXA

Jen-Martin Folz
  Director Saint-Gobain
  Director Société General and Carrefour
  Director AXA

Claude Bébéar
  Director Saint-Gobain
  Director Vivend
  Previously chairman AXA
  Director BNP Paribas

Michel Pebéreau
  Director Saint-Gobain
  Director Lafarge and Total Oil
  Chairman BNP Paribas

Denis Ranque
  Director Saint-Gobain
  Chairman and CEO Thales

(*Economist*, March 2008)

Discussion Questions

1. What are the strengths and weaknesses of cross-directorships?

2. Should cross-directorships be regulated?

entrepreneur in the company made suggestions; occasionally so did other members. The decision was formalized in a properly convened meeting of the shareholders. This is still the case in many private companies and family firms.

But as companies grew in scale, became more diverse and spread geographically, so did their public shareholders, as Berle and Means (1932) showed. It was not feasible for the large number of shareholders, with varying degrees of investment, and located around the country and sometimes the world, to influence decisions on directors' appointment or re-appointment. The directors of major listed companies were now being chosen by the existing directors, particularly the executive directors, and routinely approved by shareholders in their annual general meeting. Critics complained that boards can become self-perpetuating clubs of like-minded people, routinely chosen from small networks of influence. In England it was claimed that in some public companies directors were being selected by 'the old school tie', meaning that directors chose those who came from the same background as themselves. In the United States it was recommendations from fellow members of the country club or business school fraternities that held sway. In France it was the networks of those educated in the elite grandes ecoles who peopled both boardroom and key government posts.

The response to this apparent dilemma was to appoint a greater proportion of INEDs to boards and to require them, as members of a nominating committee, to take a more objective view on nominations for new board members. We will explore the role of the nominating committee later in this chapter.

But the issue has not been resolved. Shareholders in public listed companies still have little opportunity to influence the nomination of new directors, unless they hold a significant proportion of the voting shares. Various proposals have been put forward to enable shareholders to nominate directors. Some would have the institutional investors play a larger role. Others would allow shareholders to create and vote on a 'slate' of directors they had proposed. Another idea, from Shann Turnbull, would be for the shareholders to form a shareholders' committee, which could represent all the shareholders in dealings with the company, including nominating new directors.

Case Study 3.4 The Removal of Directors: Trans-Tec

Eight directors of Trans-Tec, a British engineering group which collapsed, were banned from being company directors under UK company law for a total of forty-two years following an investigation for presenting a false picture to the group's auditors and for intentionally producing and signing misleading or false accounts. The investigation found that the managers were unsuited to their roles.

Discussion Questions

1. Each of the TransTec directors was banned from being company director for an average of five years. Is this an appropriate punishment?

2. On the completion of the exclusion period would they be any more likely to be suitable as a director?

The Chairman and Chief Executive Roles

The roles of chairman and chief executive continue to be one of the contentious and unresolved dilemmas in corporate governance. Although many commentators refer to the 'chairman of the company', we should note that in reality the chairman is chairman of the board of directors, not the company. Company law has relatively little to say about the specific role of the chairman. It is the company's constitution that determines the way the chairman of the board is appointed (typically by a simple decision of the board), the duties of the chairman, and other aspects of the role. The chief executive (called managing director in some cases), on the other hand, is an employee of the company and, as we saw in the last chapter, a member of management.

A key question in contemporary corporate governance is whether the chairmanship and chief executive roles should be separate or combined in one person. The view of all of the codes of good practice in corporate governance is that the roles should be separate.

'*The roles of chairman and chief executive should not be exercised by the same individual. The division of responsibilities between the chairman and chief executive should be clearly established, set out in writing and agreed by the board*' (Principle A2.1 of the UK Combined Code on corporate governance). The argument is that separation, providing duality at the top of the company, produces a check and balance mechanism, avoids the potential for abuse if power is concentrated in a single person, and enables the chief executive to concentrate on managing the business whilst the chairman handles the running of the board and relations with shareholders and other non-contractual shareholders such as the government, the regulators and the media. We will explore the role of the chairman in detail in chapter 10, 'The Reality of the Boardroom'.

Despite the well honed recommendation around the world that the chairmanship and CEO should be separate, in the United States the roles are frequently combined. The arguments in favour of combined roles are that a dynamic enterprise needs just one leader, that spreading leadership duties between two people leads to conflict, and that this is the way American companies have been run very successfully for generations. In recent

---

Case Study 3.5 Marks and Spencer: Combining the Roles of Chairman and CEO

Marks and Spencer Plc, the long established and successful UK retailer, announced that '*Lord Burns will stand down as Chairman with effect from 1 June 2008*' and that '*Sir Stuart Rose (the current chief executive) is appointed Executive Chairman from the same date.*'

Investors, analysts, and media commentators were aghast. Sir Stuart had worked for the company for seventeen years and was recognized as having done a remarkable job in warding off a hostile take-over bid, improving the company's fortunes, and strategically positioning the company for the future. But combining the role of chairman and CEO was a breach of the principles of the UK Combined Code on Corporate Governance and would require the company to explain officially why it had not followed the code.

In a subsequent letter to shareholders the retiring chairman wrote:

I joined the board as Deputy Chairman in 2005 and became chairman in 2006 . . . Although a lot of new talent had come into the company, or had been developed internally, it became apparent to the board that . . . none of these would be ready to assume the role of Chief Executive by 2009. One option was to bring in a new Chief Executive from outside the organization . . . However, the retail environment started to deteriorate in the second half of 2007 . . . and it became clear that . . . a new Chief Executive was likely to be a damaging and unwelcome distraction at precisely the time when the business needed clear leadership . . . [S]everal meetings were held with major institutional shareholders. A recurring theme was concern about succession, and the need for certainty and continuity.

The Board is very conscious of the governance arguments that companies should split the roles of Chairman and Chief executive as it is undesirable to have too much concentration of authority in one person.

However in appointing Stuart as Executive Chairman the Board was aware of the need to put in place balancing controls to mitigate the governance concerns . . . accordingly the Board agreed to:

1. A limited period of appointment until 2011 when the Company will revert to the conventional model of Chairman and Chief Executive

2. The appointment of Sir David Michels as Deputy Chairman (continuing his role as Senior Independent Director)

3. Clear specification of duties of Chairman and Deputy Chairman Group Finance and Operation Director

4. Recruitment of an additional non-executive director

5. Annual voting by shareholders for Stuart's re-appointment as a director.

The company raised another furore with shareholders in June 2008 when it announced that it was lowering the target figure in the long term incentive bonus for Sir Stuart Rose, explaining that the move was an acknowledgement that the retail market had fallen and that previous year's high growth could not be maintained. The bonus scheme called for 8 percent growth plus inflation in earnings per share from 2008 to 2011 to earn a potential £4.2 million. The company said it had consulted with its ten largest shareholders and the Association of British Insurers (ABI).

Discussion Questions

1. What is your reaction to the proposal to appoint Sir Stuart Rose as Executive Chairman? What are the arguments for and against?

2. Are you convinced by the explanation from the current Chairman?

3. Will the appointment of a deputy chairman and further directors resolve the situation? Why did the board not foresee this situation and plan succession?

4. Why could the existing situation not be extended until 2011, when the company planned to appoint a new chief executive?

5. If you could advise the board, what would you suggest?

6. What are your reactions to the bonus statement?

years, following a number of dramatic and heavily reported company collapses in the US, many of them apparently due to the abuse of power by the head of the company, there have been calls from institutional investors for the roles to be separated. Not surprisingly, however, these views have been resisted by many incumbents of the combined positions, because separation would erode some of their power. Such views are often supported by their INEDs, because many of them hold the combined roles in their own companies. Interestingly, however, in the most dramatic collapse of all—Enron—the roles *were* separated.

There is no doubt that, where the roles of chairman and CEO are separated, the relationship between the chairman and the CEO is particularly important. Where it works well, as Sir Adrian Cadbury explains in his book on chairmanship, it can be a subtle, productive, and personally rewarding relationship. Where it fails, it can lead to major corporate problems and considerable personal stress.

Which raises another contentious issue in this context: should a retiring CEO be reappointed as chairman of the company's board? Those in favour point out the years of experience, knowledge, and connections that the retiring top executive could bring to the board as its chair, experience that would otherwise be lost. Those questioning the move point out potential difficulties for the new CEO. It is a rare person, having been a successful CEO, who can pass on the managerial reins to a new CEO without interfering in the day to day running of the business. As we shall see, some codes of good practice in corporate governance oppose the retiring CEO becoming chairman in that company.

Case Study 3.6 Vodafone

Institutional investors in Vodafone Plc demanded changes to the board of this European mobile telephone group. The issue surfaced when the chairman Lord MacLaurin appeared to be at loggerheads with his CEO Arun Sarin. But further investigation questioned the independence of the Deputy Chairman Paul Hazen, who was the board's senior independent director responsible for liaising with the investors. Hazen was shown to have worked with Sarin for many years at Airtouch, an American mobile business, which had been acquired by Vodafone. One institutional investor said '*Hazen is more like Sarin's mentor than an independent*'. Another commented that some of the other so-called independent directors had in fact joined the board as part of takeover agreements with companies that had been acquired by Vodafone. 'The board is being run as a Sarin fiefdom', he said. Subsequently the company added new INEDs.

Discussion Question

1. Should directors or executives of a company that has been taken over, be appointed to the board of the acquiring company? Can they be considered genuinely independent? Would your answer be different if the employee or director retired from the acquired company?

Board Structures

An issue that has been widely written about in corporate governance is the formal structure of the board. What is the appropriate balance between executive and non-executive members? What is the appropriate size for the board? Intuitively, there are four possible structures—a board with just executive directors, a board with a majority of executive directors, a board with a majority of non-executive directors, and a board with only non-executive directors. Where there is a single governing body, as in these four models, the board is known as a unitary board, in contrast with the two-tier board to be considered subsequently.

In the *all executive director board* the top managers are also the directors. (See figure 3.1.)

This structure is found today in many small, family firms and start-up businesses. Typically, the business has not reached the stage at which there is a need for non-executive directors. Directors on such boards seldom draw a distinction between their roles as managers and their duties as directors. In the minds of the directors, the company is a legal convenience, perhaps with taxation advantages and limiting liability, rather than a distinct legal entity. Even bankers providing finance to such a company often require personal guarantees from individual directors to cover loans made to the company. As we will see later, the all executive director board is also found frequently in the board structures of subsidiary companies operating in corporate groups.

In the *majority executive director board* some non-executive directors have been invited to join the board, even though they remain in the minority. (See Figure 3.2.)

The addition of non-executive directors to a board can arise for various reasons. The executive directors of a successful, growing company may feel the need for additional expertise to back up their own experience, perhaps as they enter new markets, get involved in new technologies, or face more complex managerial or financial issues. The price of accepting significant growth capital from an outside source may also result in the requirement to allow a non-executive director to represent the interests of the lender. (See the boxed case Finance House Appoints Nominee Director above.) A family firm moving into the second generation may find that, whilst some family members continue to be directly involved in the management of the firm, others are now outside the firm and shareholders only. Calls for non-executive directors to represent the non-management family shareholders

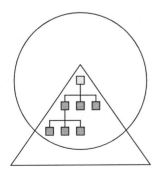

Figure 3.1 The all executive director board

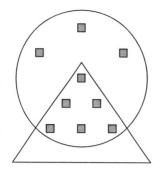

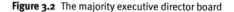

Figure 3.2 The majority executive director board

on the board may now arise. The challenges of governance in family firms will be discussed later.

However in the majority executive board, as non-executive directors are added to a board, the executive directors remain in the majority and typically continue to exercise considerable power over the company. This model reflected the typical structure of the British public listed company until the 1970s. Research has shown that, at that time, the boards of even major companies had a majority of executive directors. The conventional wisdom was that non-executive directors could be quite useful on a board, adding additional experience, perspective, and insight to discussions, that about a third non-executive directors was about right, but that the non-executives should never be in the majority. In those days executive directors wielded the power over what they perceived as '*their*' company.

However, in the United States, the United Kingdom, and similar advanced economies the boards of most significant listed companies now have a majority of non-executive directors and many of these non-executive directors are likely to be independent directors. (See figure 3.3.)

Clearly, where non-executive directors are in the majority, the culture of the board, its internal relationships and, indeed, its activities are likely to be different from boards dominated by executive directors. The typical board of a company listed in the United States will have only two or three executive directors—the chairman/CEO, the chief operating officer, and the chief finance officer, perhaps—with three or four times that number of outside directors. Nevertheless, the chairman/CEO continues to wield considerable power, because these roles are typically combined in a single person.

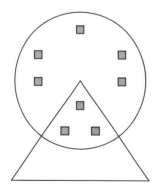

Figure 3.3 The majority non-executive director board

Consequently the outside directors are expected to provide oversight and supervision of executive activities, the achievement of corporate objectives and assurance of compliance with corporate governance requirements. Since independence criteria require outside directors to have no relationship with the company, other than the directorship, which can mean that such directors have relatively little knowledge of the company's industry or markets. So the formulation of strategy has to be led by the CEO, with the board questioning to ensure that strategic developments are in an appropriate direction and that business risks have been appropriately assessed. Critics of this type of board structure suggest that in practice, it gives too much power to the executive directors by making them responsible for strategy as well as the day to day running of the enterprise. The outside directors, they suggest, are inevitably pushed into a conformance and compliance mode, rather than contributing positively to the performance aspects of strategy formulation and policy making. '*Such board structures are pushing us towards the European two-tier board system*' one experienced director of a British public company argued.

Case Study 3.7 Board Architecture at Arcelor Mittal

The merger of steel makers Arcelor and Mittal in 2006 produced the world's largest steel company, with 330,000 employees and forecast earnings of US$15.6 billion. Arcelor had fought a long defensive battle against the hostile takeover, valued at around US$35 billion. Arcelor was incorporated in Luxembourg and had adopted European governance architecture, with a supervisory board, including employee representatives, and a management board.

Mittal was a family company with a tradition of growth through acquisition, in which the founding family still played the dominant role. Arcelor had criticized Mittal for its inadequate controls, because it had many Mittal family members and few independent directors on its board.

In the merged Arcelor Mittal company the Mittal family retained 43.5 percent of the voting equity. The new board was eighteen strong, with chairman Joseph Kinsch, who was previously chairman of Arcelor, president Lakshmi Mittal, nine independent directors, plus employee representative directors and nominee directors to reflect the interests of significant shareholders.

The General Management Board was chaired by the CEO Roland Junck, with the son of Lakshmi Mittal, Aditya Mittal as CFO.

(For more information see www.arcelormittal.com and www.mittalsteel.com)

Discussion Questions

1. What is your opinion of this board structure?

2. With eighteen members, is the board likely to prove a viable vehicle for strategic discussion or active management supervision?

3. Since the Mittal family retain 43.5% of the voting equity can an institutional investor make a significant contribution to the governance of the company?

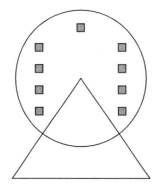

Figure 3.4 The all non-executive director board

Finally, there is an obvious fourth category of board structure: the board composed entirely of non-executive directors. (See figure 3.4.)

Such board structures are seldom found in listed public companies, but frequently in the boards of not-for-profit entities, such as charitable organizations, arts, health and sports organizations, and quangos (quasi-autonomous non-government organizations). The boards of some subsidiary companies in corporate groups may also have such a structure, where the board consists of senior executives from elsewhere in the corporate organization. Where boards have this structure, the chief executive and, perhaps, members of the management team, typically attend board meetings but are there to provide information and answer directors' questions not to be formally involved in the making of decisions. Indeed, in most cases, the constitution will provide for the board to invite managers to attend meetings, either for the entire agenda or for specific items, but reserving the right to ask them to leave and for the board to take decisions in camera.

We will explore the governance of complex corporate groups, including their governance architecture, in the next chapter.

It will be apparent to readers that, conceptually, the all non-executive board has the same structure as the European two-tier or supervisory board architecture. Figure 4 can be re-drafted to show this, as in figure 3.5.

In the German approach to corporate governance, large and public companies are required to have a two-tier board structure: the upper, supervisory board, called the *aufsichtsrat* and the lower, management board or committee, called the *vorstand*. The

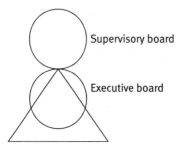

Supervisory board

Executive board

Figure 3.5 The two-tier or supervisory board

supervisory board is comprised entirely of outside directors and the management board entirely of executive directors.

Germany has long believed that the management of large companies should involve a close relationship between the workers and the company, an informal partnership between labour and capital. This process, referred to as co-determination, is enshrined in law. As a result, half of the members of supervisory boards represent the interests of the employees and are appointed through the trades' union organizations. The other supervisory board members represent the interest of the shareholders and are appointed by them.

In practice, members of the executive board attend meetings of the supervisory board, but have no vote. The executive members present their strategies, management plans, and budgets to the supervisory board for comment and approval. If necessary the supervisory board refers matters back to the executives for further consideration. The supervisory board can then review and assess subsequent managerial performance. The power of the supervisory board lies in its ability to appoint and remove members from the executive board.

The German Corporate Governance Commission launched a code of best practice (Kodex) in 2002, which provided supervisory boards with more powers over management and external audit, required details of directors' remuneration (including the criteria for performance based rewards), and gave investors more timely information. Whilst technically voluntary, some of the provisions have been enshrined in company law. Since 2003, German companies have had to issue an annual statement published online, showing whether they have complied with the code and explaining any discrepancies.

Case Study 3.8 Volkswagen's Supervisory Board

German company Volkswagen, Europe's largest carmaker, had a supervisory board. In 2005 institutional investors demanded that the chairman of the supervisory board, Herr. Piëch, resign because of alleged conflicts of interest. They claimed that H. Piëch and his family held significant shares in Porsche, who held a near 20 percent stake in Volkswagen.

German's voluntary corporate governance code states that conflicts of interest should result in the termination of a supervisory board members' mandate. H. Piëch claimed that the conflict would be managed by him leaving the room whenever any Porsche related matter was discussed. Some American institutional investors called this 'naive'. H. Piëch was strongly supported by the ten employee representatives on the twenty strong board.

Discussion Questions

1. Many boards require directors, who declare a conflict of interest, to leave the room when the relevant issue is discussed. What is your opinion of this practice? Is it 'naive' as some investors in this case claimed?

2. Given that H. Piëch was strongly supported by all ten employee representatives on the supervisory board, do the shareholder representatives on that board have grounds for complaint?

Case Study 3.9 Vodafone/Mannesmann

The first hostile takeover by a foreign firm in German corporate history occurred in 2000 when Vodafone, then a UK company, made a successful bid for the German company Mannesmann. Mannesmann used the classic German two-tier corporate governance structure with a wholly executive board appointed and overseen by a supervisory board, which had both shareholders and employee representatives.

An acrimonious meeting of the Mannesmann shareholders followed the acquisition. They claimed that severance bonuses of around £50 million paid as part of the bid negotiations to the Mannesmann head, Klaus Esser, and other top executives, were immoral, reduced the company's value and had been designed to influence the bid. 'Crooks' and 'looters' were two of the epithets hurled at members of both the executive and supervisory boards.

A member of the supervisory board, Klaus Zwickel (Head of IG Metall, the Metalworkers Union) protested that the bonuses were 'indecently high', until it was pointed out that he was present and voted in favour of them at the supervisory board meeting. Initially Vodafone said it knew nothing of the bonuses, but later conceded that the idea had come from Hong Kong based Hutchison Whampoa, one of Mannesmann's major shareholders, and that Vodafone had agreed to permit any such payments provided that they were made legally.

In Anglo-American corporate governance an open market for control, facilitating takeover activity, is seen as essential to a healthy capital market. The potential of a hostile bid for under-performing companies can act as an important motivator to boards. For over a decade, the European Union had been trying to develop Europe-wide laws that would facilitate hostile bids and restrict company defences against them. But in Germany hostile takeovers are viewed with suspicion by both management and unions. The Mannesmann case reinforced this opinion. Facing pressure from its companies and trades unions, the German government actively sabotaged the European Union proposals, offering instead its own weaker set of controls, which, effectively, permit some defensive actions if backed by the company's supervisory board. Many commentators believe that Germany has sound governance structures but sub-standard disclosure practices; calling for a process that is more transparent and facilitates an open market in corporate control.

Discussion Questions

1. Why did the Mannesmann supervisory board agree to the severance bonuses being paid to their top executives at the time of the takeover by Vodafone?

2. What role should a supervisory board take when their company is faced with a hostile takeover?

3. If an open market for control, which enables takeover activity, is essential for a healthy market, what safeguards should be built in to protect the interests of employees, shareholders, and other legitimate stakeholders in a target company?

The corporate governance architecture of Dutch companies also adopts the two-tier board. But the supervisory board has a tripartite structure—one-third representing capital, one-third employees, and the other third society at large. A companies court resolves questions about the suitability of members to represent the three interest groups.

As we saw earlier, at one time the Commission of the European Union (or European Economic Community as it then was) believed that the two-tier board should be adopted in all member states, but subsequently a more adaptable approach has been adopted. The legal framework in those countries that adopt the two-tier board model, is typically based on continental European, Napoleonic law, which is rule based rather than rooted in case law that evolves from the precedents of decided cases, as is the case in the United States, the United Kingdom, and Commonwealth countries with law derived originally from British law.

Taiwan also uses two-tier boards. In mainland China, the authorities, in creating the corporate governance structures and processes for their large number of newly privatized and listed companies, fascinatingly, require a two-tier with a supervisory board and a main board but, quite unlike the continental European model, also called for independent outside directors on the main board. We will explore corporate governance in China and other cultures in chapter 8.

Advisory committees or boards are sometimes created by companies operating internationally in different parts of the world, to give advice to the corporate directors. Typically prominent business leaders, politicians, and other influential figures from the region are invited to serve, but not given executive powers. Advisory boards were more prevalent in the 1970s and early 1980s. Subsequently, companies found that the advice they needed could be obtained more cheaply from consultants, who need be retained only as long as their advice was wanted. Some also found that advisory boards, although they had no formal executive authority, assumed an independence that created complications by making policy recommendations, which were inconsistent with group-wide needs. An advisory board might, for example, call for investment in a given country, when the board's global strategy called for disinvestment there.

Some data showing differences in corporate governance structures between various countries are shown in Table 3.1 overleaf.

Board Committees

In recent years an important development in corporate governance has been the formalization of board committees. The three principal board committees are the audit committee, the remuneration committee, and the nominating committee. These committees are standing committees of the main board established formally for specific purposes.

The Audit Committee

The independent, external auditor plays a fundamentally important role in corporate governance, reporting to the members that the information provided by the directors to the

Table 3.1 **Listed company board characteristics**

Country	Chairman/ CEO separation	Average board size	% outside directors
Unitary board model			
Australia	Very high	8	High
Belgium	High	15	High
Brazil	Low	6	Moderate
Canada	High	13	Very high
France	Nil	13	High
Hong Kong[2]	Very low	8	Low
Italy	Total	11	High
Spain	Low	12	High
Sweden	High	9	Very high
Switzerland	High	5	Very high
UK	Very high	12	High
USA	Very low	13	Very high
Two-tier board model			
France	Total	12	Very high
Germany	Total	15	Total
Netherlands	Total	7	Total
Business network model			
Japan	Total	large	Very low

shareholder members gives a true and fair view. Later in the book we will see how this role is evolving as concepts of risk management and the assessment of internal control become incorporated into traditional approaches to historical financial audit. The United States' SOX Act (which we will also study later) has also enhanced the auditor's role in companies listed in the United States and their subsidiaries around the world.

Inevitably, issues arise during an audit; for example, the valuation of inventory items, whether certain expenditures should be capitalized or written off to the profit and loss account, or concerns about the financial control systems. Obviously, every director should be aware of any significant matters that have arisen during the audit. However, since the finance director and, perhaps, the CEO tend to be closely involved with the auditors during the audit, such issues can often be resolved before the auditor writes his report and the board is consequently left in ignorance.

The idea of the audit committee, which originated in the United States in the 1970s, aimed to avoid such domination of the audit process by senior executives and provide a bridge between the external auditor and the board. Classically, the audit committee

---

[2]Though this is changing as Hong Kong lists more companies incorporated and operating in mainland China.

would be a standing committee of the main board, created under a board policy and comprised entirely or predominantly of INEDs. Typically, the audit committee would meet three or four times a year to discuss the details of the audit, to consider any contentious points that had arisen on the accounts and to receive the auditor's recommendations on audit-related matters such as management controls. The audit committee would often negotiate the audit fee and, if appropriate, recommend to the board if a change of auditor was necessary.

Today all codes of good practice in corporate governance and stock exchange listing requirements require listed companies to have audit committees, usually comprised entirely of INEDs, as we shall explore in depth in chapter 7. Moreover, the remit of many audit committees has expanded to cover the oversight of risk management, management control systems, internal audit, and corporate governance compliance.

The role and responsibilities of the audit committee should be established in writing in a charter agreed by the board, and should be regularly reviewed. The committee should set

---

Case Study 3.10 The Collapse of Arthur Andersen

Arthur Andersen, one of the world's top five accounting firms, prided itself on the quality and originality of its work. But it went dramatically out of business following a number of audit failures, including Waste Management, Worldcom, and Enron. Memorably at client company Enron, Arthur Andersen was accused of shredding papers sought by an SEC investigation, and appeared before a grand jury on charges of obstructing justice.

Clients quickly distanced themselves and many Andersen partners around the world smartly joined one of the remaining big four global audit firms. The confidence of the accounting profession, which traditionally had relied on professional self-regulation, was threatened when it realized that the market was really in control.

Subsequent concerns have been expressed about the loss of competitiveness in the audit market with a potential oligopoly of just four firms, competing for the business of the major global corporations. In the United States the Sarbanes-Oxley Act introduced new controls on the audit profession.

Discussion Questions

1. What is your opinion of the following solutions that have been suggested to the problem of auditors becoming too close to their client companies:

   • Prohibiting staff of an external auditor to join a client company (at least until the passage of a given period of time)

   • Requiring the staff leading the audit of a client company to rotate periodically

   • Requiring audit firms to change periodically?

2. Study the relevant parts of the Sarbanes-Oxley Act. Are they likely to be a cost-effective solution to the problems raised by the Enron case? (For more information on Enron see Appendix 1)

itself clear and measurable objectives, and review performance against them. The reasons for failing to meet their objectives should be diagnosed and remedied, reporting accordingly to the board.

Criticisms of audit committees include the concern that members can get too involved in executive management matters and interfere in management's legitimate responsibilities. Others complain that an audit committee can become bureaucratic and process driven rather than exercising sound commercial judgement. Concerns have also been expressed that the creation of a sub-set of the board with specific responsibility for ensuring compliance represents a move towards the European-style two-tier supervisory board, which proponents of the unitary board distrust.

The Remuneration Committee

The remuneration committee is also a sub-committee of the main board, consisting wholly or mainly of independent outside directors, which is set up with responsibility for overseeing the remuneration packages of board members, particularly the executive directors and, possibly, members of senior management.

For some years investigative media and institutional investors in both the United States and the United Kingdom have been challenging the apparently high levels of directors' remuneration. High rewards in companies with poor corporate performance were particularly suspect. In 1995, a group of City of London institutions commissioned Sir Richard Greenbury, then Chairman of Marks and Spencer Plc, to look into board level pay. The Greenbury Report provided a Code of Conduct, which has now been incorporated in the UK Combined Code, as we shall see in chapter 7.

This report recommended that companies should have remuneration committees consisting solely of independent non-executive directors. The role of the committee was, essentially, to make recommendations to the main board on the remuneration packages, including salary, fees, pension arrangements, options to acquire shares in the company, and other benefits (travel costs, use of executive jets, membership of clubs, housing costs, school fees, etc.) of the executive directors and, sometimes, other senior executives.

However, allegedly excessive director remuneration remains a concern around the world. The problem is how to provide sufficient incentive to directors in a competitive market for talent, rewarding success, whilst avoiding excesses and apparently rewarding failure. The hope is that incentives rewarding exceptional performance will align managers' interests with those of the shareholders. But rather than encouraging exceptional performance, such schemes can encourage exceptional deception, as directors manipulate share prices, revenues, or profits to meet the target criteria of the incentive scheme.

Moreover, even a remuneration committee, comprised entirely of INEDs, may not be totally independent. For example, if the members were originally nominated by the chairman or CEO, they may feel a loyalty towards them in making remuneration recommendations. If they are also themselves executive directors of other companies, recommending high rewards will tend to inflate market rates to their own benefit.

Legislation enacted in the UK in 2003 required quoted companies to publish a directors' remuneration report and put them to shareholder vote at the AGM. The report had to contain details of the members of the remuneration committee and anyone who advised that committee, a statement of the company's policy on directors' remuneration for the future, details of individual directors' remuneration, giving details of the performance criteria in incentive schemes, pensions and retirement benefits, their service contracts, and a line graph for the past five years showing how the company's performance has compared with competitors. Although shareholders vote on the report, the outcome remains advisory.

Case Study 3.11 BP and the Retirement of the Chief Executive

BP is the largest company in the British FTSE 100 index. Consequently, when in 2007 nearly a quarter of the voting shareholders showed their disapproval of the remuneration package of the outgoing chief executive, Lord Browne, the board had to take notice. Although BP chairman Peter Sutherland refused to call this a shareholder revolt, everyone else knew that it was.

Browne had spent forty-one years with the company, in his later years as chief executive, building it through aggressive acquisitions and strategic vision into an enterprise worth over £100 billion. But recent performance had been poor and there had been some safety disasters.

Browne brought forward his retirement by nearly three years before his contract ended. His remuneration package, approved by the remuneration committee, was worth £72 million. But it was a three year performance-related bonus that caused most shareholder anger, because it related to the period after he would have left the company.

Discussion Questions

1. BP's remuneration committee, comprised of independent outside directors elected by the shareholders, had recommended Lord Browne's remuneration package. The main board had accepted that recommendation. So did the significant proportion of the shareholders voting against approval have a legitimate case?

2. Would the use of independent remuneration consultants to advise the remuneration committee have improved the situation?

The Nominating Committee

There was a time in many countries when boards resembled comfortable clubs of people, well known to each other, who shared similar interests and, often, came from similar backgrounds, as we saw earlier.

The nominating committee was an attempt to prevent the board becoming a cosy club, in which the incumbent members appointed like-minded people to join their ranks. In effect it offered a check and balance mechanism designed to reduce the possibility of a dominant director, such as the chairman or CEO, pushing through their own candidates. As a sub-committee of the main board, the nominating committee is made up wholly, or mainly, of independent outside directors, to make recommendations on replacement or additional members of the board.

Unfortunately, the creation of a nominating committee does not resolve an underlying dilemma. On the one hand, an independent nominating committee can suggest potential directors with appropriate credentials, whilst avoiding claims of the old boys club. On the other hand, to be effective a board chairman needs to know, respect, and be able to work with the members of his or her board. To have members imposed on him or her could be divisive. If a board is to work together as a tough-minded, effective team, it also is just as well that they know and respect each other. Also, as we saw earlier, supposedly independent outside directors who form the committee may themselves feel a loyalty towards the chairman or CEO who nominated them.

Of the three committees recommended in the codes of good practice in corporate governance—the audit committee, the remuneration committee, and the nominating committee—it is the nominating committee that has been most resisted by boards. Neither is that surprising, given that the right to appoint to the board of directors goes to the very heart of corporate power.

Subject to their constitution, boards may create whatever other board committees they want. Faced with growing demands on directors' time, some boards form an *executive committee*, a *finance committee*, or a *general purpose committee* delegating responsibility to it for handling detailed aspects of the board's business. Such arrangements can contribute to board effectiveness, provided that the deliberations and decisions of the sub-committee are carefully minuted and reported to the main board, with opportunity for the other directors to be informed, to question and, if necessary, for the board to amend the sub-committee's decisions.

Some boards also create standing sub-committees to handle specific areas of board responsibility such as a *risk management committee*, a *corporate governance committee* or a *compliance committee*. The danger in board sub-committees is that the other directors, in effect, abdicate part of their responsibility to that committee.

Some boards also form *ad hoc committees* to be responsible for handling specific one-off issues. Examples include a committee set-up to handle the integration of two organizations following a merger between two companies, one set-up to be responsible for the handling of a public flotation of shares, or one required to report on strategic growth options by acquisition.

In setting up an ad hoc committee it is important that the objectives of the committee, the scope of its powers, and the form of its output, are carefully described in the board's policy document which creates it. Even more important is establishing how and when an ad hoc committee is to be wound up: committees have a tendency to perpetuate their existence.

In this chapter we have looked at various aspects of board level architecture—the way that the design of board structures and the use of board committees can affect the processes of corporate governance. Nevertheless, as we shall see throughout this book, it is people who really determine the outcome in governance situations. In corporate governance, personalities, politics, and power are usually more significant than systems.

REFERENCES AND FURTHER READING

Cadbury, Adrian Sir (2002) *Corporate Governance and Chairmanship: A Personal View.* New York: Oxford University Press.

Carter, Colin B. (2004) *Back to the Drawing Board: Designing Corporate Boards for a Complex World.* Boston: Harvard Business School Press.

LeBlanc, Richard and James Gillies (2005) *Inside the Boardroom.* Canada: Wiley.

Lorsch, Jay W. and Elizabeth McIver (1989) *Pawns or Potentates: The Reality of America's Corporate Boards.* Boston: Harvard Business School Press.

Mallin, Chris (2006) *International Corporate Governance* (Cases). London: Edward Elgar Publishing.

NACD (National Association of Corporate Directors) (2005) 'Audit Committees: A Practical Guide'. Report of a NACD Blue Ribbon Commission. Washington, DC: NACD.

Spira, Laura F. (2002) *The Audit Committee: Performing Corporate Governance.* Boston: Kluwer.

Turnbull, Shann (1975) *Democratising the Wealth of Nations.* Sydney: Company Directors' Association.

Wearing, Robert T. (2005) *Cases in Corporate Governance.* London: Sage.

USEFUL WEBSITES

www.austal.com/go/investors/corporate-governance/2-board-structure
An example of a company's policy on board structure.

www.cgfrc.nus.edu.sg
National University of Singapore, Corporate Governance and Financial Reporting Centre—updates on current topics in corporate governance.

www.ecgi.org
European Corporate Governance Institute—a forum for dialogue between academics, legislators, and practitioners.

www.iwep.org.cn
(click on 'English' then 'corporate governance') Institute of World Economics and Politics, Chinese Academy of Social Sciences.

PROJECTS AND EXERCISES

1. Research the work on worker (or employee) directors. The UK Bullock Report on worker directors (1977) might provide a useful starting point. What are the arguments for and against the concept?

2. You have been retained by the chairman/chief executive of a company, which is about to be floated on the stock market through an IPO. He is opposed to the advice he has received from his financial advisers that the roles of the chairman and chief executive should be separated. Prepare a report/presentation for him.

3. Major companies in some European countries adopt the two-tier board structure, with supervisory and executive boards. Advise the directors of a company incorporated in Delaware, USA, which is considering the acquisition of a German subsidiary, on two-tier boards.

SELF-TEST QUESTIONS

To confirm your grasp of the key points in this chapter try answering the following questions. Answers are at the end of the book.

1. Distinguish an independent non-executive director from an affiliated non-executive director?

2. What is an outside director?

3. What is a shadow director?

4. Can people be given the title 'director' without being formally members of a board?

5. Is the chairman legally 'chairman of the company' or 'chairman of the board of directors'?

6. Is it a good idea to appoint a retiring CEO as chairman?

7. Does company law in most jurisdictions distinguish the roles of executive and non-executive directors?

8. What was the original role of the audit committee?

9. What is a remuneration committee?

10. What is a nominating committee? What does it do?

4   Complex Corporate Structures

....

- In which we consider:
    - ownership patterns in modern companies
    - the governance of complex corporate structures
    - cross-holdings of shares: *keiretsu* and *chaebols*
    - block-holders and universal ownership
    - dual listed companies
    - dual class shares
    - listings on alternative stock markets

Thus far we have looked at governance issues in simple corporate structures in which there is one corporate entity, one governing body, and one set of shareholder members. Certainly, this was the situation in the mid-19th century when joint stock, limited liability companies were first developed. Although a few companies did merge during this period, this was achieved by creating a new company, which acquired the assets and liabilities of the merging companies, and then winding-up the original companies. Not until towards the end of the 19th century did entrepreneurs realize that a company could legitimately own shares in other companies. Since then some vastly complex corporate structures have been created. In this chapter we will look first at some of the complexities that arise with today's ownership patterns and then we will explore the governance of complex organizations.

Ownership Patterns in Modern Companies

A vital influence in the practice of corporate governance is the reality of the ownership structure. Although some texts treat the owners of listed companies as homogeneous, the actual pattern of ownership can have a major influence on corporate governance. Consider, for example, the differences of shareholder power in the following cases:

- A company in which the shares are widely spread between many individual and institutional shareholders with no one in a dominant position. Given a balanced and mixed ownership no single or group of investors is able to exercise undue influence on company affairs

- A company in which institutional shareholders, for example mutual funds, hedge funds, and pension funds, dominate. Even though no single institution holds a major share, their influence on the company can be significant

- A listed company in which a single shareholder owns a major shareholding. Such a controlling shareholder may not need to have a majority holding to exercise considerable influence, if no other shareholder has a significant holding
- A company in which large shareholders form a shareholder block and are thus able to influence events, even though none hold a majority of the voting rights. For example, such shareholder blocks are prevalent in Italy, where they can create legal agreements to work and vote together in a form of voting trust
- A family company, which is listed with outside shareholders but in which a significant proportion of the voting shares are still in family hands. Many family companies fit this category. The family shares do not need to be as high as 50 percent to exercise considerable influence: 20 or 30 percent is often sufficient, if the other shares are widely held. Most of the family companies listed in Hong Kong ensure total control by offering less than 50 percent of the voting shares to the investing public
- A company which has been floated on the stock market but which is still in the hands of the founder, who dominates even though holding less than a controlling share
- A company which is listed but has a controlling shareholder. A listed company can be the subsidiary of another major company, with less than 50 percent of its shares available to the public. We shall see examples of such companies in the next section on companies in chains and networks

It is also worth noting at this stage that, although we tend to think of a direct relationship between investor and company, in reality there can be a complex chain of intermediaries acting as agents, as we noted briefly in chapter 1. To take a not unrealistic example, the ultimate owner is an individual investing in a pension fund which:

- Invests some of its funds in a hedge fund
- Which in turn invests in a fund of funds to hedge its risk
- Which invests in a commercial property fund
- Which places some of its funds in the hands of a financial institution
- Which invests ultimately in a listed company
- But lends the shares as collateral for a deal it has made

In such a complex chain, how does the listed company demonstrate its accountability to its owners? Who is responsible for exercising corporate governance influence on the listed company? These are issues that lie behind some of the challenging questions in contemporary corporate governance.

These days most listed companies operate not as single corporate entities but through groups of companies, which can be quite complex and may include other listed companies. Let us now consider the governance of companies in such complex groups.

The Governance of Complex Corporate Structures

Complex corporate structures can be grouped into three broad categories: pyramids, in which the holding company sits on top of a pyramid of subsidiary and associate companies; chains, in which one company or shareholder group holds an interest in a string of companies; and networks, in which a set of companies owns shares in each other. To be clear on definitions:

(1) A *holding company* is a company which holds all or a dominant share of the voting rights in another company.

(2) A *subsidiary company* is a company in which another company (its holding company) holds all of its voting shares (a *wholly owned subsidiary*) or a majority of its voting shares (a *partially owned subsidiary*).

(3) An *associate company* is a company over which another company exercises dominant power, even though it does not hold a majority of the voting rights in that company, for example where the other share-holdings are widely spread.

The Governance of Pyramid Structures

The corporate pyramid is the most straightforward organizational form for a group of companies. It is the structure found most frequently in practice and is widely used by both private and public listed companies. It is also the structure widely used by international groups which own companies incorporated in a number of countries. Figure 4.1 depicts an elementary form of pyramid, showing a holding company with four subsidiaries held at two levels.

Research published over twenty years ago[1] showed that twenty companies at the top of the UK Times 1,000 list had 4,600 subsidiaries between them, an average 230 subsidiaries each. The smallest group had twelve subsidiaries, the largest a surprising 800. But, more surprising, was the number of levels (subsidiaries of subsidiaries of subsidiaries, etc.) at which the subsidiaries were held. Most held subsidiaries at two or three levels, but many had subsidiary companies at levels five or six and one even at level eleven! This had arisen because a company at level five had acquired a company which itself had subsidiaries at five levels. With the growth of globalization and cross-border holdings of companies, the situation today can be even more complex.

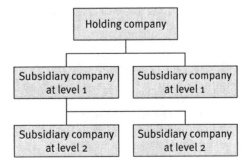

Figure 4.1 A simple pyramid structure

[1]Tricker R. I. (1984) *Corporate Governance: Practices, Procedures and Powers in British Companies and their Boards of Directors.* Aldershot, UK: Corporate Policy Group and Gower.

Why should a holding company adopt a pyramid structure, rather than operating through a single entity? There are a number of possibilities.

First, strategic positioning: a group structure can be used to bound identifiable parts of the enterprise in line with the group's corporate strategy.

Case Study 4.1 The ARE Group: Governed for a Country/Customer Based Strategy

ARE is one of Finland's leading building services, contracting and property services companies. The Group is owned by the family business Onvest Oy.Are, which operates throughout Finland. The group employs about 1,500 people.

ARE's corporate strategy is strongly customer-orientated with a major expertise in technology. It reorganized its basic operational structure to encourage people at local and nation-wide levels to work together for customers' benefit. So the holding company incorporated three regional subsidiaries in Russia (ZAO Are in St Petersburg), Estonia (AS Are in Tallinn), and Latvia (SIA ARE Lat in Riga), to operate the group's business in those countries in order to pursue the overall corporate strategy.

The board of the holding company has five members: president, chairman/CFO, an industrial counsellor, an engineer, and the corporate counsel/secretary to the board.

(See www.onvest.fi)

Discussion Questions

1. What challenges might arise with such a structure? Consider, *inter alia*, the balance of responsibility for strategic planning, policy making, executive supervision, and accountability between the holding company and subsidiary company boards; management control systems; head office directors on subsidiary company boards; intergroup trading; the allocation of holding company administrative costs; cash flow decisions; and many others.

2. How might these potential problems be overcome?

Second, legal: operating through a company incorporated in the country of operation often simplifies legal and regulatory aspects, including business regulation, contracting, employment, taxation, health and safety regulation, and so on. Incorporating a company in an offshore tax haven can also provide significant legal benefits.

Third, taxation: there can be significant tax benefits in operating through companies registered in countries where the taxation regime is lower than elsewhere. Although the tax laws of most countries seek to ensure that profits are taxed where they are earned, with tough oversight of transfer prices for goods and services passed between group companies in different countries, there are still major benefits to be gained through separate subsidiaries in differently taxed countries.

Fourth, limiting liability: creating separate entities to reduce the group's exposure to the debts of any member company. As we have already seen, the shareholders of a

---

Case Study 4.2 Incorporation in a Tax-haven: The Example of BVI

The British Virgin Islands are a group of islands situated sixty miles east of Puerto Rico in the Eastern Caribbean of which about twenty have permanent residents. The capital is located in Tortola. The British Virgin Islands are a British Overseas Territory using the United States dollar as its legal currency. The Islands constitution gives executive and legislative power to the Governor, the Executive Council, and the Legislative Council.

The British Virgin Islands (BVI) is a world leader in offshore company incorporations. BVI companies are used for a wide range of purposes, including acting as a holding company for multinational and global corporations, as trusts for asset protection, for collective investment, and to hold intellectual property. Such incorporations can offer tax benefits, limited disclosure of financial and ownership information, secrecy of intercompany dealings, and other benefits.

BVI has good communications, political and economic stability, no exchange controls, low taxation with certain classes of business exempt, no capital gains tax or wealth tax. Incorporation in BVI offers flexibility, corporate privacy and confidentiality, a pool of professional service providers, sound company law based on British law, and regulation that is reasonable but not bureaucratic. BVI is also committed to assist the international fight against money laundering.

As an indication of the importance of offshore companies, a majority of the companies listed on the Hong Kong stock market are incorporated in BVI, Bermuda, Panama or other tax havens around the world.

(See www.britishvirginislands.com)

Discussion Questions

1. List the potential advantages of incorporating in a tax haven.

2. Are there drawbacks to incorporation in a tax haven?

Consider the interests of majority (management) shareholders, minority shareholders, financial institutions and others with financial interests in the company; creditors and others contracting with the company, employees, customers, and other stakeholders.

---

company are not liable for its debts. That applies where the owner is itself a limited company. Consequently, where a group has businesses that could hazard the well-being of the group as a whole if they failed, each business can be incorporated as a separate legal entity.

In a few company law jurisdictions corporate groups are not allowed to protect themselves in this way from the failure of one member of the group. In these countries the holding company can be held liable, up the ownership structure, for the debts of subsidiaries. However, in most jurisdictions company law still shrouds each separate company with a veil that protects its owners from liability for its debts. Piercing this corporate veil is not allowed in these jurisdictions.

Case Study 4.3 Union Carbide and the Bhopal Tragedy

Group Liability Limited With Subsidiary Companies

Union Carbide India Limited (UCIL), a company incorporated in India, was established in 1934, when Union Carbide Corporation (UCC) became one of the first US companies to invest in India. UCIL shares were publicly traded on the Calcutta Stock Exchange. UCC owned about 51 percent of its stock. The remainder was owned by Indian financial institutions and private investors in India. In other words, UCIL was a subsidiary of UCC, with a large minority holding in the hands of the external shareholders.

In the late 1970s, UCIL built a plant at Bhopal to produce pesticides for use in India. Shortly after midnight on 3 December 1984, a serious leak of methyl isocyanate gas from a tank at the plant, killed about 3,800 people and left several thousand severely disabled. UCC provided interim relief funds and worked with the Bhopal community on medical and economic aid. Legal actions against the company were initiated in both the U.S. and India. Being a limited liability company meant that, under the law, UCIL was liable for its own debts not its shareholders, which included UCC. Many felt that UCC should be held responsible. Ultimately, the courts decided that legal proceedings should go before the Supreme Court of India.

In May 1989, Union Carbide (UCC) and Union Carbide India Limited (UCIL) entered into a US$470 million legal settlement with the Government of India, which represented all claimants in the case. The settlement was affirmed by the Supreme Court of India, which described it as '*just, equitable and reasonable*', and settled all claims arising out of the incident. The settlement was reached after the Supreme Court of India reviewed all US and Indian court filings, applicable law and relevant facts, and an assessment of the victims' needs. The settlement, which was larger than any previous damage award in India, was US$120 million more than plaintiffs' lawyers had told US Courts was fair. Ten days after the decision, UCC and UCIL paid in full.

In October 1993, the US Supreme Court declined to hear an appeal of a lower US court's findings, thus confirming that Bhopal victims could not sue UCC for damages in the US courts. In 1994, UCC sold its half interest in UCIL to MacLeod Russell (India) Limited of Calcutta, and UCIL was renamed Eveready Industries India, Limited. Consequently UCC no longer had any legal interest in the Bhopal site. The proceeds of the UCIL sale were placed in a trust and exclusively used to fund a hospital in Bhopal, which now provides specialist care to victims of the tragedy.

(The material in the case has been taken from Union Carbide sources. See www.bhopal.com)

Discussion Question

1. A fundamental concept of the limited liability company is that shareholders are protected from debts arising in the company in which they have invested. This applies whether the shareholder is a person or a corporate entity. Should creditors of a company, or others who have suffered damage at its hands, be able to 'pierce the corporate veil' and obtain satisfaction from the owner when this is another company?

Fifth, some companies in a corporate group may have been incorporated merely to preserve a name or to provide a legal home for a non-trading activity. Such companies are sometimes called 'letter-box' companies. Some companies in a group could also be dormant, that is they are not trading.

Case Study 4.4 Hutchison Whampoa Ltd (HWL)

HWL is a leading international corporation committed to innovation and technology with businesses spanning the globe, ranging from some of the world's biggest port operators, through significant international retailers to property development and telecommunications operations. With activities in fifty-four countries and over 220,000 employees worldwide, HWL exercises governance and management control through five flag-ship companies.

A.S. Watson & Co. Ltd (ASW) is one of the longest established and best known trading names in Asia. The company began as a small dispensary in Guangzhou, China in 1828. Today, ASW has developed into a renowned international retail and manufacturing company with a network of over 7,400 retail stores in thirty-six countries worldwide—Hong Kong, Mainland China, Taiwan, Macau, Australia, Austria, Belgium, Czech Republic, Estonia, France, Germany, Hungary, Indonesia, Ireland, Israel, Italy, Korea, Latvia, Lithuania, Luxembourg, Malaysia, Morocco, the Netherlands, the Philippines, Poland, Portugal, Romania, Russia, Singapore, Slovakia, Slovenia, Spain, Switzerland, Thailand, Turkey, and the United Kingdom.

Hutchison Port Holdings (HPH) owns the United Kingdom's busiest port, the Port of Felixstowe and operates ports in twenty-one countries throughout Asia, the Middle East, Africa, Europe, and the Americas. The Group also has an interest in HUD Group and Hongkong Salvage & Towage Company (HKST).

Hutchison Properties Ltd (HPL) was incorporated to oversee the Group's property interests, including property at Whampoa Garden Estate, Hung Hom Bay Centre, and The Harbour Front as well as development sites in Hong Kong. HPL has other property development and investment activities and also embraces the Group's hotels.

The Group also has interests in Hongkong Electric Holdings Ltd and Husky Energy, a listed Canadian based energy and energy related company, where the Group now has 34.6 percent interest. More recently, the Group has become involved in a number of power-generation and toll roads and bridges projects in Mainland China, as well as power and gas distribution businesses and global water industry in Australia and the UK through its subsidiary Cheung Kong Infrastructure.

(Information from company sources. See www.hutchison-whampoa.com)

Discussion Questions

HWL is a classic conglomerate group operating diverse businesses internationally through a pyramid of industry/market based subsidiaries and associated companies.

1. What issues can you foresee in organizing, managing, and governing such a pyramid of companies?

2. In such a group where should power lie to make strategic decisions?

Finally, many corporate groups have arrived at their complex pyramid structure through the happenchance of mergers and acquisitions. Rather than rationalize their organization structure following acquisitions and mergers, perhaps into product or regional divisions, they continue with a conglomeration of separate companies reporting through the ownership structure to the holding company. If one of the acquisitions itself has a tail of subsidiaries that increases the levels at which the holding company holds its subsidiaries.

So, what are the corporate governance implications of a group operating with a pyramid structure?

Every company in a group must obey the legal requirements of the jurisdiction in which it is incorporated. Moreover, if it is a listed company it must fulfil the listing requirements of the stock exchanges on which its shares are listed. In most cases that means that each subsidiary and associate company must have its own officers and board of directors, keep its own financial records, and file the required company reports. Of course, there are costs involved and holding companies have to evaluate the cost/benefit of their group structures.

The corporate governance implications for a director of a subsidiary or associate company operating in a pyramid structure are significant. As a director, a duty is owed to that company to follow all the corporate governance requirements of the relevant company law jurisdiction, the rules of the regulatory regime and, if a listed company, the listing requirements of the stock exchange. But, if the company is controlled through the group management control system, the director also has to accept the duties and responsibilities as a member of the management structure, recognizing that performance appraisal and reward will be determined within the management structure. This is particularly important if the subsidiary company on whose board the director serves has external minority shareholders, in which case the director must ensure that the rights of all shareholders (the external minority shareholders and the group) are recognized. This can be difficult should their interests differ, remembering that the career prospects of a director who is also a manager in the group depend on decisions taken in the group. If an independent non-executive director (INED) is appointed as a director of a subsidiary company, to ensure that the interests of minority shareholders are protected, then he or she is a nominee director with the implications already discussed.

The Governance of Chain Structures

The corporate chain is, as the name suggests, a group of companies in an ownership chain. What distinguishes this structure from a simplified form of pyramid is that the companies in the chain have other outside shareholders, as shown in figure 4.2.

The head of the chain may be an individual, a group of investors or a company. Companies in the chain could be public, listed companies or private companies.

Why is the chain structure adopted? The answer is simple: the leveraged power gained from the gearing. By investing in a chain, the head of the chain is able to exercise more influence over the companies in the chain than would be available by investing in individual companies in the chain. A chain of companies may also offer a defence to predators.

Case Study 4.5 General Electric (GE)

Governance and Management Through the Group Organization and Control Systems

General Electric (GE) is a vast, United States based, company with an international reputation for excellence in operations, performance, and corporate governance. It is organized into six businesses, each of which includes a large number of companies and other units aligned for growth. The six businesses are:

GE Industrial

The GE Industrial business provides a broad range of products and services throughout the world, including domestic appliances and lighting; a network of electrical suppliers, plastics and silicones products; and equipment services, through a large number of companies throughout the world.

GE Infrastructure

GE Infrastructure is one of the world's leading providers of fundamental technologies to developing countries, including aviation (e.g. jet engines), energy (e.g. power plants) oil and gas, rail and water process technologies.

GE Commercial Finance

GE Commercial Finance provides loans, operating leases, financing programmes, commercial insurance, and an array of other products and services aimed at enabling business worldwide to grow.

GE Money

GE Money, formerly GE Consumer Finance, is a leading provider of credit services to consumers, retailers, and automotive dealers around the world.

GE Healthcare

GE Healthcare is a leader in the development of a new paradigm of patient care dedicated to detecting disease earlier and helping physicians tailor treatment for individual patients.

NBC Universal

NBC Universal is one of the world's leading media and entertainment companies in the development, production, and marketing of entertainment, news, and information to a global audience.

Within each of these six businesses are hundreds of companies, mainly wholly owned subsidiaries, but with some associated companies and joint ventures. Management and financial control around the world is exercised through the six business units.

(See www.ge.com)

Discussion Questions

1. Explore the material on GE's website at www.ge.com. Study 'Our company', 'Our businesses', 'Governance', and 'Investor relations'.

2. What impression have you formed of corporate governance in this company?

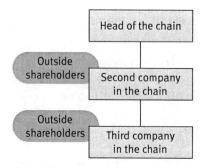

Figure 4.2 A simple chain structure

Those controlling the head of a chain are able to influence management decisions in the other companies in the chain. Take an example: a highly successful businessman and his family interests owned 34 percent of company A, which owned 40 percent of company B, which owned 36 percent of company C. Companies A, B, and C were all public companies listed on a stock exchange. The rest of the shareholdings in each company were held by the public. (See figure 4.3.)

It can be seen that in this chain of holdings, the head of the chain (A) financially has only a 5 percent holding in the company at the bottom of the chain (C)—that is 34 percent of 40 percent of 36 percent—yet is able to exercise significant influence over all the companies in the chain.

What are the governance implications for the directors serving on the boards of companies in a chain? Primarily of course, directors of a company in a chain must fulfil their duties to the company on whose board they serve under the company law, the regulatory regime, and (if listed) the stock exchange. But inevitably, with a dominant shareholder at the head of the chain, the companies in the chain need to be responsive to the requirements of that shareholder. Indeed, some of the directors may well be his nominees. But, as we have already seen when discussing nominee directors, such directors must also respect the interests of the other shareholders in their company, including any minority shareholders.

Chain structures are found in many countries in Asia, particularly where entrepreneurs and their families leverage their investment with other outside investors through a chain of companies. They are also popular in Europe and other countries, particularly where family interests dominate corporate groups. In Italy, for example, the Agnelli family in Italy, through family interests held in the limited partnership, are able to exercise considerable

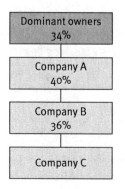

Figure 4.3 Example of chain of companies

influence over Fiat, the automobile firm, through the chain shown in the following box. This shows that, at the time of writing, Agnelli interests own 31 percent of the first company in the chain, which owns 53 percent of the second company, which owns 65 percent of the third company, which owns 30 percent of Fiat the fourth company in the chain, thus they can exert control despite actually owning less than a 4 percent financial stake (31 percent of 53 percent of 65 percent of 30 percent).

Case Study 4.6 The Agnelli Family Chain of Companies

See figure 4.4:

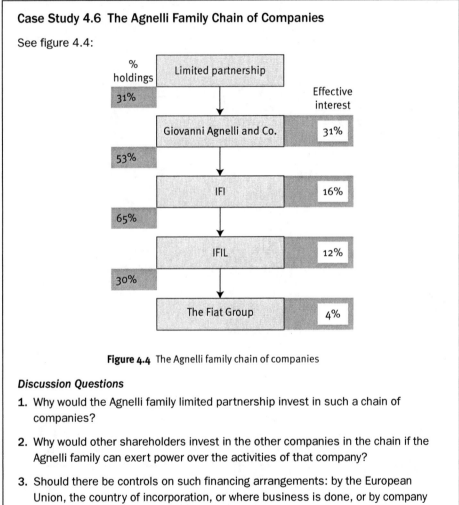

Figure 4.4 The Agnelli family chain of companies

Discussion Questions

1. Why would the Agnelli family limited partnership invest in such a chain of companies?

2. Why would other shareholders invest in the other companies in the chain if the Agnelli family can exert power over the activities of that company?

3. Should there be controls on such financing arrangements: by the European Union, the country of incorporation, or where business is done, or by company regulators, stock markets, or others?

The Governance of Network Structures

The terminology is obvious: a network structure is one in which the member companies form a network of cross-holdings, each company being a node in the network. One or more companies may be dominant or there may be no dominant member.

Case Study 4.7 The Overseas Trust Bank

When the Overseas Trust Bank, a company operating in Hong Kong, became dramatically insolvent the appointed administrators realized that the company was embedded in a network of other companies, making the establishment of ownership and creditors difficult. Eventually, investigators were able to trace something of the complex linkages and discovered that 42 percent of OTB was held through companies in the network, some private, some public. See figure 4.5:

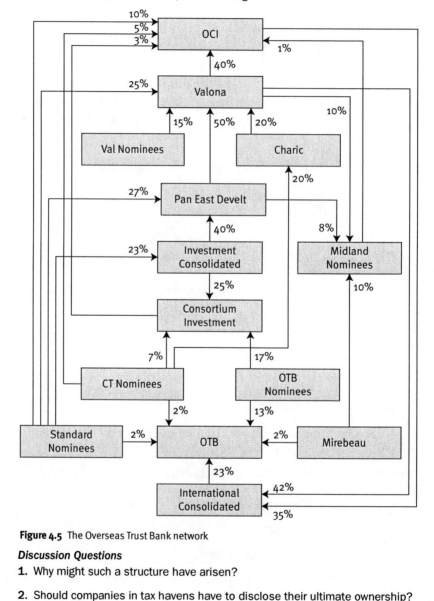

Figure 4.5 The Overseas Trust Bank network

Discussion Questions

1. Why might such a structure have arisen?

2. Should companies in tax havens have to disclose their ultimate ownership?

Why do Groups of Companies Operate in Networks?

In some cultures, Japan and South Korea for example, the network is the traditional way for corporate groups to operate, working together with mutual operations and cross-holdings of shares. We will explore the Japanese *keiretsu* and the Korean *chaebols* later in this chapter.

In the rest of the world there are a number of reasons why groups operate in networks.

First, strategic links can be created between companies to cooperate operationally. For example, companies may agree to work together, with different companies offering research and technological know-how, manufacturing capability, marketing and distribution services, or managerial capability to the others. Consequently, they may agree to exchange shares and accept cross-directorships between their boards. Such linkages can be reinforced by financial relationships, in addition to the cross-holding of shares. We will discuss the governance of joint venture companies in the next chapter.

Second, companies may network to provide mutual protection, minimizing the chance of hostile predators. With a cross-holding of shares, a potential hostile bidder has a built-in disadvantage in acquiring enough shares to pursue a bid. The Jardine Matheson Holdings case that follows provides an interesting example. Jardine Strategic Holdings is incorporated in Bermuda and listed in London, Singapore, and Bermuda. A private family based company, Jardine Matheson Holdings, owns a controlling 52 percent interest in the public company Jardine Strategic Holdings. But Jardine Strategic Holdings in turn holds 35 percent of its parent. The public company is sheltered from predators through the cross-holding which it owns in its parent company. (See Case Study 4.8 below.) In some jurisdictions company law prohibits such arangement.

Third, networks may be formed to raise funds through equity or loan financing. Pyramids and chains of companies may be buried within the network. In some cases the apparent complexity of such financing networks can result from the deals made to obtain access to funds. In other cases, however, it can reflect attempts by predators to disguise their tracks, where the take over rules restrict the building of a stake in a target company without notifying the market. Complex ownership networks may conceal the acquisition of dominant positions, at least for a while. The case of the Australian company Elders IXL that follows provides an example.

Fourth, networks can be used for taxation reasons, and to provide anonymity for the ultimate owners of companies and the protection for individuals.

Case Study 4.8 The Jardine Matheson Group

Jardine Matheson Holdings, a private family based company, owns a controlling 52 percent of Jardine Strategic Holdings, which in turn holds 35 percent of its parent company (see figure 4.6).

Jardine Strategic Holdings is a publicly listed holding company with substantial interests in Jardine Matheson, Dairy Farm, Hongkong Land, and Mandarin Oriental and has its primary share listing on the London Stock Exchange and secondary listings on the Bermuda and Singapore stock exchanges. Its shares form part of the Singapore Straits Times share index.

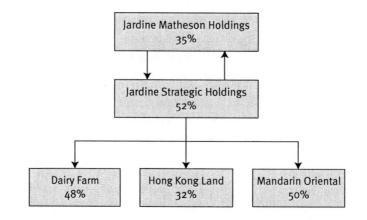

Figure 4.6 The Jardine Matheson Group (simplified—there are many other companies and cross-holdings in the group)

Dairy Farm is a leading pan-Asian retailer, with over 3,300 outlets including supermarkets, hypermarkets, health and beauty stores, convenience stores, home furnishings stores, and restaurants; employing over 62,000 people with sales over US$5 billion. Dairy Farm International Holdings Limited is incorporated in Bermuda and has its primary share listing on the London Stock Exchange, and secondary listings on the Bermuda and Singapore stock exchanges.

Hongkong Land Holdings is a leading property investment, management, and development group with a major portfolio in Hong Kong, where it owns and manages some five million square feet of prime office and retail space in the heart of the Central business district. The Group also develops high quality commercial and residential property projects elsewhere in Asia and holds a 77 percent shareholding in Singapore-listed residential property developer, MCL Land. The company is incorporated in Bermuda and also has its primary share listing on the London Stock Exchange, and secondary listings on the Bermuda and Singapore stock exchanges.

(See www.jardines.com)

Mandarin Oriental Hotel Group is an international hotel investment and management group operating more than 30 deluxe and first class hotels and resorts worldwide. The Group has equity interests in many of its properties and net assets of over US$1.5 billion. Like Dairy Farm and Hongkong Land, Mandarin Oriental International Limited is incorporated in Bermuda and has its primary listing in London, with further listings in Bermuda and Singapore.

Discussion Questions

1. Is the ownership structure depicted in this case a network, a pyramid, or a chain?

2. What is your opinion of this ownership structure?

Case Study 4.9 The Elders IXL Shareholding Network

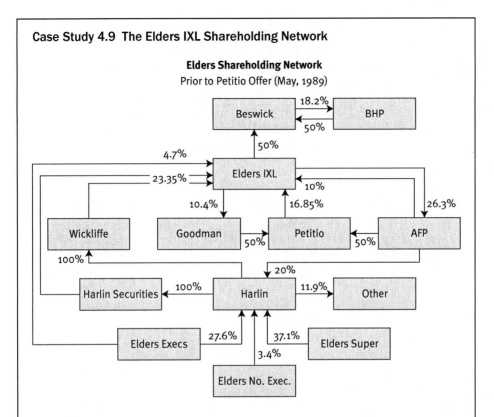

Figure 4.7 Elders IXL shareholding network

In this network the Harlin company had built up a stake in the Australian publicly listed company Elders IXL, through a complex chained network of other companies (see figure 4.7). Tracing the ownership links in the network showed the effective Harlin holding in Elders was 28 percent through Wicliffe, Harlin Securities, and Elders Execs, but that Harlin itself was partly owned by AFP, which was itself 16 percent funded by Elders (26 percent less 10 percent cross-holding).

Discussion Questions

1. Why might this network of cross-holdings have arisen or been created?

2. Whose interests does such a network serve?

3. The identification of such networks requires much investigation and can be thwarted by companies incorporated in tax havens. Should company legislation or stock exchange regulation require wider disclosure of such networks?

Figure 4.8 The Sincere Co. Ltd

Fifth, networks can be formed to share risks between companies, part of a strategy to reduce exposure to business risk. For example, Company A, B, and C exchange shares to reinforce an agreement to share risks, profits, and losses from a large construction contract in which they are all involved. We will explore the governance of companies in joint venture relationships later in this chapter.

An extreme example is shown in figure 4.8, above, in which the companies virtually owned each other. These cross-holdings would also serve to deter a hostile take-over bid for the listed holding company. As mentioned above such an ownership scheme would only be permitted in certain jurisdictions.

Sixth, networks can arise as the unintentional effect of corporate acquisition activity. Companies accept the network structure rather than incurring the costs and organizational stress of redefining the group structure and organizational systems. This can occur particularly if there are outside minority interests in some of the network companies whose interests would have to be valued and redefined in restructuring.

Finally, complex networks can arise as the result of deliberate obfuscation, to reduce a group's visibility, perhaps to confuse competitors, deter predators, or avoid the unwanted interest of the authorities. Such network designs may push at the boundaries of legality, for example in taxation, exchange controls, corporate reporting, or money laundering.

Cross-holdings of Shares: *Keiretsu* and *Chaebols*

Keiretsu are networks of Japanese companies connected through intertrading, extensive interlocking directorships, and cross-holdings of shares. Typically the network includes a financial institution. Chairmans and senior directors of companies in the *keiretsu* meet regularly and have close, informal relationships. In the past corporate governance of such Japanese groups have had a stakeholder, rather than shareholder, orientation.

Traditionally, in *keiretsu* companies the board plays a formal, even ritualistic role. Boards are large and almost entirely executive. In effect the board is the top four or five layers of the management organization. Promotion to the board, as in the West, is a mark of distinction; but, unlike the West, interpersonal competition, which has been a feature of life throughout the organization, continues on the board for promotion to the next 'level' up to the top management ranks. We will explore the cultural aspects of corporate governance in chapter 8.

Japanese companies wanting access to overseas capital have come under pressure, particularly from Western institutional investors, to adopt Anglo-American approaches to corporate governance. In particular they have called for INEDs and more transparency to provide more protection for outside investors. Of course, any Japanese company that wanted to list on a stock exchange outside Japan has to meet the regulatory requirements of that exchange.

We will explore the cultural aspects of the governance of Japanese *keiretsu* networks in chapter 8.

In other East Asian countries, which have been influenced by British company law in the past—Singapore, Malaysia, Hong Kong, for example—corporate governance requirements in their company laws, company regulations, and stock exchange listing requirements are relatively well developed. Corporate governance in China is advancing rapidly, in line with the country's rapidly growing economy. Governance in China and the work of the Chinese authorities will be also be studied in chapter 8.

In South Korea, however, another approach to corporate governance developed. After the Second World War, large conglomerate networks of companies, known as *chaebols*, were formed with close government involvement and financial support, although they tended to be dominated by a few families. Even if they had only a relatively small shareholding, a family could maintain control by using cross-ownership in subsidiary companies.

In recent years, the South Korean government sought to reduce the power of the *chaebols* by requiring them to divest some of their interests. But before the financial and economic crisis of 1997, success was limited. Subsequently, the *chaebols* found it increasingly difficult to compete with other Asian producers, because of their tradition of lifetime employment and militant trade unions, and governance changes were forced on them.

Block-holders and Universal Ownership

Where institutional investors, such as banks, financial and non-financial institutions, companies, or individuals, own a significant proportion of the voting shares in a company, and are able to act together, they form a block of shareholders. If they act as a block they may be able to influence corporate decisions, for example on corporate strategy including acquisition policy, on the appointment or dismissal of directors, and on financial strategy including dividend policy or capital restructuring.

Italian voting trusts or voting syndicates (*patti di sindacato*) are groups of large shareholders who sign an explicit legal agreement to vote together. About a third of large Italian companies are dominated by such coalitions of large shareholders. In Italy, information on all such trusts has to be registered and this knowledge is publicly available. Such voting trusts ensure continuity and stability in management strategies and policies, and prevent conflicts of interest between large shareholders. Some proponents of voting trusts argue that concentrated, rather than diverse, ownership produces more monitoring of executive management, better management discipline, and better returns. The trust agreement typically provides for a management committee to run the trust, arranges its operating procedures and finances, and confirms that no one shareholder can dominate.

Block-holders are also significant in South Korea, Russia, and China (where state related organizations provide the block) and, following privatization, from state-ownership in Spain and Poland. Indeed, listed companies in most economies are not widely held, as they are in the United States and the United Kingdom, most being controlled by families or states.

Although there are no apparent block-holders in listed companies whose shareholders are widely dispersed, it has been suggested that institutional investors could form such power blocks if they acted together on governance matters. The recently developed terminology of 'fiduciary capitalism' recognizes the potential power of financial institutions to take collective action that reflects the interests of the 'universal owners'. For example, the largest pension funds are mainly those of employees in local and state government, teachers, universities, and other public sector organizations, and employee retirement assets could be used as a power basis for action over companies.

Advocates of 'universal ownership' recognize the ability of pension and other funds working together to improve governance and long term returns, though each holds only a relatively small percentage share. The idea of universal ownership is particularly relevant where equity holdings are highly diversified without a dominant investor. The idea also recognizes the agency chain of intermediaries that often exists between listed company and ultimate investor/owner. Agents have agents, each acting as the agent for the next principal in the chain, with highly diversified roles but all bound in law by the fiduciary duty of loyalty and care. But their actions are neither transparent nor accountable. If the idea is to make a contribution, however, a universal holder mindset will be needed to provide the classical governance relationship between corporate body and its owners.

Dual Listed Companies

In a traditional takeover situation one company acquires the shares of the other, which then becomes a subsidiary or associate company of its parent holding company. In a dual listed company, by contrast, a group structure is created in which two listed companies merge but both continue to exist and share the ownership of a single operational business. The group maintains its two separate stock exchange listings with different shareholders typically in different countries. A complex set of contracts defines their relationship with an integrated top management structure and the same directors or some cross-directorships.

The benefits for dual listing include:

- Continuing existing successful businesses
- Protecting brand names
- Taxation benefits
- Sustaining national pride avoiding claims that one country is losing 'its' company to another

The disadvantages can be:

- Conflict between the two managements, for example on resource allocation
- Disagreements between the boards, unless all directors are common to both
- Legal difficulties in applying the intercompany contracts
- Challenges from shareholders about unfair benefits to the other company
- Taxation difficulties, including transfer prices for intergroup trading
- Problems if the group wants to unravel the dual listing agreements

Dual listed companies as explained above need to be distinguished from cases where a company is listed on more than one stock exchange, sometimes referred to as cross-listed or cross-held companies. Many international companies raise funds in this way, usually with a primary listing in their home country and one or more secondary listings elsewhere. For example, many Canadian companies are listed in Toronto and New York.

The case of the Carnival Corporation (US) and the Carnival Corporation Plc below provides a typical case. Other examples include BHP Billiton (Australia and UK), Investec Bank (South Africa and UK) and Unilever (Holland and UK).

Case Study 4.10 Carnival Corporation and Plc: A Dual Listed Group

Carnival Corporation and Plc is a dual listed company, with listings in New York and London. This British-American corporation is the only group in the world to be included in both the S&P 500 and the FTSE 100 indices. It is the world's largest cruise operator, with twelve cruise brands, including Carnival Cruise Lines, Princess Cruises, Holland America Line, Windstar Cruises, and Seabourn Cruise Line in North America; P&O Cruises, Cunard Line, Ocean Village Holidays, and Swan Hellenic in the United Kingdom; AIDA and A'ROSA in Germany; Costa Cruises in Southern Europe and P&O Cruises Australia in Australia.

Carnival Corporation, incoporated in Panama, is the larger of the two holding companies and is listed on the New York Stock Exchange. Before the dual listing it was the market leader in the US cruise market. Carnival Plc is listed on the London Stock Exchange and was formed from the P&O (Peninsular and Orient Steam Navigation Company's) cruise business.

(See www.carnivalcorp.com and www.carnivalukgroup.com)

Discussion Questions

1. Why has such an arrangement occurred?

2. What advantages can you see in such a dual listing?

3. Would it be better to form a third company, which acquires the shares of the other two for a consideration paid in its own shares?

Dual Class Shares

Having just discussed dual listed corporate groups, this might be a good place to mention dual class shares and to distinguish between the two. The corporate constitution (memorandum and articles of association) of a few companies provide for two classes of voting shares in which one class enjoys greater voting rights, or all the voting rights, than the other class. For example, a company might issue 'A' class shares, in which each share has one vote and 'B' class shares, in which each share has 100 votes. Dual class shares are typically issued to protect the ownership power of a dominant shareholding class, often a family, when a company is floated on the stock market. Some stock exchanges will not list companies with dual class shares, demanding shareholder democracy in which every voting share enjoys an equal voting right.

Other stock exchanges, however, do list companies with dual class shares. The founders of Google, Larry Page and Sergey Brin, exercise power through dual class shares. Though holding only around 20 percent of the equity they control around 60 percent of the votes. The Ford Motor Company has dual class shares, giving greater power to the Ford family. The Porsche and Piëch families, though owning less than half of the shares in the Porsche company, enjoy all the voting rights. Another classical example is the Wallenberg Group in Sweden. Predictably, the limited or no-voting class share trades at a discount.

Listings on Alternative Stock Markets

Some stock exchanges create a second market, often called a second board, to enable smaller, perhaps riskier, companies to raise capital. The London Stock Exchange established the Alternative Investment Market (AIM) in 1995, to raise capital and provide a market for companies from all industrial sectors and any country. Since then AIM has raised some £50 billion, through initial public offerings (IPOs) and the raising of additional capital, and now lists more than 2,300 British firms and 400 non-British, including both venture-capital backed start-ups and well-established mature organizations. Some of these companies have subsequently progressed to a listing on the main board. Although a large proportion of AIM companies are early-stage businesses and may operate in high-risk sectors, the failure rate on AIM has been relatively low, running at less than 3 percent for the four years from 2002.

Unlike the main board, AIM does not stipulate a minimum size or market capitalization, the number of shares in public hands; nor does it require a track record of quality profits and financial history. The regulatory regime for AIM companies is a succinct rule book, which is also less stringent than that of the main board.

A crucial element in the corporate governance of AIM companies is the Nominated Adviser (usually referred to as the Nomad), authorized by AIM, which all AIM companies are required to appoint. The Nomad's experience provides a quality control mechanism by checking the company's plans and certifying to the Exchange that the company is suitable and ready for listing. The Nomad assists the company during the flotation, subsequently ensures that it meets its governance obligations, and handles any ongoing market issues. The company deals with AIM through its Nomad, who advises AIM on all regulatory

Case Study 4.11 The Wallenberg Group

Corporate governance in Sweden has a number of distinctive characteristics—mandatory co-determination, high private share ownership, dual class shares, shareholders board nominating committee, and 'spheres' of private owners. The Wallenberg family forms such a sphere, owning a business empire that is more of a dynasty than a company. Now in its fifth generation of family control, and planning for the sixth, this huge empire dominates Swedish business.

The Wallenbergs own some 40 percent of the value of the Swedish stock exchange, but through dual class shares, which give greater voting rights to their shares than to others, exercise control over many companies. Their interests include around 19 percent by value, 38 percent by votes, of car maker Saab, 5 percent by value but 20 percent by votes of Ericsson, a leading telecommunications company, around 11 percent by value but 28 percent by votes of Electrolux, a white goods manufacturer, 10 percent by value and 20 percent by votes of Scania, and also major interests in Atlas Copco, ABB—a global engineering group, SEB, one of Scandinavia's largest banks, and many other companies. They also control 4 percent by value and votes of Astra Zeneca, a pharmaceutical company listed in London, where dual class shares are not permitted.

Wallenberg ownership is exercised through the Wallenberg foundations (assets US$6 billion), which exercise just under 50 percent of the votes in Investor, a public company chaired by Jacob Wallenberg, with over 100,000 other investors sharing in the family fortunes. Companies dominated by Investor are run by professional managers with their own boards of directors. However Jacob Wallenberg insists that the family are '*not just kingmakers*', as some claim, but are closely involved in the companies' corporate strategies. The governance style adopted by the Wallenbergs is based on a network of carefully fostered contacts, a policy to shift investment strategies from the past to the future as industries and technologies change, but then to stick with their companies through thick and thin. Marcus Wallenberg, in the present generation, has invested in technology firms.

The family claim that they deserve their special rights in the multiple-voting, dual class shares because of the family's role in founding and developing Swedish companies and their tradition of strong and involved ownership.

Discussion Questions

1. Swedish law and the rules of some stock exchanges permit the issuing of the dual class shares used in the Wallenberg Group. Do you think they should?

2. What is your reaction to the Wallenberg family's justification for their dual class shares, given in the last paragraph of the case?

matters. The company's broker, lawyers, auditors, and financial institution also provide support services.

The Stock Exchange of Hong Kong also offers a second board—the Growth Enterprise Market (GEM). GEM emphasizes that these are emerging companies carrying a high investment risk, with potential market volatility and no assurance that there will be a liquid market, which are thus more suitable for 'sophisticated investors'. Companies listing on GEM are not required to show a track-record of profits, or to forecast future profitability. The initial listing document must show the business objectives and activities. Quarterly operating and financial reports are required, with the directors being responsible for disclosure. The GEM is often used by Hong Kong family based companies to enable family members to capitalize on the wealth in the family business, as well as providing additional funds for corporate growth.

Singapore Exchange's secondary market, named Catalist, opened in 2008, replacing the previous Sesdaq board. Catalist aimed to attract fast-growing companies from the region, competing with London's Alternative Investment Market (AIM) for Asian listings. Approved sponsors are responsible for vetting new listings and supervising them thereafter. To be listed, companies should have a healthy financial position and prospects of profitability, but no operating or profit track record is required.

REFERENCES AND FURTHER READING

Lufkin, Joseph C. F. and David Gallagher (1990) *International Corporate Governance*. London: Euromoney Books.

Kaen, Fred R. (2003) *A Blueprint for Corporate Governance: Strategy Accountability and the Preservation of Shareholder Value*. New York: American Management Association.

Millstein, Ira M. and Salem M. Katsh (1981) *The Limits of Corporate Power: Existing Constraints on the Exercise of Corporate Discretion*. New York: Collier-Macmillan.

Wright, Robert E. (2004) *History of Corporate Governance: The Importance of Shareholder Activism*. London: Pickering and Chatto.

USEFUL WEBSITES

www.gm.com/corporate/investor_information/corp_gov/index.jsp
General Motors corporate governance documents.

www.heh.com/hehWeb/InvestorRelations/CorporateGovernance/Index_en.htm
Hong Kong Electric corporate governance report.

www.lensadvisors.com/docs/corp_gov_principles.pdf
Royal Dutch Shell corporate governance principles.

www.microsoft.com/about/companyinformation
(click on 'corporate governance') Microsoft's corporate governance practices.

www.unilever.com/ourcompany/investorcentre/corp_governance
Unilever investors' site—follow links to 'corporate governance'.

PROJECTS AND EXERCISES

Explore the corporate structure of some companies operating in your country. Most listed companies provide a wealth of information on their websites about their businesses, organization structures, and corporate governance arrangements as well as financial information. In particular discover:

- Where are the companies in the group incorporated? Where are their shares listed?

- Are these cases of networks, pyramids, or chained structures?

- What is your opinion on the quality of disclosure on the group structure and corporate governance arrangements?

SELF-TEST QUESTIONS

To confirm your grasp of the key points in this chapter try answering the following questions. Answers are at the end of the book.

1. Distinguish a holding company, a wholly owned, a partly owned subsidiary company, and an associated company.

2. Why might a company incorporate in an off-shore jurisdiction?

3. Explain 'piercing the corporate veil'.

4. Why do groups adopt a chain structure?

5. What are some of the distinguishing features of the governance of a *keiretsu*?

6. What is a *chaebol*?

7. What is a dual listed company?

8. Why might companies consider entering into a joint venture agreement?

9. Can companies hold shares in themselves? Give examples from the chapter.

5   The Governance of Private Companies and Other Corporate Entities

....

* In which we consider:
    - the governance of subsidiary and associated companies
    - the governance of family controlled companies
    - the governance of hedge funds, private equity firms, and sovereign wealth funds
    - the governance of joint ventures
    - the governance of NGOs and non-profit corporate entities
    - the governance of partnerships and limited liability partnerships

The Governance of Subsidiary and Associated Companies

Some definitions first:

* A holding company is the company at the head of a group pyramid of companies. Its board of directors is often called the 'main board'
* A subsidiary company is one in which the holding or parent company holds all or a majority of the voting shares in that company
* An associated company is one in which the holding company, though not holding a majority of the shares, has sufficient interests to control it and determine its actions

The governance of subsidiary and associated companies raises some interesting issues. Essentially, the holding company determines the governance structure and processes of the companies in its group.

As we saw in chapter 4 there are broadly two distinct options in governing and managing a group of companies:

(1) Group-company self-governance, allowing each company in the group to govern itself and manage its own affairs, subject to overall group-wide policies and resource allocation. Control is exercised through the group's shareholdings, emphasizing the decision making autonomy of the board of each subsidiary company. This will often be adopted in a conglomerate group in which the companies run diverse businesses.

(2) Group-wide governance, treating the group companies as divisions or departments of the holding company and controlling through the group's management control system; in other words, emphasizing management through the group management organization structure and management control systems, not governance through the boards of each subsidiary.

Group-company Self-governance

The first approach, delegating decision making power to the group's subsidiary company boards, requires each subsidiary in the group to act as an autonomous company, subject to policy requirements and resource allocations determined by its shareholder, the holding company. In other words, the directors of each subsidiary company are expected to run their company as an autonomous entity, within group policies, to meet the performance criteria required by the group.

With group-company self-governance the structure and membership of the subsidiary and associate company boards becomes important. The holding company has the option of drawing the directors of subsidiary companies from:

- The group holding company, who might or might not be on the main board
- The management of the subsidiary company
- The management in other group companies (as in the Singapore Airways case below)
- Outside the group

The benefits of drawing subsidiary company directors from other companies in the group include the opportunity for cross-group coordination, the sharing of expertise, training, and development of future main board directors, management development, and the building of group norms and culture.

In associate companies, and in subsidiaries with outside minority interests, it would be normal to find nominee directors representing the interests of the outside shareholders.

Group-wide Governance

In the second approach, the group holding company imposes management control systems and organization structures on the entire group operations, which transcend the operations of the individual subsidiary companies. The control system divides the group into appropriate operating units, which may or may not map onto the subsidiary company structure. Group resources are allocated to these performance units through the management control system, performance criteria are laid down for management of each unit and outputs monitored. The power to make decisions throughout the group is delegated along the lines of the management control system not the legal structure of the subsidiaries.

With group-wide governance the members of subsidiary company boards are typically drawn from the management of group head office and the subsidiary company, because

Case Study 5.1 Singapore Airlines

Singapore Airlines (SIA) is the national airline of Singapore and is ranked 17th in Fortune's list of the world's most admired companies. The SIA Group has some twenty-five subsidiary companies and thirty associated airline-related businesses in its group including:

Table 5.1 **The SIA Group**

Company	Activity	Relationship	% holding
SIA Engineering Co. Ltd	Airline engineering	subsidiary	82
SilkAir (Singapore) Private Ltd	Airline	subsidiary	100
Singapore Airlines Cargo Private Ltd	Cargo airline	subsidiary	100
Singapore Airport Terminal Services Ltd	Terminal services group	subsidiary	82
Singapore Flying College Private Ltd	Flight school	subsidiary	100
Tiger Airways Private Ltd	Airline	associate	49
Virgin Atlantic Ltd	Airline group	associate	49

The boards of the subsidiary companies include top executives of that subsidiary and non-executive directors drawn from other group companies. The boards of the associate companies have nominees from SIA and the other shareholders as well as independent outside directors.

(See www.singaporeair.com, go to investor relations)

Discussion Questions

1. What advantages might accrue from having subsidiary company directors drawn from other parts of the SIA Group?

2. Could there be any disadvantages to the Group or individual subsidiary companies?

power lies in the management organization structure throughout the group, not in the boardrooms of the subsidiary companies.

For example, in figure 5.1 the holding company manages their group through a group organization structure with two divisions A and B. Their management control system, consequently, will monitor the management of the divisions. Managers have their responsibilities delegated down through the levels of management in the organization structure and are accountable back up that structure. Managers owe their primary allegiance to their line manager, not the directors of the subsidiary company of which their business unit may be part.

You might ask why such holding companies controlling through the group management system have subsidiary companies at all. The reasons could be legal—the ability to contract

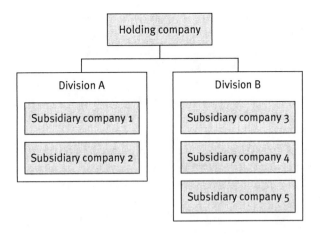

Figure 5.1 Control through a group management control system

under the laws of the state in which the subsidiary is incorporated and operates; taxation—the opportunity to reduce taxation in high tax regimes; strategic positioning—to protect a brand name or other strategic benefit; or risk reduction—to obtain the benefit of limited liability. Because such subsidiaries are legal entities, they must, of course, fulfil their legal reporting and taxation requirements. But power lies in the management organization structure throughout the group not in the boardrooms of the subsidiary companies.

The Governance of Family Controlled Companies

As we have seen, in the early days of the joint stock limited liability company, all companies were public companies, incorporated to raise capital from outside investors. Today most companies around the world are private companies, providing taxation benefits to the proprietors (because corporation tax is often preferable to personal income tax) and giving them the benefit of limited liability. A large proportion of these private companies are owned and controlled by families or the founders. In Asia, India, and Latin America some 95 percent of companies are family owned. The importance of the small and medium sized enterprise in Italy, Spain, and other European countries, and the 'Mittlestand' medium sized companies in Germany, demonstrate the significance of family controlled businesses in Europe. Of course, family owned companies are not necessarily small or medium sized. Some very large companies in Asia, Latin America, and Europe are family owned. Neither are these family firm companies always private: in France one in four of the listed companies on the CAC40 stock market index are family controlled.

The governance of family controlled private companies raises some interesting issues. Tracing the evolution of ownership and control in a typical family firm will highlight some of them.

Initially, a small company may be incorporated for a business start-up or to take over an existing sole-trader or partnership business. At this stage the shareholders are also likely to be the directors, who may be the entrepreneurs starting a business, the partners in an existing firm, or the family members involved in the enterprise. At this early stage the key issue is likely to be survival. Many companies fail within the first two or three years. Thereafter the focus shifts to maintaining success and further growth. In the early years of the family company, management and governance tend to be intertwined, because both are being done by the same people. The running of the business and its internal management, as well as the governance tasks of strategy formulation, policy making, periodic supervision, and accountability are all in the heads of the owner/managers.

The next stage of governance comes as the company survives and then thrives. A need for additional expertise is recognized, perhaps marketing, financial, or international skills, and knowledge, which the existing directors and top management lack. But the company cannot yet afford to employ a full time executive in this field. So they invite an outside director with the skills, experience, and network contacts to join the board. This is cheaper in the short term than hiring a consultant, although a consultant is much easier to be let go when his or her usefulness has ended.

A further stage can involve the reward of an executive directorship to long serving executives, who have contributed significantly to the success of the firm. Such appointments can provide reward, recognition, and prestige.

Then the business may find that it needs additional capital, because plough-back profits are no longer sufficient to fund its rate of growth. Additional capital is needed. Private equity capital may be raised producing the demand for an outside nominee director. Or the company may gear up, adding a loan partner who also requires a presence on the board.

Now a crucial stage can occur. Junior family members, who have been involved in management and are successful then deserve a place on the board. Such an appointment rewards success but can trigger family resentments.

Then the penultimate issue occurs: the need to move into the second generation. A typical solution is for the senior family member in the second generation, who is experienced in the management, to assume the senior executive role, while the founder/parent figure assumes the role of chairman of the board. But experience shows that such a switch is very difficult to achieve successfully. The new chairman is often unable to drop his executive decision making role for an advisory one to his successor.

The final succession issue occurs as the founders' shares pass to the next generation. Often by this stage the family is split between those children involved in management and those who are just share-owners. For example, one branch of the family—brother number one and a sister, perhaps, who are involved in management, and another branch of the family, perhaps brother number two, who is not involved in the company other than as a shareholder. This situation produces a major headache for some families.

The non-management members of the family want to maximize dividends so that they can benefit from their stake in the company. By contrast the management family members want to limit dividends, plough the money into the business, and maximize their personal remuneration and benefits (cars, travel, living expenses, etc.). If the company wants to change strategy—perhaps to make a major capital investment, to sell-off a part of the business or acquire another company, the interests of the management family members may well differ from those of the non-management members.

How might this dilemma be overcome? Some family company experts recommend setting up a family council, consisting of all the family members who own shares (management and non-management), which meets prior to shareholder meetings to identify issues that affect family members and to resolve them in the best interest of the family as a whole. In this way potentially acrimonious issues can be resolved before the formal meeting of shareholders and directors.

In the family controlled company the challenge is to incorporate sound corporate governance practices which, on the one hand, ensure continuing professional management whilst, on the other hand, preserving family unity. Of course many successful family controlled companies never reach this stage. The company is sold and the capital distributed within the family before the succession issue arises.

The Governance of Hedge Funds, Private Equity Firms, and Sovereign Wealth Funds

Hedge Funds

As the name suggests, the essential element of a hedge fund is to provide its investors with a hedge against future uncertainty. For example, the manager of a normal fund might invest in shares in, say, the commercial property sector because he or she believes that there will be significant growth there. A hedge fund manager might also buy such shares but will complement the purchase by selling short an equivalent value of other stocks (that is by selling shares that have been borrowed for a fee, buying them back later). If the price raises the purchase of the commercial property shares will show a profit, if the market falls the shorted shares will compensate for the loss. So whichever way the market moves the fund is hedged. Of course, the fund is still at risk of losing money if the prices at which it bought and sold have been misjudged. Moreover, in reality hedge funds are involved in much more complex trades than these and are typically highly geared, increasing their exposure.

Large sums of money are provided to hedge fund managers by sophisticated rich individuals who have been attracted by the fund's prospectus, the fund managers, and their track record. Institutional investors, including some public and corporate pension funds, also invest in hedge funds to improve their overall performance, subject to the aims of the fund.

Hedge funds may take positions in commodities, buy equity shares, trade in debt, invest in futures, such as energy futures, sugar prices, carbon emission prices, even the weather, or make other exotic contracts, whilst using all the tools in the contemporary financial management tool box, such as economic forecasting, statistical analysis, mathematical modelling, gearing, short-selling, securitization, and more. The massive sums often involved in hedge fund investments can result in spectacular profits and, of course, correspondingly devastating losses. But the aim of most hedge funds is to produce consistent returns, although that has proved difficult for many funds following the 2008 financial market crash. Sensible investors further spread their exposure by investing in a basket of hedge funds.

It is estimated that there were more than 10,000 hedge funds around the world. Of course, only the strong survived the 2008 global financial crisis. The most successful funds are often closed to new investors. The majority trade along raising new investment as necessary and trying to provide sustained returns. The least successful fail and lose their investors' money. The case of Long Term Capital Management, which did just that, is summarized below.

Case Study 5.2 Long Term Capital Management (LTCM)

LTCM was a hedge fund founded in 1994 by John Meriwether and included board members Myron Scholes and Robert Merton who had shared the Nobel Prize in economics. Initially the fund was highly successful and became an example for the hedge fund industry.

The company developed mathematical models to arbitrage deals in American, Japanese, and European government fixed-interest bonds. Profit was made by buying some bonds and short-selling others as prices narrowed. As the firm prospered it generated more investment than could be used for these arbitrage opportunities and began to undertake trading decisions beyond its experience, including options and merger arbitrage.

The 1997 East Asian financial crisis produced significant losses. Then in 1998 the Russian Government defaulted on their bonds. Holders of European and Japanese bonds, fearing further defaults, transferred to US Treasury bonds and the previous arbitrage opportunities used by LTCM reversed. The firm lost nearly US$2 billion of its capital.

Fearing a chain reaction in the financial markets, the Federal Reserve Bank organized a bail-out by major creditor institutions of over US$3.5 billion. The banks participating in the bail-out received 90 percent of the hedge fund and an independent supervisory board was created. The LTCM fund was wound up in 2000. Some of the positions formerly held by LTCM were eventually liquidated at a small profit to the bail-out institutions. The fear remained, however, that the intervention by the Federal Reserve might encourage other institutions in the future to take risks in the belief that they would be bailed out.

Discussion Questions

1. Should the Federal Reserve Bank have arranged the bail-out of LTCM?

2. Compare and contrast the 2008 case of Northern Rock Bank in the UK.

Hedge funds typically make heavy use of gearing, thus increasing their potential return and their exposure to risk. If investments are successful the firm reaches break-even between revenues and costs earlier and thereafter contributes more rapidly to investors' profit. Conversely, if investments are unsuccessful, the fund reaches break-even more slowly, because it still has to meet the interest costs, and the investors are saddled with a loss.

Some politicians around the world have expressed suspicion of hedge funds. Germany's Deputy Chancellor called hedge funds 'locusts', when blaming them for the hostile takeover of German companies. Others claimed hedge funds forced Britain out of the European Exchange Rate Mechanism in 1992. Malaysia's Prime Minister blamed hedge funds for the East Asian financial crisis in the late 1990s. The Long Term Capital Management case (see See Case Study 5.2) was accused of destabilizing the US market. In each case there were other forces at work.

Other criticisms of the governance of hedge funds include their concern for privacy, the lack of disclosure on matters such as their investment strategies and profitability, the extraordinary earnings of successful fund managers both from fees and percentages on gains, and that share traders are not responsible shareholders but only interested in the short term. At the societal level there is also the fear that, as we saw with banks around the world during the sub-prime mortgage crisis in 2007/8, things can spiral downwards. The collapse of one fund could affect the others by driving down prices on the market, triggering margin calls, forcing more selling, driving prices still lower, with more margin calls and more losses, until funds collapse and the pension funds providing the capital and the banks providing the gearing funds would be hit.

Compared with the heavy regulation of listed companies, the hedge fund industry is relatively unregulated, except for controls on the financial viability and available wealth of those allowed to invest. Of course hedge fund managers have to abide by insider-dealing laws and stock exchange regulations when they trade in equities. There have been calls for regulation or voluntary codes. The International Corporate Governance Network supports the creation of a code of best practice for hedge funds, based on the 'comply or explain' principal. Others call for information on hedge funds indebtedness and society's exposure to risk, rather than requiring them to disclose their business models, their complex statistical programmes, or their investment strategies.

Case Study 5.3 The Man Group Plc

The Man Group was founded in London by James Man over 200 years ago as a brokerage business. Since 1987, it has run hedge funds that generate strong risk-adjusted returns, constructing its multi-manager hedge fund portfolios to exploit market inefficiencies with low risk. Its clients include some of the most significant institutional investors around the world. Man Group Plc is incorporated in the UK, is quoted on the London Stock Exchange, and is a constituent of the FTSE 100 Index. The company employs over 1,600 people with offices in London, Chicago, Dubai, Hong Kong, New York, Switzerland, Sydney, Tokyo, and Toronto. US$72 billion assets were under management in 2008.

The Group explains its managed futures investment programmes as follows:

Man Investments programmes are quantitative and primarily directional in nature, meaning they seek to identify and take advantage of upward and downward price trends. Investment rules are executed within a systematic framework. Trading takes place around-the-clock and real time price information is used to respond to price moves across a diverse range of global markets encompassing stock indices, bonds, currencies, short-term interest rates and commodities. The instruments traded are primarily futures and OTC foreign exchange forwards and metal contracts . . . always underpinned by a strong research ethic. Refinements to the investment process have been as much a feature as the continuity of the investment philosophy and principles—diversification, discipline, efficiency, rigorous risk control, and ongoing research.

The Group further outlines its global activities as:

Man Global Strategies Division constructs and manages hedge style and multi-strategy portfolios, including the portfolios for Man Investments structured products. It also creates customised portfolios in conjunction with institutional partners operating in local markets around the world. Man Global Strategies focuses on hedge fund styles with favourable performance characteristics and then develops and blends diversified portfolios both within and between styles. It has a team dedicated specifically to identifying managers with complementary performance characteristics, and strives to establish close associations with the managers it selects. In focusing on robust investment solutions in hedge funds, leveraged finance and convertible bonds the Group places a premium on skill-based strategies with predictable outcomes and clearly definable added value. The Group has succeeded in developing a structured investment model in which investment selection, portfolio construction, risk management and investment service functions are modularised, which enables it to galvanise the full potential of alternative strategies as well as leverage the creativity and expertise of its highly qualified investment professionals. Drawing on extensive know-how in different investment disciplines and established relationships within the alternative investment community, the various teams are able to access high quality managers and practitioners. Attracted by its reliable, ISO-certified investment process, and proven track record of solid absolute returns, a range of insurance companies, pension funds and corporations have chosen the Man Group to fulfil their varied alternative investment requirements.

The Oxford-Man Institute of Quantitative Finance at the University of Oxford is funded by the Man Group. The group also sponsors the Booker Prize for Fiction.

(See the Man Group's corporate website www.mangroupplc.com)

Discussion Questions

1. Do you understand what the Man Group does?

2. What is an 'ISO-certified investment process'?

3. Draft an explanation of their activities for someone who does not understand financial markets.

Private Equity Firms

Private equity firms operate funds that can invest massively in the acquisition of limited companies. These can include listed companies, which are taken private thus avoiding the public company disclosure requirements of the stock market and corporate regulators.

These funds may also provide venture capital to grow existing businesses or start-up new ventures, and some also seek special investment opportunities, such as buying a failing company from which value can be realized.

Private equity firms seek capital for their funds mainly from institutional investors, including state and corporate pension funds, banks and other financial institutions, and from rich individuals. Some states restrict investment in such funds to accredited investors who are able to shoulder the risk. Usually investors subscribe to a specific fund managed by a firm, becoming a limited partner in the fund, rather than becoming an investor in the firm itself. Investors in such limited partnerships recognize that their funds can be locked in for a long period, that the risk is high with the potential to lose their entire investment, and that they therefore expect high returns. Some private equity funds spread their risk by investing in a range of other private equity funds, which are often called a fund of funds. The managers of private equity firms may also invest their own money in their own funds, typically providing up to 5 percent of the overall capital.

Mergers and acquisition activity in the United States and the United Kingdom reached an all-time high prior to the sub-prime lending crisis in 2007/8. Much of this growth in acquisition activity was due to private equity institutions acquiring control of previously listed companies. In the United States, many well-known companies have been helped by private equity investment, including Apple Computers, Avis, Dr. Pepper, FedEx, and Microsoft.

In the United Kingdom the Automobile Association is owned by private equity and more recently some other well-known public companies came into private equity ownership, including Boots the Chemist, Hilton Hotels, and the EMI music business. Britain has probably gone further than any country in allowing its core companies to be sold to overseas interests—Thames Water is now owned by a German company, London Electricity by a French company, and the ownership of the British Airports Authority, which runs all the major UK airports, is Spanish.

Typically private equity funds generate returns on their investments by the sale of acquired business to other interests, or by floating the acquired company through an initial public offering.

Private equity is a notoriously secretive sector. Firms do not usually publish information on their history, their ownership, the senior members of their management and advisory teams, or their investment strategy. Private equity funds also provide little indication on the partners in the fund, or their capacity to invest. Nor do they disclose the portfolio of companies in the fund, other than to their investors.

However, a few private equity firms have been floated as public companies and are listed on stock markets. In these cases more information is available on the overall funding, but not of individual funds, nor their investors. A splendid example is shown in the vignette case of Blackstone that follows.

Some commentators have felt that the acquisition of listed companies by private equity interests would dilute stock markets through 'privatization'. In fact, such developments could be seen as a return to the earlier 19th century model of joint stock companies, when a handful of external shareholders invested in a public company, elected the directors and held them to account for their stewardship.

Typically, private equity firms are unregulated, other than within the company and banking regulations and laws of the relevant jurisdiction. Calls for more transparency and greater

Case Study 5.4 The Blackstone Group

Peter G. Peterson and Stephen A. Schwarzman founded The Blackstone Group with a shared secretary and a balance sheet of US$400,000 in 1985. Today Blackstone is a leading global alternative asset manager and provider of financial advisory services listed on the New York Stock Exchange with total assets under management of nearly US$100 billion in 2007. The asset management businesses includes the management of:

- Corporate private equity funds
- Real estate opportunity funds
- Marketable alternative asset management funds, including:

> funds of hedge funds
> mezzanine funds
> senior debt vehicles
> proprietary hedge funds
> closed-end mutual funds

The corporate private equity operation, established in 1987, is a global business with 98 investment professionals and offices in New York, London, Mumbai, and Hong Kong, and is a world leader in private equity investing, having managed five general private equity funds as well as one specialized fund focusing on communications-related investments.

From an operation focused in the early years on consummating leveraged buyout acquisitions of US based companies, the company has grown into a business pursuing transactions throughout the world and executing not only typical leveraged buyout acquisitions of seasoned companies but also transactions involving start-up businesses in established industries, turnarounds, minority investments, corporate partnerships, and industry consolidations, in all cases in strictly friendly transactions supported by the subject company's board of directors.

In total, the corporate private equity operation has raised around US$36 billion in capital since 1987 and has invested in approximately 121 companies in a variety of industries and countries. In 2007, the corporate private equity funds had some US$32.7 billion of assets under management with significant equity investments in 44 different companies.

(See www.blackstone.com)

Discussion Questions

1. Why do you think that the Blackstone group has been able to grow in just over twenty years from US$0.2 million to US$32 billion?

2. Find out what is meant by funds of hedge funds, mezzanine funds, senior debt vehicles, proprietary hedge funds, closed-end mutual funds.

3. Explain leveraged buyout acquisitions, seasoned companies, start-up businesses, established industries, turnarounds, minority investments, corporate partnerships, and industry consolidations.

4. Is Blackstone's policy only to handle 'strictly friendly transactions supported by the subject company's board of directors' sound?

disclosure are sometimes heard on the grounds of potential conflicts of interest, finance market stability, or public interest, particularly when a well-known listed company disappears under the veil of private equity. The response of private equity interests is, predictably, that their responsibility is to the owners of their firm and the investors in their funds. Greater exposure of their funding, strategies, or portfolios would inhibit the private deals which enable private equity to generate impressive returns on the back of significant risk.

Private equity firms operate private equity funds that can invest massively in the acquisition of other limited companies, sometimes listed companies which are taken private thus avoiding the public company disclosure requirements of the stock market and corporate regulators.

The strengths of private equity investment also reflect its potential weaknesses. In essence these can be summarized as:

- High gearing, which increases volatility and risk. Private equity firms are typically highly leveraged, using interest-bearing debt rather than equity capital for growth
- A strategic orientation towards financial rather than business strategies. In other words, private equity investors are more interested in realizing value from under-performing companies and under-valued assets, than acting in the best long term interests of the companies in their portfolio
- Cost reduction policies, seen by some as stripping out costs without regard for other stakeholders, particularly staff and customers
- The disposal of unnecessary assets, sometimes described by others as asset-stripping or 'selling the family silver'
- The use of tax advantages on the sale of entities in some tax jurisdictions and
- The charging of high fees and top management remuneration

Sir David Walker's voluntary code for private equity firms (see below) applies only to the UK although many private equity deals involve cross-border deals.

Box 5.1 Sir David Walker's Voluntary Code for UK Private Equity Firms

An equity firm should publish, either as an annual review or as a regular update on its website, information including:

- A description of the way in which an entity authorized by the Financial Services Authority fits into the firm of which it is a part with an indication of the firm's history and investment approach
- A commitment to conform to the guidelines on a 'comply or explain' basis and to promote conformity on the part of the portfolio companies owned by its fund(s)
- An indication of the leadership of the UK element of the firm, identifying the most senior members of the management or advisory team and confirmation that arrangements are in place to deal appropriately with conflicts of interest
- A description of the UK companies in the firm's portfolio
- A categorization of the limited partners in the fund(s) that invest or have a designated capability to invest in companies that would be UK portfolio companies.

Sovereign-wealth Funds

Surging Asian exports and high oil prices in the Middle East have generated massive surpluses. In some developing Arab and Asian countries state-owned funds have been used to recycle some of these surpluses by investing in companies in developed countries. These sovereign-wealth funds have invested in telecoms, technology, real estate, ports and transport operations, and significantly in the financial sectors, particularly in the United States and Europe. The following table gives an indication of the scale involved.

Morgan Stanley estimates that nearly US$3 trillion has been invested so far through major sovereign-wealth funds. Admittedly, this only represents some 2 percent of the world's traded securities, but if emerging economies continue to thrive their sovereign-wealth funds have the potential to grow quickly.

Sovereign-wealth funds raise two basic corporate governance issues:

• Shortcomings of the funds' governance

• The strategic potential of the sovereign nation to exert power over its investments

Table 5.2 **Examples of some of the larger sovereign-wealth funds**

Sovereign-wealth investing country	Funds invested US$ billion (estimate 2008)
Kuwait	
– Reserve Fund for Future Generations	250
Norway government	
– National pension fund	380
Peoples' Republic of China	
– China Investment Corporation	200
– China Development Bank	150
– Citic	60
Saudi Arabia	
– various funds	300
Singapore	
– Temasek Holdings	100
– GIC	100
United Arab Emirates	
– Abu Dhabi Investment Authority	875

Source: Morgan Stanley (2008).

Criticisms of the corporate governance of these funds include complaints that they lack transparency and are secretive, neither stating their objectives nor disclosing their portfolios, that they lack accountability to anyone other than their government paymasters, and that they are inadequately regulated. Unlike most other corporate entities they are not accountable to their members, shareholders, or regulators. Neither are they accountable directly to the citizens or voters in their sovereign nation.

Concerns about the strategic intent of sovereign nations include the worries that they may not be driven solely by a financial motive and that financial markets could be manipulated, because with its enormous wealth a fund could detrimentally affect financial markets.

Others see a potential abuse of power if sovereign-wealth funds use their investments to exercise strategic, possibly political, power around the world, for example promoting or protecting their own national champions, restricting competition, or using the investment as a pawn in a diplomatic wrangle.

For example, they fear that a sovereign-wealth fund with a controlling stake in a European or American bank might threaten to withhold funds unless the country acceded to its demands; or having acquired an oil or mineral producer, close it down to protect their own industries. Although running a company for political rather than economic reasons could well prove expensive.

A predictable nationalistic and protectionist backlash, expressing concerns about 'national treasures' such as energy, airlines, ports, and utilities being owned by foreigners, has been heard in developed nations. The United States Congress objected to the proposed Kuwait ownership of US port management and to China owning a US oil firm. However, it would be somewhat hypocritical to erect national barriers to inward investment from developing countries when expecting access to their developing markets. On the positive side Singapore, Kuwait, and South Korea provided a multi-billion dollar lifeline to Citigroup and Merrill Lynch, two banks which had lost massively in America's sub-prime credit crisis in 2008, which helped to stabilize the financial markets. China also has a significant stake in the American private equity firm the Blackstone Group (see previous case).

Investment managers of some sovereign-wealth funds say their strategy limits them to minority stakes, so that they do not get locked in to a massive investment, which could involve them in governance responsibilities and which they might have difficulty selling.

The governance of sovereign-wealth funds is likely to remain in focus for some time. As Bob Monks has commented: '*sovereign wealth investors raise all the questions of ownership power and responsibilities*'. In the longer term some international agreement may be reached, with a code of conduct for sovereign funds, perhaps regulated by an international body such as the International Monetary Fund.

The Governance of Joint Ventures

Joint ventures between companies, or strategic alliances as some call them, have been the preferred way for many companies to enter markets, transfer technology, procure supplies, obtain finance, share management skills, manufacture products around the world, or share risk on an international scale. Sometimes the partners in a joint venture are competitors in other fields.

Many joint ventures involve the incorporation of a joint venture company owned by the two or more partners in the joint venture. Top management of such joint venture companies are often drawn from among the senior management of the partners.

Governing joint venture companies can present special challenges. As in the Teletronic Riches case above, disagreements not envisaged in the initial joint venture agreement can arise between the partners. Directors then face conflicts of interest between their responsibilities to the joint venture company and to the partner company that employs them.

Case Study 5.5 Teletronic Riches Ltd

Teletronic Riches Limited was a joint venture company set up between Litchfield Teletronics Limited (henceforth Litchfield), a UK company, and Great Riches Limited (henceforth Riches), a company based in Hong Kong, though incorporated in Bermuda. Riches was quoted on the Hong Kong stock exchange, although 66 percent of the voting stock was owned by Albert Li Cheuk Yan and his family. Litchfield was the wholly owned subsidiary of a US based public company, listed on the NASDAQ stock exchange.

The joint venture had been set up to manufacture the Teletronic range of integrated fax, phone, and recording machines in Shenzen, China. In the joint venture agreement Litchfield would provide technological know-how, specialist manufacturing equipment, and the top management. Riches would introduce the manufacturing site, labour, and local management. Both sides put up an equal amount of working capital and would share equally in profits. The entire output was to be supplied to Litchfield for distribution through their worldwide marketing organization, except for sales to the market in China, where Riches were given the rights.

Litchfield and Riches had equal share holdings and voting rights, and each appointed three members to the board. Teletronic's managing director, Bill Torrington, was also made a member of the board. He had run a very successful division of Litchfield in the UK and in 1997 was seconded to Teletronics on a five-year contract. He expected, when the joint venture was successful, to become a director of the Litchfield main board on his return to England.

Initially, all went well, but after three years tensions emerged. Relations between the two sets of directors on the Teletronic board were frosty. The Riches nominated directors complained that the venture was not being given the latest products or technology. The Litchfield directors claimed that their company's products, made in Shenzen, were being sold throughout Asia, in contravention of the JV agreement.

Bill Torrington found himself in an impossible position. He wanted what was good for Teletronics, but his Litchfield colleagues expected him to side with them. His career prospects were on the line.

Discussion Question

1. What should Bill Torrington do?

Moreover, many joint venture companies are incorporated in foreign jurisdictions, with diverse and different company laws and regulatory regimes, and have overseas partners with different cultural expectations.

A crucial aspect of the governance of joint venture companies is to realize that only matters concerning the joint venture can properly be handled by the joint venture company board. Issues affecting the relationship between the joint venture partners, such as those in the Teletronic Riches case, cannot be resolved at the joint venture company level. They need to be handled at the level of the joint venture partners, if necessary revising the joint venture agreement.

The composition of the board of joint venture companies needs to be considered carefully and written into the joint venture agreement: how many representative directors from each side and whether independent non-executive directors (INEDs) are desirable. Although many joint venture companies do appoint the managing director or CEO of the joint venture to the board, to avoid Bill Torrington's dilemma in the Teletronic case, others now appoint representative directors from the partner companies, plus INEDs in some cases, with the joint venture project manager attending meetings in a non-voting, non-partisan way.

The Governance of NGOs and Non-profit Corporate Entities

It is now widely recognized that all corporate entities need sound corporate governance, not just limited companies. This includes organizations in the voluntary and community sectors, such as education authorities, hospital trusts, sports organizations, and other not-for-profit entities; non-governmental organizations, such as public sector corporations, quangos; and cooperatives. They all need to be appropriately organized and managed, and they all need to be well governed.

The typical distinguishing features of such organizations are that:

- They are working for the public good (not the benefit of shareholders).
- Their aims reflect community objectives (not long term growth and bottom-line profit)
- Their legal status is rooted in the law of trusts, charities, cooperatives, or other legal acts (not company law)
- Their form can take various legal structures (other than a limited company)
- Their underpinning constitution determines their form and purpose (not a corporate memorandum and articles)
- Governance is provided by a governing body, which can be known variously as a council, board of trustees, management committee etc. (not as a board of directors)
- Their performance is measured by the achievement of multiple goals and is often difficult to measure. They have a 'multiple bottom line' rather than a single financial profitability measure
- Their governing body is often large and drawn entirely from outside, non-executive members (unlike the size and structure of corporate boards with their executive and non-executive directors)

- Their objectives can conflict: for example, a hospital may find that it cannot simultaneously deliver the highest performance on patient care and medical standards, financial effectiveness, administrative efficiency, staff welfare, and community approval
- Nomination to the governing body may come from members, funding bodies including the state, representative bodies (staff, beneficiaries, funding bodies, the local community etc.), subject to the constitution. Difficult conflicts of interest can arise where governing body members are 'representative' of interest groups associated with the organization
- The top executive and the top management team are typically invited to attend meetings of the governing body, make reports and answer questions, but are seldom voting members of it (unlike the corporate sector where the CEO and other senior executive directors are usually board members)
- Membership of the governing body is usually voluntary and unpaid, with no fees, remuneration, or capital gains, subject perhaps to reasonable expenses (again unlike the corporate sector)
- Trustees are the guardian angels of a voluntary organization, watching over its activities, and need to be competent, informed, but personally disinterested

In the UK public sector, an independent commission for good governance in public services, chaired by Sir Alan Langlands, produced a good governance standard for public services in 2005. The standard argued that good governance means:

(1) Focusing on the organization's purpose and on outcomes for citizens and service users.

(2) Performing effectively in clearly defined functions and roles.

(3) Promoting values for the whole organization and demonstrating values of good governance through behaviour.

(4) Taking informed, transparent decisions and managing risk.

(5) Developing the capacity and capability of the governing body to be effective.

(6) Engaging stakeholders and making accountability real.

In the voluntary and community sector, the UK Charity Commission, also in 2005, published a non-mandatory code for good governance for the voluntary and community sector. Working with the National Council for Voluntary Organisations (www.ncvo-vol.org.uk) the following 'hallmarks' of good charity trusteeship were suggested.

Board Leadership

Organizations should be led and controlled by an effective board of trustees which collectively ensures delivery of its aims, sets its strategic direction and upholds its values. The board has ultimate responsibility for ensuring that the organization is well run, solvent, and delivering the desired outcomes; further the board should focus on strategic direction and avoid becoming involved in day-to-day operations, unless strategic and operational roles of individuals are separated.

Board Control

The board is responsible and accountable for monitoring and ensuring that the organization is performing well, including compliance with its constitution, the law, and regulatory requirements. The board should maintain and regularly review the organization's internal controls, policies, and procedures for reporting performance, and organization risk management . . . Principles of equality and diversity should be upheld and the organization should be fair and open to all sections of the community in its activities.

The High Performance Board

The board should have and achieve clear responsibilities and functions, with a statement of trustees' duties and responsibilities, which the trustees understand. The board should have a diverse range of skills, experience, and knowledge and make the most effective use of trustees' time and abilities. Induction, training, and ongoing support should be available to trustees, along with appropriate information and advice. The board is responsible for the supervision, support, appraisal, and remuneration of its chief executive.

Board Review and Renewal

The board should periodically review its own effectiveness, and that of its committees and the organization as a whole.

Board Delegation

The board should set out the functions of its sub-committees, the chief executive, and other staff in clear, delegated authorities. The terms of reference and roles should be clear and the delegation effective.

Board and Trustee Integrity

Individual trustees and the board as a whole should act according to the highest ethical standards and ensure that any conflicts of interest are properly disclosed and handled. Trustees must not benefit from their position beyond that allowed by the constitution and the law.

Board Openness

The board should be open, responsive, and accountable to the organizations' members, beneficiaries, other users, partners, and all those with an interest in its work . . . Stakeholder communication should be effective, and key stakeholders should be involved in the organization's planning and decision making.

In earlier days charities relied on values in society to ensure that their trustees behaved appropriately. Today, given the greater diversity of voluntary and community organizations, their many aims, and changing social norms, in some parts of the world more use is being made of codes and legal sanctions.

In the United States, even though the SOX Act does not formally apply to non-profits, SOX standards are being applied to not-for-profit entities. In California SOX-like standards have been imposed on all large non-profits.

> **Box 5.2 New York Stock Exchange (NYSE)**
>
> The New York Attorney General had overall (though rarely exercised) supervisory authority over the non-profit sector in the state. The New York Stock Exchange was a non-profit corporation. The Attorney General, Eliot Spitzer, brought an action against the CEO of the NYSE, Dick Grasso, and the chairman of its compensation committee alleging that his retirement compensation was excessive had SOX standards been applied.

Some problems that are frequently found in the governance of voluntary and community organizations include:

- Founders of the organization who become permanent members of the governing body
- Stagnant membership of the board
- Board members elected by representative groups who have conflicts of interest
- Boards packed with representative members who are well meaning but contribute little
- Lack of board members with necessary skills, knowledge, or experience
- Failure to keep board members informed
- Failure to induct new board members and update other board members
- Inadequate control systems, performance measures, and monitoring of executive actions
- Lack of a strategic focus and failure to rethink strategies as circumstances change
- Poor chairmanship of the board, lack of leadership, and interpersonal politics

Some community and voluntary sector organizations include limited companies within their organization structure, for example running a mail order catalogue company to raise funds and make a profit. Such companies, of course, must abide by company law, regulation, and governance codes as appropriate. The UK has created two legal forms for such companies—the Community Interest Company and the Incorporated Charitable Company.

The key criterion for board membership of a voluntary or community organization should be merit and contribution, not representation and status. In many communities the importance of the voluntary sector is growing. In some countries more governmental funds are being made available to such organizations with related calls for wider accountability and transparency. Inevitably there is a growing need to recognize the vital significance of sound corporate governance.

The Governance of Partnerships and Limited Liability Partnerships

A partnership is a legal organizational form in which two or more people agree to join together to achieve common goals under a partnership agreement that determines the contribution that each partner is required to make to the partnership, the way the partnership will be governed and managed, and the way profits and losses will be shared. Typically partners are personally liable for the debts of the partnership. A partnership is not a company and in most jurisdictions operates under specific partnership law. The partnership organizational form has a long tradition and has shown itself to be robust and flexible. Around the world professional practices, in accountancy and medicine for example, have adopted the partnership form for many years.

A partnership has fewer constraints and lower requirements for reporting than a company. As a result partners are free to decide how they want to govern their partnership. In a small partnership with relatively few partners, the normal form of governance is through a meeting of all the partners. In larger practices, with many partners and, particularly if they are geographically spread, the partnership may decide to appoint a managing partner and a governing body, perhaps called an executive or management committee, which meets regularly to manage partnership affairs, with a periodic, perhaps annual, meeting of the entire partnership to accept the accounts, to transact business reserved to the meeting, and to appoint members to the governing body.

In the past, some partnership law put a limit on the maximum number of partners allowed in a partnership. But this law has been relaxed in some jurisdictions and partnerships there are now large and international. As a result, partners can find themselves personally exposed to the partnership risks of a widely spread and diverse partnership practice, without being personally able to influence partnership decision, except though periodic voting for members of the governing body. This was the case when the international accountancy partnership Arthur Andersen found itself financially exposed in the collapse of Enron.

Case Study 5.6 More on the Collapse of the Andersen Partnership

Arthur Andersen was one of the big five global accounting practices. Operating in most countries in the world, the firm provided audit, accountancy, and consultancy services to their client companies. The firm had developed many pioneering accounting practices and systems. Their reputation, and certainly the partnership's self-image, was as the international leader of the profession.

Then in the early years of the 21st century things went badly wrong. Some of their major US clients—Waste Management, Worldcom, and Enron—became spectacularly insolvent and the auditor was claimed to be less than blameless. The claims for damages from disgruntled creditors and shareholders of the failed companies threatened the financial viability of the Andersen firm. The American firm was also found guilty of destroying evidence, although that verdict was quashed on appeal.

But the question was whether the Andersen partnership was based in America, or were the partners in the Andersen practices around the world also exposed? Some claimed that the partnerships were legally distinct, but in the event, the rapid loss of clients in countries around the world and partners leaving for other firms, resulted in the failure of the global practice and the end of the Arthur Andersen partnership.

Discussion Questions

1. Why did the accountancy firm Arthur Andersen collapse?

2. Why was the question 'whether the Andersen partnership was based in America, or were the partners in the Andersen practices around the world' important?

Following the Enron and Andersen debacle, a call to limit the exposure of audit firms to unlimited actions for damages in such cases was widely heard. It was further suggested that many claimants sued the auditors, even though they might have had only a relatively small part in the overall collapse, because they had 'deep pockets' as a result of insurance cover, whereas the directors of the company, who might have been far more culpable, had only their private resources.

Some countries have now provided for a form of limited liability partnership (LLP). This governance vehicle gives the benefits of limited liability to the members but allows the flexibility of organizing as a traditional partnership. The governance of an LLP is similar to that of a partnership: members provide the capital, contribute personally, and share profits and losses. To give some protection to those dealing with a limited partnership, however, the disclosure requirements tend to be more stringent than for a traditional partnership, and similar to those of a company. For example, in the UK, LLPs are required to have a registered office, file an annual return with financial accounts, and notify changes to their membership.

REFERENCES AND FURTHER READING

Bleicher, K. and H. Paul (1986) 'Corporate Governance Systems in a Multinational Environment: Who Knows Best?' *Management International Review*, 26(3) (Summary in 'Corporate Governance Update', *Corporate Governance: An International Review*, April 1993, Vol. 1).

Burrough, Bryan and John Helyar (1990) *Barbarians at the Gate: The Fall of RJR Nabisco*. New York: Harper & Row. (The story of two private equity firms—Forstmann Little and Kohlberg Kravis Roberts—and their aggressive US$25 billion takeover of RJR Nabisco.)

Cornforth, C. (2003) *The Governance of Public and Non-profit Organizations: What do Boards Do?* London: Routledge.

Solomon, Jill (2004, 2007) *Corporate Governance and Accountability*. Chichester: Wiley.

USEFUL WEBSITES

www.charity-commission.gov.uk
Information on governance in voluntary and community organizations.

www.gcgf.org
The World Bank's and OECD corporate governance programme.

www.hkgem.com
Hong Kong Stock Exchange Growth Enterprise Market (GEM).

www.ifc.org/ifcext/corporategovernance.nsf/Content/CG_Tools
The IFC/World Bank offer a number of corporate governance tools for family and founder owned unlisted companies, listed companies, financial institutions, privatized transition economy companies, and state owned enterprises.

www.londonstockexchange.com
Listing rules including the Alternative Investment Market (AIM).

www.mapnp.org/library/boards/boards.htm
Free Management Library guidelines for not-for-profit organizations.

www.ncvo-vol.org.uk
www.swd.gov.hk/doc/ngo/corp-gov-eng.pdf
Leading your NGO board (Canada).

PROJECTS AND EXERCISES

1. Explore the Internet for information on voluntary and community organizations and NGOs in your country. Draft a report to the government on the extent to which they appear to conform to international norms on corporate governance.

2. Draft an explanatory paper and presentation for the chairman of a voluntary or community organization in your country explaining what is needed for successful corporate governance in his or her organization.

SELF-TEST QUESTIONS

To confirm your grasp of the key points in this chapter try answering the following questions. Answers are at the end of the book.

1. Should the managing director/CEO of a joint venture company, who is also employed by one of the joint venture partners, be a member of the joint venture company board?

2. How are partnerships governed?

3. What is a limited liability partnership?

4. Explain the differences between associated, subsidiary, and holding company.

5. Explain the two distinct options in governing and managing a group of companies.

6. What are the benefits of drawing subsidiary company directors from other companies in the group.

7. Explain what a family council is and does in a family company.

8. Explain what a sovereign-wealth fund is and which countries have been particularly involved.

9. What are some of the sectors in which sovereign-funds have invested?

10. List some of the distinguishing characteristics of a not for profit corporate entity.

6   Functions of the Board

- In which we consider:
  - the functions of the board
  - corporate transparency
  - the delegation of board functions to management
  - balancing the board's performance and conformance roles

The Functions of the Board

A simple framework was introduced in chapter 2 that gave an overview of the functions of the board, showing its responsibility to be looking inwards at the enterprise and outwards to the firm's external situation, focusing on the past, the present, and the strategic future (see figure 6.1).

It should be noted that the terminology used here—of corporate strategy leading to corporate policy—is the usage adopted in the business world. In government circles, at both national and local levels, the terminology tends to be reversed with policy statements leading to strategic initiatives. Here we will adopt the business usage.

In fact boards can and do delegate some part of these activities to management, through the CEO or managing director, as depicted in figure 6.2. Later in this chapter we will discuss how a balance is achieved between board and management.

Figure 6.1 The basic board functions

Figure 6.2 Board functions working through management

We can now explore each of the four functions in more detail to see what they involve.

Strategy Formulation

Who is responsible for formulating strategy in the modern company? Most people would not hesitate in their reply—'*top management, of course—the CEO and the management team*'. That is the conventional wisdom in Western companies. But what then is the role of the board of directors? Clearly, this question cannot have a simple answer. Boards dominated by executive directors have been accused of '*marking their own examination papers*'. But in boards with a preponderance of outside directors, the question is frequently asked whether they can really know enough about the company and its industry to make a realistic contribution to strategic thinking. Some also question whether they can find sufficient time to make a worthwhile input to strategy, particularly since some of them may be CEOs of companies in their own right.

Directors are called directors because they direct: one of their primary duties is to ensure that their enterprise is heading in the right direction. The board which does not have a shared view of the company's future direction and purpose, what some call a corporate vision, cannot develop an effective corporate strategy. Strategy formulation is the process of generating and reviewing alternative longer term directions for the firm that lead towards the achievement of its purpose. Strategy formulation may involve senior management and consultants, but should certainly involve the board members.

Many companies attempt to encapsulate this sense of purpose and direction in a mission statement. Some directors feel that their mission statement provides a concrete statement of the company's purpose, aims, and direction, which can inspire employees and inform customers and other stakeholders. If it is to guide strategic decisions, such a mission statement needs to be a clear but succinct indication of the purpose and strategic intent of the enterprise.

Other directors, however, feel that written mission statements are at best a bland public relations exercise and at worst an exercise in futility. Certainly, unless directors believe in and link their mission with their strategic decisions, a public mission statement for customers or a sign on the wall for employees can achieve little.

Box 6.1 Examples of Mission Statements

McDonald's: *'McDonald's vision is to be the world's best quick service restaurant experience. Being the best means providing outstanding quality, service, cleanliness, and value, so that we make every customer in every restaurant smile.'*

J. Sainsbury, a UK retailer: *'Our mission is to be the consumer's first choice for food, delivering products of outstanding quality and great service at a competitive cost through working faster, simpler, and together.'*

The Ford Motor Company: *'To become the world's leading consumer-company for automotive products and services.'*

General Electric: *'We bring good things to life.'*

Microsoft changed its mission statement from: *'To empower people through great software—any time, any place, and on any device'* to: *'To enable people and businesses throughout the world to realize their full potential.'*

A traditional approach to strategic planning, still adopted by a few companies, is long range planning. Essentially long range planning involves an exercise in which the annual budget process is rolled forward over a longer strategic time horizon, perhaps three to five years. At least this approach forces boards to focus on the longer term. But the drawbacks are apparent. The planner is, conceptually, inside the organization looking out. The approach fails to take a strategic perspective, perpetuating the existing business, rather than recognizing potential strategic changes in technology, markets, or competition, and ignoring the economic, political, and social context.

To formulate strategy effectively the strategic planner needs to be, conceptually, above the enterprise looking down, able to see the enterprise in its strategic context, including the industry, the market, customers and competitors, products, and services, wherever the company operates and to identify the wider political, economic, social, and technological context (what some commentators call PEST analysis). Figure 2.8 in chapter 2, which shows the scope of corporate governance, can be expanded to depict the scope of strategy formulation.

A well known metaphor refers to the ability to perceive the enterprise in the context of ever-widening circles of influence as 'helicopter vision', explaining that when on the ground the helicopter pilot can see the ground in great detail, but not very far horizontally. As the helicopter rises the pilot's horizons widen, but the detail gets less. In fact, to think with helicopter vision is not difficult: the challenge is to determine the appropriate level at which to view the territory.

A more penetrating approach to strategic analysis than long range planning is the widely used SWOT (strengths, weaknesses, opportunities, and threats) analysis, which seeks to relate the internal situation in the firm with its external strategic context.

An example of the outcome of a SWOT analysis will explain this. In the analysis that follows, drawn from the experiences of a realtor (real estate agent), the ideas were generated during a half-day strategy seminar attended by the directors and top management from the firm's regional offices. The chart represents a synthesis of the ideas produced by small working groups.

Box 6.2 SWOT Analysis for a Long Established Realtor (Estate Agent)

Strengths

- We have a well-known and respected brand name
- We have a good market share where we are represented
- We have been successful for thirty-five years
- Both sellers and buyers respect our business methods
- Our leaflets and adverts for promoting properties are successful
- We have a large and experienced staff
- We have a reputation as a good employer
- We have effective financial and management control systems

Weaknesses

- High overheads, particularly rents and salaries
- Overheads rising
- Cash flow erratic
- Slow to respond to new clients—pressure of work
- Insufficient time with clients
- Higher management authority required for decisions—slows the contract process and stifles staff initiative
- Our website is still being developed
- Telephone inquiries not well handled
- Staff turnover—experienced staff being poached
- Organizational inertia—slow to change direction—over-confidence

Opportunities

- Our business sector is expanding
  - Growth in sales of new house builds and existing properties
- Commercial property sector sales not yet in portfolio
- Many opportunities for development of new client services
- Our competitors may be slow to adopt new technologies

Threats

- Competition rife
  - High street offices, national franchised chains, private sales
- Vulnerable to Internet—developments unpredictable
- New ways to buy and sell houses erodes our position
- Developments in technology changes the basics of the business
- A new strategy by a large competitor ruins our market position
- More government controls and charges on property transfers

The strategic situation facing the firm, both internally and externally, is certainly highlighted by this analysis. What emerges is a picture of a long established, successful, but over-bureaucratic, firm in the real estate business facing vulnerability with an increasingly competitive market, driven by franchised high street chains and a shift towards property sales through the Internet. The self-confidence rooted in past success, the difficulty of adapting to change, and the need to develop a sense of urgency for strategic change, are apparent.

The SWOT methodology offers the prospect of building on strengths, whilst working to eliminate or at least mitigate internal weaknesses, exploiting external opportunities faster than other firms and moving to minimize the effect of external threats. A SWOT analysis tends to focus attention on the existing business, looking for threats that it might face and opportunities it could pursue. The limitations can include a failure to identify what is driving change in the market, the technology, or the economic situation and thus the ability to respond adequately. It can also overlook the firm's exposure to risk.

A SWOT analysis exercise can provide a penetrating experience for those involved and produce valuable information for board deliberations, but it does little to identify causes and effects of strategic change and suggest alternatives. In the real estate case above the SWOT analysis does not generate strategic possibilities such as growth through acquisition, perhaps by franchising the firm's brand, merger (collaborating with rather than fighting the opposition), buying into another franchise, and/or investing in buying/selling operations through the Internet.

Surprisingly, many boards fail to devote enough time and attention to strategy formulation, as we will see later. Directors in a professionally led board will have a strategic focus with relevant up-to-date information about the internal situation in the company, appropriate information about the firm's external context, both the immediate operating situation (its industry, competitors, customers, products, operations, and financial situation), and the overall environment (the political, economic, social, and technological contexts).

Moreover, directors on professionally-led boards have an ability to think strategically. What is meant by the ability to think strategically? General Sun Tse, a Chinese leader in the Chou/Zhou dynasty in the first millennium BC, was one of the finest strategic minds the world has ever known. He called for the strategist to be able to '*think with the mind of the enemy*'. In business terms, that means identifying existing and potential competitors, understanding their strategic situation, and thinking through the strategies that they might be pursuing. What would our directors hear if they were flies on the wall of the competitor's boardroom?

To understand the strategic situation affecting a company we need to appreciate the forces that determine its competitiveness within that company's industry. Sometimes they will be harsh because of massive competitive pressures, for example in a mature 'smokestack industry' facing competition from alternative products and processes produced in economically cheaper countries or environmentally friendlier circumstances. Or sometimes the pressure to change may be benign because the growth of market size leaves all the players in that sector with operational and production demands—not competitive pressure.

> **Case Study 6.1 IBM's Failure to Appreciate Microsoft Strategy**
>
> The well known company Microsoft, which was originally known as MicroSoft, was founded in New Mexico in 1975 by Bill Gates and Paul Allen to develop and sell BASIC interpreters for the Altair 8800. In the mid-1980s, IBM agreed to license that software for their PCs, not to buy the product or the company. IBM believed that their main interest lay with large main-frame computers. In effect this strategic decision committed the world to using Microsoft Windows software for the foreseeable future.
>
> Microsoft was then able to dominate the home computer market with MS-DOS. Later, when the company was launched through an IPO, Bill Gates became one of the world's richest men and many of his colleagues, millionaires.
>
> *Discussion Questions*
>
> **1.** By hindsight it is easy to see IBM's strategic failing, but at the time why did they fail?
>
> **2.** Do you think that Microsoft had a strategy to dominate the world's PC and laptop software?

Professor Michael Porter[1] of the Harvard Business School has provided a number of analytical frameworks that can give an understanding of the strategic situation. In one, he focuses on the value added by a company to its products and services. In another, often referred to as the five forces model, he challenges a company's assumptions about its immediate strategic environment:

(1) Who is currently competing in our market?

- How are they currently competing—price, service, quality, etc.?
- How does that compare with the value added by this business?

(2) What strategic powers do our upstream suppliers of goods and services have?

- Are they able to exercise strategic influence on us—by pricing, supply, etc.?

(3) What strategic powers do our downstream distributors and ultimate customers have?

- Are they able to exercise strategic influence on us—by price demands, etc.?
- Who are our customers—types, location, volume etc.?
- What customer needs do we satisfy?

(4) Could our customers' needs be met in other ways—with substitute goods or services?

(5) Could other firms enter the market?

- What is keeping them out—high entry costs, know-how, low margins, etc.?

---

[1]Porter, Michael E. (1980) *Competitive Strategy: Techniques for Analyzing Industries and Competitors.* New York: The Free Press.

Porter, Michael E. (1985) *Competitive Advantage: Creating and Sustaining Superior Performance.* New York: The Free Press.

This emphasis on the strategic environment of the company, rather than its internal situation, reflects the advice of General Sun Tse, mentioned earlier, to '*think with the mind of the enemy*'. Directors that are thinking strategically try to understand the strategic situation of the competitors, and deduce what strategies they are pursuing. This is very different from reacting operationally. Crucial questions include:

- Who are the competitors?
- What is their current strategic situation?
- What is their current strategy—how are they currently competing?
- What are their capabilities—both strengths and weaknesses?
- What assumptions do they hold about themselves and their market?

What attitudes do their directors and top management have compared with ours?

- Are they satisfied with their present market/financial position?
- Where might the competitors be vulnerable?
- What strategies could they pursue in the future?
- What is the likelihood?
- How might they react to strategic shifts that we might make?

Professional directors understand the importance of such information, and well run boards ensure that they have access to it. Unless directors have a similar view of their firm's strategic situation, they cannot formulate objective strategy. Later in this chapter we will see how much emphasis boards tend to put on strategy formulation and some of the ways they have of maximizing this effort.

Critics of Porter's approach to strategy formulation argue that, by focusing on the company's external competitive environment, the strengths of a company's internal resource may be under-utilized and its strategies be over-influenced by market conditions. By contrast, a currently popular alternative, often known as resource based theory, sees a firm as a collection of resources and capabilities that need to be utilized to create a winning strategy. The resources could include access to capital, employee skills, unique products or services, managerial talent and experience, equipment and buildings, or goodwill. This resource based perspective seeks to find a fit between a firm's internal capabilities and its external market situation that will produce a competitive advantage.

Policy Making

Strategies remain nothing more than statements of intent or dreams until they are turned into operational plans. To make strategies operational, companies need policies, procedures, plans, and, in some cases, projects. The policies, procedures, and plans provide the criteria against which the board can subsequently monitor management's performance and fulfil their duty to supervise executive management.

Policies can be thought of as the rules, systems, and procedures that are laid down by the board to guide and constrain executive management. Obviously, the details of corporate polices depend on the scale, diversity, and type of operation.

Top management may play a large part in the development of policies and in their implementation. In other cases, the board may delegate much of the policy making to the CEO and top executive team. But the board must ensure that appropriate policies are in place, functioning effectively, and regularly reviewed in the light of changing circumstances.

There are some matters that a board may decide should not be delegated to management, decisions that they want to keep to themselves. In such cases the board creates a

---

Case Study 6.2 South American Resources Ltd: Board Policy on Reserved Powers

Decisions Which Must be Taken at Board Level and Cannot be Delegated

- Approval of overall corporate strategy and direction
- Major business acquisitions or disposals
- Approval of investment projects (over US$1 million)
- Board appointments and removals (executive and outside directors)
- Directors' remuneration policy
- Terms and appointment of CEO and top executives
- Appraisal of CEO and top executives
- Significant dealings with government and the media
- Remuneration and selection of auditors
- Approval of interim and final financial statements
- Significant changes to accounting policies
- Terms of reference for board committees
- Appointments to board committees
- Fundamental changes to employee pension scheme rules
- Main treasury policies
  e.g. on gearing, borrowing limits, currency exposure
- Corporate risk management
- Significant changes to corporate control systems

Discussion Questions

1. Do you see any basic problems with the application of this policy in South American Resources?

2. If you were an independent outside director on the board, what further decisions would you want to retain to the board, to ensure that you knew what was going on and could contribute appropriately?

3. Are there any board decisions in this list that you would delegate to management?

policy on reserved powers—decisions that are reserved to the board and that only the directors can take. This is illustrated in case study 6.2 on the previous page.

Other policies may be developed by management and, if appropriate, be approved by the board. The following examples of policies will illustrate:

(1)   Marketing policies
  • Product or service polices—amplifying strategy on market sector
  • Pricing policy
  • Distribution policy

(2)   Operational policies
  • Technology policy—reflecting the strategy on hi-tech/low tech etc.
  • Production or service provision policies
  • Location policy

(3)   Financial policies
  • Credit policy
  • Borrowing policy
  • Policy on gearing or leverage
  • Policy on accounting standards to be adopted in all countries

(4)   Risk assessment and management policies
  • Business catastrophe recognition and continuity management
  • Strategic risk assessment and management
  • Financial exposure
  • Employment, health and safety risk management
  • Product risk management and contingency policies

(5)   Labour relations and employment policies
  • Staff terms and conditions policy
  • Trades union policy
  • Health and safety policies

(6)   IT policies
  • IT operational and management policies
  • Policy on IT security and confidentiality
  • Staff use of network policy

(7)   Merger and acquisition policies.

Policies need to be closely related to and flow from the company's strategies.

Risk management policies are of particular importance at board level, because in recent years, corporate governance codes have expressly recognized directors' responsibility to ensure that risk management polices are in place, and that risks are adequately assessed. We will explore this issue further in chapter 14.

Having set the corporate policies, or approved those proposed by top management, the board needs to ensure that appropriate management systems are in place to make these policies operational. That means appropriate management procedures and plans, including project plans, resource allocation plans, and operational budgets, all reinforced by effective management information and control systems.

Strategy formulation and policy making together form the board level performance role. This is a fundamental component of the work of a unitary board; whereas in a two-tier board the responsibility falls to the management board.

We now come to the conformance roles—executive monitoring and supervision, and accountability. Again this is a fundamental part of the work of a unitary board; whereas in a two-tier board the conformance role is the responsibility of the supervisory board.

Supervising Executive Activities

Almost all corporate entities, large and small, use financial measures and accounting systems as the primary means of monitoring the state of the enterprise and the performance of its managers. At the very least this is likely to include a balance sheet and profit and loss (or revenue and expenditure) account. To be able to keep a better track of executive activities many boards also rely on regular reports from a budgetary control system. Budgetary control systems compare actual revenues and expenditures against budgeted revenues and expenditures. The initial development of cost centres and their budgets enable management at all levels to be involved in the budgeting process, with the resultant motivation to achieve the planned performance.

Obviously, budgetary control systems are expressed in terms of costs and revenues. A more sophisticated approach to financially based controls involves the creation of profit centres within a firm. Managers responsible for such profit centres can now be motivated by and held accountable for the profit performance of their unit, possibly including return on investment criteria.

A further refinement is a management control system which applies multiple performance measures to business units. An example will illustrate:

Box 6.3 A Multiple Measure Management Control System

The board of a company with profit responsible divisions required its divisional managers to perform appropriately on ten criteria:

- Profitability—return on investment in that division
- Growth in market share, revenues, and profit
- Customer satisfaction
- Capital expenditure project performance
- Management development and succession planning
- Product and service development
- Employee training, labour turnover, and employee attitudes

- Contributing to the group's corporate social responsibility
- Risk monitoring and management
- Balancing the short term with the long term

Responsible executives were expected to perform well on all ten criteria continuously. Failure to maintain planned performance on any one criterion required an explanation at board level.

Management control systems that use criteria beyond financial measures may have problems with quantifying some of the criteria. Judgement may be required in the measurement of difficult concepts such as customer satisfaction or employee attitudes. However, such systems do exist and some boards rely on their output.

To reduce the reports presented to the board some firms rely on exception reporting in which only significant variations from planned performance have occurred and board level attention is required.

Further consideration of management control systems needs to be through specialist literature in that field. In chapter 12 we will explore board level information in greater depth.

However, before leaving the use of management control systems to enable a board to fulfil its responsibility to monitor and supervise management, we should note a particular dilemma, known as sub-optimization. Where units of an organization are held responsible for the achievement of specific criteria, in seeking to meet the required performance measure each unit will tend to take action which helps it to achieve its own objectives but which is potentially detrimental to the organization as a whole. Directors need to be sensitive to such actions when setting and assessing subsidiary company, divisional, or unit performance measures. In chapter 9, when we consider theories of corporate governance, we will see that sub-optimization is a special case of the agency dilemma. Examples of sub-optimization are legion. We will explore the idea further in chapter 9 when discussing theories of corporate governance. For now a few examples will illustrate:

Case Study 6.3   Examples of Sub-optimization

1. In an automotive company the engine division made the engines that were built into the car division's product. The management control system was based on divisional profitability. Consequently, the transfer price between the engine and the car division was crucial, the engine division wanting the highest price, the car division the lowest. Faced with a disagreement, the engine division threatened to place orders for engines with an outside supplier, whilst the engine division decided to sell its production outside the group. Referring the issue to top management resolved the matter but only at the price of removing responsibility from the divisional managers for their own divisional performance.

2. In a health organization with many hospitals, the governing board decreed that hospital performance would be judged, inter alia, on the speed that patients

were discharged. The result was a dramatic rise in emergency re-admissions. So the board changed the criterion to measure bed occupancy rates, at which beds became blocked with patients who could have been discharged earlier. Even a system of multiple performance measures still encouraged sub-optimal behaviour.

3. In a chain of retail stores, the head office used a budgetary control system to monitor store-by-store level management and report store-by-store performance to the board. Directors visiting some stores, however, found that though the managers were hitting their budget expenditure and turnover targets in the short term, they were not investing in appropriate staff training, store maintenance, or local promotion because that would increase their costs without increasing the measurable store performance in the short term. Some store managers recognized the longer term implications of their sub-optimal actions but hoped to get their performance related bonus, even promotion to a bigger store, before the adverse results became apparent.

Discussion Question

1. Identify other examples of sub-optimal behaviour from your own experience. Consider not-for-profit entities, for example in education, health-care, or public services, as well as businesses.

Accountability

To whom is a board accountable? Universally, the answer is: the members of that corporate entity. In the case of a joint stock, limited liability company, the members are those shareholders with voting rights. In a cooperative society, the members are those with voting rights under the constitution. In a professional body, the members are those paid-up and qualified to vote under the rules of that association.

The level and detail of reporting required will be determined by the constitution of the organization, the laws under which it is incorporated and the demands of any regulating authority. In the case of the limited liability company, the required accountability is laid down in the Companies Acts, often in considerable detail. Companies may provide more than this legal requirement: they may not disclose less. Companies whose shares are listed on a stock exchange also have to meet that exchange's requirements for disclosure and the regulatory authorities rules.

However, in recent years a view has been gaining currency that boards, particularly of significant organizations which have the potential to affect a lot of people by their behaviour, should recognize some accountability to a wider range of stakeholders. We will discuss stakeholder thinking in chapter 9, when we reach theories and philosophies of corporate governance. For now, it should be noted that many companies recognize this wider responsibility and seek to provide relevant information to a range of connected stakeholders—employees, customers, and the media, for example. Other companies go further and recognize a responsibility to account to the community at large. We will explore corporate social responsibility (CSR) reporting, much of which is often qualitative and non-financial, in chapter 15.

But a few companies take a strictly legal view, arguing that, provided they obey the laws of the countries in which they operate, they owe no wider duty of disclosure or accountability to stakeholder groups. If a society expects such wider accountability it is up to the legislature to enact laws accordingly, they argue.

We have now reviewed, albeit briefly, the nature of the four activities which make up the board's activities. Notice that there is a dynamic to them: strategy formulation is a process which leads to the making of policies (and related management procedures, projects, and plans), which provide the basis for executive monitoring and supervision, the results of which form the basis of the accountability that a board has to fulfil. This process, in turn, provides an essential input into the next round of strategy formulation.

Before leaving accountability, we should focus a little more on what is now involved in corporate reporting.

Corporate Transparency

Traditionally boards used the audited, historical financial accounts to tell shareholders the story of their stewardship. Today, listed companies are expected to say far more, not only about how the company has been performing, but to tell the story behind its current performance and to anticipate its future. Moreover, a whole raft of stakeholders is likely to be interested, and the medium of communication will include the Internet as well as the printed word. The narrative has become as important as the numbers.

Indeed, with today's complex financial reporting requirements and standards, the interpretation of accounts and their voluminous footnotes has become well nigh impossible unless one is a financial expert. Surveys have shown that many readers of annual reports now rely more on the commentary than the accounts.

The need to publish such narrative information can present the chairman, the other board members, and the company secretary with some real challenges. What information should be included and in how much detail? Might any of the information raise false hopes or mislead the stock market and therefore be share price sensitive? Could any information be useful to existing or prospective competitors?

The typical narrative reports, supporting the financial and audit report, include at least the chairman's statement, the directors' report, and a corporate governance report.

The chairman's statement is often the most read part, because it provides a summary of the company's overall performance, its strategic orientation and says something about its intentions. The directors' report is likely to contain more detailed management analysis on, for example, products and services, staff, international markets and competition, the corporate mission, values, strategies, and plans. The corporate governance report must contain at least the minimum required by the relevant corporate governance code and listing rules, and may provide a wider discussion on the company's position on governance matters such as corporate social responsibility and sustainability.

A sound narrative will contain at least:

- A balanced review of the business of the company
- A comprehensive analysis of key financial and operating performance indicators
- An explanation of the principal risks facing the company
- Details of any significant events that the company has experienced recently (for example, a major acquisition, a damaging fire, or a change of CEO)
- An indication of any planned future developments
- A statement about the company's relationships with key stakeholders, including employees, customers, and suppliers
- A report on the company's policies on corporate social responsibility and sustainability

The crucial questions that readers want to have answered are:

- What creates value in the company?
- What makes it profitable?
- What is the risk in the business?
- What is affecting the company's prospects?

The answers show how the directors see their company and builds up a picture of the real position it is in. The directors might see the dominant future issue being in products (for example, a car manufacturer's ideas on future models and pollution controls), customers (for example, the thinking a retailer has on the effect of Internet trading), patents (for example, a pharmaceutical company's hopes for a new drug), rights (for example, an airlines concerns about landing rights), goodwill (for example, the value of a brand name), human capital (for example, the significance of skilled staff in an IT company). Such intangible resources, though vital to a company, are seldom on the balance sheet, although IFRS3 (International Financial Reporting Standard) on business combinations does require the value of intangibles acquired in a takeover to be identified.

Some stock exchanges provide guidelines on what to include in the narrative commentary in a company's report. The International Accounting Standards Board, discussing the basic principles of a good management commentary, calls for *'forward-looking information that focuses on generating value for investors'*.

Overall, the aim of the narrative should be to inform the market, both existing and potential shareholders, on the position and trends facing the company. It should be balanced and objective, clear and concise, unbiased and transparent, and mention all significant possible future changes. The material factors that influence results need to be disclosed. Undue optimism and public relations 'spin' should be avoided. In discussing future expectations, ranges and probabilities can be used instead of absolute predictions. Companies that are seen to have published realistic assessments will become trusted, which in the longer term adds value.

Some stock exchanges have 'safe harbour' provisions in their rules to protect directors from legal actions over statements or omissions in their commentaries, and some Companies Acts limit liability unless statements are untrue, or misleading, in bad faith, reckless, or dishonest.

Auditors do not normally report on narrative statements but are required to ensure that the commentary is not materially inconsistent with the audited figures. Commentaries are not a substitute for the financial accounts; they should be complementary.

The trend towards greater corporate transparency is worldwide, and companies that are seen to be open will be recognized and, ultimately, rewarded.

The Delegation of Board Functions to Management

The interplay between the board and management raises a crucial aspect of corporate governance. Subject to the articles and any regulatory demands, boards have considerable freedom to delegate responsibilities to management. In figure 6.2, below, as we saw earlier in this chapter, the relationship between the board's work and that of the CEO and his or her management team is at the heart of the four governance functions of the board.

Figure 6.2 Board functions working through management

The cell of management involvement in the centre of the quadrant in figure 6.2 can be small and relatively insignificant, with the directors making most executive decisions; or it can be large, with the directors expecting top management to make a major contribution to some or all of the four governance functions.

Some examples will illustrate.

Box 6.4 Examples of the Interplay Between the Board and Top Management

Strategy Formulation

The Beaumont Executive Press Ltd was a small publisher based in Oxford, England. There were two directors who formulated strategy and made all the strategic decisions between them. They decided which materials to publish, where to market, and how the business was financed. There was no delegation to others in the company, indeed many of the other operational functions were outsourced to specialist firms. The two directors, who were also the owners of the company, determined the corporate strategy and identified the business risks they were prepared to take.

By contrast, the board of General Motors delegates most of the responsibility for formulating strategy to their operational divisions. The operating divisions produce strategies and project proposals that are put to the main board for approval and funding. The largely INED board are not experts in the automotive industry. Their role is to question the strategic proposals, raise concerns about level of R&D, product developments, competitor situation, pricing policy, technological developments, and so on, and probe the exposure to risk. The main board's strategic decisions are largely about the allocation of resources to fund divisional strategies in the light of overall group strategy.

Policy Making

The Vigilance of Brixham Preservation Co. Ltd is a company incorporated to restore and run a heritage sailing trawler in one of England's few remaining fishing ports. All policies are made by the board. Since only cruise skippers are paid and the company is run by volunteers there is no management to be involved in policy making.

By contrast, in conglomerate Hutchison Whampoa (for more information see the case in chapter 4) only group financial policy, top management staff policies, and a few broad group management policies are made at main board level. Policy making follows the formulation of strategy at subsidiary company levels.

Executive Monitoring and Supervision

The Rainbow Hospice Inc. is a charitable foundation involved in the provision of care in terminal illness. The board consists entirely of INED volunteers. The chief executive attends board meetings but is not a director. The board receives a monthly statement on the financial and cash/bank position, reports on projects such as new building works and new equipment, drug use reports, details of complaints from staff, patients, and their relatives. Directors also study the incidents book which records health and safety breaches, and receives a written report on patient care and an oral report on staff from the chief executive. Directors then question him on matters that concern them, such as variances from budget plans, and any others from the information they have been given. The chief executive complains that the directors are too involved in the day to day running of the hospice, and from time to time individual directors even give instructions to the nursing staff.

By contrast, the directors of General Motors also receive detailed reports of the performance of each of the subsidiary companies in the group, supported by briefings from appropriate executives. They seek clarification and raise questions about matters that concern them. They discuss apparent problems with executives attending board meetings and, following discussions between themselves, call for more information or approve the current executive performance.

Accountability

The board of a leading boarding school in Canada is comprised entirely of INEDs. The headmaster and the bursar attend board meetings to provide information and advice. The report to the owners of the school comes from the board and it is the board that is held accountable for performance, including the appointment, monitoring, and if necessary, removal of the head and senior staff.

> By contrast, in General Electric (for more information see the case in chapter 4), the chairman and directors accept a primary responsibility for the periodic report and accounts to shareholders, and the chairman of the board and the chairman of the audit committee address and respond to questions at shareholders meetings. The senior outside director is also available to respond to shareholder issues. But senior financial management is also significantly involved in dealings with shareholders, regulators, and the financial media. Much detailed accountability work is delegated to the finance and the shareholder relations functions.

These examples bring us to an important question—where do boards focus their attention and how do they balance their time between the four basic functions of the board?

Unsurprisingly, research shows that boards vary significantly in the way they carry out their functions. In a company with an all executive board, the directors virtually combine governance with the top management functions and it can be difficult to separate the two. In other cases, particularly in the board of a holding company which has delegated much of the strategy formulation and policy making in the group to its subsidiary companies, the dominant focus is on setting overall strategies and policies at group level, the internal supervision of the group, and external accountability.

However, research has also shown that there is a basic difference between what experienced directors believe should happen and what does happen in practice. Asked for their opinion on how a board *should* divide its time and effort at board level, directors in the vast majority of cases suggest that the major focus should be on strategy formulation. A typical allocation of time in these studies is shown in figure 6.3.

Notice that they believe that most of emphasis of the board's work should be on the right-hand performance aspects of the board's work (63%). They also see the focus of the board's work being predominantly on the company in its outside context (62%). In this idealized world, directors think that the left-hand conformance should be relegated to a less significant role (37%), with executive supervision taking no more than

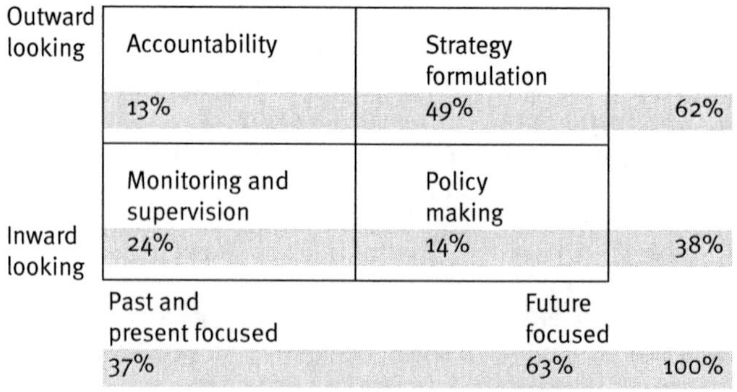

Outward looking	Accountability 13%	Strategy formulation 49%	62%
Inward looking	Monitoring and supervision 24%	Policy making 14%	38%
	Past and present focused 37%	Future focused 63%	100%

Figure 6.3 Normative balance of board functions. How directors suggest boards *should* balance their activities

Outward looking	Accountability 22%	Strategy formulation 23%	45%
Inward looking	Monitoring and supervision 41%	Policy making 14%	55%
	Past and present focused 63%	Future focused 37%	100%

Figure 6.4 Reported balance of board functions. How directors believe boards *do* balance their activities

a quarter of their time and accountability to external stakeholders a relatively insignificant 13 percent.

However, asked to draw on their own experiences of how boards actually *do* focus their time and effort, directors produce data that resembles the results shown in figure 6.4.

In the real world of experience, the emphasis of the board's work swings to the left-hand conformance aspects of the board's work (63%). They also see the focus of the board's work predominantly focusing inside the company (55%).

This exercise, asking directors to give their normative views on board activity, then their actual experience, has been conducted with hundreds of directors around the world. Although, of course, there is a spread of responses reflecting the different situations that can face boards, broadly the results seldom differ from those shown in figures 6.3 and 6.4. Directors almost always believe the greater emphasis should be on the performance roles, particularly strategy formulation, but report that in practice the emphasis tends to be on conformance, particularly executive monitoring and reacting to internal short term problems.

Explanations, though varying in detail, have a consistent similarity.

Events arise that the board could not have foreseen ('a major discrepancy in the stock position', 'the death of the CFO', 'a massive budget deficit', 'the competitor unexpectedly launched a brand new service that was taking away our clients', 'a potential take-over bid'), so we have to spend more time on executive supervision.

In recent years directors have also reported the need to give a greater emphasis to accountability, partly due to greater regulatory demands and partly due to pressure from society ('shareholder expectations', 'stakeholder demands', 'the media', 'CSR needs').

Of course these results apply to unitary boards, in which directors have to fulfil both the performance and the conformance roles. In the two-tier board, the roles are separated between the management and the supervisory boards.

Nevertheless, directors often do recognize the need to find more time to concentrate on strategy formulation. In some cases boards achieve this by actively devoting part of each meeting to strategic issues, by deciding to devote the entire board meeting to strategy, or by holding a strategy seminar—a day or two at which the board can be briefed on the strategic situation, discuss the implications, think about alternatives, evaluate and move towards a shared strategic vision, which will lead to new strategic plans and action in due course.

Experience has suggested a number of useful pointers in running a board strategy seminar or workshop; see the guidelines for a board strategy workshop below:

Box 6.5 Guidelines for a Board Strategy Seminar or Workshop

- Leadership by the board chairman
- Careful planning, well in advance
- Ensure a time when all directors can attend
- Fix a location where all directors can participate
- Define the objectives clearly, for example:
  - To explore the strategic situation
  - To discuss the implications
  - To consider alternative strategies
  - To determine the next steps to be taken
    (but not to take strategic decisions immediately)
- All directors must be fully informed about the objectives
- All directors should be supportive of the event
- All directors need briefing with relevant data in advance
- Do not hold the event in the boardroom (the boardroom culture is decision orientated)
- Decide who is going to run the event (this need not be the chairman—consider the senior INED, a past director, a specialist outside consultant)
- Decide whether other people should be invited to participate (senior executives to brief the directors, external experts to give briefings, experts to contribute to process)
- At the first session establish the ground-rules
  - This is not a board meeting to make decisions
  - Rather a free-ranging exchange of views and insights
  - Strategic decisions will not be made: the place for that is in the normal board meeting after appropriate analysis, reports, and evaluation have taken place
- During the session
  - Call for imaginative contributions however unusual
  - Discourage negative comment ('we tried that—it won't work', 'never in a month of Sundays!', 'no good for us')
- The output of the strategy session should be an agreed list of next actions, and who is responsible for taking them and by when.

Balancing the Board's Performance and Conformance Roles

We see, therefore, that every board faces a challenge to strike a reasonable balance between strategy formulation and policy making, the performance roles, on the one hand, and executive supervision and accountability, the conformance roles on the other. Typically the time of directors is under pressure. The way that the time available to a board and its committees is allocated is, therefore, crucial. It is also fundamental to the way that the board approaches corporate governance. The problem is that the more a board concentrates its efforts on the conformance activities—management supervision and accountability—the more that board comes to see its work as ensuring compliance with the corporate governance requirements of respective codes, regulations, and law.

In fact, some directors do believe that corporate governance is essentially about compliance. They see their role as the supervision of management and ensuring accountability to legitimate stakeholders. In other words, they emphasize the conformance side of the conformance/performance dichotomy. The formulation of strategy and policy making is then largely delegated to top management. By focusing on compliance, such boards tend to see corporate governance activities as an expense and wonder whether it is cost-effective.

In a board with a large majority of independent outside directors the focus on conformance can become inevitable, if directors believe that their ability to contribute to strategy formulation and policy making is limited. The performance activities are then delegated to top management. In a two-tier board, of course, this separation is complete, with the management board running the business, responsible for performance, whilst the supervisory board oversees that performance and ensures accountability.

Some boards, on the other hand, recognize that they are responsible for balancing conformance activities with their commitment and contribution to performance. Directors are called directors because they are responsible for directing the company, ensuring that it is heading in the right direction, aware of the risks, establishing the way ahead. That means sensibly balancing performance with conformance activities.

One unfortunate effect of the necessary introduction of corporate governance principles and codes, rules, and regulations is the danger that boards, by concentrating on conformance, overlook their principle mission, which is to direct the enterprise. That means being involved in strategy formulation and policy making.

The responsibility for determining the board's agenda, ensuring that sufficient time is allocated to each of the four functions and balancing these activities, lies with the board chairman. Sensibly, he or she will seek advice from the company secretary and the chief executive. Moreover, in a professionally led board every director will have the opportunity to suggest items that the board should discuss and to express concerns about the balance of the board's deliberations. One chairman actually asks each of his directors to write to him every year about ways to improve his performance as chairman and to suggest matters that need more board attention. But not many chairmen are this professional.

In the next chapter we will study the codes of corporate governance principles and good practice around the world and see how the emphasis on conformance and compliance might have arisen.

REFERENCES AND SELECTED READING

Kakabadse, Andrew and Nada (2007) *Leading the Board*. London: Palgrave Macmillan.

McNulty, T. J. (2003) *Creating Accountability Within the Board: The Work of the Effective Non-executive Director*. London: DTI.

NACD (National Association of Corporate Directors) (2005) 'Role of the Board on Corporate Strategy'. Report of a NACD Blue Ribbon Commission. Washington, DC: NACD.

Steinberg, Richard M. (2000) *Corporate Governance and the Board: What Works Best*. London: Internal Auditors Research Foundation.

Tarantino, Anthony (2007) 'Manager's Guide to Compliance: Sarbanes-Oxley, COSO, ERM, COBIT, IFRS, BASEL II, OMB's A-123, ASX 10', *OECD Principles, Turnbull Guidance, Best Practices, and Case Studies*. London: Wiley.

USEFUL WEBSITES

acc6.its.brooklyn.cuny.edu/~phalsall/texts/artofwar.html
Chinese General Sun Tse on the Art of War.

www.bplans.com/dp/missionstatement.cfm
On writing a mission statement.

www.dilbert.com/comics/dilbert/games/career/bin/ms.cgi
Mission statement generator.

www.mindtools.com/pages/article/newTMC_05.htm
More on SWOT analysis.

myphliputil.pearsoncmg.com/student/bp_turban_introec_1/MissStmt.html
Explaining mission statements.

PROJECTS AND EXERCISES

1. Review the mission statements of leading companies, including those listed earlier in this chapter and others found on company websites. Do you think that they really add anything to the strategy formulation process? Is there a danger that they could become merely part of the public relations effort of an organization? If so, how might this be avoided? Could they contribute to corporate culture and the creation of a common approach to management decision making?

2. Undertake a strategic assessment of an organization to which you have access. Use both SWOT analysis and a review of the competitive strategic environment of the entity. Prepare a report/presentation for the governing body of that organization.

3. Review the management control systems and the reporting to the board for an organization to which you have access.

4. Identify the strategy formulation, policy making, executive monitoring and supervision, and accountability activities in other organizations with which you are familiar or from which you can obtain information.

SELF-TEST QUESTIONS

To confirm your grasp of the key points in this chapter try answering the following questions. Answers are at the end of the book.

1. Define strategy formulation.

2. What is a mission statement?

3. Why might long range planning not be a useful tool for strategy formulation?

4. What are the five forces in the five forces model?

5. What is resource based strategic theory?

6. What are corporate policies?

7. Name some management control systems that can be used by directors to monitor management performance.

8. What is sub-optimization?

9. To whom is a board accountable?

10. What is exception reporting?

Part 2

Policies

7 Corporate Governance Codes

....

- In which we consider:
  - from Cadbury to the Combined Code: United Kingdom
  - codes in other countries
  - the Sarbanes-Oxley Act: United States of America
  - principles or prescription: the governance debate
  - codes from international agencies
  - codes from institutional investors
  - company codes
  - codes for the public and voluntary sectors
  - codes for individual directors
  - compliance with corporate governance codes
- Appendix : Corporate Governance Codes around the World

The past few years have seen an explosion of interest in corporate governance throughout the world. Prior to the corporate collapses of the 1980s (see boxed case studies) corporate governance was not even a phrase that was used. Around the world company regulation was based on a mixture of company law, corporate regulation (mainly filing and disclosure requirements), and accounting standards, and for public listed companies the stock exchanges' rules.

In the United States, companies have to abide by the law of that state in which they are incorporated, and follow the US generally accepted accounting principles (GAAP). In addition, listed companies have to meet the demands of the Securities and Exchange Commission (SEC), which was set up in the 1930s, to protect the interests of investors and regulate the securities market, following unacceptable domination of major companies by their management. In 1997, the Business Roundtable, which takes a pro-business perspective, produced a Statement on Corporate Governance. In 2001, a Blue Ribbon Commission set up by the National Association of Corporate Directors published the report 'Director Professionalism'. A year later, the American Law Institute published a set of General Principles on corporate governance, which generated a debate on the regulation of boards and directors, with the Business Roundtable contributing their views in a further report the same year, as did the Council of Institutional Investors which published proposals, *Core Policies and Principles of Corporate Governance*, also in 2002.

In most other countries companies are incorporated at the federal level and have to abide by their country's company law, accounting standards, and, for listed companies, stock exchange regulations. The first specific set of recommendations on good corporate governance practice was produced in the UK in 1992, and most financially significant countries now have a set of corporate governance principles or a code of good corporate governance practice.

In this chapter we are going to review the corporate governance codes published in the UK, because they have been influential in the development of codes around the world, and the impact of the Sarbanes-Oxley (SOX) Act in the US, because this has probably been the most influential piece of company legislation to date. Then we study other codes developed around the world. Inevitably, this material lacks some of the case examples of previous chapters, but it is important for the serious student of corporate governance.

From Cadbury to the Combined Code: United Kingdom

Britain produced the first corporate governance report and subsequently has produced more than any other country. So we start our review of corporate governance codes in Britain.

Box 7.1 Corporate Governance Codes in the United Kingdom

- Cadbury (December 1992)
- Greenbury (July 1995)
- Hampel (January 1998)
- UK Combined Code (1998)
- Turnbull (1999, revised October 2005)
- Higgs (January 2003)
- Smith (July 2003)
- Tyson (June 2003)
- Revised UK Combined Code (July 2003)
- Myners (December 2004)
- Revised UK Combined Code (June 2006)

The Cadbury Report (1992) was produced by a committee chaired by Sir Adrian Cadbury in response to a series of corporate failures in the United Kingdom. It was entitled 'The Financial Aspects of Corporate Governance', and was not intended to be a comprehensive review of the subject as Sir Arian subsequently emphasized. However, the Cadbury Report did call for:

- The wider use of independent non-executive directors
- The introduction of an audit committee of the board with a minimum of three non-executive directors with a majority of them independent

- The division of responsibilities between the chairman of the board and the chief executive. But, if the roles were combined in a single person, the board should have a strong independent element
- The use of a remuneration committee of the board to oversee executive rewards
- The introduction of a nomination committee with independent directors to propose new board members and
- Adherence to a detailed code of best practice

It is interesting to note, that despite being written more than fifteen years ago, this report contained many proposals that remain at the heart of today's corporate governance thinking.

The Greenbury Report (1995) addressed issues of directors' remuneration, then as now a matter of concern to directors, the media, and society at large. The Greenbury Report recommended that:

- The remuneration committees of companies should consist solely of independent non-executive directors
- The chairman of the remuneration committee should respond to shareholders' questions at the AGM
- Annual reports should include details of all director rewards—naming each director
- Directors' contracts should run for no more than a year to avoid excessive golden handshakes
- Share option schemes for directors should be linked to long term corporate performance

The Hampel Report (1998) was a response to a suggestion in the Cadbury Report that a review should be undertaken after a few years experience. The Hampel Report proposed that:

- Good corporate governance needs broad principles not prescriptive rules
- Compliance with sound governance practices, such as the separation of board chairmanship from chief executive, should be flexible and relevant to each company's individual circumstances
- Governance should not be reduced to what the report called a 'box-ticking' exercise
- The unitary board is totally accepted in the UK. There is no interest in alternative governance structures or processes such as two-tier boards
- The board is accountable to the company's shareholders. There is no case for redefining directors' responsibilities to other stakeholder groups
- Self-regulation is the preferred approach to corporate governance. There is no need for more company legislation

The Hampel Committee consisted mainly of directors of major public companies and their professional advisers. Predictably, therefore, it did not criticize contemporary corporate governance practices, neither did it advocate any measures which would further limit directors' power to make unfettered decisions, nor widen the scope of their accountability. In fact it reduced the force of the original Cadbury proposals by suggesting greater 'flexibility'. It was also strident in its insistence that British companies did not want two-tier boards, rejected calls for broader accountability to stakeholder groups beyond the shareholders, and did not need any more legislation. Shortly after the report was published the British Government announced a new fundamental review of UK company law.

The Cadbury, Greenbury, and Hampel committees were set up by City of London institutions, that is, by the UK's financial sector. The codes were essentially voluntary and applied principally to listed companies, although it was suggested that many of the recommendations could be applied to private companies.

In 1998, the Cadbury, Greenbury, and Hampel proposals were consolidated into the UK Combined Code, which was incorporated into the London Stock Exchange's listing rules. This Combined Code set out standards of good practice on matters such as board composition, director remuneration, accountability, and audit in relation to shareholders. All companies incorporated in the UK and listed on the main market of the London Stock Exchange were now required to report on how they had applied the principles in the Combined Code in their annual report to shareholders. In this report, companies had to confirm that they had complied with the Code's provisions or, if they had not, to provide explanations.

Although the code had no legislative basis and enforcement, failure to meet its requirements could lead to de-listing from the Exchange. De-listing, however, would tend to disadvantage the very shareholders whom the corporate governance codes were designed to protect, so de-listing was a last resort (and in fact never used). The Stock Exchange relied on informal guidance to companies.

The requirement to '*apply the code or explain why not*' has become the philosophical underpinning of most corporate governance codes around the world, as we shall see. This approach, however, is contrary to the thinking that emerged in the United States, following the enactment of the Sarbanes-Oxley Act in 2002, which required companies and their directors to report that they have obeyed the law or risk prosecution and significant penalties including imprisonment.

The UK Turnbull Report (1999) elaborated a call in the Hampel Report for companies to have appropriate internal controls. It set out how directors of UK listed companies should comply with the combined code requirements about internal controls, including financial, operational, compliance, and risk management. The report recognized that risk assessment was vital and recommended that:

- Reporting on internal controls became an integral part of the corporate governance process

Thus two new dimensions, enterprise risk analysis and risk management, and internal management controls were added to the field of corporate governance.

The UK Higgs Report (2003) re-examined corporate governance in British companies ten years after the Cadbury Report. The proposals sharpened the requirements in the previous codes, in particular recommending that in listed companies:

- At least half the board should comprise independent non-executive directors
- All members of the audit and remuneration committees and a majority of the members of the nomination committee should be independent non-executive directors

- The role of chief executive should always be completely separate from that of chairman
- Director recruitment should be rigorous, formal, and transparent
- Executive directors should not hold more than one non-executive directorship of a FTSE (Financial Times Stock Exchange) 100 company
- Boards should evaluate the performance of directors and board committees annually, and have a comprehensive induction programme
- Boards should have a senior independent director to liaise with shareholders

It can be seen that Higgs had strengthened requirements of the combined code; in particular, amplifying the demand for INEDs on the board and in board committees, insisting that the roles of board chairman and CEO should never be combined, that director appointments had to be more transparent, and that directors' and board committees' performance should be evaluated annually—a particularly contentious proposal at the time for many directors.

The Higgs Report had been commissioned by the Labour Government, rather than the financial institutions, with the remit to see how '*more independent and more active non-executives, drawn from a wider pool of talent, could play their part in raising productivity*'. Some of Derek Higgs' initial proposals were contentious. Among the proposals that were *not* accepted were:

- A ban on chief executives moving into the chair of their own company
- A ban on chairmen heading the nomination committee of their own board
- A ban on anyone being chairman of more than one FTSE 100 company
- A call for regular meetings between the senior independent director and shareholders

The UK Smith Report (2003) looked at the work of the audit committees, a key element in corporate governance concepts. Among the proposals, Sir Robert Smith called for:

- A strengthening of the role of the audit committee
- All members of the audit committee should be independent
- At least one member of the committee should have significant, recent, and relevant financial experience
- The audit committee should recommend the selection of the external auditor
- An audit committee report should be included in the annual report to shareholders
- The chairman of the audit committee should attend the AGM to answer shareholders' questions

Once again the demands of corporate governance had been amplified, in this case by insisting (as the Higgs Report had) that the audit committee had only independent non-executive directors (INEDs), at least one of whom was financially literate and up-to-date, and by specifically giving the committee and its chairman a role in the annual report and shareholders' general meeting.

The UK Tyson Report (2003) focused on the recruitment and development of non-executive directors. It called for:

- More professionalism and transparency in the recruitment of directors

- The introduction of director induction and training
- Use of a wider catchment area for outside directors, who could be recruited from, what the report called, the 'marzipan layer' of senior executives, that is those just below board level, in unlisted companies, as well as consultancies and organizations in the non-commercial sector

A revised version of the UK Combined Code was published in 2003 by the Financial Reporting Council which by this time had taken over regulatory responsibility from the London Stock Exchange. In this edition of the code the corporate governance requirements were grouped under four headings—independence, diligence, professional development, and board performance evaluation. The broad principles were as follows.

On Independence

- At least half the board, excluding the chairman, should be non-executive directors who are independent of the company
- Audit committees and remuneration committees should be formed entirely with independent directors
- The majority of nomination committee members should also be independent
- The definition of independence included:
  - Not being employed by the company in the past five years
  - Having no material business relationship with the company in the past three years
  - Not having a significant shareholding
  - Not having served on the board for more than nine years
- Chief executives should not go on to become chairman of their own company, because that could compromise their independence

On Diligence

- Non-executive directors should disclose their other commitments to ensure that they have sufficient time
- Directors' appointments should be rigorous and transparent
- No individual should chair more than one FTSE 100 company

On Professional Development

- All directors should receive induction training
- All directors should have regular updates on relevant skills, knowledge, and familiarity with the company

On Boards' Performance Evaluation

- Boards should undertake an annual evaluation of their own performance
- There should also be an annual assessment of the performance of individual directors and of the main board committees

The revised combined code also had sections on remuneration committees and audit committees, increasing their roles in monitoring the integrity of the published financial statements and reinforcing the independence of the outside auditor.

Notice that the standard expectations of corporate governance had once again been sharpened. In the revised combined code at least half the board should be INEDs, independence was defined more rigorously, all directors should have induction and training, and evaluation of board performance was required.

The UK Myners Report (2004) addressed the responsibilities of institutional investors. Writing about his report, Paul Myners said:

good corporate governance is essential to all forms of business. It provides checks and balances that ensure that firms are run efficiently and meet the objectives of their owners, whether shareholders or the members of a life mutual. It also has limitations . . . I have recognized that risk is inherent in the conduct of business . . . The recommendations aim to achieve greater accountability by life mutuals to their members . . . This includes measures . . . promoting better internal scrutiny of management by firm's boards as well as the role of the Financial Services Authority (FSA), the UK's financial regulatory body.

In 2006, the FSA made some minor revisions to the UK Combined Code, principally:

- Amending the existing restriction on the company chairman serving on the remuneration committee, enabling him to do so where considered independent on appointment as chairman, although it was recommended that he should not also chair the committee
- Providing a 'vote withheld' option on proxy appointment forms to enable shareholders to indicate if they have reservations on a resolution but did not wish to vote against. A 'vote withheld' was not a vote in law and was not counted in the calculation of the proportion of the votes for and against the resolution
- Recommending that companies publish the details of proxies lodged at a general meeting on their website where votes are taken on a show of hands

Codes in Other Countries

The UK Cadbury Report was produced in response to company collapses and what were seen as failings in corporate governance, particularly the domination of boards by powerful individuals. The Cadbury Report was the first, but other countries, which were also experiencing problems of company collapses due to inadequate corporate governance, soon followed with their own version of corporate governance codes. Subsequently, most other economically significant countries have published some form of corporate governance guidelines, recommendations, or principles.

The following list demonstrates the current state of play around the world. Consider the date of the latest report and see how the approach has evolved in some countries. Also notice the originator of the reports—an official commission set up by the government, the securities regulating authority as part of the corporate regulatory process, the stock exchange as a requirement of the listing rules, or sometimes an independent industrial federation, or the local Institute of Directors. Because of their emergent and rapidly changing situation, we will study corporate governance codes in China and Russia in chapter 8.

The texts of many of the above reports are available on the Internet, the majority with an English version. Insights from the corporate governance codes of various countries can be enlightening.

Australia has been a pioneer in corporate governance developments. As the entry above shows, the first Australian report on corporate governance was written by Fred Hilmer in 1992. He called it *Strictly Boardroom*, after the film about competitive ballroom dancing in which compliance with the rules had stifled initiative. This, Hilmer argued, would happen to companies if corporate governance was focused on compliance. '*The Board's key role is to ensure that the board is continuously and effectively striving for above average performance, taking account of risk (which) is not to deny the board's additional role with respect to shareholder protection.*'

Following the Hilmer work, Henry Bosch wrote a study in 1995 and a corporate governance report for the public sector was produced in 1997. In March 2003, the Australian Stock Exchange (ASX) Corporate Governance Council produced 'Principles of Good Corporate Governance and Best Practice Recommendations', which added some new dimensions to the concept of corporate governance. This work offered the following essential corporate governance principles, suggesting that a company should:

(1) Lay solid foundations for management and oversight
   - Recognize and publish the respective roles and responsibilities of board and management

(2) Structure the board to add value
   - Have a board of an effective composition, size, and commitment to adequately discharge its responsibilities and duties

(3) Promote ethical and responsible decision making
   - Actively promote ethical and responsible decision making

(4) Safeguard integrity in financial reporting
   - Have a structure to independently verify and safeguard the integrity of the company's financial reporting

(5) Make timely and balanced disclosure
   - Promote timely and balanced disclosure of all material matters concerning the company

(6) Respect the rights of shareholders
   - Respect the rights of shareholders and facilitate the effective exercise of those rights

(7) Recognize and manage risk

– Establish a sound system of risk oversight and management and internal control

(8) Encourage enhanced performance

– Fairly review and actively encourage enhanced board and management effectiveness

(9) Remunerate fairly and responsibly

– Ensure that the level and composition of remuneration is sufficient and reasonable and that its relationship to corporate and individual performance is defined

(10) Recognize the legitimate interests of stakeholders

– Recognize the legal and other obligations to all legitimate stakeholders

The 2003 ASX Principles usefully define independence in a director in ways that are far more detailed than the original notion of '*having no interests that could affect objective judgement*':

An independent director is a non-executive director (i.e. is not a member of management) who:

1. is not a substantial shareholder of the company or an officer of, or otherwise associated directly with, a substantial shareholder of the company

2. within the last three years has not been employed in an executive capacity by the company or another group company, or been a director after ceasing to hold any such employment

3. within the last three years has not been a principal of a material professional adviser or a material consultant to the company or another group company, or an employee materially associated with the service provided

4. is not a material supplier or customer of the company or other group member, or an officer of, or otherwise associated directly or indirectly with, a material supplier or customer

5. has no material contractual relationship with the company or another group member other than as a director of the company

6. has not served on the board for a period which could, or could reasonably be perceived to, materially interfere with the director's ability to act in the best interests of the company

7. is free from any interest and any business or other relationship which could, or could reasonably be perceived to, materially interfere with the director's ability to act in the best interests of the company.

The second King report from South Africa, took an advanced view on the need for companies to take an inclusive view of their relationships, not only with shareholders, but other groups in society affected by their activities.

Emerging economies have been driven by entrepreneurs, who take business risks and initiatives. With successful companies come successful economies. Without satisfactory levels of profitability in a company, not only will investors who cannot earn an acceptable return on their investment look to alternative opportunities, but it is unlikely that the other stakeholders will have an enduring interest in the company.

The key challenge for good corporate citizenship is to seek an appropriate balance between enterprise (performance) and constraints (conformance), so taking into account the expectations of shareowners for reasonable capital growth and the responsibility concerning the interests of other stakeholders in the company.

The Canadian Saucier Report also took a performance orientated view of the nature of corporate governance: '*The objective of good governance is to promote strong, viable and competitive corporations.*'

A committed, cohesive and effective board adds value, first and foremost, by selecting the right CEO for the company. Beyond this, the board contributes to value by:

- setting the broad parameters within which the management team operates, including in particular, strategic planning and risk management, and communication policy
- coaching the CEO and the management team
- monitoring and assessing performance, setting the CEO's compensation, taking remedial action where warranted, including replacing the CEO
- providing assurance to shareholders and stakeholders about the integrity of the corporation's reported financial performance.

Case Study 7.1 Marconi

The UK group Marconi plc grew out of GEC, a company built by Lord Weinstock, who bequeathed a set of solid, if unadventurous, manufacturing businesses, with large reserves of cash. On his retirement Marconi adopted a different strategy—to invest in high-tech enterprises. Within a few years, all the cash had been spent and the company was over £4 billion in debt. Worse, many of its investments were disasters. In July 2001, the company suspended trading in its shares, warning that profits were likely to halve to around £350 million. The company's share price fell and the chief executive, Lord Simpson, met strong opposition to his proposal that executive share options should be re-priced to reflect the fall.

Throughout August 2001, the company refused to comment on rumours that things were much worse. No advice was given to investors, the stock exchange, or the Financial Services Authority. Then in September 2001, the scale of the disaster became clear, when a loss of £327 million for the three months to June was announced. Various operating explanations were forthcoming. The downturn in the high-tech market was global. The internal control systems had failed to identify financial problems fast enough. The corporate centre was out of touch with its struggling divisions. The opinion that this was a case of poor business judgement, not of poor corporate governance, smacked of complacency.

Where was the board during this developing debacle? The case raises questions far beyond strategic and operational mismanagement. The issues go to the heart of the board structure and director competence. The case for non-executive directors argues that their independence allows them to question top management and make tough-minded calls for change if necessary. Subsequently, some Marconi non-executive directors claimed that they had questioned both the strategic direction and the financial situation of the company, but had not received the necessary information. Nevertheless, all directors have the duty to insist that they have the information necessary to understand and make decisions.

But were the Marconi outside directors truly independent? Lord Simpson of Dunkeld was Marconi's chief executive; he was also a non-executive director of ICI and of the Royal Bank of Scotland, one of Marconi's bankers. Sir Roger Hurn, the chairman of the Marconi board, was also chairman of Prudential Assurance, a major shareholder in Marconi, a non-executive director of ICI, and a non-executive of Glaxo-SmithKline (as was fellow director Derek Botham). The non-executive directors included Sir Bill Castell, chief executive of Nycam, formerly finance director at ICI; John Mayo, previously finance director of ICI and its associate Zeneca; and Derek Bonham, chairman of Cadbury Schweppes and Imperial Tobacco, who had only recently been appointed to the board.

A board meeting was called to face the situation, which one director described as 'Britain's greatest industrial disaster for decades'. Decisive action was needed. Bonham, as senior non-executive director, took charge. By the end of the meeting both the chief executive Simpson and the chairman Hurn had been replaced.

Discussion Questions

1. Did the personal connections between some of the directors make this a cosy club, its members too close to ask awkward questions, demand satisfactory answers, and insist on decisive action?

2. Some non-executive directors claimed that they had questioned both the strategic direction and the financial situation of the company, but had not received the necessary information. What should they have done then?

3. Subsequently commentators on the Marconi debacle commented that the case pinpointed the dangers of cronyism and cross-directorships. But benefits can come from directors who know each other well and serve on a number of other boards. What do you think?

The Sarbanes-Oxley Act: United States of America

In the United States the main driver of change has not been voluntary codes or stock exchange listing requirements but legislation. As we have already seen, companies in the United States are incorporated in a specific state and the state company laws and regulations apply to them. Each state tends to guard its own rights jealously. Consequently, companies cannot be incorporated at the federal level, as in other countries.

But since 1933, there *has* been strong federal oversight of the securities market, through the Securities and Exchange Commission (SEC). Over the years the SEC developed an extensive corporate governance regime for America's listed companies. A number of reports contributed to these developments, including the 1978 Cohen Commission Report from the American Institute of Certified Public Accountants (AICPA) on auditors' responsibilities; the 1987 Treadway Report, from the National Commission of Fraudulent

Reporting, again from the AICPA; and the 1992 COSO Report offering an integrated framework for internal control (COSO is the Committee of Sponsoring Organizations of the Treadway Commission of the AICPA).

In 1997, the Business Roundtable, representing the leaders of major US companies, produced a statement on Corporate Governance; in 1999, the New York Stock Exchange and the National Association of Securities Dealers published a 'Blue Ribbon Report' on improving the effectiveness of corporate audit committees; and in 2001, the National Association of Corporate Directors also wrote a 'Blue Ribbon Report', this time on director professionalism.

Between the establishment of the SEC and the collapse of Enron, regulators and business people in the United States were quietly confident that the US corporate governance framework and accounting standards were world leaders. The system seemed to work, met state and federal concerns, and equated the rule of law with regulation through stock exchanges' listing rules to protect investors, and balanced transparency and disclosure with unnecessary and costly bureaucracy.

The expectation was that the rest of the world would gradually converge with this approach to corporate governance. Indeed, some American institutional investors proposed changes to corporate governance practices in Germany, Japan, and other countries to ensure this convergence.

Then the corporate collapses of the 1990s and the early 2000s came. The boxed cases of Tyco, Waste Management, WorldCom, and Enron demonstrate the problems that then emerged. As a consequence, the Sarbanes-Oxley Act, named after US Senator Paul Sarbanes and US Representative Michael Oxley who promoted the bill, was passed in 2002. This was the most significant change in federal securities law since the 1930s.

In 2002, post the Enron and Arthur Andersen debacle, the Sarbanes-Oxley Act was incorporated into the New York Stock Exchange's new corporate governance rules of 2003 and 2004. Simultaneously, in 2002 the Council of Institutional Investors published *Core Policies and Principles of Corporate Governance*, followed by the American Law Institute's 'General Principles, Positions and Explanatory Notes', and the Business Roundtable's 'Principles of Corporate Governance'.

The SOX Act applied criminal and civil penalties for non-compliance, required certification of internal auditing, and increased financial disclosure. It applied to all public US companies and non-US companies listed in the United States. All public-traded companies were now required to submit an annual report about their internal accounting controls to the US Securities and Exchange Commission.

Section 302 of the Act mandates a set of internal procedures designed to ensure accurate financial disclosure. The signing officers must certify that they are '*responsible for establishing and maintaining internal controls*' and

have designed such internal controls to ensure that material information relating to the company and its consolidated subsidiaries is made known to such officers by others within those entities, particularly during the period in which the periodic reports are being prepared.

The officers must '*have evaluated the effectiveness of the company's internal controls as of a date within 90 days prior to the report*' and '*have presented in the report their conclusions about the effectiveness of their internal controls based on their evaluation as of that date*'.

Section 404 has attracted much criticism, particularly on the unexpectedly high cost of compliance. The section requires management to produce a report on the company's internal controls as part of the annual report, affirming '*the responsibility of management for establishing and maintaining an adequate internal control structure and procedures for financial reporting*'. The report must also '*contain an assessment of the effectiveness of the*

Case Study 7.2 General Electric (GE)

As we saw in an earlier case, GE was one of America's largest and most successful groups, operating in the electrical appliance, power generation, aircraft engine, and financial sectors. Under Jack Welch's leadership GE became an icon for business success. After his retirement concerns were expressed about the accounting methods used by the financial arm of the group. His own retirement benefits, including the use of the company's plane, also came under scrutiny, not because of information disclosed in EC filings, but through information supplied by his wife in divorce proceedings.

In 2003, Welch's successor, Jeffrey Immelt proposed changes to GE's corporate governance, which were designed to strengthen the board's oversight of management and to serve the long term interests of shareowners, employees, and other stake-holders. He claimed that these changes went beyond the Sarbannes-Oxley Act and the New York Stock Exchange Principles on Corporate Governance. Disclosure and transparency would be improved. Two-thirds of the directors would be genuinely inde-pendent. The chair of the compensation committee would serve as presiding director and chair at least three meetings each year of the 'non-employee directors'.

In December each year the CEO would discuss future strategic, risk, and integrity issues with the board, which would schedule discussions on these topics over the year. Each director would visit two GE plants a year without members of senior management present. Outside directors who are CEOs should not serve on more than two other pub-lic company boards and other directors should not serve on more than four. Two outside directors stepped down because the aggregate business that their firms had with GE exceeded more than 1% of their revenues, the limit set for independence.

(See www.ge.com/company/citizenship/compliance/index.html)

Discussion Questions

1. During his time at the helm of GE Jack Welch was revered as an icon of business success. Why do you think his successor found it necessary to make such sweeping changes to GE's corporate governance practices?

2. What do you think of the chairman's proposal that the CEO would discuss future strategic, risk, and integrity issues with the board, which would then schedule discussions on these topics over the following year.

3. What is your opinion of the limit set by GE for independence in its outside directors, that the aggregate business that the director's firm had with GE should not exceed more than 1% of their revenues.

internal control structure and procedures . . . for financial reporting'. Independent external auditors must also attest to management's internal control assessment, pursuant to the new SEC rules. This has proved to be an expensive requirement. The cost of compliance has been shown to be at least ten times higher than the original SEC estimate.

The act further established:

- New standards for boards and their audit committees
- New accountability standards and criminal penalties for management
- New independence standards for external auditors
- A new Public Company Accounting Oversight Board (PCAOB), to oversee public accounting firms and issue accounting standards overseen by the SEC

The SOX legislation has been incorporated into the listing rules of the New York Stock Exchange. The SOX Act has undoubtedly forced a massive concentration on corporate governance in the United States. Compliance added large costs to companies listed in the US and companies associated with them, brought significant fees to legal and accounting firms, and spawned a new corporate governance advisory and training industry. Some companies based overseas have delisted, others have dropped plans to list. More positively, many US companies report benefits from SOX compliance, including better accountability of individuals, reduced risk of financial fraud, and improved accuracy in financial reports.

In 2004, the Committee of Sponsoring Organizations of the Treadway Commission published *New Enterprise Risk Management: An Integrated Framework.*

Principles or Prescription: The Governance Debate

The 2002 Sarbanes-Oxley Act reinforced a crucial distinction between the regulation of corporate governance in the United States and that of most other countries in the financially advanced world.

The SOX Act requires companies listed in the United States and their directors to report that they have obeyed the law or risk prosecution, subject to significant penalties, including imprisonment. In other words the basic approach to corporate governance practice in the US is based on rules enshrined in state regulation and law.

By contrast, in the European Union, Commonwealth countries, and throughout most of the rest of the world, the underlying philosophy of corporate governance relies on self-regulation and voluntary compliance with a set of principles. In other words companies are expected to follow a voluntary code or explain why they have not, what the Australians neatly call the *'if not, why not?'* approach.

This fundamental dichotomy—between the rule based US approach and the principles based approach adopted in the rest of the world—goes to the heart of corporate governance philosophy. We will discuss the issue further in chapter 8 on the theories of corporate governance.

Codes from International Agencies

In addition to the codes developed in specific countries to guide boards and to regulate corporate governance in those countries, a number of international agencies have published principles and codes.

Organisation for Economic Development and Co-operation (OECD)

The OECD has produced sets of Principles that are intended to assist governments in their efforts to evaluate and improve the legal, international, and regulatory framework for corporate governance in their countries and to provide guidance and suggestions to stock exchanges, investors, corporations, and others that have a role in the process of developing good corporate governance. The Principles are intended to provide the basis for the development of good corporate governance in a country. Against the backdrop of major corporate scandals, including Enron, the OECD Council of Ministers has recognized the need to survey developments and regularly update the Principles.

The OECD Principles have developed over time:

- Guidelines on Corporate Governance of State-owned Enterprises December 2004
- OECD Principles of Corporate Governance April 2004 (see extract below)
- OECD Principles of Corporate Governance May 1999

The OECD Principles of Corporate Governance

(1) *Ensuring the basis for an effective corporate governance framework.* The corporate governance framework should promote transparent and efficient markets, be consistent with the rule of law and clearly articulate the division of responsibilities among different supervisory, regulatory, and enforcement authorities.

(2) *The rights of shareholders and key ownership functions.* The corporate governance framework should protect and facilitate the exercise of shareholders' rights.

(3) *The equitable treatment of shareholders.* The corporate governance framework should ensure the equitable treatment of shareholders, including minority and foreign shareholders. All shareholders should have the opportunity to obtain redress for violation of their rights.

(4) *The role of stakeholders in corporate governance.* The corporate governance framework should recognize the rights of stakeholders established by law or through mutual agreements and encourage active cooperation between the corporations and stakeholders in creating wealth, jobs, and sustainability of financially sound enterprises.

(5) *Disclosure and transparency.* The corporate governance framework should ensure that timely and accurate disclosure is made on all material matters regarding the corporation, including the financial situation, performance, ownership, and governance of the company.

(6) *The responsibilities of the board.* The corporate governance framework should ensure the strategic guidance of the company, the effective monitoring of management by the board, and the board's accountability to the company and the shareholders.

The International Corporate Governance Network (ICGN)

ICGN was founded in 1999 at the instigation of major institutional investors, companies, financial intermediaries, academics, and other interested parties. Its objective is to facilitate dialogue including adopting guidelines and has applauded the OECD Principles.

The World Bank and the International Monetary Fund (IMF), with the United Nations has a programme on Reports on the Observance of Standards and Codes (ROSC) and is charged with assessing the application of the OECD Principles of Corporate Governance. The goal of the ROSC initiative is to identify weaknesses that may contribute to a country's economic and financial vulnerability. Each Corporate Governance ROSC assessment reviews the country's legal and regulatory framework, as well as the practices and compliance of its listed firms, and assesses the framework relative to an internationally accepted benchmark.

Commonwealth Association for Corporate Governance

Unlike the OECD Principles, which are addressed to nation states seeking to regulate corporate governance in their country, the Commonwealth Association for Corporate Governance (CACG) Guidelines: Principles for Corporate Governance in the Commonwealth, November 1999, are aimed at the level of the individual company.

Principles for Corporate Governance in the Commonwealth

Part one—Executive Summary of Guidelines

The board should:

Principle 1—exercise leadership, enterprise, integrity and judgement in directing the corporation so as to achieve continuing prosperity for the corporation and to act in the best interests of the business enterprise in a manner based on transparency, accountability and responsibility;

Principle 2—ensure that through a managed and effective process, board appointments are made that provide a mix of proficient directors, each of whom is able to add value and to bring independent judgement to bear on the decision-making process;

Principle 3—determine the corporation's purpose and values, determine the strategy to achieve its purpose and to implement its values in order to ensure that it survives and thrives, and ensure that procedures and practices are in place that protect the corporation's assets and reputation;

Principle 4—monitor and evaluate the implementation of strategies, policies, management performance criteria and business plans;

Principle 5—ensure that the corporation complies with all relevant laws, regulations and codes of best business practice;

Principle 6—ensure that the corporation communicates with shareholders and other stakeholders effectively;

Principle 7—serve the legitimate interest of the shareholders of the corporation and account to them fully;

Principle 8—identify the corporation's internal and external stakeholders and agree a policy, or policies, determining how the corporation should relate to them;

Principle 9—ensure that no person or a block of persons has unfettered power and that there is an appropriate balance of power and authority on the board which is, inter alia, reflected by separating the roles of the chief executive officer and the chairman, and by having a balance between executive and non-executive directors.

Principle 10—regularly review processes and procedures to ensure the effectiveness of its internal systems of control, so that its decision making capability and the accuracy of its reporting and financial results are maintained at a high level at all times;

Principle 11—regularly assess its performance and effectiveness as a whole, and that of the individual directors, including the chief executive officer;

Principle 12—appoint the chief executive officer and at least participate in the appointment of senior management, ensure motivation, and the protection of intellectual capital intrinsic to the corporation, ensure that there is adequate training for management and employees, and a succession plan for senior management.

Principle 13—ensure that all technology and systems used in the corporation are adequate to properly run the business and for it to remain a meaningful competitor;

Principle 14—identify key risk areas and key performance indicators of the business enterprise and monitor these factors;

Principle 15—ensure annually that the corporation will continue as a going concern for its next fiscal year.

International Corporate Governance Network (ICGN)

The International Corporate Governance Network was founded in 1995 at the instigation of major institutional investors, major companies, financial intermediaries, academics, and other parties interested in the development of global corporate governance practices. One of its objectives is to facilitate international dialogue on issues of concern to investors. Statements from ICGN include:

- Statement on Global Corporate Governance Principles, July 2005
- Enhancing Corporate Governance for Banking Organisations, September 1999
- Statement on Global Corporate Governance Principles, July 1999

Codes from Institutional Investors

Some major institutional investors and organizations representing them have also offered their views on corporate governance codes. For example:

- CalPERS Global Corporate Governance Principles, 1997

- Teachers Insurance and Annuity Association—College Retirement Equities Fun, Policy Statement on Corporate Governance, March 2000
- The Hermes Principles, Hermes Pensions Management Ltd, 2002

CalPERS, the California Public Employees' Retirement System, was a pioneer and has developed corporate governance principles for France, Germany, Japan, the United Kingdom, and the United States, and international and global guidelines, which tend to build on the OECD Principles.

The principles espoused by Hermes, an international fund manager follow.

Case Study 7.3 The Hermes Principles

Hermes' overriding requirement is that companies be run in the long term interests of shareholders. Companies adhering to this principle will not only benefit their shareholders, but also we would argue, the wider economy in which the company and its shareholders participate. We believe a company run in the long term interest of its shareholders will need to manage effectively relationships with its employees, suppliers and customers, to behave ethically and have regard for the environment and society as a whole.

Communication

Principle 1: Companies should seek an honest, open and ongoing dialogue with shareholders. They should clearly communicate the plans they are pursuing and the likely financial and wider consequences of those plans. Ideally goals, plans, and progress should be discussed in the annual report and accounts.

Financial

Principle 2: Companies should have appropriate measures and systems in place to ensure that they know which activities and competencies contribute most to maximizing shareholder value.

Principle 3: Companies should ensure all investment plans have been honestly and critically tested in terms of their ability to deliver long term shareholder value.

Principle 4: Companies should allocate capital for investment by seeking fully and creatively to exploit opportunities for growth within their core businesses rather than seeking unrelated diversification. This is particularly true when considering acquisitive growth.

Principle 5: Companies should have performance evaluation and incentive systems designed cost-effectively to incentivize management to deliver long term shareholder value.

Principle 6: Companies should have an efficient capital structure which will maximize the long term cost of capital.

Strategic

Principle 7: Companies should have and continue to develop coherent strategies for each business unit. These should ideally be expressed in terms of market prospects and of the competitive advantage the business has in exploiting these prospects. The company should understand the factors which drive market growth, and the particular strengths which underpin the competitive position.

Principle 8: Companies should be able to explain why they are the best 'parent' of the businesses they run. Where they are not best parent they should be developing plans to resolve the issue.

Social, ethical, and environmental

Principle 9: Companies should manage effectively relationships with their employees, suppliers, and customers and with others who have a legitimate interest in the company's activities. Companies should behave ethically and have regard for the environment and society as a whole.

Principle 10: Companies should support voluntary and statutory measures which minimize the externalization of costs to the detriment of society at large.

(www.hermes.co.uk/pdf/corporate_governance/Hermes_Principles.pdf)

Discussion Questions

1. Do you agree with Hermes' overriding requirement that 'companies (should) be run in the long term interests of shareholders'?

2. Do you also agree with the further sentiment that 'a company run in the long term interest of its shareholders will need to manage effectively relationships with its employees, suppliers and customers, to behave ethically and have regard for the environment and society as a whole'?

3. Can you improve on these ten principles?

Notice how these principles are written from the point of view of shareholders, emphasize maximizing shareholder value and even give strategic advice (companies should *exploit opportunities for growth within their core businesses rather than seeking unrelated diversification*).

Company Codes

In addition to sets of principles and codes at the international, national, and institutional levels described above, some major companies have published their own set of corporate governance policies. Among the first was General Motors in 1994, following a disastrous performance and board re-structuring. This code contained detailed provisions on:

(1) Selection and composition of the board
   - Board membership criteria
   - Selection of new directors
   - Extending an invitation to a potential director to join the board

- Resignation policy relating to majority voting for directors
- Director orientation and continuing education

(2) Board leadership
- Selection of chairman and chief executive officer
- Chair of the directors and corporate governance committee

(3) Board composition and performance
- Size of the board
- Mix of management and independent directors
- Board definition of independence in directors
- Former chairman and CEO board membership
- Directors who change their present job responsibility
- Limits on outside board membership
- Meeting attendance
- Term limits and retirement age
- Board compensation
- Loans to directors and executive officers
- Stock ownership by non-management directors
- Meetings of independent directors
- Role of the presiding director
- Access to outside advisors
- Assessing the board performance
- Ethics and conflicts of interest
- Confidentiality
- Board's interaction with advisors, institutional investors, press, customers, etc.

(4) Board's relationship to senior management
- Regular attendance of non-directors at board meetings
- Board access to senior management

(5) Meeting procedures
- Selection of agenda items for board meetings
- Board materials distributed in advance
- Board presentations

(6) Board committee matters
- The board committees
- Committees performance evaluation
- Assignment and rotation of committee members
- Frequency and length of committee meetings

- Committee agenda
(7) Leadership development
    - formal evaluation of the chairman and CEO
    - Succession planning
    - Management development

CalPers, the US institutional investor, circulated the GM code to major public companies and in the next decade thousands of US companies adopted corporate governance policies or guidelines. In 2002, the New York Stock Exchange required all listed companies to adopt corporate governance guidelines and post them on their websites, so there are now thousands of examples in the public domain.

Codes for the Public and Voluntary Sectors

The UK Independent Commission for Good Governance in Public Services, chaired by Sir Alan Langlands, published a Good Governance Standard for Public Services in 2005. The Standard had six primary components:

Good governance means:

1. focusing on the organization's purpose and outcomes for citizens and service users
2. performing effectively in clearly defined functions and roles
3. promoting values for the whole organization and demonstrating the values of good governance through behaviour
4. taking informed, transparent decisions and managing risk
5. developing the capacity and capability of the governing body to be effective
6. engaging stakeholders and making accountability real.

Also in 2005, the UK Institute of Chartered Secretaries published a Code of Governance for the Voluntary and Community Sector. The main principles cover:

(1) Board leadership—the organization to be led by effective board of trustees, setting strategic direction, delivering its objectives and upholding its values.

(2) Board in control—responsibility of trustees as a board to be collectively responsible and accountable for monitoring and ensuring that the organization is performing well, ensuring relevant internal controls, compliance, prudence risk management, equality and diversity.

(3) High performance board—the board to have clear responsibilities and functions, including principles on trustee duties, board information, skills, and experience, and the relationship with the chief executive.

(4) Board review and renewal—board to review its own and the organization's effectiveness, with trustee and staff appraisals.

(5)   Board delegation—board to set out delegated functions of sub-committees, chief executive, officers, and agents.

(6)   Board and trustee integrity—board and individual trustees to adopt high ethical standards and ensure conflicts of interest recognized and handled.

(7)   Board openness—board to be open, responsive, and accountable to users, beneficiaries, members, partners, and others with an interest in its work.

Codes for Individual Directors

Finally, it should be noted that codes have also been drawn up for individual directors, particularly non-executive directors. We will explore these later.

Compliance with Corporate Governance Codes

In the early days compliance with corporate governance codes was voluntary. Exhortation to adopt the spirit of the codes came from financial institutions, the media, directors' professional bodies, and academic commentators. Some institutional investors applied specific pressure. But it was in the boardrooms that decisions were taken on the extent of following the relevant code.

Then, in a number of countries, the relevant code was incorporated into stock exchange listing agreements. Conformity with the code became a condition of listing. In most countries, as we have already seen, compliance remained voluntary with the company required to explain why, if it chose not to follow the code. In other words, companies conform with the code either by following its requirements or explaining why they have not. In a growing number of jurisdictions companies were now required to make a corporate governance report to their members, confirming that they had complied with the corporate governance requirements.

The exception to the voluntary, principles based approach to corporate governance regulation, as we also saw, is in the United States, which adopted a legal rule based approach.

The clear preference in business communities around the world, other than in the United States, is still for voluntary compliance and the avoidance of legislation, as the UK Hampel Report had indicated. However, revised companies law in some jurisdictions, including Australia (1997 updated 2006), the UK (2006) and China (2006), such as clarifying directors' duties, has sharpened the legal position.

The responsibility for ensuring compliance with these new listing requirements and laws in listed companies often fell to the company secretary; but in some companies a new management function appeared—the compliance officer. Moreover, given the importance which was now being placed on the new rules, many boards entrusted the new responsibility to their audit committee. Others created a new board compliance committee.

REFERENCES AND FURTHER READING

Charkham, Jonathan P. (1994) *Keeping Good Company: A Study of Corporate Governance in 5 Countries (Germany, France, Japan, the USA and the UK)*. Oxford: Oxford University Press.

Gordon, Jeffrey N. and Mark J. Roe (2004) *Convergence and Persistence in Corporate Governance*. New York: Cambridge University Press.

Lee, Thomas A. (2004) *Financial Reporting and Corporate Governance*. London: John Wiley.

Jones, Ian and Michael Pollitt (2004) 'Understanding How Issues in Corporate Governance Develop: Cadbury Report to Higgs Review', *Corporate Governance: An International Review*, 12(2).

USEFUL WEBSITES

www.frc.org.uk/corporate/combinedcode.cfm
The UK Combined Code in full.

www.bus.ualberta.ca/ccgi
Canadian Corporate Governance Institute.

www.calpers-governance.org/forumhome.asp
CalPERS (proactive US pension fund) corporate governance forum.

www.ccg.uts.edu.au
Centre for Corporate Governance UTS Sydney Australia.

www.gm.com/corporate/investor_information
General Motors corporate governance guidelines.

www.ecgi.org/codes/all_codes.php
Index of corporate governance codes around the world with access to texts.

www.ecgi.org/codes/documents/hermes_principles.pdf
Hermes (proactive UK institutional investor) corporate governance principles.

www.frc.org.uk
UK Financial Reporting Council for latest on UK codes.

news.findlaw.com/hdocs/docs/gwbush/sarbanesoxley072302.pdf
The Sarbanes-Oxley Act in full.

www.soxlaw.com/introduction.htm
The Sarbanes-Oxley Act outline with key sections including 404.

PROJECTS AND EXERCISES

1. Use the Internet to explore some of the corporate governance codes around the world in the appendix to this chapter. Compare and contrast the codes in some countries that you find interesting.

2. Prepare an essay/report/presentation on the 'principles or prescription' corporate governance debate. Do you believe that corporate governance codes will converge on one or the other underlying paradigm?

3. Are there basic differences between codes of corporate governance good practice for joint stock, limited-liability companies and those for the public and voluntary sectors?

SELF-TEST QUESTIONS

To confirm your grasp of the key points in this chapter try answering the following questions. Answers are at the end of the book.

1. What were the key recommendations of the first ever code of corporate governance—the Cadbury code?

2. What are the UK Combined Code requirements on (a) professional development and (b) performance evaluation?

3. What is the role of the OECD Principles of Corporate Governance?

4. What do the Hermes Principles have to say about a company's relationships with stakeholders?

5. What does section 404 of the Sarbanes-Oxley Act require?

6. What do the Hermes Principles have to say about a company's strategy formulation?

7. How does the Sarbanes-Oxley Act define an INED?

8. What is the minimum number of members of an audit committee under the Sarbanes-Oxley Act? What qualifications should they have?

9. Is it necessary for companies covered by the Sarbanes-Oxley Act to adopt and disclose a code of business conduct and ethics for directors, officers, and employees?

10. What are the responsibilities of the board according to the OECD Principles?

Appendix to Chapter 7
Corporate Governance Codes around the World

International

- The Auditor's Procedures in Response to Assessed Risk, International Standard on Auditing (#330), International Federation of Accountants (IFAC), New York, 2005
- Understanding the Entity and its Environment and Assessing the Risks of Material Mis-statement, International Standard on Auditing (#315), International Federation of Accountants (IFAC), New York, 2005
- Communication of Auditing Matters with those charged with Governance, International Standard on Auditing (#260), International Federation of Accountants (IFAC), New York, 2005
- Principles of Corporate Governance, Organisation for Economic Co-operation and Development (OECD), Paris, 1999 and 2004
- Principles of Auditor Independence and the Role of Corporate Governance in Monitoring an Auditor's Independence, International Organization of Securities Commissions (IOSCO), Madrid, 2002
- Corporate Governance—a framework for implementation (Iskander and Chamlou), World Bank, Washington, 2000

Africa

Kenya

- Principles for Corporate Governance in Kenya, Private Sector Corporate Governance Trust, 2002
- Sample Code of Best Practice for Corporate Governance, Private Sector Corporate Governance Trust, 2002

South Africa

- King II Report on Corporate Governance for South Africa, Institute of Directors in South Africa, 2002
- King I Report on Corporate Governance for South Africa, Institute of Directors in South Africa, 1994

Australia and New Zealand

Australia

- Principles of Good Corporate Governance and Best Practice Recommendations, Australian Stock Market ASX Corporate Governance Council, March 2003
- Corporate Governance—Volume One: In Principle, Audit Office of New South Wales, Sydney, June 1997
- Corporate Governance—Volume Two: In Practice, Audit Office of New South Wales, Sydney, June 1997
- Bosch Report, Australian Financial Institutions, Sydney, 1995
- Strictly Boardroom, Fred Hilmer, InfoAustralia, 1992

New Zealand

- Corporate Governance in New Zealand: Principles and Guidelines, The New Zealand Securities Commission, Wellington, February/March 2004
- Corporate Governance Principles, The New Zealand Securities Commission, November 2003

Asia

Bangladesh

- The Code of Corporate Governance for Bangladesh, Bangladesh Enterprise Institute, March 2004

Hong Kong

- Hong Kong Stock Exchange and Hong Kong Institute of Directors joint statement on explanations required on a director's resignation, May 2007
- Hong Kong Code on Corporate Governance, Stock Exchange of Hong Kong, November 2004
- Model Code for Securities Transactions by Directors of Listed Companies: Basic Principles, Hong Kong Stock Exchange, 2001
- Corporate Governance Disclosure in Annual Reports, Hong Kong Society of Accountants, 2001
- Code of Best Practice, Hong Kong Stock Exchange, 1999

India

- Report of the Kumar Mangalam Birla Committee on Corporate Governance, Securities and Exchange Board of India, 2000
- Desirable Corporate Governance in India—A Code, Confederation of Indian Industry, 1998

Indonesia

- Code for Good Corporate Governance, the National Committee on Corporate Governance, 2001
- Code for Good Corporate Governance, the National Committee on Corporate Governance, 2000

Japan

- Principles of Corporate Governance for Listed Companies, Tokyo Stock Exchange, April 2004
- Revised Corporate Governance Principles, Japan Corporate Governance Forum, October 2001
- Corporate Governance Principles: A Japanese view, Committee of the Corporate Governance Forum of Japan, Tokyo, October 1997
- Urgent Recommendations Concerning Corporate Governance, Japan Federation of Economic Organisations (Keidanen), September 1997

Malaysia

- Malaysian Code on Corporate Governance, Securities Commission Malaysia, March 2000

Pakistan

- Code of Corporate Governance (Revised), the Securities and Exchange Commission of Pakistan, March 2002
- Stock Exchange Code of Corporate Governance, the Securities and Exchange Commission of Pakistan, March 2002

Philippines

- Code of Proper Practices for Directors, Institute of Corporate Directors, March 2000

Singapore

- The Monetary Authority of Singapore and the Singapore Stock Exchange joint statement dissolving the Council of Corporate Disclosure and Governance, and jointly assuming responsibility for overseeing corporate governance of listed companies, May 2007
- Code of Corporate Governance, Council on Corporate Disclosure and Governance, July 2005
- Revisions to the Code of Corporate Governance, December 2004
- Code of Corporate Governance, March 2001

South Korea

- Code of Best Practice for Corporate Governance, Committee on Corporate Governance, September 1999

Taiwan

- Taiwan Corporate Governance Best-Practice Principles, Taiwan Stock Exchange, GreTai Securities Market, 2002

Thailand

- Code of Best Practice for Directors of Listed Companies, the Stock Exchange of Thailand, October 2002
- Best Practice Guidelines for Audit Committee, the Stock Exchange of Thailand, June 1999
- The Code of Best Practice for Directors of Listed Companies, the Stock Exchange of Thailand, January 1998

Europe

European Union

- European Corporate Governance Forum created to encourage co-ordination and convergence of national codes, June 2007
- Directive on the formation of public companies and the maintenance and alteration of their capital, September 2006
- Directive on cross-border mergers, October 2005
- Discussion paper on the Financial Reporting and Auditing Aspects of Corporate Governance, Féderation des Experts Comptables Européens, 2003

- Final Report of high level Group of company law experts, chair Jaap Winter, corporate governance and the modernisation of European company law, November 2002
- Euroshareholders Corporate Governance Guidelines, the European Shareholders Group, February 2002
- Recommendations on Auditor Independence, EU, 2002
- Statute for a European Company, October 2001
- Principles and Recommendations, European Association of Securities Dealers (now APCIMS-EASD), Corporate Governance Committee EASD, May 2000
- Corporate Governance Guidelines 2000, European Shareholders Group (Euroshareholders), February 2000
- Sound business standards and corporate practices: A set of guidelines, European Bank for Reconstruction and Development (EBRD), September 1997
- The Role, Position and Liability of the Statutory Auditor in Europe, EU Commission, 1996
- Report of Centre for European Studies Working Party, CEPS, Brussels, 1995

Austria

- Austrian Code of Corporate Governance, Austrian Working Group on Corporate Governance, January 2006
- Austrian Code of Corporate Governance, Austrian Working Group on Corporate Governance, February 2005
- Austrian Code of Corporate Governance, Austrian Working Group on Corporate Governance, November 2002

Belgium

- Code Buysse: Corporate governance for non-listed companies, Commission Corporate Governance pour les entreprises non cotées, September 2005
- Belgian Corporate Governance Code, Corporate Governance Committee, December 2004
- Director's Charter, Directors Foundation (Fondation des Administrateurs), January 2000
- Guidelines on Corporate Governance Reporting, La Commission Bancaire et Financière, November 1999
- Corporate governance for Belgian listed companies (the Cardon Report), Belgian Corporate Governance Commission
- Commission Bancaire et Financière, December 1998
- Corporate Governance—Recommendations, Federation of Belgian Enterprises, January 1998

Cyprus

- Cyprus Corporate Governance Code (2nd edn), Cyprus Stock Exchange, March 2006
- Corporate Governance Code, Cyprus Stock Exchange, September 2002

Czech Republic

- Revised Corporate Governance Code based on the OECD Principles, Czech Securities Commission, June 2004
- Corporate Governance Code based on the OECD Principles, Czech Securities Commission, February 2001

Denmark

- Revised Recommendations for Corporate Governance in Denmark, Copenhagen Stock Exchange Committee on Corporate Governance, August 2005
- Report on Corporate Governance in Denmark, Copenhagen Stock Exchange Committee on Corporate Governance, December 2003
- The Nørby Committee's report on Corporate Governance in Denmark, Copenhagen Stock Exchange, December 2001
- Guidelines on good management of a listed company (Corporate Governance), Danish Shareholders Association, February 2000

Estonia

- Corporate Governance Recommendations, Financial Supervision Authority and Tallinn Stock Exchange, January 2006

Finland

- Improving Corporate Governance of Unlisted Companies, Central Chamber of Commerce of Finland, January 2006
- Corporate Governance Recommendations for Listed Companies, HEX Plc, Central Chamber of Commerce of Finland, Confederation of Finnish Industry and Employers, December 2003

France

- Recommandations sur le gouvernement d'entreprise, L'Association Française de la Gestion Financière (AFG), March 2004
- The Corporate Governance of Listed Corporations, MEDEF and Association Française des Entreprises Privées (AFEP), October 2003

- Promoting Better Corporate Governance in Listed Companies, AFEP-AGREF/ MEDEF, September 2002
- Viénot II Report, Mouvement des Entreprises de France (MEDEF) [formerly CNPF] and Association Française des Enterprises Privees (AFEP), July 1999
- Recommendations on Corporate Governance, AFG-ASFFI Commission on Corporate Governance , June 1998
- Viénot I Report, Conseil National du Patronat Français (CNPF) and Association Française des Entreprises Privees (AFEP), June 1995

Germany

- Amendment to the German Corporate Governance Code (the Cromme Code), Government Commission German Corporate Governance Code, June 2005
- Corporate Governance Code for Asset Management Companies, The German Working Group on Corporate Governance for Asset Managers, April 2005
- Amendment to the German Corporate Governance Code (the Cromme Code), Government Commission German Corporate Governance Code, May 2003
- The German Corporate Governance Code (the Cromme Code), German Corporate Governance Kodex, February 2002 (Government Commission amendment 2003)
- Baums Commission Report, Bericht der Regierungskommission Corporate Governance, July 2001
- German Code of Corporate Governance, Berliner Initiativkreis, June 2000
- Corporate Governance Rules for German Quoted Companies, German Panel on Corporate Governance, January 2000
- DSW Guidelines, Deutsche Schutzvereinigung für Wertpapierbesitz e.V., June 1998
- Gesetz zur Kontrolle und Transparenz im Unternehmensbereich (KonTraG), Deutsche Bundestag—German Ministry of Justice, March 1998

Greece

- Principles of Corporate Governance, Federation of Greek Industries, July 2001
- Principles on Corporate Governance in Greece: Recommendations for its Competitive Transformation, Committee on Corporate Governance in Greece (under the coordination of the Capital Market Commission), October 1999

Holland (The Netherlands)

- Handbook of Corporate Governance, Corporate Governance Research Foundation for Pensionfunds (SCGOP), 2004
- The Dutch corporate governance code (the Tabaksblat Code), Corporate Governance Committee, December 2003

- Handbook of Corporate Governance, The Foundation for Corporate Governance Research for Pension Funds (Stichting Corporate Governance Onderzoek voor Pensioenfondsen—SCGOP), August 2001
- Government Governance; Corporate governance in the public sector, why and how? The Netherlands Ministry of Finance Government Audit Policy Directorate (DAR), November 2000
- Peters Report—Corporate Governance in the Netherlands, Committee on Corporate Governance, July 1997

Hungary

- Corporate Governance Recommendations, Budapest Stock Exchange, February 2002

Iceland

- Guidelines on Corporate Governance, The Iceland Stock Exchange (ICEX), Iceland Chamber of Commerce, Confederation of Icelandic Employers, March 2004

Ireland

- Corporate Governance, Share Option and Other Incentive Schemes, Irish Association of Investment Managers, March 1999

Italy

- Corporate Governance Code (Codice di Autodisciplina), Comitato per la Corporate Governance, Borsa Italiana, March 2006
- Handbook on Corporate Governance Reports, Associazione fra le società italiane per azioni (Assonime), February 2004
- Corporate Governance Code (il Codice di Autodisciplina delle società quotate rivisitato), Committee for the Corporate Governance of Listed Companies, Borsa Italiana, July 2002
- Report & Code of Conduct (the Preda Report), Committee for the Corporate Governance of Listed Companies, Borsa Italiana, October 1999
- Testo Unico sulle disposizioni in materia di intermediazione, based on Draghi Proposals, February 1998

Latvia

- Principles of Corporate Governance and Recommendations on their Implementation, Riga Stock Exchange, December 2005

Lithuania

- Corporate Governance Code for the Companies listed on the National Stock Exchange of Lithuania, National Stock Exchange of Lithuania, April 2003

Luxembourg

- The Ten Principles of Corporate Governance of the Luxembourg Stock Exchange, April 2006

Malta

- Principles of Good Corporate Governance: Revised Code for Issuers of Listed Securities, Malta Financial Services Authority (MFSA), November 2005
- Principles of Good Corporate Governance for Public Interest Companies, MFSA, November 2005
- Principles of Good Corporate Governance, Malta Stock Exchange, October 2001

Norway

- The Norwegian Code of Practice for Corporate Governance (Revised 2005), Norwegian Corporate Governance Board, December 2005
- The Norwegian Code of Practice for Corporate Governance, December 2004

Poland

- Best Practices in Public Companies 2005, The Best Practices Committee of the Warsaw Stock Exchange in association with the Corporate Governance Forum, October 2004
- Best Practices in Public Companies in 2002, The Best Practices Committee at Corporate Governance Forum, July 2002
- The Corporate Governance Code for Polish Listed Companies (the Gdańsk Code), The Polish Corporate Governance Forum, June 2002

Portugal

- White Book on Corporate Governance in Portugal, Instituto Português de Corporate Governance, February 2006
- Recommendations on Corporate Governance, Comissão do Mercado de Valores Mobiliários (CMVM), November 2003
- Recommendations on Corporate Governance, Comissão do Mercado de Valores Mobiliários (CNMV), November 1999

Romania

- Corporate Governance Code in Romania, International Center for Entrepreneurial Studies, University of Bucharest, 24 June 2000

Slovakia

- Corporate Governance Code (Based on the OECD Principles), Bratislava Stock Exchange, September 2002

Slovenia

- Corporate Governance Code, Ljubljana Stock Exchange, Managers' Association of Slovenia, Association of the Supervisory Board Members of Slovenia, December 2005
- Corporate Governance Code, Ljubljana Stock Exchange, Association of Supervisory Board Members of Slovenia, Managers' Association of Slovenia, March 2004

Spain

- Code of Ethics for Companies, Instituto de Consejeros-Administradores, April 2006
- Draft Unified Code of Recommendations for the Good Governance, Comision Nacional del Mercado de Valores (CNMV), January 2006
- IC-A: Principles of Good Corporate Governance, Instituto de Consejeros-Administradores, December 2004
- Decálogo del Directivo, Instituto Español de Analistas Financieros (IEAF), May 2004
- The Aldama report, Special Commission, January 2003
- Código de Buen Gobierno, Special Commission, February 1998
- Círculo de Empresarios October 1996

Sweden

- Swedish Code of Corporate Governance Report of the Code Group, The Codes Group, December 2004
- Corporate Governance Policy, The Swedish Industry and Commerce Stock Exchange Committee (Naringslivets Borskommitte—NBK), October 2001
- Swedish Academy of Directors, Sveriges Aktiesparares Riksförbund (The Swedish Shareholders' Association), 1994

Switzerland

- Swiss Code of Best Practice for Corporate Governance, Swiss Business Federation, June 2002
- Corporate Governance Directive, SWX Swiss Exchange, June 2002

Turkey

- Corporate Governance Principles, The Capital Markets Board of Turkey, June 2003

Ukraine

- Ukrainian Corporate Governance Principles, Ukrainian Securities Commission, June 2003

United Kingdom

(See the list of corporate governance reports and the UK Combined Code listed earlier in this chapter)

North America

Canada

- Corporate Governance: A guide to good disclosure, Toronto Stock Exchange, December 2003
- Beyond Compliance: Building a Governance Culture (Saucier Report), Joint Committee on Corporate Governance, November 2001
- Five Years to the *Dey*, Toronto Stock Exchange and Institute of Corporate Directors, June 1999 (Mr Dey was the author of the 1994 report)
- Building on Strength: Improving Governance and Accountability in Canada's Voluntary Sector, Panel for Accountability and Governance in the Voluntary Sector, February 1999
- Where Were The Directors? Guidelines for Improved Corporate Governance in Canada, (the Dey Report),The Toronto Stock Exchange, December 1994

Jamaica

- Code of Corporate Governance, Private Sector Organisation of Jamaica, October 2005

Mexico

- Código de Mejores Prácticas Corporativas, July 1999

United States of America

- Asset Manager Code of Professional Conduct, Centre for Financial Market Integrity, November 2004
- Enterprise Risk Management—integrated framework, Committee of Sponsoring Organizations of the Treadway Commission, New York, 2004

- Amendments to the Corporate Governance Rules, NYSE, August 2004
- Corporate Governance Rules, New York Stock Exchange, November 2003
- Commission on Public Trust and Private Enterprise Findings and Recommendations: Part 2: Corporate Governance, the Conference Board, New York, 2003
- Sarbanes-Oxley Act 2002
- Corporate Governance Rule Proposals, New York Stock Exchange, August 2002
- Principles of Corporate Governance, the Business Roundtable, May 2002
- Core Policies, Principles of Corporate Governance: Analysis & Recommendations, Council of Institutional Investors, 2002
- General Principles, Positions & Explanatory Notes, American Law Institute, March 2002
- Blue Ribbon Report on Director Professionalism, National Association of Corporate Directors, 2001
- Blue Ribbon Report on Improving the Effectiveness of Corporate Audit Committees, New York Stock Exchange and National Association of Securities Dealers, New York, 1999
- Statement on Corporate Governance, The Business Roundtable, September 1997
- Internal Control Integrated Framework, (the COSO Report), Committee of Sponsoring Organizations of the Treadway Commission, American Institute of Certified Public Accountants, New York, 1992
- Report on the National Commission of Fraudulent reporting, (the Treadway Report), American Institute of Certified Public Accountants, New York, 1987
- Commission on Auditors' Responsibilities, (the Cohen Commission Report), American Institute of Certified Public Accountants New York, 1978

South America

- Latin American Corporate Governance, the Latin America Corporate Governance Roundtable White Paper, 2003

Brazil

- Code of Best Practice of Corporate Governance, Instituto Brasileiro de Governança Corporativa ('IBGC'), March 2004
- Recomendações sobre Governança Corporativa, Comissão de Valores Mobiliários, June 2002
- Code of Best Practice of Corporate Governance, Instituto Brasileiro de Governança Corporativa ('IBGC'), May 1999

Trinidad and Tobago

- Corporate Governance Guideline, Central Bank of Trinidad and Tobago, May 2006

8　Models of Corporate Governance

....

- In which we consider:
  - how context and culture affect corporate governance
  - the American rule based model
  - the United Kingdom/Commonwealth principles based model
  - the Continental European two-tier model
  - the Japanese business network model
  - the Asian family based model
  - corporate governance in mainland China
  - corporate governance in Russia
  - corporate governance in India
  - corporate governance in the Middle East
  - corporate governance: convergence or differentiation?
  - institutions necessary for successful corporate governance

How Context and Culture Affect Corporate Governance

In chapter 3, we identified various board structures, including the unitary board and the two-tier board. In chapter 4, we read about the Japanese *keiretsu* form of networked organization and the Korean *chaebols*. In this chapter, we ask how such differences have arisen and whether corporate governance systems around the world are converging as some suggest.

Two primary influences can be suggested for some fundamental differences in corporate governance around the world: context and culture. Looking first at the context in which corporate governance is practised, we review the implications of different patterns of ownership, alternative markets for corporate control, and different ways of financing corporate entities. Then we will look at cultural influences on corporate governance.

Patterns of Ownership

The pattern of ownership in listed companies around the world varies dramatically. Where a relatively high proportion of shares in a company are held by external shareholders, the directors need to recognize their potential power. Contrariwise, where there is a significant

Table 8.1 **Balance of listed company ownership**

Country	Individuals	Institutional investors	Banks and government	Holding company	Foreign
Australia	20%	34%	4%	11%	31%
Canada	15%	38%	8%	14%	25%
France	23%	12%	14%	14%	37%
Germany	17%	15%	17%	39%	12%
Italy	18%	14%	40%	18%	10%
Japan	20%	21%	23%	28%	8%
Sweden	23%	30%	8%	9%	30%
Netherlands	14%	21%	1%	23%	41%
UK	19%	58%	5%	2%	16%
USA	51%	41%	3%	0%	5%

owner, such as a holding company, or where a dominant shareholding is held by a government or a bank, the directors need to respond to their expectations. Table 8.1 above shows the proportion of voting shares held by individuals, institutional investors, banks and government, holding companies, and overseas investors, country by country.

Notice, how in the United States individuals and institutional investors together account for 92 percent of the shareholdings and in the UK 77 percent, whereas in France it is only 35 percent. In fact, the dispersed ownership found in UK and US companies is the exception rather than the norm around the world. The impact of foreign investors in countries such as the Netherlands (41%) can influence boards of companies listed there. In Germany, Japan, and the Netherlands many listed companies are held within corporate groups and their boards find themselves responsible to a holding company. In the case of foreign ownership, some of these shareholdings are in the hands of an overseas parent company, in other cases the holdings may be dispersed among many shareholders.

Obviously, in the longer term the pattern of ownership fundamentally affects the ability of a board to exercise power over a company. In a company that has a wide spread of shareholders, a board will have more freedom to act on its own initiative than in one whose shares are dominated by a block of investors. Boards need to be acutely aware of which parties have the potential to influence their decisions. Unfortunately some commentators on corporate governance fail to make this distinction.

Markets for Corporate Control

In countries with a high proportion of external investors, as in the USA and the UK, boards can be faced with a hostile takeover bid and a consequential loss of their control. In other words, the market for corporate control is strong. Merger and acquisition activity is likely to be widespread. In countries with a relatively low proportion of external investors, the market for corporate control will be weaker, and merger and acquisition activity less.

Hostile takeover bids in British companies have been commonplace for over fifty years: the first contested takeover bid for a German company occurred in the 1990s.

Financing Corporate Entities

In countries where equity markets are relatively large, with high liquidity and significant turnover, such as the United States and the United Kingdom, shareholdings are often widely spread. So power over a company ultimately lies with the voting shareholders. In other countries, however, where stock markets are relatively small, companies can be financed in other ways, often by non-equity loan capital. In companies which have leveraged their equity capital, with high equity/loan gearing, ultimate power over the company may be in the hands of the lender.

Culture Influences on Corporate Governance

Intuitively, board level behaviour differs from culture to culture. Later in this chapter we will see how, around the world, board relationships and activities vary, directors' expectations differ, and individual directors behave differently. So, apparently, corporate governance has a cultural component. Not everyone agrees. David Webb, a Western commentator based in Hong Kong, has written:

People who defend bad corporate governance on the grounds of Asian values or some cultural difference are talking nonsense. Yes, there is a different structure of ownership; it's somewhat Victorian in that most companies (in Asia) are family controlled, but had I been around in Victorian times in England I think I would have seen similar bad corporate governance.

The position taken in this book is that cultural differences do exist and, whilst they should not be used to defend poor governance practices, failure to appreciate their significance is myopic. We will now review the context and culture of corporate governance using five basic models: the American model, the United Kingdom/Commonwealth model, the Continental European model, the Japanese business network model, and the Asian family based model.

The American Rule Based Model

In the early days of corporate governance thinking experts tended to write about the Anglo-American (or Anglo-Saxon) unitary board model of corporate governance and contrasted it with the Continental two-tier board model. Indeed, many expected a convergence of corporate governance practices towards the American model, not least because of the availability of American capital to invest around the world and the resultant influence of US governance practices. In recent years, however, some fundamental differences have appeared between the United States perspective and that of the United Kingdom/ Commonwealth model, as we will discuss later.

The American model reflects corporate governance practices required in the United States of America and the influence of the US on other countries. As we have seen, companies in the US are incorporated in individual states and subject to those states' company law and corporate regulation. Investor protection, auditing requirements, and financial disclosure of public companies, however, are federal responsibilities, predominantly overseen by the Securities and Exchange Commission (SEC). Company law is based on common law, which is rooted in legislation that evolves with a continually-growing body of case-law at both the federal and the state level.

The basic governance model in the United States is the unitary board with a predominance of independent outside directors. The SEC and stock exchange listing requirements also call for mandatory board audit, nomination, and remuneration committees, as in the UK/Commonwealth model.

In the United States, shareholders have little influence on board membership, other than expressing dissatisfaction by not voting, selling their shares or resorting to litigation. By contrast, in the United Kingdom/Commonwealth shareholders with 10 percent of the voting rights in a public company can force an extraordinary meeting and vote on strategic decisions or the removal of a director. Even though that seldom occurs, the possibility can affect board actions.

Similarly, whereas in the United Kingdom/Commonwealth model the roles of the board chairman and the chief executive officer are separated, in the United States they are often held by the same person. Although there have been some calls for separation (as we saw in the Walt Disney case in chapter 3). The board of Exxon Mobil has resisted a strong bid from shareholders in recent years to split the roles of chairman and chief executive; but, even if passed by a majority of shareholders voting, the decision would not be binding on the board.

But a more fundamental distinction has developed in recent years between the US model of corporate governance and that of the UK/Commonwealth model. The US model is 'rule based', in effect with the regulators asking *'is this legal?'* The UK/Commonwealth model is 'principles based', with the regulators asking *'is this right?'*

In the United States governance is regulated by legal statute and mandatory rules, which are inherently inflexible. Litigation levels are high. Directors face legal penalties for non-compliance. The 2002 Sarbanes-Oxley Act strengthened this emphasis on governance under penalty of law, with disclosure requirements that proved more expensive and burdensome than expected. The role of the regulators is to ensure that the rules are being obeyed. The American financial markets are the largest and most liquid in the world, but their lead, particularly in IPOs, has been eroded.

The United Kingdom/Commonwealth Principles Based Model

The law that recognized the incorporation of the joint stock, shareholder limited liability company originated in the United Kingdom around 1850. (Purists might argue that France can claim a slightly earlier form of legal incorporation, but that only granted limited liability to investors who were not involved in managing the company.) The influence of the old British Empire, in the later part of the 19th and early 20th centuries, meant that UK company law influenced the development of company law in Australia, Canada,

India, New Zealand, South Africa, Singapore, and indeed throughout what is now known as the Commonwealth.

As in the American model, company law in the UK/Commonwealth model is based on common law, rooted in legislation extended by case-law.

But, by contrast with the American model, in the United Kingdom/Commonwealth countries corporate governance is 'principles based'. Codes of corporate governance principle or good practice determine board responsibilities, not the rule of law. Companies are required to report that they have followed the governance principles laid down in the codes or explain why they have not. Consequently, this model is often referred to as the 'comply or explain' approach to corporate governance.

Self-regulation is the underlying theme. Compliance is voluntary, with the sanctions being the exposure of corporate governance failings to the market and, ultimately, delisting from the stock exchange. The role of the regulators is to ensure that investors and potential investors have accurate information on which to base their judgements.

Throughout the Commonwealth, corporate governance codes for listed companies, though differing slightly in detail, all call for independent non-executive or outside directors, audit, remuneration, and nomination committees, and high levels of transparency and accountability. The UK/Commonwealth codes require a separation between chairman and CEO.

Case Study 8.1 TYCO

Dennis Kozlowski became chief executive of Tyco in 1992. Treating the company as a private fiefdom, he siphoned off some hundreds of millions in private expenditure, including an infamous gold and burgundy shower curtain, allegedly costing £6,000 and a lavish US$2 million toga party on a Mediterranean island for his wife's birthday. His compliant board gave Kozlowski a contract saying that he would not be dismissed if convicted of a felony, unless it directly damaged the company. Subsequently it transpired that he had also authorized funding of US$4 million to support a chair in corporate governance at Cambridge University. He claimed that this was jointly funded by the company and himself. Some irate Tyco shareholders, hoping to retrieve some of their squandered funds, tried to recover these University funds. But the powers behind the chair of corporate governance insisted that they would hang on to the cash, no matter how tainted by corporate excess it might be, they could put it to good use, although they did have difficulty in finding a suitable incumbent. In 2005, Kozlowski was fined US$70 million and jailed for up to 25 years.

Discussion Question

1. What should a board do to ensure that a CEO does not treat the company as a private fiefdom? Recognize that the CEO probably played a major part in the appointment of the other directors. Furthermore, resignation from the board may have little effect on the CEO's behaviour.

The principles based versus the rule based view of governance is also reflected in accounting standards. The UK/Commonwealth countries apply standards that are predominantly based on international accounting standards, which emphasize compliance with principles. In the United States, the GAAP (Generally Accepted Accounting Principles) standards call for compliance with rules. There are signs that the US is moving towards international standards (the SEC recently dropped its requirement for foreign companies listed in America to reconcile their international standard accounts with GAAP accounts). But progress may be slow.

The Continental European Two-tier Model

Company law in Continental European countries is typically rule based. In France, for example, it is based on Napoleonic law, in which required corporate behaviour is determined by legally binding rules and evolves by further legislation, not by the precedents of case based common law.

Finance markets tend to be smaller and less liquid. The market for corporate control is weak. Bank and loan finance is widely used to fund companies and banks wield more influence on corporate affairs, particularly in Germany. Investors tend to be more concentrated, often with dominant family shareholdings, particularly in France and Italy. As we have seen earlier, gearing chains of companies are used to leverage controlling shareholders' investment, particularly in Italy.

Two-tier boards, explained in chapter 3, are required in Germany and Holland and are found in France and Italy. Moreover, in line with the social contract found in many European societies, corporate governance practices frequently have a social component. For example, the co-determination rules in Germany require one half of the supervisory board to represent labour, with employee representative directors elected through the trades unions, the other half to represent capital, elected by the shareholders. Many countries in the European Union also require works councils in which representatives of the employees wield power. The European company (the *Societas Europaea*) enacted under the rules of the European Union, mentioned earlier, provides for either Anglo-American or Continental European approaches.

Criticisms of the Continental European model of corporate governance differ significantly from those of the US and the UK models. Some argue that the management board is inevitably dominated by top management and lacks the information inputs, advice, and wise counselling that can be provided by outside independent non-executive directors in a unitary board.

Others question the effectiveness of supervisory boards, their lack of real power, and their ability effectively to control the management board. Other critics argue that the representative character of the supervisory board provides the potential for conflicts of interest.

There was a time when countries which employed the two-tier board believed that this was a superior model to the unitary board. Indeed, at one time the European Union tried to impose this model on all companies in member states—a proposal strongly resisted in the unitary board countries. Today, the limitations of each model are more widely recognized.

Case Study 8.2 Siemens AG

Siemens is Europe's largest engineering group, manufacturing a diverse range of products from power plants to home appliances, computers to railway engines. Head-quartered in Germany, the company has a two-tier board.

In 2007, the chief executive Klaus Kleinfeld challenged the supervisory board to renew his contract or accept his resignation. The proposal failed to get the necessary votes in the supervisory board and he resigned.

Previously, Kleinfeld had successfully run Siemens American operations, listing the company on the New York Stock Exchange in the process. He had served as an outside director on the boards of the major bank Citigroup and the American aluminium company Alcoa. He was recognized as a capable leader. Under his guidance the Siemens Group had recently reported a 10% increase in revenue and a 36% increase in profits.

But both the union and the shareholder representatives on the supervisory board disliked his aggressive management style. Rumours about him circulated among board members. Heinrich von Pierer, the head of the supervisory board resigned and was replaced by Gerhard Cromme, a pioneer of corporate governance reform in Germany.

Kleinfeld's problems, according to the *Economist*, were the lack of allies in Germany's chummy corporate elite and '*his American management methods, which seemed brash to industrialists and union representatives who were more used to Germany's consensual style of corporate leadership*'.

(*Economist*, 28 April 2007 and www.siemens.com)

Discussion Question

1. What might Kleinfeld have done to avoid resigning?

The Japanese Business Network Model

Keiretsu are networks of companies in Japan connected through cross-holdings and with interlocking directorships, as we saw in chapter 4. Member companies tend to intertrade extensively. Frequently the network includes a financial institution.

The classical model of the *keiretsu* reflects the social cohesion within Japanese society, emphasizing unity throughout the organization, non-adversarial relationships, lifetime employment, enterprise unions, personnel policies encouraging commitment, initiation into the corporate family, decision making by consensus, cross-functional training, and with promotion based on loyalty and social compatibility as well as performance. This model is currently under pressure, as we will see, but first let us review this traditional approach to corporate governance in Japan.

In the classical *keiretsu* model, boards of directors tend to be large and are, in effect, the top layers of the management pyramid. People speak of being 'promoted to the board'. The tendency for managers to progress through an organization on tenure rather than performance, means that the mediocre can reach board level.

A few of the directors might have served with other companies in the *keiretsu* network, and in that sense be able to represent the interests of suppliers or downstream agents; others might have been appointed to the company's ranks on retirement from the *keiretsu's* bankers, or even from amongst the industry's government regulators (known as a *amakaduri* or 'descent from heaven').

But independent non-executive directors, in the Western sense, would be unusual. Many Japanese do not see the need for such intervention 'from the outside'. Indeed, they have difficulty in understanding how outside directors operate. '*How can outsiders possibly know enough about the company to make a contribution,*' they question, '*when the other directors have spent their lives working for the company? How can an outsider be sensitive to the corporate culture? They might even damage the harmony of the group.*'

Japanese company law does provide for independent outside directors, where they exist, to form a separate committee outside the board. Although the basic governance model is of a unitary board, this committee could be seen as a form of supervisory board. Recently, some independent outside directors have been appointed, usually under pressure from international investors.

The Japanese *ringi* approach to communication encourages dialogue up and down the management hierarchy leading over time to an agreed position. This means that boards tend to be decision-ratifying bodies rather than decision initiating and decision taking forums, as in the West. Indeed, in some companies meetings of the entire board tend to be ceremonial, with honourable titles used on social occasions, although that aspect of society is in transition.

Chairmen and senior directors of companies in the *keiretsu* meet regularly and have close, informal relationships. Meetings of the managing directors with the directors in their teams are also crucial, as are the informal relationships between the top echelons of the board. Ultimate power lies with the top managers, particularly the president and the chairman.

The Japanese commercial code calls for 'representative directors' to be elected by the board. Whereas, from a Western viewpoint, these might be expected to represent the interests of various stakeholders in the firm, their actual role is to represent the company in its dealings with outside parties such as the government, banks, and other companies in the industry. Typically the representative directors include the chairman and president and other top directors. The code also calls for the appointment of individuals as full time statutory auditors. They report to the board on any financial problems or infringements of the company code or the company articles. They can call for information from other directors and company employees and can convene special meetings of the board. These internal board-level auditors, of course, liaise with the external professional auditors.

Traditionally investors have played a relatively small part in corporate affairs. The classical model of Japanese corporate governance had a stakeholder not a shareholder orientation. Power lay within the *keiretsu* network. There was no market for corporate control since hostile takeover bids were virtually unknown.

However, in the past decade the extent of cross-holdings of shares between companies has fallen, and in 2007, the first apparently hostile takeover in the Tokyo Stock Exchange was reported. The Japanese Pension Fund Association, which has 29 million members and over US$100 in assets, has tried to put pressure on boards by calling for a return on equity of at least 8%. But the effect has been marginal to date.

With the Japanese economy facing stagnation in the 1990s, traditional approaches to corporate governance were questioned. A corporate governance debate developed and the bank based, stakeholder orientated, rather than shareholder, corporate governance model came under scrutiny. The poorly performing economy had weakened many of the banks at the heart of *keiretsu*. Globalization of markets and finance put further pressure on companies. The paternalistic relationship between company and lifetime 'salary-man' slowly began to crumble. Some companies came under pressure from institutional investors abroad.

Company laws were then redrafted to permit a more US style of corporate governance. But few firms have yet embraced them. More emphasis has, however, been placed on shareholders, with board restructuring and directors receiving performance incentives. Some companies experimented with alternative, hybrid forms of governance structure. Consequently, there is now more diversity in the approaches to corporate governance in Japan, although changes tend to be gradual and incremental. But some do expect moves towards the US or UK/Commonwealth models, as Japan responds to the pressures of the globalization of business and finance.

Signs of movement included calls in 2008 by eight international investment funds for greater shareholder democracy, and a report from the Japanese Council for Economic and Fiscal Policy to the prime minister proposing that anti-takeover defences be discouraged and the takeover of Japanese firms be made easier.

In a 2008 report, the Asian Corporate Governance Association provided a critique of corporate governance in Japan:

We believe that sound corporate governance is essential to the creation of a more internationally competitive corporate sector in Japan and to the longer-term growth of the Japanese economy and its capital markets. While a number of leading companies in Japan have made strides in corporate governance in recent years, we submit that the system of governance in most listed companies is not meeting the needs of stakeholders or the nation at large in three ways:

- By not providing for adequate supervision of corporate strategy;
- By protecting management from the discipline of the market, thus rendering the development of a healthy and efficient market in corporate control all but impossible;
- By failing to provide the returns that are vitally necessary to protect Japan's social safety net— its pension system.

The Asian Family Based Model

Two types of family capital based system can be identified in Asia—that of the 'overseas Chinese' and the *chaebol* groups in South Korea. 'Overseas Chinese' is the term used to describe Chinese business people who over the years, as a result of the Chinese Diaspora from the mainland, are now fundamental to the business life of South East

Asia. Many companies in the significant Asian economies, Singapore, Taiwan, Malaysia, Thailand, Indonesia, Hong Kong, and the Philippines are in the hands of a relatively small number of Chinese families. For example, nearly half of the share capital invested in Malaysian companies is owned by Chinese residents and a quarter by foreign controlled companies.

Overseas Chinese

In the governance of overseas Chinese companies the board tends to play a supportive role to the real exercise of power, which is exercised through relationships between the key players, particularly between the dominant head of the family and other family members in key top management positions. Some of these companies are quite diverse groups with considerable delegation of power to the subsidiary unit but with the owner-manager, or a family orientated small group still holding a strategic hand on the tiller.

Research into the management of overseas Chinese companies has suggested some distinguishing characteristics, which may help to interpret the evidence on governance practices. These studies suggest that overseas Chinese firms are:

- Family centric with close family control
- Controlled through an equity stake kept within the family
- Entrepreneurial often with a dominant entrepreneur so that decision making is centralized, with close personal links emphasizing trust and control
- Paternalistic in management style, in a social fabric dependent on relationships and social harmony, avoiding confrontation and the risk of the loss of 'face'
- Strategically intuitive with the business seen as more of a succession of contracts or ventures, relying on intuition, superstition, and tough-minded bargaining rather than strategic plans, brand-creation, and quantitative analysis.

Even where such a company is listed, the outside shareholdings are in a minority, which can sometimes cause problems with related party transactions.

Hong Kong and Singapore

In Hong Kong and Singapore corporate governance is a fascinating melange of Anglo-American and Asian ideas. The corporate governance systems in both territories are an outgrowth of British company law and are amongst the more advanced in Asia. The Hong Kong stock market is the larger and most companies listed there are family firms with control firmly kept within the family, or mainland China based corporations. Although the Hong Kong regulatory authorities require a minimum of three independent non-executive directors, the heads of some family companies see little value in them. Their secretive, authoritarian, and family-centric approach to business does not lend itself to outside directors who might disagree with their decisions. Further, evidence of abnormal dealing prior to acquisition or merger activity suggests insider dealing. Incidentally, most Hong Kong listed companies are incorporated in Bermuda or the Cayman Islands, so that, whilst Hong

Kong listing rules and takeover code apply, Hong Kong companies' ordinances do not (other than those applying to overseas companies).

As the Far Eastern Economic Review commented:

Instead of strategy, the successful Hong Kong businessman has a modus operandi that is orientated towards the short term: endless opportunism is backed by a determination to narrow the odds. Their empires grow amoebae like, feeding on whatever comes to hand. The only predictable direction of growth is outwards.

The Singapore corporate governance code, like those in most Asian countries, is based on a 'comply or explain' approach, and calls for independent directors, audit committees, director training, and so on. Compliance is high, although companies listed on the SESDAQ (Stock Exchange of Singapore Dealing and Automated Quotation System) market, which is now called the Catalyst market, tend only to meet the minimum requirements unlike companies listed on the Singapore main board. In Singapore, the government is a significant player in the market, using government funds and those of the state pension fund to own and control significant companies incorporated there. (We briefly mentioned this in chapter 5 under the heading of 'Sovereign Funds'.)

Recognizing the importance of corporate governance to the long term development of Asian economies and capital markets, the Asian Corporate Governance Association (ACGA) was founded in 1999, as an independent, non-profit membership organization dedicated to working with investors, companies, and regulators in the implementation of effective corporate governance practices throughout Asia.

South Korea

Chaebol groups in South Korea developed following the Second World War, when the government advanced loans on attractive terms to family based firms to stimulate economic revival. Over time some of these family firms prospered and have become large groupings of associated companies. Even *chaebol* companies that are listed are often still controlled by the dominant owner-family interests. Even though companies attracted outside capital, family domination was maintained predominantly through insider boards. Attempts to introduce independent outside directors into South Korean boards have had only limited effect against the entrenched power of the existing block owners. At times this has led to protests from employees and social unrest. In recent years the South Korean Government has endeavoured to reduce the power of the *chaebols*, through enforced sales of companies in the groups, with limited results.

Can any conclusions be drawn from this comparison of Western corporate governance with Asian attitudes and practices? In the Western approach to corporate governance, it is the board, per se, that is the basis of legitimate power over the corporation. Stewardship, agency, and stakeholder theories all presume that the locus of power lies with the governing body—the board of directors, as we will explore in more detail in chapter 10. Even though the board may choose to delegate powers to the CEO, top management, or board committees, the board remains responsible. In the Asian approach to corporate governance the approach is more organic, with the relationships between key players legitimizing power.

Corporate Governance in Mainland China

In a country with strong central control, in which the National People's Congress, the State Council and the Communist Party play significant roles in the governance of enterprises, share ownership is not the obvious basis for governance power. Yet the People's Republic of China is developing an innovative corporate governance regime. Consequently, we will study the evolution of corporate governance in that country. The historical context is important.

The Communist revolution began in 1927, and in 1949 the Communists took over, proclaiming state ownership over the means of production. Private property and incorporated companies were forbidden. The first five-year plan, from 1953 to 1957, applied to all major economic sectors, particularly heavy industry.

At the beginning of 1958, Chairman Mao Tse Tung initiated the Great Leap Forward with the intention of making the country self-sufficient. Millions of farmers, peasants, and city workers were relocated. Massive economic dislocation resulted. Moreover, poor agricultural production coupled with natural disasters caused serious famines. The Cultural Revolution began in 1966 and lasted a decade. Communes were reorganized and many state owned enterprises (SOEs) were created, most needing state subsidy.

In the 1970s, a new leader, Deng Xiao Ping, introduced a form of market economy, but with a centralized, communist-state orientation. Under the 'Four Modernizations' campaign farmers, had an incentive to increase agricultural production, some agriculture collectives were privatized, and small private businesses appeared.

The industrial SOEs, which were in effect large bureaucracies, continued to receive their production and distribution orders from state planners. SOE employees benefited from housing, medical care, and schooling for their children, with the government providing benefits for maternity, injury, disability, and old age. Many SOEs were heavily subsidized and the government gave them easy access to bank financing, partly to pay for the social welfare needs of the workers. The concept of company, legal entity, or corporation did not appear in the Chinese language at that time.

The Emergence of Company Law and Governance in China

Between 1984 and 1993, a transitional model of governance for SOEs was introduced to increase productivity and profitability throughout China, giving them more autonomy. In 1994, a new Corporate Law provided for the restructuring of traditional large and medium-sized SOEs as legal entities, establishing a modern corporate system. These laws transformed SOEs into corporations by clearly defining their asset boundaries and their ownership, set up the board of directors to represent owners' interests, and created a dual system with a management board and a board of supervisors. Company law was improved in 1999 and 2006.

In 1988, the State Council of the People's Republic of China, advised by OECD experts, produced a set of corporate governance directives for SOE reform, which included the following proposals:

- A clear, flexible legal framework for property rights
- Rules for the establishment and the smooth and transparent functioning of commercial companies
- Equitable requirements of entry into markets and for competition between firms

- The transparent resolution of disputes between private parties and the state to enforce property rights and increase investor confidence
- A focus on fighting corruption and economic crime

In September 1999, the Fourth Plenary session of the 15th Chinese Communist Party's Central Committee took a vital decision on enterprise reform, in what was termed a '*strategic adjustment*' of the state sector, agreeing that the state should be '*withdrawing from what should be withdrawn*'. Interestingly, corporate governance was recognized as being at the core of the modern enterprise system. The 16th Congress of the Party called for a joint stock system with the state controlling critical enterprises, whilst other SOEs continued their corporate reforms. Many small and medium-sized firms were transformed into non-state owned enterprises, and some SOEs were restructured prior to stock market listing.

Some of the reformed corporate entities were floated on the two China stock markets in Shanghai and Shenzen (a city across the border from Hong Kong), which had been set up in 1991 and 1992 respectively. After due diligence studies on their financial standing, a few China companies were listed in Hong Kong or other stock exchanges around the world. Some listed 'through the back door' in Hong Kong, by acquiring a non-trading listed company and backing a China business into this shell. By 2007, 143 domestic China companies were listed abroad, 126 of them in Hong Kong. A Securities Law enacted in 1998 was updated in 2005.

The evolution of share-owning capitalism in China has led to the creation of a number of different categories of share:

- *A shares*, which are listed in China and can be held and traded only by residents of China. They are denominated in the Chinese currency renminbi
- *B shares*, which are also listed in China and denominated in renminbi, but designated for foreign investors and traded in foreign currency. In recent years the prices of A and B shares have been converging, and the intention is for the distinctions eventually to disappear
- *H shares*, which are shares of China based companies listed on the Hong Kong Stock Exchange. The highest rated H shares are known as red chips
- *N shares*, which are shares of China based companies listed on the New York Stock Exchange
- *L shares*, which are shares of China based companies listed on the London Stock Exchange

In the early days, many listed companies were dominated by their majority internal shareholders, who tended to represent state, provincial, or local governments. They nominated the directors for confirmation by the other shareholders. Board membership overlapped management, control by insiders was a widespread problem, and the major shareholders controlled shareholders meetings. Sometimes this governance structure enabled dominant shareholders to transfer interests and make connected (related-party) deals with the company at the expense of medium and small shareholders.

The roles and responsibilities of key players were often unclear and internal management control measures were not clearly established. Since the duties of the board and top management were often vague, the chairman sometimes usurped the chief executive's role, and the chief executive encroached on the work of the chief operations officer and divisional heads. In some cases, information was manipulated, delayed, even falsified. Performance assessment of individual directors was immature and not necessarily linked to incentives. Reviews of the performance of the board and its committees were rarely undertaken. Worse, the supposedly independent audit firms were not experienced and not always independent, sometimes hiding rather than disclosing financial problems.

A World Bank/IFC survey in 1999 of 257 companies listed on the Shanghai Stock Exchange found that two-thirds of all directors were executive directors most holding senior management positions, less than 5 percent had any degree of independence, and very few companies had yet to establish audit committees.

In 2001, the China Securities Regulatory Commission (CSRC) formulated some basic norms of corporate governance, promoting the separation of listed companies from controlling shareholders. These CSRC proposals included guidelines for establishing independent boards of directors in listed companies. At least one-third of the board should consist of independent directors, and include at least one accounting professional, although initially there was a lack of suitable people. Independent directors could be nominated by the board of directors, the board of supervisors, or any shareholders holding 5 percent of the shares. China also became a member of the World Trade Organization in 2001.

In 2002, a Code of Corporate Governance for listed companies was formulated. This included basic principles for the protection of investors' rights, basic behaviour rules, and standards for directors, supervisors, and senior management. The code was intended to be the major measuring standard for evaluating listed companies' corporate governance structure.

A guidance note issued by the CSRC in 2002 required each listed company to have at least two independent directors and by June 2003 at least one-third of the board should be independent directors. In 2005, CSRC allowed listed companies to remunerate managers with shares and stock options.

In 2006, a fundamental review of Chinese company law was enacted, creating two types of limited company—the limited liability company (LLC private companies) and the joint stock company (JSC public companies), bringing the legal context much in line with the company law of other countries. For example, the responsibilities of company (board) secretaries were established. A new corporate bankruptcy law was enacted in 2007 which applied to SOEs, foreign investment enterprises, and domestic companies.

Contemporary Corporate Governance in China

Over the past twenty years China has achieved remarkable economic growth, becoming the largest and fastest growing emerging country economy in the world. This reflects the policy of economic reforms progressively shifting from a centralized command-economy to a market economy. Consequently there has been a decline in state-owned enterprises, although the state typically maintains a significant ownership share and influence in the privatized companies.

The broad structure of governance of listed companies in China is shown in the following figure 8.1. Typically the state is the controlling shareholder.

China has created a unique form of corporate governance structure—a management board of directors, with some independent outside directors, and a board of supervisors, with both employee and other members—thus combining elements of both the German-style two-tier board model and the unitary board use of independent outside directors, as well as recognizing China's traditional concept of employees being masters of enterprises.

However, unlike the German model, which calls for an equal number of shareholder and employee representatives under the German co-determination law, Chinese company law

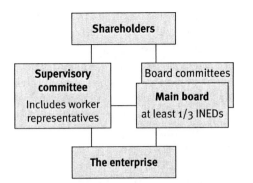

Figure 8.1 The board structure of governance of listed companies in China

does not specify the proportion of shareholders' representatives and employees' representatives on boards of supervisors, other than requiring at least a third to be worker representatives, with corporate charters stipulating the proportion.

Moreover, whereas the supervisory board in the German model sits between the shareholders and the management board, in the Chinese model the supervisory board has no responsibility on the shareholders behalf for return on investment. Neither does the supervisory board in China have the power to hire and fire directors as in the German case. Consequently the supervisory power of the Chinese supervisory board is relatively soft and seeks to act through influence.

Some commentators have suggested that China's model is more closely aligned to the Japanese model, which although essentially a unitary board system provides for the independent outside directors on the board to form a separate committee outside the board.

The following figure 8.2 attempts to differentiate the models:

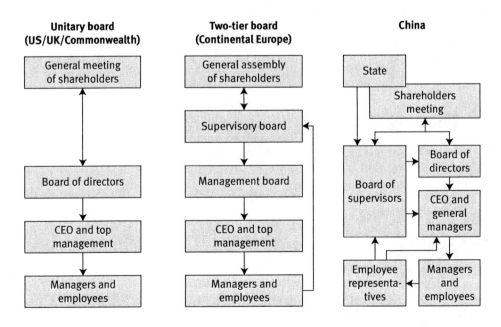

Figure 8.2 Differentiation of models of corporate governance

Officially, the board of supervisors oversees finances, ensures the due diligence of directors and senior management personnel, safeguards company assets, reduces company's risks, and protects shareholders' interests. The board of supervisors can nominate an external auditing firm to the shareholders' meeting and members have the right to inquire about the operating status of the company under an obligation of confidentiality. If necessary, the board of supervisors can hire independent institutions to assist in the committee's work. In practice, leaders of companies' political party committees have tended to take the chair and vice chair of their companies' boards of supervisors.

However, as Professor Tong Lu, Director of the Chinese Center for Corporate Governance, at the Chinese Academy of Social Sciences has written: '*supervisory boards are often more "decorative" than functional . . . . with room for improvement in their effectiveness*'. Boards of supervisors generally meet less often than boards of directors and their meetings are less well attended. Published announcements by supervisory boards show that they rarely contest decisions made by boards of directors and company executives. Moreover, boards of supervisors are often unable to supervise directors and managers because their members have less professional experience and education.

Listed companies now are required to disclose information regarding corporate governance including (but not limited to):

- The members and structure of the board of directors and the supervisory board
- The performance and evaluation of the board of directors and the supervisory board
- The performance and evaluation of the independent directors, including their attendance at board of directors' meetings, their issuance of independent opinions, and their opinions regarding related party transactions and appointment and removal of directors and senior management personnel
- The composition and work of the specialized committees of the board of directors
- The actual state of corporate governance of the company, the gap between the company's corporate governance and the Codes, and the reasons for the gap
- Specific plans and measures to improve corporate governance

The State's Control of Listed Companies

The state at the national or provincial level has maintained ownership control of most of China's listed companies. In other words the overall regulatory structure can be depicted as shown in figure 8.3:

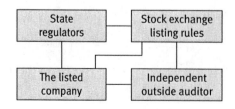

Figure 8.3 The overall regulatory structure

The lines of control from various state and provincial authorities can be numerous, as reflected in figure 8.4:

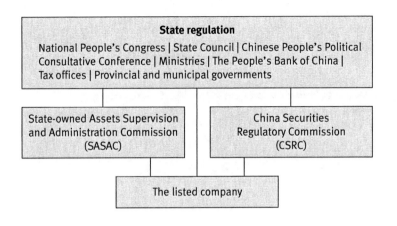

State regulation

National People's Congress | State Council | Chinese People's Political Consultative Conference | Ministries | The People's Bank of China | Tax offices | Provincial and municipal governments

State-owned Assets Supervision and Administration Commission (SASAC)

China Securities Regulatory Commission (CSRC)

The listed company

Figure 8.4 The lines of control

The People's Bank of China, the tax offices, the ministry responsible for the industry in which the company operates, and other state and provincial officials act in what they see as the interests of the state and the people, for example, by regulating supplies and prices, taking action to avoid unacceptable economic or social stress including unemployment, bankruptcy, corruption, financial pressures on the state economy, or undesirable competition between state enterprises.

The State-owned Assets Supervision and Administration Commission of the State Council (SASAC) holds the China Government's shareholding in all China's listed companies (other than those in the finance sector). In 2008, total assets were over US$1.56 trillion. So SASAC is the largest institutional shareholder in the world, with eight in the *Fortune* list of the world's top 500 companies. SASAC ensures that the State's interests are represented in the activities of China's listed companies, including the appointment of directors and top executives to state majority owned companies.

A 2006 mandate from SASAC called for governance reforms in large SOEs, including the creation of boards with outside directors, sound internal controls, and comprehensive enterprise risk management. SASAC is a Commission of the State Council and wields considerable power over the SOEs.

The China Securities Regulatory Commission of the State Council (CSRC) is the Chinese Government's corporate regulator. CSRC issues the corporate governance code and other corporate governance regulations, and publishes regular reports on corporate governance reform and performance in China. CSRC also liaises closely with the management of the stock exchanges in Shanghai and Shenzen, and with those exchanges overseas which list China stock. The CSRC is a regulatory body, with powers analogous to the SEC in the United States, with the prime aim of investor protection.

The Governance of Other China Companies

Of course, the dawning of the market economy in China has also produced many private enterprises (PEs) and foreign-invested enterprises (FIEs), many of them joint ventures with Chinese partners. A 2007 study by the executive-search firm Heidrick & Struggles with Fudan University pointed out that Chinese boards vary significantly depending on whether they are SOEs, PEs, or FIEs.

The study found that the board structures varied as follows:

Table 8.2 **Variation in Chinese boards between SOEs, PEs, or FIEs**

n =	Type of enterprise	Shareholder directors	Independent directors	Executive directors	Employee directors
40	State-owned (SOE)	40%	31%	24%	5%
21	Private enterprises (PE)	23%	29%	45%	3%
21	Foreign-invested enterprises (FIE)	51%	26%	23%	0

Source: Study by Heidrick & Struggles with Fudan University, 2007.

On PE boards they found that '*like Chinese society, patriarchy prevails*', similar to the cultural context of the Asian family based model already discussed. '*The tendency of a weak board and strong chairman is common, and boards tend to be tight-knot groups built on business or personal networks. Independent directors tend to be brought in to fulfil legal requirements and are limited to advisory roles.*' In foreign-invested enterprises the high proportion of shareholder directors reflected the interests of local and overseas investors and joint venture partners. Employee directors in SOEs, the report suggested were often opposed to corporate reform, resulting in protracted negotiations on the board. The independent directors were drawn principally from universities (35%), the professions (25%), the relevant industry (21%), and government (15%). Very few directors were foreign nationals and those that were tended to come from Taiwan or Hong Kong. The average board size of the SOEs and FIEs in the study was nine.

On separating the roles of chairman and CEO, predictably, the SOEs were more likely to split the roles as shown in the following table:

Table 8.3 **The likelihood of separation or combination of roles of chairman and CEO by SOEs, PEs, and FIEs**

n =	Type of enterprise	Chairman split from CEO	Chairman/CEO combined
40	State-owned (SOE)	74%	26%
21	Private enterprises (PE)	62%	36%
21	Foreign-invested enterprises (FIE)	57%	43%

The Future of Corporate Governance in China

Two decades ago Chinese corporate governance was virtually non-existent. Given the dramatic and sustained economic growth since, the CSRC has done a remarkable job in developing law, rules, and regulation, and introducing appropriate corporate governance attitudes. China is also attempting to bring its accounting and auditing rules in line with international standards, whilst making allowances for SOEs in a transitional economy.

But challenges still remain. The CSRC suffers from being both the promoter of the investment market and its regulator, although this can be the case in other markets, too. A potential overlap in the jurisdiction of SASAC and CSRC also has to be resolved. Other problems include the identification, training, and development of independent directors; the potential influence of members of the Communist party, particularly where directors are also members of a company's Party Committee; and changing attitudes from the previous centralized state directed decision making to a market orientated perspective.

The legal system, although it has ancient traditions, is somewhat lacking in transparency and predictability. The training of judges is embryonic. The opportunity to bring private legal action against companies is limited, although a new contract arbitration law was enacted in 2008, which set up a framework for resolving disputes. The Supreme People's Court and the People's Courts around the country act primarily in what is seen as the interests of the people, in other words, of the state. The recognition of contractual and corporate relationships tends to be limited, and enforcing legal judgments can be problematic.

Although corruption and rigorous penalties (including the death penalty) for wrongdoers are widely reported in the Chinese press, the law against commercial corruption is not widely enforced. China lacks an independent body to fight corruption, such as the Independent Commission against Corruption in the Hong Kong SAR. Groups of highly placed executives and bureaucrats, as well as individuals at all levels, can be involved. Expropriation, poor accounting, insider dealing, market manipulation, and fraud remain potential risks.

Future directions for corporate governance in China, according to Li Zhaoxi,[1] are towards emphasizing the power of shareholders with the 'insiders' losing their ability to dominate, and reviewing the supervisory system, which is increasingly seen as rather ineffective, towards a unitary model with the supervisory role assumed by the audit committee of independent directors.

Case Study 8.3 China Sinopec

China Petroleum & Chemical Corporation (Sinopec) is a China-based integrated energy and chemical company. Sinopec was set up in 2000, under the Company Law of the People's Republic of China, and that year issued 16.78 billion shares in Hong Kong, New York, and London, raising close to US$3.4 billion. In 2001, the company floated a further 2.8 billion 'A' shares on Shanghai Stock Exchange. In 2007, Sinopec's total number of shares was 86.7 billion, of which 75.84 percent was held by the State, 19.35 percent by international share holders, and 4.81 percent by investors in China.

---

[1] Li Zhaoxi, Enterprise Research Institute, Development Research Centre of the State Council, 2007.

The business covers oil and gas exploration, development, production, and marketing; oil refining; production and sales of petrochemicals, chemical fibres, chemical fertilizers, and other chemical products. It is China's largest producer of oil products and major petrochemical products and the second largest producer of crude oil. Sinopec is a dominant brand in China, and its gas stations, which are modern with courteous staff, are found around the country. Sinopec was ranked 17th in the Global Top 500, by its core assets and operating revenue, in the *Fortune* magazine list of 2006.

Similar to its international peers, Sinopec has set up a standardized structure of corporate governance and adopted a management system of centralized decision making, delegated authorities in management and business operations handled by specialized business units. It has more than eighty subsidiaries and branches including wholly owned, equity holding, and equity participating companies, engaging in oil and gas exploration and production, refining, chemicals, marketing, R&D, and foreign trade.

Sinopec bases its corporate governance on the Code of Corporate Governance for Listed Companies issued by the China Securities and Regulatory Commission (CSRC), the Company Law of the People's Republic of China, the mandatory provisions for the Articles of Association of Companies to be listed overseas, the guidelines for the Articles of Association of Listed Companies, standards of Corporate Governance of Listed Companies, Sinopec's Articles of Association, and other governing regulations in the countries where Sinopec is listed. In China, the regulation and enforcement of a company's corporate governance is primarily the responsibility of the Board of Directors and the Supervisory Committee.

Prior to it's listing, Sinopec restructured its board to satisfy both overseas regulators and the state government. It installed a two-tier system with a Board of Directors and a Supervisory Board (which Sinopec translates in English as the supervisory committee).

The Board of Directors has eleven members, with a chairman, a vice-chairman, a president, three senior vice presidents, two executive directors, and three independent non-executive directors.

There is an audit committee, which reports to the management board, not to the supervisory committee. The supervisory committee has nine members, with a chairman, four employee representative supervisors, and four other members.

(For more information on Sinopec see their informative website
http://english.sinopec.com/investor_center/)

Discussion Question

1. What is your opinion of the corporate governance structure at Sinopec? Consider the role of the Supervisory Committee, its relationship with the Board of Directors, and (unlike the Continental European model of the two-tier board) the inclusion of three independent non-executive members.

Corporate Governance in Russia

Some of the Eastern European transitional economies, including Hungary, Poland, and the previous Eastern Germany, took a similar approach to China in privatizing their state enterprises creating companies whose shares were sold to external strategic investors, often foreign investment institutions.

Russia, however, along with Bulgaria and the Czech Republic, took a different approach. Many Russian citizens were dubious about privatization, holding old soviet beliefs that industry should be run by the state, that everyone should be guaranteed a job, and that incomes should be controlled. Recognizing the need to overcome such resistance and make changes irreversible, during the 1990s, the state attempted to transfer ownership to the people through three forms of voucher privatization:

(1) The free distribution of vouchers to all Russian citizens, which could be exchanged for company shares or invested in voucher investment funds. Although all citizens were supposed to have equal shares, insiders often benefited, particularly incumbent management who were given bonus shares to overcome resistance.

(2) Investment tenders, in which investors had to make substantial investments to redevelop companies. There was little or no state monitoring or control, which led to deception, with investment proposals that were not undertaken or fictitious.

(3) Loan-for-shares auctions—the government provided finance from the federal budget for the purchase of shares in public companies that were put up for auction, such as Yukos, Sibneft, and Lukoil. Fraudulent practices, violence, and social injustice were rife and many of the major businesses that emerged were dominated by relatively few people, many of them now very rich. Small banks evolved into major financial institutions and industrial groups.

Ownership concentration was high, typically involving the previous managers. The minority shareholders, who included members of the public and foreign investment institutions, saw their rights violated by these dominant interests.

Some Russian companies were floated on foreign stock exchanges, mainly London and New York. Of course, these companies had to comply with the listing agreements reflecting the corporate governance requirements of the countries concerned, including independent directors, board committees, and corporate governance compliance reports.

The first federal law on joint-stock companies in Russia was enacted in 1995, followed by securities laws in 1996, and laws on the protection of rights and legal interests of investors in the securities market three years later in 1999. Shareholders with at least 2 percent of the voting rights gained the right to introduce items to the agenda of shareholders' meetings and to nominate candidates for the board. Shareholders with 1 percent could file a complaint against the board or specific directors for damages to the company caused by their actions. In 1998, a new bankruptcy law was enacted.

But there were problems with implementation, not least because many directors felt that they owed their allegiance, not to the shareholders as a whole, but to the controlling shareholders who had nominated and in effect appointed them. Although the law called for directors to act reasonably and in good faith towards the company, neither directors nor the courts had relevant experience. Moreover, state interests could take precedence. The need for director training and board development was apparent.

In the early stages of privatization, the state was inevitably involved in the process, but companies tended to adopt the unitary board structure, with some independent outside directors, reflecting the US and UK/Commonwealth models based on the rule of law and regulation by the stock market. Unfortunately, the company and securities law that was enacted did not reflect the way companies were typically run.

But in 1998, Russia faced a major financial crisis, the state defaulted on government bonds, the currency was devalued, and rising oil prices provided the opportunity for the existing owners to consolidate their control.

Faced with the domination of many boards by insider and controlling shareholder interests and widespread corruption, there was a call for better understanding of corporate governance. In 2000, a Centre for Business Ethics and Corporate Governance was founded to encourage corporate governance reform in Russia. The OECD, through their Centre for Co-operation with Non-members, offered advice and created the Russian Corporate Governance Roundtable, which brought together an influential network of Russian and international policy makers. The Roundtable produced a white paper for reform in corporate governance in Russia in 2002 and a report on improving the transparency of related

---

Case Study 8.4 Gazprom

Gazprom is the largest natural gas company in the world, supplying the entire needs of Eastern Europe and a large percentage of the gas used in Turkey, Austria, Germany, Italy, and France. It is the largest company in Russia and the third largest in the world by market capitalization.

In the days of the Soviet Union, Gazprom was part of the oil and gas ministry but was incorporated as a company in 1992. Gazprom was partially privatized in 1994, the state retaining 40 percent. Workers and management received 15 percent and other shares were offered to Russian citizens through the voucher system. But trading was regulated and the balance was sold by investment tender, which management was able to control. Evidence emerged of abuse by controlling shareholders, dubious trading, and asset-stripping to entities controlled by friends and relatives. In 1996, Gazprom offered 1 percent of its equity to investors abroad and equity in the form of London Depository Receipts and a large bond issue in the US, which were successful.

The close relationship with government, which existed during the presidency of Boris Yeltsin, was strengthened when Vladimir Putin assumed the role. (See the Yukos case for more information.) Reforms in management and changes at board level occurred. In 2001, Gazprom acquired NTV the Russian independent television station and, in 2005, purchased Izvestia the influential Russian newspaper. Its attempts to buy Yukos and Rosneft, two other influential energy companies, failed. In 2005, Gazprom acquired Sibneft thus consolidating its position as a global energy giant.

The Gazprom Board of Directors has eleven members: the chairman is the First Deputy Prime Minister of the Russian Federation and the deputy chairman is the Chairman of the Gazprom Management Committee. The Management Committee has seventeen members, the heads of various group operating companies and functional sections.

(For more information see www.gazprom.com)

Discussion Questions

1. What is your overall impression of the privatization process employed by Gazprom?

2. How might it have been improved?

Case Study 8.5 Yukos

The Yukos Oil Company, founded by Mikhail B. Khodorkovsky in 1993, acquired vast assets from the privatization of Russia's state enterprises. Yukos owned and operated oil and gas fields, oil refineries, and pipelines across Russia and Central Europe and was the largest non-state oil company in Russia, producing around 20 percent of Russian oil. At its peak in mid-2003, Yukos was worth more than US$40 billion.

But within two years the company had been seized by the state with the company claiming '*an unprecedented campaign of illegal, discriminatory and disproportionate tax claims escalating into raids and confiscation, culminating in intimidation and arrests . . .*' and Mikhail Khodorkovsky was in jail in Siberia. The Yukos story is long, complex, and still controversial. In this vignette case we see the need for the state's approval for the exercise of corporate governance power.

The Yeltsin Years

Following the dissolution of the Soviet Union, Boris Yeltsin became President of Russia in 1991, with a mission to turn a Communist centrally planned economy into a capitalist market economy. The 1990s proved to be a turbulent period in Russian history. The economic reforms came too slowly and the living standards of many people were devastated, especially those dependent on Soviet-era state subsidies.

In 1998, Russia's economy collapsed, bringing economic chaos, humiliation, and suffering. The state was unable to pay its workers. With their personal savings destroyed, millions of Russians were plunged into poverty. The currency fell 70 percent, Russia defaulted on its foreign debt, and the International Monetary Fund (IMF) bailed the country out with loans of US$40 billion, but with demanding conditions.

However, a few people were able to enrich themselves during the decade. Called oligarchs, or the 'novi Russki', they benefited from the privatization of Russian state assets. They became super-rich, lived extravagantly, imported expensive cars, and travelled the world. The era also saw the rise of a middle class, unthinkable in soviet days. Unexpectedly Yeltsin resigned at the end of 1999, passing the presidency to Vladimir Putin, a former secret service chief.

The Putin Era

Putin's first term of office was a significant success. He was able to end the chaotic excesses of the Yeltsin years and brought millions out of poverty. Under the watchful eye of the IMF, Russia repaid her international loans. The people developed a new confidence and in 2004, Putin was re-elected with a huge majority.

As the journal *Prospect* said in 2005:

> Putin agrees that the Soviet system did not work, but still calls its collapse a tragedy. He is probably closer to the thoughts and feelings of ordinary people than any other Russian leader in history. Putin has never disguised his intention to build a modified version of the authoritarian, centralised Russian state under which the Russians have been governed, mostly badly, for six centuries . . .

Inevitably, Putin saw the privatized entities as a problem and thought that the oligarchs were a potential threat to his plans.

Yukos and Mikhail Khodorkovsky

In 2003, Mikhail Khodorkovsky was said to be Russia's richest man. In August 2003, Yukos announced an agreement to combine Yukos with Sibneft, Russia's 5th largest oil company, 73 percent owned by the Russian state company Gazprom. Sibneft was led by billionaire oligarch Roman Abramovich, Governor of Russia's remote Chuotka region, owner of London's Chelsea football club, and claimed by *Forbes* magazine now to be Russia's richest man with US$14.7 billion.

In 2004, Khodorkovsky was charged with seven counts of fraud, embezzlement, forgery, and tax evasion following a raid on his office and the seizure of about half of the company's stock by the Russian authorities. Yukos was charged with tax evasion, although the company claimed its use of tax havens was legal at the time. Khodorkovsky was found guilty and jailed in October 2004. He repeatedly described his imprisonment as a political strike against him by President Vladimir Putin resulting from his interest in seeking the Russian presidency. Some of the stock was returned, and it was traded again on international exchanges.

Khodorkovsky resigned as CEO of Yukos in November 2004. His shares in the company were frozen by prosecutors. The assets of Yukos were then confiscated by the Russian revenue authorities and sold to state-company Gazprom and Rosneft for US $80 billion, including the business Yugansk—the crown jewel of Yukos, and assets in a Netherlands holding company. Rosneft shares were listed in London in July 2006.

The Council of Europe complained: '*Intimidating action by different law-enforcement agencies against Yukos and its business partners and other institutions linked to Mr Khodorkovsky and his associates and the careful preparation of this action in terms of public relations, taken together, give a picture of a co-ordinated attack by the state.*'

In 2006, the company GML, formerly Menatep (a majority international shareholder in Yukos) brought a lawsuit in the United States against the Russian Federation, demanding US$50 billion, accusing the Kremlin of discrimination against Yukos, for example valuing Yugansk on the basis of an oil price of US$30 a barrel, although the current price was US$70. The action failed because of problems of jurisdiction.

In 2006, Yukos creditors rejected a rescue plan and voted to make Yukos bankrupt, recognizing that it would be impossible to restore solvency; Rosneft took the remaining assets.

The Future

The rise in oil prices around the world, driven by production scarcity and rapidly growing demand in China and India, brought significant economic benefits to Russia, which was now flush with reserves. A new confidence pervaded the country and its leaders. Energy was used as a powerful instrument of foreign policy, replacing the Soviet Union's previous military power. Directors of some of these state enterprises were colleagues of Putin in his earlier career, members of the former secret police, '*siloviki*'. Gazprom, the state holding company for oil and gas assets played a major role in this strategy.

Discussion Question

1. What lessons might be learned from the Yukos case about corporate governance in Russia?

party transactions in 2005. The International Finance Corporation, working with the World Bank, also produced a corporate governance manual for Russia including drafts for a corporate charter, director contracts, and by-laws on shareholder meetings, the corporate secretary, proxy voting and the board of directors. Russia also formed an Independent Directors Association.

Under the company law and corporate governance code recommendations, companies are governed by the general shareholders meeting which elects the members of the board through cumulative voting, a board of directors (sometimes confusingly called the supervisory board) with both independent directors and management directors, and an executive (or management) committee. The audit committee reports to the board, whose chairman is not allowed to be the head of the executive committee.

Today there is more transparency, standards for corporate governance are more widely understood, many of the original managers have been changed, and loss through unfair practices has been reduced.

But with the presidency of Vladimir Putin, the role of the state has expanded and government influence over some companies has increased. Some ownership has been transferred back to the state by expropriation or by acquisition in the market. For a discussion of the state's role in corporate governance in Russia see the Gazprom and Yukos cases that follow.

Corporate Governance in India

As with China and Russia, history has played a part in the development of corporate governance in India. Originally a member of the British Empire ('the jewel in the crown'), like Hong Kong and Singapore, India benefited from the early creation of government administrative processes, with the rule of law including a body of company law backed by a reliable judiciary. A drawback was the accompanying bureaucracy.

Following independence the country took a socialist road, with large state-owned enterprises and the public sector dominating the economy. Bureaucracy grew and inefficiency, corruption, and nepotism flourished.

By the 1990s, the need for India to develop its business infrastructure and attract capital was recognized. Better corporate governance of companies and improved regulation of its stock markets was needed. In 1992, Parliament created the Securities and Exchange Board of India.

The first corporate governance code was published in 1998, but by the Confederation of Indian Industry (CII) entitled *Desirable Corporate Governance*. Unlike codes in some other countries, the CII code did not make statements of principle but addressed specific business issues in India. Focused on the governance of listed companies, the code called for '*professionally competent, independent non-executive directors*' to constitute at least 30 percent of the board if the chairman is a non-executive director and at least 50 percent where the chairman and the managing director were the same person. Non-executive directors should '*play a material role in corporate decision making and maximising long-term shareholder value (becoming) active participants in boards, not passive advisers*'. No one should hold directorships in more than ten listed companies. The code also called for audit committees. The code was exhortatory and was not endorsed by the regulatory body, or incorporated into the listing rules.

A year later in 1999, a government committee, chaired by Shri Kumar Manalam Biria, a businessman, released India's National Code on Corporate Governance. Reflecting international standards, the code was approved by the Securities and Exchange Board of India (SEBI) and incorporated into stock exchange listing rules.

Corporate governance standards in India's top-tier listed companies, such as Infosys and the major banks, are high. As we have seen, the original 1998 code was the outcome of voluntary action by the Confederation of Indian Industry. But this commitment is not yet general. Small and medium capital companies are largely unconvinced of the value of corporate governance activities and expenditures.

As in other parts of the world, interest in corporate governance in India was a reaction to corporate scandals, often involving stock price manipulation, for example the Harshad Mehta scam and the so-called vanishing company scam. As the Central Vigilance Commissioner, N. Vittal, said in the Tata Memorial Lecture in 2002:

I find that the legal and administrative environment in India provides excellent scope for corrupt practices in business. As a result unless a management is committed to be honest and observe the principles of propriety, the atmosphere is too tempting to observe good corporate governance in practice.

The government set up a task force in 2000, under the chairmanship of Dr Sanjeev Reddy, to 'sharpen India's global competitive edge'. In 2002, reflecting international concern at the fall-out from the USA Enron debacle, the government set up a high-level committee chaired by Shri Naresh Chandra to examine corporate auditing and independent directors. The report called for independent directors to represent at least 50 percent of the board of listed companies, strengthened the definition of independence and called for the rotation of audit partners (but not audit firms).

A further committee, chaired by Shri Narayana Murthy, chairman of Infosys, was set up in 2003 by the Securities and Exchange Board (SEBI) to 'evaluate the adequacy of existing corporate governance practices'. Audit committees, risk management, director remuneration, codes of conduct, and the role of independent directors were all addressed.

The Indian Companies Act of 1956 was amended in 1999 to improve shareholder rights, and in 2000 to require audit committees. In 2002, a committee reported on a revision of the 1956 Act. In 2005, an expert committee on company law, chaired by Dr J. J. Irani of Tata Industries, reported but has not yet led to a new act.

In 2007, the government issued guidelines on corporate governance in central public sector enterprises covering the composition of boards, audit committees, management of group companies, accounting standards, and risk management.

In many companies in India, those in the public sector, multinationals, and private sector companies, boards find themselves dominated by majority shareholders. Pre-emption rights for minority shareholders are frequently ignored. Competent regulators and capital market action are needed to protect minority investors.

A corporate governance rating by the Asian Corporate Governance Association in 2007 assessed India's corporate governance as 'fair to poor'. As can be seen from the efforts listed above, corporate governance standards and regulations have improved over the years, but implementation of regulations and the application of best practices have tended to be slower. The formation of committees has generated more enthusiasm than the application of their recommendations.

Corruption remains entrenched, not least in government administration. India ranked seventy out of 150 countries in the 2006 index of corruption perceptions. Distrust of government is high, with bureaucracy and red tape sometimes stifling entrepreneurial flair. The Ministry of Company Affairs and the Securities and Exchange Board need more competent staff experienced in corporate governance matters. But the rapid economic growth and potential of India suggest that the next few years will see significant changes in both attitude and practice.

Corporate Governance in the Middle East

The states that are typically grouped together as the Middle East and North Africa (MENA) are:

Table 8.4 **The MENA states**

Algeria	Jordan	Morocco	Tunisia
Bahrein	Kuwait	Oman	United Arab Emirates (Abu Dhabi, Dubai, and five other states)
Egypt	Lebanon	Qatar	

Broadly, these countries have relatively low GDPs and slow industrial growth. In recent years the oil producing countries, benefiting from rising oil prices, have generated large surpluses, which have been deposited abroad. Banking reforms have attempted to channel some of these savings into local growth, but domestic financial markets are emergent. States also appreciate the need to attract inward investment and, therefore, recognize the importance of sound corporate governance. The capital markets are emergent, small, and illiquid. Consequently the market for corporate control is poor. Of course there are exceptions to such general observations: for example Dubai is making massive investments in tourism and property, whilst attempting to become an international financial centre.

Businesses in the region can be typified as having:

- Concentrated ownership, with strong family ownership of both private and listed companies or state ownership
- Dominant family oversight and control, with leadership from the head of the family, entrepreneurial decision making, opaque communications, and relationship based trading
- Debt financing in which bank financing is often more than shareholders' equity
- Banking sector equity investment, with banks holding significant shares in companies

The legal underpinnings around the region vary interestingly. In the Gulf States, Egypt, and Jordan jurisdictions are orientated towards common law, reflecting earlier UK/ Commonwealth influences. Elsewhere, jurisdictions have adopted European style civil law. Throughout the region, company and securities laws exist but are evolving to meet changing circumstances. But the most significant legal influence is the over-arching Islamic

Shariah law introducing religious rules and interpretations, which can affect attitudes towards contracts, property rights, and borrowing. Essentially, finance is based on the principle that charging interest is improper and that both sides of a deal must share risks.

The framework for corporate governance is broadly in place, although development is at an early stage and implementation and enforcement varied. Government securities commissions have also created different sets of rules.

The Organisation for Economic Co-operation and Development, through the MENA/OECD Investment Programme has sponsored an important study of corporate governance in the region, analysing the position in each country and recommending developments. Essentially, the OECD has recommended the adoption of rule based corporate governance because of the state of financial markets, the lack of experience, and poor corporate discipline. In other words, they call for legal and regulatory control not self-control by management, shareholders, and creditors (for detailed information see www.oecd.org/mena/investment).

Corporate Governance: Convergence or Differentiation?

Are corporate governance practices around the world converging? This is a question that is often posed by corporate governance practitioners, and frequently answered in the affirmative. Certainly, there are many forces that could lead towards convergence, as the following factors show:

(1) *Corporate governance codes of good practice* around the world have a striking similarity, which is not surprising given the way they have been influenced by each other. Though different in detail, all emphasize the importance of independence, transparency, and accountability. The codes published by international bodies, such as the World Bank, the Commonwealth of Nations, and OECD, clearly encourage convergence. The corporate governance policies and practices of major corporations operating around the world can also be global influences.

(2) *Securities regulations* for the world's listed companies are certainly converging. The International Organisation of Securities Commissions (IOSCO), which now has the bulk of the world's securities regulatory bodies in membership, encourages convergence. For example, its members have agreed to exchange information on unusual trades, thus making the activities of global insider trading more hazardous.

(3) *International accounting standards* are also leading towards convergence. The International Accounting Standards Committee (IASC) and the International Auditing Practices Committee (IPAC) have close links with IOSCO and are further forces working towards international harmonization and standardization of financial reporting and auditing standards. US General Accepted Accounting Principles (GAAP), though some way from harmonization, are clearly moving in that direction.

In 2007, the US Securities and Exchange Commission announced that US companies could adopt international accounting standards in lieu of US GAAPs. However, American accountants and regulators are accustomed to a rule based regime and international standards are principles based requiring judgement rather than adherence to prescriptive regulations.

(4) *Global concentration of audit practices* into just four firms, since the demise of Arthur Andersen, encourages convergence. Major corporations in most countries, wanting to have the name of one of the four principal firms on their audit reports, are then inevitably locked into that firm's worldwide audit, risk analysis, and other governance practices.

(5) *Globalization* of companies is also, obviously, a force for convergence. Firms that are truly global in strategic outlook, with production, service provision, added-value chain, markets, and customers worldwide, calling on international sources of finance, whose shares are held around the world, are moving towards common effective, transparent, and accountable governance practices. Unfortunately, the composition of the boards of the parent companies of such groups seldom reflects such globalization, being still dominated by nationals of the country of incorporation. However, the proportion of 'foreign' directors (i.e. not nationals of the home country), though small, has been increasing. Companies such as Arcelor incorporated in Belgium, Novartis in Switzerland, Cable and Wireless in the UK, and ABN Amro in the Netherlands do have a significant proportion of directors who are not from the 'home country'. Significantly, no companies incorporated in the United States figure in this list.

(6) *Raising capital on overseas stock exchanges* clearly encourages convergence as listing companies are required to conform to the listing rules of that market. Although the governance requirements of stock exchanges around the world differ in detail, they are moving towards internationally accepted norms through IOSCO, as we saw above. Cross-border mergers of stock exchanges, for example the links between New York and Euronext (Paris, Brussels, Lisbon, Amsterdam), accelerate this trend.

(7) *International institutional investors*, such as CalPers, explicitly demand various corporate governance practices if they are to invest in a specific country or company. Institutional investors with an international portfolio have been an important force for convergence. As developing and transitional countries grow, generate, and plough back their own funds, of course, the call for inward investment will decline, along with the influence of the overseas institutions.

(8) *Research publications, international conferences and professional journals* can also be significant contributors to the convergence of corporate governance thinking and practice.

However, despite all these forces pushing towards convergence, there are others which, if not direct factors for divergence, at least cause differentiation between countries, jurisdictions, and markets.

(9) *Legal differences* in company law, contract law, and bankruptcy law between jurisdictions affect corporate governance practices. Differences between the case law traditions of the US, UK, and Commonwealth countries, the codified law of Continental Europe, Japan, and China distinguish corporate governance outcomes, as we have seen.

(10) *Standards in the legal process*, too, can differ. Some countries have weak judicial systems. Their courts may have limited powers and be unreliable. Not all judiciaries are separate from the legislature. The state or political activities can be involved in

jurisprudence. In some countries bringing a company law case can be difficult and, even with a favourable judgment, obtaining satisfaction well nigh impossible.

(11) *Stock market differences* in market capitalization, liquidity, and markets for corporate control affect governance practices, as we saw earlier. Obviously, financial markets vary significantly in their scale and sophistication, affecting their governance influence.

(12) *Ownership structures* also vary between countries, with some countries having predominantly family based firms, others have external investors but the proportion of individual against institutional investors differ, whilst some adopt complex networked, chained, or pyramid structures.

(13) *History, culture, and ethnic groupings* have produced different board structures and governance practices, as we have also seen. Contrasts between corporate governance in Japan with her *keiretsu*, Continental European countries, with the two-tier board structures and worker co-determination, and the family domination of overseas Chinese, even in listed companies, in countries throughout the Far East, emphasizes the differences. Views differ on ownership rights and the basis of shareholder power.

The concept of the company was Western, rooted in the notion of shareholder democracy, the stewardship of directors, and trust—the belief that directors recognize a fiduciary duty to their company. But today's corporate structures have outgrown that simple notion. The corporate concept is now rooted in law, and the legitimacy of the corporate entity rests on regulation and litigation. The Western world has created the most expensive and litigious corporate regulatory regime the world has yet seen. This is not the only approach; and certainly not necessarily the best. The Asian reliance on relationships and trust in governing the enterprise may be closer to the original concept. There is a need to rethink the underlying idea of the corporation, contingent with the reality of power that can (or could) be wielded. Such a concept would need to be built on a pluralistic, rather than an ethnocentric, foundation if it is to be applicable to the corporate groups and strategic alliance networks that are now emerging as the basis of the business world of the future.

Institutions Necessary for Successful Corporate Governance

Having seen some of the different ways countries and cultures apply corporate governance, we can now identify the institutional arrangements that are needed to support successful governance. These include:

- A reliable legal system including an independent judiciary, courts that are bias and corruption free, and judgments that are enforceable, free of state or other political pressures
- A stock market with liquidity, international standing, and institutional investors
- Financial institutions, including brokers, sponsors for new issues, and financial advisers
- Regulatory authorities including securities and futures market regulators
- A companies registry that facilitates comprehensive disclosure, with high levels of transparency
- Accounting and legal professions that are internationally respected, able to discipline their members, and ensure compliance with accounting standards and legal requirements

- Auditing firms that are professional, reliable, and independent of their clients
- Professional organizations such as director and company secretary qualifying and disciplining bodies
- Educational institutions able to educate and train for relevant qualifications
- Consulting organizations able to advise companies and directors
- Financial and corporate governance training, plus continuous professional development
- Corporate governance research reported in academic and professional publications

Obviously, in many countries, particularly those with emergent economies, not all of these institutions yet exist, and where they do are still in the process of being developed. Moreover, even in those countries recognized as having relatively high standards of corporate governance, there are opportunities for further development and improvement. However, taking a longitudinal view, it is interesting to see just how far many countries have come in developing their corporate governance infrastructure in a relatively few years.

REFERENCES AND SELECTED READING

Accounting Standards Steering Committee (1975) *The Corporate Report: A Discussion Paper Published for Comment.* London: Institute of Chartered Accountants in England and Wales.

Aoki, Masahiko, Gregory Jackson and Hideaki Miyajima (2007) *Corporate Governance in Japan: Institutional Change and Organizational Diversity.* New York: Oxford University Press.

Batra, Sumant, Kesar Dass and Associates (2008) *India: National Experience with Managing Related Party Transactions. The 2008 Asian Round Table on Corporate Governance.* Hong Kong: OECD.

Filatotchev, I. and M. Wright (eds.) (2005) *Corporate Governance Life-Cycle.* London: Elgar.

Hesterly, William S., Julia Liebeskind and Todd R. Zenger (1990) 'Organizational Economics: An Impending Revolution in Organization Theory?' *The Academy of Management Review,* July, 15(3).

Ho Kai Leong (ed.) (2005) *Reforming Corporate Governance in South East Asia.* Singapore: Institute of South East Asia Studies. Available at: pubsunit@iseas.edu.sg

ISI Publications (2004) *The Practitioners' Guide to Corporate Governance in Asia.* Available at: www.BooksonBiz.com

McCarthy, Daniel, Sheila Puffer and Stanislav Vladimirovich (2004) *Corporate Governance in Russia.* London: Edward Elgar Publishing.

Nader, Ralph and Mark Green (1980) *The Case for a Corporate Democracy Act of 1980.* Washington, DC: Public Citizens Congress Watch, et al.

Ohmae, Kenichi (1986) *The Mind of the Strategist.* London: Penguin.

Pfeffer, Jeffrey (1992) *Managing with Power: Politics and Influence in Organizations.* Boston, MA: Harvard Business School Press.

Spencer, Anne (1983) *On the Edge of the Organization: The Role of the Outside Director.* Hoboken, NJ: Wiley.

Steger, Ulrich (2004), *Mastering Global Corporate Governance.* Hoboken, NJ: Wiley.

Watanabee, Shigeru and Isao Yamamoto (1993) 'Corporate Governance in Japan: Ways to Improve Low Profitability', *Corporate Governance: An International Review,* October, 1(4).

World Bank and IFC (2002) *Corporate Governance in China,* Washington, DC: World Bank and IFC .

Yu Guang Hua (2007) *Comparative Corporate Governance in China.* Hong Kong: Routledge.

Zhang, Weidong (2008) *Related Transactions: Analysis of China's Listed Companies. The 2008 Asian Round Table on Corporate Governance, China.* Shanghai: OECD Hong Kong SAR, Shanghai Stock Exchange Research Center.

USEFUL WEBSITES

Worldwide

www.acga-asia.org
Asian Corporate Governance Association.

www.gcgf.org
Global Corporate Governance Forum of the World Bank.

www.ifc.org/corporategovernance
International Finance Corporation (IFC) a member of the World Bank.

www.iggn.org
The International Corporate Governance Network.

www.iosco.org
International Organisation of Securities Commissions (IOSCO).

www.oecd.org
Organisation for Economic Co-operation and Development (key 'browse' and 'topic').

Australia

www.asic.gov.au
Australian Securities and Investments Commission.

www.australian-corporate-governance.com.au
Chartered Secretaries of Australia.

www.asx.com.au
Australian Securities Exchange (ASX).

Europe

www.ecgi.org
European Corporate Governance Institute.

www.icgn.org
International Corporate Governance Network.

Asia

www.acga-asia.org
Asian Corporate Governance Association—working with investors, companies, and regulators for effective corporate governance throughout Asia.

www.adb.org
Asian Development Bank (for governance see 'topics').

www.clsa.com
CG Watch—corporate governance in Asia.

China

www.cicpa.org.cn
The Chinese Institute of Certified Public Accountants.

www.csrc.gov.cn
China Securities Regulatory Commission.

www.mof.gov.cn
Ministry of Finance.

www.pbc.gov.cn
People's Bank of China. China's central bank and banking regulator.

www.sse.com.cn
Shanghai Stock Exchange.

www.szse.cn
Shenzen Stock Exchange.

Hong Kong SAR of China

www.fstb.gov.hk
Financial Services and Treasury Bureau

www.hkex.com.hk
Hong Kong Exchange.

www.hkgem.com
Hong Kong Growth Enterprises Market.

www.hkicpa.org.hk
Hong Kong Institute of Certified Public Accountants.

www.hkics.org.hk
Institute of Chartered Secretaries.

www.hkma.gov.hk
Hong Kong Monetary Authority.

www.icac.org.hk
Independent Commission against Corruption.

www.icris.cr.gov.hk
Hong Kong Integrated Companies Registry Information System.

www.info.gov.hk/idt
Insider Dealing Tribunal in Hong Kong, describes remit and investigations.

www.sfc.hk
Securities and Futures Commission—the securities regulator.

www.webb-site.com
Commentary by David Webb on Hong Kong's corporate governance. Valuable source of reference to corporate governance in Hong Kong.

India

www.academyofcg.org

www.bseindia.com
Stock Exchange Mumbai.

www.cfcg.net
Institute of Directors' Centre for Corporate Governance.

cvc.nic.in
Central Vigilance Commission.

cbi.nic.in
Central Bureau of Investigation.

finmin.nic.in
Ministry of Finance.

www.icai.org
Institute of Chartered Accountants.

www.icsi.edu
Institute of Company Secretaries of India.

www.iodonline.com
Institute of Directors in India.

www.nseindia.com
National Stock Exchange of India.

rbi.org.in
Reserve Bank of India.

www.sebi.gov.in
Securities and Exchange Board of India.

Japan

www.fsa.go.jp
Financial Services Agency.

www.fsa.go.jp
Certified Public Accountants Oversight Board.

www.fsa.go.jp
Securities and Exchange Surveillance Commission.

www.jcgf.org
Japan Corporate Governance Forum—issued the first governance code.

www.jcgr.org
Japan Corporate Governance Research Institute.

www.mof.go.jp
Ministry of Finance in Japan.

www.keidanren.or.jp
Japanese Business Federation with information on governance in Japan.

www.rieti.go.jp
Corporate Governance Japan—on-line governance forum established by government.

www.tse.or.jp/english
Tokyo Stock Exchange.

Middle East

www.hawkamah.org
Hawkamah, The Institute for Corporate Governance.

Russia

www.cfbe.ru
Corporate Governance—Russia.

www.corp-gov.org
Corporate governance in Russia—World Bank Russia Round Table.

www.ethicsrussia.org
Centre for Business Ethics.

www.iclg.ru/english
Institute of Corporate Law and Corporate Governance—Russia.

www.nand.ru
(click on 'English') Independent Directors Association.

Russia.trade.gov/goodgovernance/CorpGovManual.asp
Russia Corporate Governance Manual—IFC and International Trade Administration (US Department of Commerce).

Singapore

www.accountants.org.sg
Singapore's national accounting profession.

www.acra.gov.sg
Companies registry and public accountants board.

www.ccdg.gov.sg
Council on Corporate Disclosure and Governance.

www.cgfrc.nus.edu.sg
National University of Singapore's Corporate Governance and Financial Reporting Centre.

www.mas.gov.sg
Monetary Authority of Singapore. Central Bank and securities regulator.

www.sgx.com
Singapore stock exchange.

www.temasekholdings.com.sg
Singapore government's investment arm.

UK

www.companieshouse.gov.uk
Registrar of Companies.

www.fsa.gov.uk
(search on 'corporate governance') Financial Services Authority.

www.icaew.co.uk
Institute of Chartered Accountants in England and Wales.

www.londonstockexchange.com
London Stock Exchange.

Note: For other corporate governance websites in the UK see lists at end of chapters.

USA

www.aicpa.org
American Institute of Certified Public Accountants.

www.cii.org
Council of Institutional Investors.

www.corp.delaware.gov
USA State of Delaware.

www.governanceprofessionals.org
American Society of Corporate Secretaries.

www.nasdaq.com
NASDAQ Stock Exchange (National Association of Securities Dealers Automated Quotation System).

www.nyse.com
New York Stock Exchange.

www.sec.gov
Securities and Exchange Commission.

Note: For other corporate governance web sites in the USA see lists at end of chapters.

PROJECTS AND EXERCISES

1. A distinction is drawn in the text between the American rule based model and the United Kingdom/Commonwealth principles based model of corporate governance. Which, if either, is likely to prevail in the long term?

2. Research the approaches that were adopted in the privatization of state enterprises in Russia and in China. What were the strengths and weaknesses of each approach? Which has been the more successful?

3. Prepare a report/presentation distinguishing the characteristics of corporate governance around the world.

SELF-TEST QUESTIONS

To confirm your grasp of the key points in this chapter try answering the following questions. Answers are at the end of the book.

1. Distinguish the Anglo-American model of corporate governance from the Continental European.

2. Does the UK or the USA have the greater proportion of individual, as against institutional, investors?

3. Describe the Japanese business network, *keiretsu*, model.

4. Name some characteristics of the Overseas Chinese family business.

5. Explain 'listing through the back door'.

6. Describe the development of strategy in a Japanese *keiretsu* company.

7. What institutions are necessary for successful corporate governance?

8. Identify some forces for convergence in corporate governance around the world.

9. Identify some forces for differentiation in corporate governance around the world.

10. What value links the original Western concept of the corporation with the contemporary Asian attitude?

9   Theories and Philosophies of Corporate Governance

....

- In which we consider
  - the agency dilemma
  - agency theory
  - transaction cost economics
  - stewardship theory
  - resource dependency theory
  - managerial and class hegemony
  - psychological and organizational perspectives
  - the societal perspective: stakeholder philosophies
  - differing boundaries and levels: systems theory
  - a subject in search of its paradigm

The Agency Dilemma

A fundamental challenge underlying all corporate governance affairs is not new, as we saw in chapter 1: '*The directors of companies, being managers of other people's money, cannot be expected to watch over it with the same vigilance with which they watch over their own*' (Smith 1776).

This is the agency problem. In its simplest form, whenever the owner of wealth (the principal) contracts with someone else (the agent) to manage his or her affairs the agency dilemma arises. How to ensure that the agent acts solely in the interest of the principal is the challenge. In the 18th and 19th centuries many contracts were, indeed, between a single principal and a single agent—trading ventures, construction projects, running a factory.

The arrival of the joint stock, limited liability company in the mid-19th century increased the number of principals (shareholders) and their agents (directors). The number and increasing diversity of the shareholders in public companies meant, moreover, that the interests of shareholders were no longer homogeneous. As Berle and Means (1932) showed in their influential analysis, as listed companies grew and their shareholders became more diverse, the separation between owners and directors magnified and power shifted towards the directors, which some of them abused.

Today agency relationships in public companies can be complex. For example, an individual owner might invest funds through a financial adviser, who invests the funds in a mutual fund or investment trust, which in turn seeks to gear its portfolio by investing in a hedge fund, which invests its resources in a range of equities, property, commodities, and other hedge funds. Tracing the agency chain in such cases can be difficult and establishing the exposure to agency risk well nigh impossible. However, the agency dilemma potential exists throughout the chain. The demands for reporting, transparency, accountability, audit, independent directors, and the other requirements of company law and securities legislation, plus requirements of regulators and stock exchange rules, and the calls of the corporate governance codes are all responses to the agency dilemma. Indeed, the conceptual underpinning of corporate governance codes around the world and the demands of company law for checks and balances is the need to respond to the agency dilemma.

The practice of stock borrowing, used by sophisticated investors such as hedge funds, means that, not only can the fund benefit from a fall in a share's value, but can also use the share's voting rights. They can thus build up a significant stake, in fact up to the level at which they, and any other fund acting in concert with them, would be required to make a public offer for the company. In other words, it is possible to acquire voting rights in a company without owning or investing in its stock. This is a long way from the original concept of the joint-stock company. It also raises a potential dilemma for directors: are they the stewards of the interests of the long term traditional shareholders, or short term activist institutions? Their interests are unlikely to be the same.

Neither is the agency problem limited to relations between investors in listed companies and their agents. The agency dilemma can occur in private companies, joint ventures, not-for-profit organizations, professional institutions, and governmental bodies. Wherever there is a separation between the members and the governing body put in place to protect their interests and deliver the required outcomes the agency dilemma will arise and corporate governance issues exist. The members could be the shareholders in a company, the members of a professional institution or a trades union, a group of owners in a cooperative, or the holding company in a corporate group: the governing body might be called the board of directors, the council, the committee, the governing body, or the holding company. But whatever names are used, whenever responsibility for activities and assets are delegated by those in the principal position to those in the agent situation, the agency dilemma will arise.

For example, consider a pyramid group of companies. The board of the holding company decides to operate the group with profit-responsible subsidiary companies in organizational divisions. The board believes that motivation and commitment will be maximized if the directors of each subsidiary are held responsible for generating profits and are measured by their company's annual return on investment (ROI). The opportunities for the subsidiary company directors to take decisions beneficial to the subsidiary but detrimental to the group are legion—for example by postponing longer term decisions on research and development, management development, or maintenance to improve the profit, or by manipulating the asset base in the ROI calculation. If the subsidiaries inter trade the opportunities multiply. In chapter 6, we saw the example of subsidiary company A, which manufactures a component that is incorporated into subsidiary company B's product. Company A needs a transfer price at which to sell to company B. Of course, A wants the highest price to maximize its profits, while B wants the lowest to maximize its returns. If they cannot agree, company B may buy in the open market, leaving A with under recovered overheads. Conversely company A may sell to the market, leaving B with insecure supply. Referring the transfer price decision to the holding company might resolve the dilemma but at the cost of removing the decision making authority of the directors of A and B. This situation is typical in decentralized groups and called sub-optimization by some authorities. In effect, it reflects the agency dilemma.

The agency problem can also arise in not-for-profit entities. Consider the British National Health Service (NHS). The responsible government ministry—the Department of Health—contracts with Regional Health Authorities to deliver the required health services in the community through hospitals and other institutions. In turn the Regional Health Authorities contract with each hospital, setting standards and targets to measure achievement. For example, they might call for a hospital to improve its bed occupancy rate, thus encouraging the hospital governors to keep patients in longer than really necessary. Conversely, the Authority might call for a speedy return of patients to the street, resulting in rising emergency re-admissions. In fact, the NHS promulgates a large list of performance measures with quantifiable outputs in an attempt to reduce the agency dilemma. But success is only partial because the agents always find ways of benefiting their entity to the detriment of the whole system.

Agency Theory

Agency theory looks at corporate governance practices and behaviour through the lens of the agency dilemma. In essence, the theory perceives the governance relationship as a contract between shareholder (the principal) and director (the agent). Directors, it is argued, seeking to maximize their own personal benefit, take actions that are advantageous to themselves but detrimental to the shareholders.

Essentially, trust involves an agreement between parties with asymmetrical access to information. In companies, of course, the directors know far more about the enterprise than the shareholders, who must trust them. This is the underpinning concept of the joint stock limited liability company. As we have seen, the shareholders trust the directors to be stewards of their funds. The agency theory of corporate governance takes a less sanguine view of directors' behaviour. (See figure 9.1.)

As the early proponents of agency theory, Jensen and Meckling (1976), explained:

agency theory involves a contract under which one or more persons (the shareholders) engage another person (the directors) to perform some service on their behalf which includes delegating some decision making authority to the agent. If both parties to the relationship are utility maximizers there is good reason to believe the agent will not always act in the best interests of the principal.

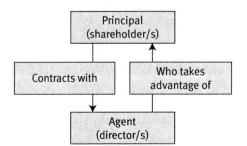

Figure 9.1 The governance relationship

Anecdotal evidence of such behaviour is not hard to find. There are a myriad cases in which directors treat a listed public company as though it was their own property, exploiting their position, receiving unsanctioned benefits, and taking remuneration unrelated to their performance to the shareholders' detriment. Bob Monks (2008), a shareholder activist, reckons that trillions of dollars of shareholders' wealth have been wrongly extracted from US corporations over the years by directors abusing their power.

Directors may also take a different view to that of their shareholders on corporate risk. After all, it is not their money they are risking. Of course, successful management involves taking controlled risks. But directors might hazard corporate funds on riskier ventures, a hostile takeover bid for example, than many of their shareholders would expect or want. Potential investors can only judge the ability of the board level decision makers and their risk profile from the company prospectus, reports, and past performance.

A further agency problem is asymmetrical access to information. Directors know far more about the corporate situation than the shareholders. Indeed, shareholders have to rely on the directors to decide what information they should have, over and above the minimum required by regulation and company law.

Agency theory has been developed within the discipline of financial economics. Jensen elaborated his original work in Fama and Jensen (1983). Most scholarly research in corporate governance has used this theoretical approach. Looking at corporate governance through the agency lens enables researchers to explore relationships between governance processes and corporate performance. In other words, they test the hypothesis that there is a causal link between governance systems, put in place to control the agent, and the effect on the interests of the principal. For example, a study might test whether a statistically significant correlation exists between long term corporate performance and, say, the proportion of INEDs to executive directors.

Agency theory offers a statistically rigorous insight into corporate governance processes. Because of its simplicity and the availability of both reliable data and statistical tests, agency theory has provided a powerful approach to corporate governance theory building.

Agency theory focuses at the level of shareholders and boards as entities. Board level activities and inter personal relations between directors are treated as a black box. Consequently, researchers do not need access to the boardroom or to individual directors. Most agency theoretical research uses data about governance practices and company performance that are readily available in the public domain using, for example, directors' reports and audited company accounts. Much of this information is also summarized by corporate type, industry, country, and other relevant attributes.

Does Good Corporate Governance Produce Better Corporate Performance?

Serious scholarship has been able to demonstrate some linkages between company performance and various attributes of governance, such as the use of independent outside directors, board structure and size, or audit committee activities. However, it has to be said that so far the evidence is weak and most conclusions inconclusive, apart from the ABI study to be described shortly.

Indeed, in some cases where a positive relationship has been shown between good governance and better performance, other scholars have reworked the data to draw contrary conclusions. More convincing evidence of a relationship between good corporate governance practices and company performance comes from the behaviour of institutional investors who are prepared to pay a premium for companies they judge to have good governance because they feel it reduces their exposure to risk.

However, a significant study was published by the Association of British Insurers (ABI) in 2008 (Selvaggi and Upton 2008),[1] which suggests that there *is* a robust causal relationship between good corporate governance and superior company performance.

ABI represents the interest of insurance companies in the UK, who tend to invest long term, reflecting their need to meet long term obligations. The ABI Institutional Voting Service provides information to their members to enable them to judge the quality of companies' governance performance and identify problems. A data base has been developed that shows the extent to which listed UK companies comply with the provision of the UK Combined Code, and adds expert judgements on other aspects of governance systems found in, for example, articles of association, remuneration reports, long term top management incentives, share dilution activities, waiver of takeover rules, and pre-emption rights.

A point is awarded for every governance failure, producing a numeric score with a zero score being ideal up to a theoretical maximum of forty-two if a company failed on every criteria. In their reports to their members ABI draws attention to corporate governance concerns through a colour code: in blue-top companies there are no areas of concern, in amber-top companies some concerns, for example, abnormal salary increases, whereas in red-top companies there are major concerns, for example if the non-executive directors did not meet the independence criteria, or where an executive director serves on the audit committee.

The study draws on the governance scores of 361 companies in the FTSE All-share index over the five years 2002 to 2007. The performance criteria used in the study are return on assets and 'TobinQ' that is the market value of a company divided by the accounting replacement value of its assets (a result between 0 and 1 indicates that the market value of the company fails to reflect the accounting value of its assets).

Regression analysis is used to test relationships between the corporate governance criteria and corporate performance. The multi-variate econometric methodology used allows the determination of relationships between various factors simultaneously.

The study shows a clear connection between good governance and both good company performance and share price levels. Companies with poor governance show a strong negative impact on performance. Moreover companies that are red-topped repeatedly under perform the rest by 2 to 5 percent a year in terms of industry-adjusted return on assets.

The study also suggests that it is good corporate governance that leads to better performance, not the other way round. Further, well governed companies deliver higher returns when adjusted for risk and the volatility of their share price returns is lower. The study also discovered that the impact of governance on performance was long-term. Lags of between two and three years between poor governance and inferior performance were found.

---

[1] www.abi.org.uk/BookShop/ResearchReports/Research_Feb_08.pdf

This study clearly suggests that sound governance does have a positive effect on profitability and boosts share price. In other words, it shows that governance expenditure can be cost-effective.

However, the issue is not yet determined, as Bhagat et al. (2007) explain, citing methodological shortcomings in existing papers:

Financial economists and commercial providers of governance services have in recent years created measures of the quality of firms' corporate governance . . . there is no consistent relation between governance indices and measures of corporate performance. Namely, there is no one 'best' measure of corporate governance: the most effective governance institution appears to depend on context, and on firms' specific circumstances.

(We will review various indices of corporate governance in chapter 13.)

Criticisms of Agency Theory

Some critics of agency theory cite its relatively narrow theoretical scope. To study the intricacies of corporate governance in terms of contracts between principals and agents, they argue, is naive. They express concern at a focus on purely quantitative metrics, such as board structure or corporate compensation packages, or on the building of a governance index through a 'box-ticking approach' where compliance with governance criteria mechanically feeds into a broad governance index, which is then compared with some measure(s) of corporate performance.

Such critics believe that board behaviour does not consist of sets of contractual relationships, but is influenced by inter personal behaviour, group dynamics, and political intrigue. They question whether the subtle and complex dynamics of board behaviour lend themselves to measurement and numerical analysis. As Ada Demb wrote in 1993, '*statistical methods will not explain the reality of the boardroom*'.

Other contemporary scholarship has discovered that not only does increasing governance conformance and compliance not necessarily add to corporate performance—it can actually detract. Muth and Donaldson (1997) challenged the findings of other agency theoretical research. Boards with well connected, executive directors perform better, they found, than those that followed corporate governance codes on the use of independent directors.

Other critics have challenged the shareholder/director agency model as simplistic in practice. Where, for example, the ultimate beneficial owner has invested through a pension fund, which invests in a hedge fund, which invests in a private equity company, which places funds in the hands of a financial institution, which invests in the shares of a listed company but lends them as collateral for another transaction, who is agent for whom they ask? These days, they say, pension funds, hedge funds, and other institutional investors can behave like imperial traders, even corporate raiders, rather than the long term investors perceived by the agency paradigm. Also the short term outlook of stock markets in the UK and USA may produce different agency relationships from the longer term and bank related investment seen in countries such as Germany and Japan.

But there is also a deeper issue. Inherent in agency theory is a philosophical, moral assumption about the nature of man. The theory assumes that people are self-interested not altruistic. They cannot be expected to look after the interests of others. In other words, directors cannot be trusted. The legal concept of the corporation, and the basis of steward-ship theory, as we shall see, takes the opposite view.

In summary, critics of agency theory argue that it has been erected on a single, question-able abstraction that governance involves a contract between two parties, and is based on a dubious conjectural morality that people maximize their personal utility.

Nevertheless, agency theoretical research remains the mainstay of published papers in corporate governance for the past two decades, and is the conceptual underpinning of the ABI study described above. An interesting research frontier of the subject bridges the dis-ciplines of economics and law, applying the agency theoretical insights of economics to the legal context of the corporation.

Transaction Cost Economics

Closely related to agency theory, transaction cost economics was derived from original work in 1937, by Coarse. He recognized that a firm could save costs by undertaking activ-ities within the organization rather than externally. In other words the firm would get goods or services at a lower price than in the market place.

However, as a firm grows there comes a point at which the external market becomes cheaper. Williamson (1975 and 1988) built on Coarse's work, arguing that large corporate groups could overcome disadvantages of scale by '*the choice of governance structures*'.

Transaction cost economics, therefore, focuses on the cost of enforcement or check and balance mechanisms, such as internal and external audit controls, information disclosure, independent outside directors, the separation of board chairmanship from CEO, risk analysis, and audit, nomination, and remuneration committees. The argument is then ad-vanced that such enforcement costs should be incurred to the point at which the increase in costs equals the reduction of the potential loss from non-compliance.

Stiles and Taylor (2001) observed that '*both transaction cost economics and agency the-ories are concerned with managerial discretion and both assume that managers are given to opportunism (self-interest seeking) and moral hazard, and that managers operate under bounded rationality*'. In other words, directors and top management act in their own best interests, not necessarily in those of the shareholders. But transaction cost analysis focuses on governance structures and mechanisms, whereas agency theory sees the firm as a set of contracts.

The underlying discipline of transaction cost economics, like agency theory, is financial economics. Although the focus is different the level of abstraction is similar, being at the level of the firm and its governance structures rather than board level behaviour. Again re-search results have been inconclusive, possibly because the complexity within organiza-tions is ignored. For a seminal review of the earlier contributions of financial economics to corporate governance knowledge see Shleifer and Vishny (1997).

Stewardship Theory

Stewardship theory looks at governance through a different lens from agency theory, re-flecting the original legal view of the corporation. As we saw in chapter 1, the joint stock company with limited liability for its share holding investors, was an elegantly simple and

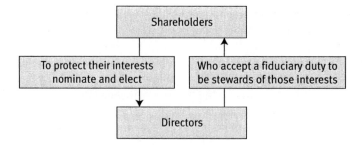

Figure 9.2 The shareholder/director relationship

eminently successful development of the mid-19th century. The limited liability company has provided capital, encouraged business growth, secured employment, provided innovation in industry and commerce, and created untold wealth over more than 150 years. This model proved robust and adaptable. Indeed, its great flexibility has led to the huge proliferation, diversity, and complexity of corporate types and structures today.

In essence, each company is incorporated as a separate legal entity. The share holding members of the company nominate and appoint the directors, who then act as stewards for their interests. The directors report to them on the results of that stewardship, subject to a report from an independent auditor that the accounts show a true and fair view. Ownership is the basis of power over the corporation. Directors have a fiduciary duty to act as stewards of the shareholders' interest. Inherent in the concept of the company is the belief that directors can be trusted. (See figure 9.2.)

Stewardship theory reflects the classical ideas of corporate governance. Directors' legal duty is to their shareholders not to themselves, or to other interest groups. Contrary to agency theory, stewardship theory believes that directors do not always act in a way that maximizes their own personal interests: they can and do act responsibly with independence and integrity. As Lord Cairns said in the London High Court in 1874, '*no man, acting as agent, can be allowed to put himself into a position in which his interest and his duty will be in conflict*'. Stewardship theorists argue that, clearly, this is what most directors actually do. Of course, some fail, but this does not invalidate the basic concept.

Stewardship exponents recognize that directors need to recognize the interests of customers, employees, suppliers, and other legitimate stakeholders, but under the law their first responsibility is to the shareholders. They argue that conflicts of interest between stakeholder groups and the company should be met by competitive pressures in free markets, backed by legislation and legal controls to protect customers (monopoly and competition law), employees (employment law, health and safety law), consumers (product safety law, consumer protection law), suppliers (contract law, credit payment law) and society (environmental law, health and safety law, taxation law). We will explore so called stakeholder theory later in this chapter and the growing interest corporate social responsibility and a wider range of responsibilities for directors in chapter 15.

The underpinning disciplines in stewardship theory are legal and organizational studies. By reflecting the legal model, stewardship theory provides precise boundaries for the company, clearly identifying its assets and liabilities, its shareholders, and its directors. As we saw in chapter 4, it facilitates the description of complex pyramids, chains, and networks of corporate groups.

Criticisms of Stewardship Theory

Critics of stewardship theory point out that the de facto situation in modern corporations is quite different from the 19th century model. They argue that the concept of a set of shareholders owning a single company and appointing its directors is naive in modern circumstances. In listed companies, they point out, shareholders have become remote from the company and do not nominate the directors. Financial reports, they suggest, have become intelligible only to experts. Consolidated group accounts, recording the finances of modern entities, complicate rather than explain complex groups. Complex corporations lack transparency and their directors are not really accountable to shareholders.

Other critics of stewardship theory point out that, because the theory is rooted in law, it is normative. It emphasizes what should be done, or even exhorts. It is not, they argue, predictive and is unable to show causal relationships between specific behaviours and corporate performance.

Mallin (2004) makes a further important point on the relevance of stewardship thinking. The fundamental concept of the joint stock, limited liability company provides the conceptual underpinning of company law in the US, the UK, and many other jurisdictions around the world influenced by their early days in the British empire. Here common law prevails based on legal principles enhanced by the precedents of case law and relying on independent judges and juries. As a result, the rights of shareholders, particularly minorities, have been protected and in these countries the shareholder base in many public companies is diversified. In other countries, in continental Europe and Latin America, for example, civil law prevails, which has less flexibility, does not learn from precedent, and is often administered by judges who are civil servants. As a result, laws are more codified and there is less protection for minorities and consequently share ownership is less widespread with many companies still dominated by dominant shareholder and family interests.

After the corporate collapses in the late 20th and early 21st centuries, many commentators felt that the trust directors owed under the stewardship model had been undermined, and this erosion of trust adversely affected the well-being of investors, employees, and communities. Questions about the commitment of boards to members' interests surfaced. Nevertheless, stewardship theory remains the legal foundation for companies' legislation all round the world. It is also an inherent underpinning of corporate governance codes.

A recent theoretical development recognizes the naivety, in the modern investment world, of the 19th century model of shareholder capitalism in which joint stock, limited liability companies are owned by a handful of individual shareholders. Referred to as a theory of universal ownership, this view of fiduciary capitalism recognizes that modern listed companies, particularly in liquid markets, such as the US and the UK, are typically held by a highly diversified set of equity holders, including holdings concentrated in the hands of a few large institutional investors.

In the US, the hundred largest financial institutions hold over 50 percent of all publicly held equity. In the UK, there is a similar concentration of ownership, as we saw in the last chapter. Since these large institutions have massive funds to invest, they need to buy shares across the board, effectively indexing the market as a whole. They are also likely to be investing in a wide range of equities, across geographical and emerging markets, and through a range of investment instruments, including hedge funds.

Consequently, such institutional investors, the theory argues, now play an essential role in corporate governance and should assume a responsibility for overseeing governance issues, and abide by principles of responsible investment, including collective action if necessary (see www.unpri.org).

Critics of this approach point out that institutional investors such as pension funds are run by trustees whose accountability is not always apparent and seldom challenged, whose interests do not align with those of fund beneficiaries, and who may use investment funds to protect themselves from claims for negligence.

Resource Dependency Theory

Resource dependency theory takes a strategic view of corporate governance. It sees the governing body of a corporate entity as the lynch pin between a company and the resources it needs to achieve its objectives. These resources could include, for example, links to relevant markets including potential customers and competitors, access to capital and other sources of finance, provision of know-how and technology, and relationships with business, political, and other societal networks and elites.

The directors are viewed as boundary-spanning nodes of networks able to connect the business to its strategic environment. Studies from this perspective focus on the interdependence of companies in a market and can serve to reduce uncertainty in corporate decisions. The theory finds its roots in organization theories, for example Pfeffer (1972).

The theory of social networks recognizes that those involved in corporate governance processes are often linked through networks. Individuals at the nodes may have things in common including, perhaps, social standing, class, income, education, institutional or corporate links, and so on. Lifestyle theory, focusing on the backgrounds of key players, has also been used. Some individuals in the networks, such as the chairman or CEO, may be pivotal nodes in a number of networks, increasing their communication leverage. Such social networks can enhance or adversely interfere with independent and objective governance activities. Identifying such networks and monitoring their activities provides another insight into governance processes and powers.

Managerial and Class Hegemony

This perspective on the governance of companies focuses on the view that directors have of themselves and its impact on their behaviour and corporate governance implications. Directors in some companies perceive themselves as an elite group. This self-perception encourages them to behave in an elite way, dominating both the company organization and its external linkages. Top management appointments ensure that newcomers fit into that elite and sustain its image. Similarly new independent directors are likely to be nominated and appointed only if they sustain the dominance of the ruling group.

Class hegemony recognizes that directors' self-image can affect board behaviour and performance. Further executive directors, with their own self-image bolstered by access to information, knowledge of ongoing operations, and decision making power, may dominate board decisions.

The theories of managerial and class hegemony are rooted in the socio-political disciplines, but have used case research, allied with biographical analysis, to produce some penetrating insights into corporate governance. Essentially, these studies see corporate governance as an inter personal, political process.

Lorsch and McGiver (1989), in their work *Pawns or Potentates: The Reality of the American Board*, focused on some realities that are not illuminated by either agency or stewardship theories. Demb and Neubauer (1992) drew on European experience in their book *The Corporate Board: Confronting the Paradoxes*. Monks and Minow (1995) in *Corporate Governance* drew on their experiences as relationship investors and shareholder activists, whilst Monks (1998) *The Emperor's Nightingale: Restoring the Integrity of the Corporation* made an informed and outspoken criticism of the excessive power that he alleges American chief executives hold.

Research in this field requires access to individual directors. The researcher needs to link the information derived from interviews with their interpretation in a way that is neither too tenuous nor expecting the reader to take too much on trust. How to overcome this concern? In one of the few books that successfully explored board behaviour through interviews, LeBlanc and Gillies (2005) provided sets of quotations from different directors, grouped by topic. This device gave credibility to their conclusions because the reader saw a number of different comments on the same subject.

Problems with studies from this perspective include obtaining access to directors and interpreting the data received from interview and observation. The national culture within which the directors operate can also be a primary driving force in affecting results.

Critics of the case approach to the study of corporate governance complain that the evidence is statistically irrelevant, largely anecdotal, and can be influenced by all sorts of personal prejudice, self-centred reporting, and biased insights. The counter-argument is that corporate governance involves a political process, with human beings expressing themselves—more art than a statistically controlled group activity.

Psychological and Organizational Perspectives

Both agency and stewardship theories, as we have seen, view corporate governance at the level of the firm, being concerned with relationships between owners and directors. Agency theory focuses on the shareholder/director relationship; stewardship theory focuses, inter alia, on companies, their shareholders, external auditors, boards of directors, and board committees. Resource dependency and class/managerial hegemony theories again take a firm level focus.

Individual players, with their different mindsets, personalities, and foibles, do not appear in these theoretical paradigms. But practitioners recognize that knowing what goes on in the boardroom and during interactions between directors is vital to understanding corporate governance.

Empirical investigation is obviously needed. But, though experienced directors and chairmen offer plenty of anecdotal evidence, there has been little empirical research to date. Why? Access to directors and boards can be difficult. Directors may believe that secrecy is vital to protect strategic plans, guard trade secrets, and for the listed company to avoid a leak of stock-market price-sensitive information. Some boards may also resist access from investigators to preserve inter personal relationships within the board, to prevent the presence of an outsider changing board level interactions, and to avoid unwanted media interest. Individual directors might also be concerned to prevent damaging information leaking out affecting their reputations or, worse, generating law suits.

A few researchers have attempted to study board level behaviour as an interpersonal process. Realizing that such processes are a critical element in corporate governance, they have not been prepared to treat the board as a black box. Consequently, they have researched board dynamics, considering the board as a team, or reviewing board behaviour as a political process. Their research approaches have included interviews, questionnaires, case studies, and simulation.

A challenge to the researcher using empirical face-to-face interviews is how to analyse, interpret, and draw conclusions from the data in a way that is convincing and preferably replicable, whilst avoiding the interpolation of the researcher's personal perceptions, preconceptions, and prejudices. This is a problem not faced by the agency theoreticians' elegant statistical analysis of published mass-data that is already in the public domain.

Psychological theory adopts the level of abstraction of individual directors, focusing on how they construe and interpret their worlds. Corporate governance research from a psychological perspective seeks to understand how individual directors perceive their board level work and what they believe leads to effective performance. Not much research has been done in corporate governance at this level.

Cognitive maps, produced by repertory grid techniques, can be used to chart directors' mindsets. Studies of cognition, perception, and thought processes can enable personal constructs and frames of reference to be identified. Core perceptual dimensions can be traced to find out how directors construe their board level activities. Deep-seated values that influence perceptions and affect decisions can be explored.

Constructs of language, using the language of the director not words imposed by the researcher, can help to describe and interpret board level experiences. If words such as involvement, leadership, participation, reputation, or teamwork, are used by the director, or moral values such as trust, harmony, and ethical standards mentioned, then these become the frame of reference for the researcher. In other words, attributes and roles identified by directors are used to understand their work and understand what they believe makes for an effective board.

Psychological theories have yet to make a significant impact in understanding corporate governance, but the relevance of individuals at board level in the overall governance process suggests that this field has potential.

Organization theories have also been relatively slow to focus on issues at board level, probably because of the problems with access to data. In practice, boards of directors appeared on few organization charts. Most organizational studies took a managerial perspective and assumed that organization structures peaked with the chief executive. However, in recent years there have been some contributions from the psychology of behavioural and leadership studies and the sociology of organizational and managerial work.

Viewing corporate governance from a longitudinal perspective has also provided some insights. Filatotchev and Wright (2005) collected material looking at the evolution of corporate governance practices over the life cycles of enterprises and institutions. The significance of learning and knowledge at board level and the managing of transitional stages were seen to be important.

Further light has been thrown onto corporate governance from the perspective of political economics. Roe (2003), writing about political and social conflict in corporations and the institutions of corporate governance, shows how a nation's political economy interacts with its legal structures and financial markets. In particular he demonstrates that in some democracies, such as Continental Europe after the Second World War, the concentration of shareholders has a political explanation.

Game theory has also been applied to corporate governance issues. For example, Masahiko Aoki at Stanford has developed a conceptual and analytical framework to make comparative studies of corporate governance in Japan and China.

The Societal Perspective: Stakeholder Philosophies

Finally, we turn to perspectives on corporate governance at a societal level, so-called stakeholder theory. This is concerned with values and beliefs about the appropriate relationships between the individual, the enterprise, and the state. It involves a discourse on the balance of responsibility, accountability, and power throughout society. It is not a predictive theory that can be researched. Consequently, this societal view of corporate governance is probably better thought of as a philosophy rather than a theory.

Companies, stakeholder advocates argue, should recognize a responsibility to *all* those affected by companies' decisions, including customers, employees, and managers, partners in the supply chain, bankers, shareholders, the local community, broader societal interests for the environment and the state. Companies owe a duty to all those affected by their behaviour, they argue. Some advocates go further and call for directors to be accountable and responsible to a wide range of stakeholders far beyond companies' current company law responsibility to shareholders. Such responsible behaviour, the stakeholder advocates argue, should be the price society demands from companies for the privilege of incorporation, granting shareholders limited liability for the company's debts.

In 1975, the UK the Accounting Standards Steering Committee produced a discussion paper, the 'Corporate Report', which recommended that all large economic entities should produce regular accountability reports to all stakeholder groups whose interests might be affected by the decisions of that entity. The political implications of such a heroic idea quickly relegated the report to the files.

In the United States, proposals for new company ordinances, including stakeholder accountability, came from Ralph Nader, who tussled with the boardroom-orientated Business Roundtable in 1970.

In 1980, Nader and Green argued, emotively, that:

[Giant corporations] can spend decisive amounts to determine which towns thrive and which gather cobwebs, corrupt or help overthrow foreign governments, develop technology that takes lives or saves lives . . . [The giant corporation] is largely unaccountable to its constituencies—shareholders, workers, consumers, local communities, taxpayers, small businesses, future generations.

A year later Millstein and Katsch commented more thoughtfully:

This strident and partisan concept of substantially unrestrained corporate power and discretion is, in a more moderate form, among the most important fundamental public concerns within large corporations . . . at issue is whether the nation . . . will accept larger private corporate size, accelerate the decline of pluralism by regulating or by giving greater responsibility to government, or by requiring fundamental changes in the internal governance structure of our major corporations.

Stakeholder thinking faded in the free market, 'growth and greed' attitudes of the 1980s. But in the more environmentally and socially concerned world of the 1990s and early 21st century the ideas again appeared, for example in corporate social responsibility and sustainability reporting (which we will discuss in chapter 15). The interest is also reflected in socially-aware mutual funds, which limit their investment to companies deemed to adopt suitable business strategies.

The Royal Society of Arts in England, published a report in 1999 entitled *Tomorrow's Company,* which advocated wider recognition of corporate responsibility to stakeholders such as suppliers, customers, and employees. The chairman of the committee producing this report, Sir Stuart Hampson, who was also chairman of the John Lewis Partnership—a company run as an employee's partnership wrote:

Shareholder value is the imperative commanding a lot of attention, but you cannot create shareholder value by talking to your shareholders. You create it by looking at the four drivers of a successful business: how good you are at involving and motivating your staff; how close you are to your customers; how good you are at removing wastage from the supply chain and maintaining good relations with suppliers; what your reputation is in the community at large. We don't believe that the board is there purely to create shareholder value. I'm sure nobody leaps out of bed in the morning and says 'I want to create shareholder value!' It's unrealistic.

Sternberg (1997) argued that stakeholder ideas are fundamentally flawed, strongly advocating the ownership rights perspective. Potential conflicts between the expectations of different stakeholders were irreconcilable, she argued, boards need a single responsibility—to their shareholders. Turnbull (1997:2) took the opposite view, advancing the benefits of a broader cybernetic (and stakeholder) view. Expectations of companies around the world are changing with growing demands for better consumer, environmental, and societal behaviour.

The 1998 UK Hampel Committee dismissed stakeholder notions, saying: 'directors are responsible for relations with stakeholders, but are accountable to the shareholders', a view supporting stakeholder theory and reflecting the conventional wisdom in boardrooms in both the UK and the USA. Roberto Goizuetta, a former head of Coca-Cola, captured the issue:

saying that we work for our shareholders may sound simplistic—but we frequently see companies that have forgotten the reason they exist. They may even try to be all things to all people and serve many masters in many different ways. In any event they miss their primary calling, which is to stick to the business of creating value for their owners.

As Pettigrew sagely commented in 1997 '*the old cry of "what about the workers?" is being replaced by a new call "what about the stakeholders?"*' Nevertheless, it is important to distinguish directors' accountability from their responsibility.

But overshadowing agency, stewardship, stakeholder, and the other theoretical perspectives are also some basic unresolved issues at a meta-philosophical level. Every theory of corporate governance needs to be founded on a view on the legitimate relationship between the individual and society. Where does the desirable balance lie between the rights, responsibilities, and powers of the individual, the enterprise, and the state? Opinions vary significantly by culture, political context, and social system. Moreover, they have been evolving throughout history. All systems of governance must seek an appropriate balance between the interests of self and society. That applies to corporate governance just as it does to governance in other areas of society.

Differing Boundaries and Levels: Systems Theory

We have seen that the disciplines contributing to the study of corporate governance to date include financial economics, law, accountancy, management studies, organizational behaviour, sociology, politics, and, perhaps, philosophy. The two dominant contenders for theoretical insight, agency and stewardship theories, are properly based on bounded models of reality—agency theory on an economic perspective, stewardship theory on a legal one. Inevitably each perspective is limited. Each theory sees the world through a different lens.

Changing the metaphor, each of the various theoretical perspectives on corporate governance can be visualized as a spotlight lighting up part of the stage on which the corporate governance action is being played (see figure 9.3). Some spotlights illuminate one part of the stage, others throw light on another area and from a different angle. Each theoretical spotlight leaves some players and part of the action in darkness.

Some theories focus on the shareholders and the board as a whole with its standing-committees, perhaps including the external auditors; other theories focus on individual directors on the board and the interactions between them; yet other theories take the perspective of the stock markets, investors, and regulators; while at the highest level the political situation, the economic impact, and the cultural context come into view, along with legislatures, states, and international agencies. As yet there is no theoretical floodlight that

Figure 9.3 Spotlights on the corporate governance stage

adequately lights the whole stage, illuminating all the players, and showing their relationships and the action.

Systems theory takes a similar approach to understanding situations. All phenomena can be perceived and classified as a hierarchy of systems. For example, consider road traffic, which can be thought of as a set of systems—the overall road traffic system, a specific vehicle, the engine of that vehicle, the carburettor in the engine, the molecules that make up a component of that carburettor—each system offers an appropriate way of thinking about parts of the overall road transport system. Each is useful in context, none tell the whole story.

Systems theory offers a useful way of looking at a situation. The classical view of systems uses three criteria to identify a system:

- The system's boundaries, that is determining what is to be considered as within the system itself and what in the system's environment. Systems are man-made artefacts to help understand a situation. Moreover, each system can be further broken down to suit the needs of the user

- The system's level of abstraction, that is the level at which the system is perceived and the amount of detail treated within it

- The system's function, that is what occurs between the system's inputs and outputs

So what are the boundaries of corporate governance? Cochran and Wartick in the first bibliography of corporate governance published in 1988 suggested that: '*Corporate governance is an umbrella term that includes specific issues arising from interactions among senior management, shareholders, boards of directors, and other corporate stakeholders.*'

In chapter 1, we adopted the simple expedient of defining corporate governance as being about the exercise of power over corporate entities. This way we did not have to identify the players nor define boundaries for their action. But now we do have to be more precise as we explore the perspectives of various theoretical positions that different scholars have taken on the subject of corporate governance.

What should be in the system, what should be its boundaries? We have a choice—individual directors, corporate entities, their owners or members, their governing bodies, intermediaries in the governance chain, auditors, regulators, laws, culture, national and international organizations, and all the other stakeholders affected by the actions of those corporate entities.

Judging from the reams of academic literature, views clearly differ on the scope of corporate governance. As we have seen, for some it is about principles and good practice on matters such as board structures and membership, the independence of directors, the use of audit, remuneration, and nominating committees and generally about board level effectiveness. For others, corporate governance is about the relationship between owners and corporations, about the exercise of power by shareholders, particularly institutional investors who, in recent years, have shown themselves capable of removing dominant executives, restructuring boards, and influencing strategic direction. Whilst for others, corporate governance is about the social responsibilities corporations owe to a wide set of stakeholders beyond the boards classical fiduciary duty to the shareholders—responsibilities and accountabilities to employees, customers, lenders, suppliers, the local community, and society at large.

Some researchers have gone beyond the use of systems theory as a convenient analogy, applying systems analysis techniques to corporate governance processes. Such analytical tools have proved useful in describing governance activities with some rigour. Cybernetics, the study of communication and control in man and machine, which distinguishes adaptive and mechanistic feedback and regulation, and adds the concept of requisite variety in the design of effective systems, has also proved a valuable adjunct to systems approaches. A potentially significant law of cybernetics is the law of requisite variety, which recognizes that control in a complex system needs sufficient levels and number of regulating devices. So it is with corporate governance.

The approach we adopt in this book is well described by Clarke (2007) when he suggests that theoretical perspectives on boards and governance can best be seen as 'multiple theoretical lenses' with which to view the subject.

A Subject in Search of its Paradigm

As we have seen, agency theory is rooted in the belief that agents are utility maximizers, and therefore cannot be relied on to act in the best interests of their principals. Put simply: directors cannot be trusted. Stewardship theory is rooted in the belief that directors accept a fiduciary duty to act in the best interest of the owners who have entrusted their funds to them. In other words: directors can be trusted. Which is true?

Karl Popper, in his seminal work on scientific proof, argued that a scientific proposition could not be proved to be absolutely true, but a single contrary result would be shown to be false. Both agency and stewardship theories fail Popper's test of scientific truth because each can readily be shown to be false in specific circumstances.

Corporate governance, as yet, does not have a single widely accepted theoretical base nor a commonly accepted paradigm. In the words of Pettigrew (1992): '*corporate governance lacks any form of coherence, either empirically, methodologically or theoretically with only piecemeal attempts to try and understand and explain how the modern corporation is run*'.

In the original concept of the corporation, as we have seen, directors were appointed by, and were usually in direct contact with, their shareholders. Shareholder democracy had meaning and shareholders could participate. (Admittedly some rogue entrepreneurs took advantage of their shareholders, but investment always involves risk.) But the concept of the corporation no longer works in that way. Directors in many large companies have become distant from the ultimate owners. Layers of brokers, agents, shareholding companies, institutional investors including hedge funds with borrowed shares, pension funds, mutual funds, and banks come between boards and their company's ultimate owners. In Western cultures a new governing elite has emerged. Self-enriching and self-perpetuating these corporate directors wield the power, and reap the rewards, that were previously reserved to ruling monarchs and their aristocracy.

The 1990s saw a dramatic surge in academic interest in corporate governance. Unfortunately, research has so far failed to offer a convincing explanation of how corporate governance works and has contributed little to the practice of the subject. All of the significant professional developments have been responses to corporate corruption and collapse, not to research findings and theory building. The Sarbanes-Oxley Act in the United States, the corporate governance codes in all economically developed nations, and the corporate governance institutions formed in many emerging economies have been based on the experience and conventional wisdom of company directors and their advisers, not from the conclusions of rigorous academic research.

Part of the problem, from a theoretical perspective, is the lack of clearly articulated understanding and definition of various governance related terms. For example, the discussion of the 'Anglo-American' approach to corporate governance, usually meaning one based on common law, becomes woolly when the underlying philosophies of governance in the two systems are seen to be significantly different, one being principles based the other rule based. Another example is in the use of the term 'outside' director, when the incumbent could be totally independent of the company (and thus know little about it!), independent as defined by various governance codes, or connected with the company in some way other than as an executive.

Today, the frontiers of corporate governance are being pushed out rapidly. The importance of good governance is recognized by investors and regulators. Governance now affects global finance markets. The significance of governance for the long term success of enterprise, in addition to sound management, is understood by business leaders. Directors and boards are facing up to the challenges.

But the theoretical underpinnings of the subject are weak. The subject lacks a conceptual framework that adequately reflects the reality of corporate governance.

The theoretical perspectives focus on different levels of abstraction: for some the relevant system covers the financial markets, for others it is the governing body, and yet others individual chairman, CEOs, and directors are in the frame.

As we have seen, corporate governance codes reflect the conventional wisdom of best practice in listed companies. There is a paucity of new conceptual thinking about corporate governance. Scholars need to break out of their preconceptions of corporate entities seen as legal entities or in terms of relationships between corporate entity and stakeholders, or of man as a utility-maximizing contract maker, and build a theory that adequately reflects the world experienced by those actually involved at board level.

To present a comprehensive and coherent view of governance arrangements and structures around the world, corporate governance theory needs a taxonomy of organizational types—public, private, family, subsidiary associate, joint venture, complex ownership structures; and pyramids, chains, nets, and the rest—to distinguish very different power bases and governance systems. Systems theory and cybernetic based control system concepts such as networks, system boundaries, goals, and sub-optimization might provide insights.

The creation of a general theory of corporate governance is certainly premature and probably over-optimistic but such a theory would need to embrace:

- The relationship between individual, enterprise, and state
- A broader definition of corporate entities to cover every organization where governance and management are separate from the members
- A mapping of all the elements that affect and are affected by the governance of such organizations
- The expectations, requirements, and demands of each participant

- The duties and responsibilities of each participant
- The powers, sanctions, and accountabilities of each participant

At the moment various theoretical insights cast light on different aspects of the play, as we have seen above, highlighting some, leaving others in the shadow. We need a viewpoint that will light up the entire stage, all of the players, and the entire action.

To return to our earlier traffic system analogy, the overall operation of such a system depends on controls at three levels:

- Level 1—the regulatory level with laws, regulations and rules.
  - At this level conformance is mandatory, for example in the UK '*keep to the left of the road and at a roundabout give way to traffic coming from the right*'. The actions of those involved are policed. There are sanctions and penalties for failing to obey.
  - Notice the legal and cultural dependency at this level, for example in the USA '*keep to the right of the road*' and '*what is a roundabout?*'
- Level 2—the advisory level involving voluntary codes of conduct.
  - At this level the responsibility becomes a matter of generally accepted responsible behaviour, for example '*respect other road users*' and '*look out for hazards—children, dogs, obstacles in the road*'.
- Level 3—the personal level concerning individual beliefs and behaviour.
  - At this level personal value systems are involved, including courtesy, concern for others, socially aware behaviour, and trust.

The practice of corporate governance needs controls at similar levels. But to date the emphasis has been on levels one and two:

- The regulatory level—laws, regulations, rules
- The advisory level—voluntary codes of conduct

What has been missing is any focus on personal behaviour rooted in basic values— morality, honesty, integrity, decency, concern for others, respect, trust. The challenge for research and writing on corporate governance, whilst extending knowledge at the regulatory and advisory level, is to break into the black box of the boardroom and focus on board level activities, directors' behaviour, and board leadership.

Case Study 9.1 Drexel Burnham Lambert

This Wall Street securities trading firm was at the heart of the predator takeover market in the 1980s, using high return, high risk 'junk' bonds. It provided the base for the insider dealing activities of Ivan Boesky and provided the setting for the nefarious activities of Dennis Levine and Michael Milken.

Dennis Levine, then in his 20s, discovered that insider trading was easy and apparently fool-proof. In his job he had access to information about prospective financial deals. Now exchange that knowledge with an executive in another bank who knew about *that* bank's deals, trade the shares under a pseudo-name in the Bahamas, open an account in a Swiss bank and, bingo, the compliance authorities would never know.

Later, he grew over-confident—some might say greedy. He took a position in a company, for which his own company was preparing a bid and made US$1.3 million. But he under-estimated the capabilities of government investigators, acting with the cooperation of securities regulators (particularly IOSCO). Levine pleaded guilty, gave evidence against his colleagues, and was sentenced to two years imprisonment and a fine of US$362,000. Further he had to make restitution to the SEC of US$11.6 million in insider trading profits and was barred from employment in the securities business for life.

Michael Milken was charged with racketeering and securities fraud. He agreed to plead guilty to six felonies, paid US$600 million in restitution and was sentenced to ten years in prison. One of the effects of these activities was a growing interest in corporate governance.

In 1988 the Drexel firm pleaded guilty to six securities felonies and paid a record US$650 million in retribution. In 1990 it filed for the protection of the Bankruptcy Court.

Discussion Questions

1. Milken had to make restitution to the SEC of US$11.6 million in insider trading profits. Who had suffered as Milken made these insider trading profits? Why is insider trading considered a crime by the regulatory authorities?

2. Which theoretical insights can illuminate this case?

REFERENCES AND FURTHER READING

Aoki Masahiko (2001) *Toward a Comparative Institutional Analysis.* Cambridge, MA: MIT Press.

Berle, Adolf A. and Gardiner C. Means (1932) *The Modern Corporation and Private Property.* London: Macmillan. (Edition revised by Adolf Berle (1967) New York: Columbia University, Harcourt, Brace and World.)

Bhagat, Sanjai, Brian J. Bolton and Roberta Romano (2007) 'The Promise and Peril in Corporate Governance Indices', 7 October, ECGI working paper no. 89/2007, Social Science Research Network. Available at: www.ssrn.com/abstract=1019921

Clarke, Thomas (2004) *Theories of Corporate Governance: The Philosophical Foundations of Corporate Governance.* New York: Routledge.

—— (2007) *International Corporate Governance: A Comparative Approach.* London: Routledge.

Coarse, Ronald H. (1937) *The Nature of the Firm.* New York: Economica N.S.4. (Reprinted in Stigler, G. J. and K. E. Boulding (eds.) (1952) *Readings in Price Theory.* Homewood, IL: Irwin.)

Cochran, Philip L. and Steven L. Wartick (1988) *Corporate Governance: A Review of the Literature.* New Jersey: Financial Executives Research Foundation, Morristown.

Demsetz, Harold (1988) 'The Theory of the Firm Revisited', *Journal of Law, Economics and Organization,* Spring.

Donaldson, L. and J. H. Davis (1992) 'Stewardship Theory or Agency Theory: CEO Governance and Shareholder Returns', *Australian Journal of Management,* 16(1).

Fama, Eugene and Michael Jensen (1983) 'Separation of Ownership and Control', *Journal of Law and Economics,* June, 26.

Filatotchev, Igor and Mike Wright (eds.) (2005) *The Life Cycle of Corporate Governance.* Cheltenham: Edward Elgar.

Gomez, Pierre-Yves and Harry Korine (2008) *Entrepreneurs and Democracy: A Political Theory of Corporate Governance*. Cambridge: Cambridge University Press.

Jensen, Michael (1986) 'Agency Costs of Free Cash Flow, Corporate Finance and Takeovers', *American Economic Review*, May, 76.

——William Meckling (1976) 'Theory of the Firm: Managerial Behavior, Agency Costs and Ownership Structure', *Journal of Financial Economics*, October, 3(4).

Jensen, Michael C. (2000) *A Theory of the Firm: Governance, Residual Claims and Organizational Forms*. Cambridge, MA: Harvard University Press.

LeBlanc, Richard and James Gillies (2005) *Inside the Boardroom*. Toronto: Wiley.

Mallin, Christine A. (2007) *Corporate Governance*. Oxford: Oxford University Press.

Mintzberg, Henry (1983) *Power In and Around Organizations*. Englewood Cliffs, NJ: Prentice-Hall.

—— (1984) 'Who Should Control the Corporation?', *California Management Review*, Fall, XXVII.

Monks, Robert A. G. (1998) *The Emperor's Nightingale: Restoring the Integrity of the Corporation*. Oxford: Capstone Publishing.

—— (2008) *Corpocracy: How CEOs and the Business Roundtable Hijacked the World's Greatest Wealth Machine*. Hoboken, NJ: Wiley.

Muth, Melinda M. and Lex Donaldson (1998) 'Stewardship Theory and Board Structure: A Contingency Approach', *Corporate Governance: An International Review*, January, 6(1).

Pfeffer, Jeffrey (1972) 'Size and Composition of Corporate Boards of Directors: The Organization and its Environment', *Administrative Science Quarterly*, 17, 218.

Pettigrew, Andrew (1992) 'On Studying Managerial Elites', *Strategic Management Journal*, 13.

Roe, Mark J. (2003) *Political Determinants of Corporate Governance*, Clarendon Lectures in Management Studies series. Oxford: Oxford University Press.

Shleifer, A. and Vishny, R. (1997) 'A Survey of Corporate Governance', *Journal of Finance*, June, 52(2), 737–83.

Selvaggi, Mariano and James Upton (2008) 'Governance and Performance in Corporate Britain', ABI research paper no. 7, February, Association of British Insurers, London.

Stiles, P. and B. Taylor (2001) *Boards at Work: How Directors View their Roles and Responsibilities*. Oxford: Oxford University Press.

Thomsen, Steen (2008) *Introduction to Corporate Governance*. Copenhagen: DJOF Publishing.

Tirole, Jean (1996) *The Theory of Corporate Finance*. Princeton: Princeton University Press, chap. 1.

Williamson, Oliver E. (1975) *Markets and Hierarchy*. New York: Free Press.

—— (1996) *The Mechanisms of Governance*. New York: Oxford University Press.

Williamson, Oliver (1988) 'The Logic of Economic Organization', *Journal of Law, Economics and Organization*, Spring, 4.

USEFUL WEBSITES

www.baacgsig.qub.ac.uk
Corporate governance research.

www.berr.gov.uk/bbf/corp-gov-research/page15049.html
UK Government initiative on research in corporate governance.

www.business.bham.ac.uk/ccgr
Centre for Corporate Governance Research, Birmingham University Business School.

www.businessandlaw.vu.edu.au/cicgr
Centre for International Corporate Governance Research, Australia.

www.conference-board.org/knowledge/govern
The Conference Board (USA) Corporate Governance Center.

www.ecgi.org
European Corporate Governance Institute.

www.london.edu/centreforcorporategovernance.html
London Business School, Centre for Corporate Governance.

www.unpri.org
Universal principles of responsible investment.

PROJECTS AND EXERCISES

1. Prepare a paper/presentation analysing the various theories that have been applied to an understanding of corporate governance. Are they in conflict or are they, rather, different perspectives on the basic phenomena?

2. The text suggests that '*All major developments in the field (of corporate governance), including the codes of good practice and the American SOX Act, have been responses to corporate crises. The codes and principles of corporate governance have been created by business leaders based on their experience and conventional wisdom about what counts as good practice.*' Do you agree? Is this a sound approach: what might be the draw-backs?

3. Do you agree or disagree that Roberto Goizuetta, a former head of Coca-Cola, captured the issue, when he said: '*saying that we work for our shareholders may sound simplistic—but we frequently see companies that have forgotten the reason they exist. They may even try to be all things to all people and serve many masters in many different ways. In any event they miss their primary calling, which is to stick to the business of creating value for their owners*'?

SELF-TEST QUESTIONS

To confirm your grasp of the key points in this chapter try answering the following questions. Answers are at the end of the book.

1. What is a fundamental difference between agency theory and stewardship theory?

2. What is a fundamental difference between stewardship theory and stakeholder philosophy?

Part 3

Practices

10   The Reality of the Boardroom

- In which we consider:
    - how people, power, and politics affect practice
    - sources of governance power
    - games directors play and the manipulation of meetings
    - board styles
    - the significance of the chairman
    - implementing corporate governance below board level

In the first two sections of this book we have focused on the underlying principles and policies of corporate governance. We turn now to the realities of the boardroom. In the third and final part of the book we look at the practices of corporate governance.

How People, Power, and Politics Affect Practice

Until they have served on a board, people may well imagine that directors behave rationally, that board level discussions are analytical, and that decisions are reached after a careful consideration of alternatives. Not often. Experience of board meetings, or of the activities of any governing body for that matter, shows that reality can be quite different. Directors' behaviour is influenced by interpersonal relationships, by perceptions of position and prestige, and by the processes of power. Board and committee meetings involve a political process. In fact, corporate governance is more about human behaviour than about structures and strictures, rules and regulations. Corporate governance involves the use of power. It is a political process.

The standing and prestige of board members does not guarantee a successful board. Members of Enron's audit committee included one of the best known American accounting academics, as well as a member of the British House of Lords and chairman of the UK Press Complaints Council.

In board activities much depends on board leadership and the way the directors work together. Sound boards have sound leaders. Good leaders create successful teams. It has been said that '*outside directors never know enough about the business to be useful and inside directors always know too much to be independent*'. Successful boards avoid this claim, with all directors, both executive and non-executive, forming a cohesive team in which

independent, tough-minded individuals work together, with trust and mutual understanding, to achieve common goals.

By contrast, poorly performing boards are likely to have weak leadership and members
with little commitment, focus, or time. Some directors may lack interest or, worse, be motivated by self-interest; others may be complacent, arrogant, or dominating, some may be
easily led or weak-willed failing to speak out when disagreeing with a board decision, and
a few may be incompetent. We will consider the experience, skills, and knowledge that
make for a successful director in the next chapter.

Sources of Governance Power

As we have seen, corporate governance can be thought of as the way power is exercised over
corporate entities. The issue now is how that power is derived, who wields it, and how it is
used. What is power? Mary Parker Follet's definition will serve us well: '*power is the ability
to make things happen*'.

The fundamental legal power of the board derives from the members who have delegated the running of the company to their directors. This power is reinforced by authority
derived from the company's constitution backed up by company law. However, a board can
also find itself influenced in a number of ways, for example:

- By a dominant shareholder or group of shareholders putting pressure on the board. For
  example, the board of a wholly owned subsidiary company must conform to the business policies, plans, and investment decisions made by the group holding company

- From the threat of a potential takeover. In a public company quoted on a liquid financial market the ambitions of predators through the market for corporate control can be
  a constant source of power over a board's behaviour

- By the prospect of litigation. In today's litigious climate the threat of significant law suits
  from customers (e.g. claiming damages for faulty product or service), from employees
  (e.g. suing for damages from heath hazards), or competitors (e.g. alleging infringement
  of patents or copyright), can concentrate a board's collective mind

- Through the influence of the auditors. An independent external auditor's threat to qual-
  ify the audit report, unless significant changes are made to the declared profit, perhaps
  because of disputed asset valuations, backdated share options, or unrecorded exposure
  to risk, is likely to affect a board's deliberations

- From the effects of legislation and regulation. The prospect of new rules regulating the
  way the company does its business (immigration controls on employees, tariff barriers,
  corporation tax changes, for example) are bound to influence a board's deliberations

- From media pressure and other external exhortation. Recent years have seen a significant increase in the interest an investigative media has in companies; and external lobbyists, interests groups, and institutional investors may all seek to exert power over a
  board's thinking

- From the risk of damage to personal reputations. Directors' decisions can be affected by individual directors' concerns about their exposure to risk, both financial and reputational

- By a dominant or charismatic leader. As we will see later, the effect of the chairman, chief executive, or other board member exerting leadership can have dramatic effects on other members and on the way the board acts, and, obviously

- Through changing business circumstances

How a board handles these potential influences is a mark of its professionalism. But in addition to external sources exerting power over a company and the decisions of its board, individual directors can also wield personal power over board matters.

The power of individual directors also derives from a variety of sources, for example:

- Personality power, in other words the power wielded by a charismatic or a dominant individual over other members of the board

- Knowledge power, that is the power derived from access to information, skills, or experiences not available to the other directors. For example, the influence that an INED, who is also a director of an international bank, has when the board is discussing the effect changes in currency rates might have on the company's finances

- Sanction power, which is the power that exists if a director can apply some sanction to the company or to other directors. For example, in a joint venture company the possibility of one partner removing access to an essential source of supply, or in a family company the threat of the parent to cut his or her child from the parent's will

- Political power, that is the ability of directors to play boardroom games, which we will briefly consider in the next section

- Interpersonal power that one person might have over another because of their relationship, for example where a father and son serve on the same board, or private knowledge that one director has about another

- Organizational power derived from position in the organizational hierarchy. For example, a CEO inevitably has potential power over other executive directors because managerially they work for him or her and their prospects depend on that relationship

- Networking power derived from contacts and acquaintances of value to the company and useful in board decisions. This power is captured in the well known phrase: '*it's not what you know but who you know that matters in this world*'.

- Societal power derived from a position of influence in society. A well respected and connected member of society may be able to influence decisions to the company's benefit and public opinion about company activities. That is why retiring politicians are offered board positions, and why 'cooling-off' periods are written into their contracts.

- Ownership power and the ability to determine board membership. A director who is also either the majority shareholder in a company or his or her nominee has undoubted influence on board deliberations, even though the right to hire or fire other directors may seldom be mentioned

- Representative power delegated from an external power source such as an institutional investor, a joint venture partner, or in a not-for-profit entity the members

Games Directors Play and the Manipulation of Meetings

Board level processes, the conduct of meetings, and interactions between directors, above all, involve communication. Deconstructing directors' comments, mainly spoken but sometimes written, can identify many layers of underlying meaning. What a director says, and even more significantly what he or she chooses not to say, can demonstrate his or her understanding of and involvement in a topic under discussion. At a higher level of abstraction it can illustrate his or her views on that subject. But it may also illuminate his or her personal beliefs and values, opinions of other members of the board, and sensitivity to what other people are feeling.

In board level dialogue, the manner and form of communication is significant. Many board members are powerful people, with high self-esteem, and big egos. Some are arrogant, self-opinionated, or boastful—a few may be bullies. But others can be diffident, insecure, and shy. Being a good listener is a hallmark of an effective director. Sensitivity to the views of colleagues, hearing not only what they say but deducing why they are saying it creates a climate of mutual trust.

Of course, being a good advocate for an issue under discussion, being able to advance a case clearly, concisely, and with conviction is also an important attribute. So is the ability to debate contentious issues, in which others hold contrary views. The effective director is aware that if a person's proposals are rudely attacked he or she is more likely to counterattack than have a change of mind. Politeness has its place in the boardroom.

In badly led boards, personalities and political manoeuvring can prevail and directors will play games. An awareness of some of these games can help create a board culture in which they become apparent and are stopped. In a light-hearted review, here are a few of the games directors play.

Alliances
Two or more members of the board conspire together to influence a board decision. For example, two executive directors, each responsible for an operating division in a group, work together to prevent the introduction of a proposed management control system that would result in greater transparency of their divisional activities: however, they both agree to argue their case on the grounds that the system would prove expensive and that cost would outweigh any benefit.

Coalitions and Cabals
Groups of directors work together, inside and outside the boardroom, to bring about a specific outcome to a board decision. Coalition building involves the canvassing of support for an issue informally outside the boardroom so that there is a sufficient consensus when the matter is discussed formally in the boardroom. For example, a group of directors in a not-for-profit company incorporated to run a sports facility opposed plans to build a new swimming pool. The members of this clique were all non-swimmers, and refused to sanction other expenditure unless the swimming pool plan was dropped.

Cronyism
Relationships between directors can influence decisions on the basis of personal relationships not the rational merits of the case. Cronyism can produce decisions that are not in the best interest of the company. For example, three directors on the board of a listed company were all members of the same country club. They tended to support each other in board discussions, all favouring the same outcome and opposing the same alternatives. Cronyism can affect an entire board. For example, a director declared a personal interest in a tender for a project being discussed by the board. He was asked to leave the room during the discussion of that contract. But the board decided to support this bid because of their personal relationships with that director, even though the bid was not the most worthy.

Deal Making
Agreements made outside the boardroom between two or more directors to achieve a specific outcome on a board issue. Deal making is a classic game, usually involving compromise. The medical members of a hospital board agreed, during a private dinner, to put pressure on the board to acquire some new sophisticated medical equipment they wanted. They were successful, even though there were more pressing needs for the available funds, including cleaning equipment for the wards.

Divide and Rule
When a contentious issue is being discussed, the outcome wanted by one faction is more likely to be achieved if the other directors can be divided into a number of disagreeing factions. This is a ploy adopted from the chair in some boards. Divide and rule can be a dirty game, in which the player sees the chance to set one director against another, or groups of directors against each other. An issue in the financial accounts might be used, for example, to divide the executive directors, the non-executive directors, and the auditors from each other, in order to achieve an entirely different personal aim. For example, a senior INED serving on the board of a Canadian cooperative advanced arguments that divided the board into three groups reflecting the views of the various representative groups—suppliers, customers, and the administration—thus he could push through the strategy he wanted.

Empire Building
Usually adopted by executive directors, empire building involves the misuse of privileged access to information, people, or other resources to acquire power over organizational territory. The process can involve intrigue, battles, and conquests. Take the example of a company in the IT consulting business, which acquired a marketing company to promote its business. The operations director of the IT company moved his staff to the more palatial offices of the marketing company, took over its fleet of cars, and argued in the board meeting that his deputy should also become a board member, because of his enlarged portfolio of responsibilities.

Half Truths

By presenting only part of the information on an issue before the board, an unscrupulous director can bias the discussion in favour of his or her own preferred result. Whilst the director does not actually lie, the half truth obscures the full story. For example, an executive director argued strongly in favour of his own project, presenting impressive cost/benefit information in support, but failing totally to mention that the risk of stoppage to the firm's entire operation would be significantly increased.

Hidden Agendas

An individual director offers a convincing argument in support of a particular line in a board discussion without adding that additional outcomes to his or her advantage would then arise—the hidden agenda. Hidden agendas usually involve the pursuit of secret goals that benefit a director's own interests or further his or her own career against the interest of the organization as a whole. In other words, the ploy is another example of the agency dilemma. For example, in advocating a contract to acquire services for a joint venture, a director on the joint venture company board failed to mention that this contract would bring significant sales discounts on products bought by one of the joint venture partners—his employer.

Lobbying

Lobbying involves attempts to influence directors, or those in a position to influence directors, usually outside the boardroom. Consider the implications when a director of a consulting practice sought out the wife of the CEO of a client company during a cocktail party and encouraged her to persuade her husband to accept a quotation.

Log Rolling

Two or more directors colluding, to their mutual benefit, is a classic board level game. For example two executive directors in a manufacturing company came to an agreement before the board meeting. The first would enthusiastically support an investment proposal benefiting the second, whilst the second would offer mitigating arguments during the review of the poor budgetary performance of the first.

Propaganda

Propaganda is the dissemination of information to support a cause, without attempting to show the complete picture. The chief executive of a finance institution made a PowerPoint presentation to his board, advocating the introduction of a new derivative-based product, without once mentioning the word 'risk'. Unfortunately, none of the non-executive directors raised the question, the board approved the proposal, and a year later the company had to issue a profit warning following losses on the new product.

Rival Camps

Rival camps is an extreme case of coalitions and cabals, where there are opposing factions on a board. Hostilities, spies, and double agents can be involved. The board of a *Fortune 500* company were totally split on a proposal led by the chairman/CEO's proposal to bid for a rival company. Leaders of each faction emerged and the two groups began to hold separate meetings, to brief the press independently, and to talk with institutional investors about their own perspectives on the bid.

Scaremongering

Scaremongering is used by some directors to emphasize the downside risks in a board decision, casting doubts on the situation without presenting a balanced perspective, thus attempting to have the proposal turned down. As a director in a multinational manufacturing group argued convincingly, when the board were considering building a new manufacturing facility in another country, '*we shall have nothing but labour troubles, high taxes, if we locate there, and possibly government interference . . . and who knows what might happen if the present government falls? We could find all our assets nationalized without recompense.*' A risk assessment would have shown the probability of these future uncertain events to be low.

Snowing

Snowing involves deluging any director who asks for more information on a topic with masses of data, thus confusing the situation and hiding any cracks. This game is usually played by executive directors on unsuspecting outside directors.

Spinning

Spinning, a form of gaming developed at governmental level, intentionally presents a distorted view of a person or a situation, in a way that favours the spinner's interests. In corporate governance, spinning can be carried out at the level of board committees, the board as a whole, the shareholders, or the media.

Sponsorship

Sponsorship is support by a powerful director for another director, often a newly elected director, usually for their joint benefit. For example, the long-serving director of the Australian subsidiary of an American global group commented during a board meeting '*Mr. Chairman, I'll have a word with Robert (a new director) after the meeting to explain how we handle these things. As you know I've a lot of experience of this type of situation and what we've done in the past.*' In the ensuing discussion the experienced director relayed a lot of gossip about the ways of the board and its chairman to his own future benefit.

Sub-optimization

Sub-optimization occurs when a director supports a part of the organization to the detriment of the company as a whole. We have explored this situation already, both when considering the agency dilemma and in group management control systems.

Some executive directors suffer from tunnel vision, because they are too closely involved with a functional department, division, or subsidiary company. Others may have a myopic view of the situation because they would be personally affected by the outcome. An independent evaluation of the overall strategic situation and top management performance by outside directors can help to overcome such problems.

Window Dressing

Window dressing includes making a fine external show of sound corporate governance principles and practice, whist minimizing failures. Some companies' mission statements, social responsibility and sustainable reports, and core principles suffer from window dressing. Window dressing can also involve showing financial results in the best possible light, whilst hiding weaknesses, although this runs the risk of an adverse audit report or worse.

One of the problems facing companies publishing non-financial statements to shareholders, such as those required in an operating review, can give rise to concerns about window dressing. Information about strategic intentions is open to optimistic presentation and is not amenable to conventional audit. Contrariwise, few boards are likely to expose their shareholders to information about potential risks facing the company from competitors, predators, or other uncertain future events.

Notice that most of the 'games' described involve the subtleties of communication and interpersonal relations. Most of the tactics are not illegal, do not amount to fraud, nor are they inherently dishonest. They are a means to achieving directors' personal preferences. Notice, too, that many of these 'games' are commonplace in the world of government, where they are considered legitimate. Indeed in some boards, too, game playing becomes an art form and board meetings more like the deliberations of an adversarial parliament. Strong chairmanship can reduce the disadvantages of game playing, unless of course the chairman is also playing games! The ideal is a well led professional board team working together with integrity, where directors understand and trust each other, and therefore do not need to resort to game playing.

Before leaving the topic of board level politics, here are a few more light-hearted thoughts on the board level game of manipulating meetings.

Meeting Manipulation

There are a number of devices that directors have been known to use to achieve the results they want in meetings. These include:

- *Management of the agenda* which determines what is and is not discussed. Influencing the agenda is a powerful weapon and experienced chairmen will ensure that they remain in control

- *Challenging the minutes* of the last meeting at the start of the next meeting. This device can be used to re-open discussion of an item that was resolved, against the manipulator's interests, previously. Strong chairmanship prevents such activities

- *Hijacking the chair*, in other words taking over the running of the meeting. This can only work if the chairman is new or ineffective

- *Refocusing the debate* when the tenor of the meeting is running against the manipulator's interests. There are a number of devices that can be used. Talking around the subject, whilst shifting the discussion onto favourable ground, is a particular skill of the meeting manipulator. Profound irrelevance is his or her stock in trade. But filibustering to run the discussion out of time will seldom work in the boardroom

- *The 'put-down'* involves the skilful introduction of doubt when responding to a proposal before the board. Good put-downs often adopt an air of superiority, as in '*we discussed this matter before you joined the board and decided against it*'.

- *Presenting ideas in the context of other people's* can be powerful: '*I was inclined to believe . . . until I heard X, now I am sure we should . . .*' The fact that X was advocating something quite different is not the point.

- *Summarizing* the discussion thus far can be used to emphasize favourable points and down-play others: '*What the meeting seems to be saying is . . .*'

- *Pre-determining the outcome* is an extension of the summarizing device used to foreclose discussion by stating the outcome of a decision, preferably in Latin, as in: '*Chairman, we seem to have reached the decision nem con*' (nemine contradicente: no one against), whether anyone is against or not

- *A challenge*, when a discussion seems to be flowing against the manipulator's interests, can be persuasive. '*On a point of order, chairman*' is a call, which if offered with sufficient challenge and conviction will stop an orator in full flight. Strictly, points of order are only relevant if there are standing orders covering the running of the meeting; but that will not deter a skilful meeting manipulator

- *A call to the chair* that the discussion has strayed from the point of the agenda item, that irrelevant issues are being raised, or that the discussion would be more appropriate under another item, can be used to deflect an ongoing discussion that is moving against the manipulator's interests

- *'Any other business'* on the agenda can also be used to re-open debate or introduce new items. However, the chairman may insist that only items previously notified can be discussed and that no papers can be tabled. No matter. The manipulator will use the agendum '*date of the next meeting*' to introduce a new topic, explain the issue, hand out the papers, express an opinion, or suggest further discussion, or the formation of a sub-committee with him or her in the chair. '*We need to look into this issue with the care and attention it deserves*', ensuring that the sub-committee has a majority of those who favour the idea

- *Calling for a postponement of discussion* until the next meeting, on the grounds of the lack of information, the need for more reflection, or until an absent member is present, can also be used to postpone a decision that seems likely to be decided against the manipulator's interests

- *Calling for an adjournment of the meeting* is a heavier version of the postponement device
- *Lack of a quorum* can be used to stymie a decision, if the articles of association or the rulebook specify a quorum, the lack of a quorum will prevent further decision making
- Finally, the *management of the minutes* can provide a crucial opportunity to manipulate a meeting

---

Box 10.1 A Few Thoughts on Boardroom Communication

- *'In my experience . . .'* is one of the most over-used phrases in board discussions. The issue is whether that experience is relevant
- *'To tell you the honest truth . . . '* should ring warning bells about the veracity of the information
- *'. . . trust me on this'* is a phrase frequently used to avoid rational debate
- *'These financials are a load of rubbish'*—some comments invite retaliation rather than rational dialogue
- *'That'll never work in a month of Sundays . . .'*—attacking proposals on the table is usually less productive than offering alternatives—*'I wonder whether we might also consider . . .'*

Some will say that this section on game playing and meeting manipulation takes a cynical view of board level interaction. Others will believe that it more closely mirrors their own experience of boardroom life than explorations of board structures and codes of good governance practice. What is undoubtedly true is that the reality of boardroom life involves people, power, and politics as much as rigorous analysis and rational debate.

Board Styles

It is apparent that boards differ considerably in their culture and their style. Some boards are highly professional in their operations, with experienced, well informed, and collaborative directors, often holding strong views and engaging in tough-minded but amicable debate. Outside directors are closely involved in decision making and share a common view of the corporate strategy. Deliberations in such boards tend to seek consensus and votes are rarely taken. The boards of many listed companies in Western cultures fall into this group. We recognized some significant differences in board culture in other countries in chapter 8.

However, even in Western cultures the behaviour of boards is not always professional. For example, board culture can evolve into a comfortable, convivial relationship between the directors. Outside directors may ask questions but not probe in depth, and offer suggestions but never challenge the executive. In board deliberations such directors tend to support each other and do not have tough-minded exchanges. In such companies the climate in the boardroom is cosy, in fact, more like that of a country club.

Case Study 10.1 Independent Insurance

In June 2001, the board of the UK company Independent Insurance was told by advisers PricewaterhouseCoopers (PWC) that the company was insolvent, its liabilities exceeding its reserves and assets by a quarter of a billion pounds. A provisional liquidator was appointed. Yet only six months earlier Independent Insurance appeared to be worth over £1 billion.

The company had been floated on the stock market in 1993 and many analysts favoured the shares. The last published accounts in 2000 showed an operating profit of £40 million, although cash outflow was somewhat higher, and the auditors, KPMG, reported that the accounts showed a true and fair view of the state of the company's affairs. Actuaries, hired to review the company's exposure to risk, claimed that the reserves made reasonable allowance for possible claims. Annual returns were duly filed with Companies House and the Financial Services Authorities. Six months later the company had collapsed.

What went wrong? Where were the checks and balances supposed to be provided by the board with independent directors, the auditors, the actuaries, the analysts, and the regulators?

For fourteen years Michael Bright had been managing director of Independent Insurance. A man of undoubted entrepreneurial flair, he had many fans in the City of London for his unique way of doing business and the company's '*superior underwriting strength*'. But he was a forceful and charismatic character and, as his reputation grew, he became less and less willing to brook challenges to his authority.

One by one his fellow executive directors left. Robert McCracken, head of British regional business left in 1997; Keith Rutter, responsible for liability underwriting, in 1998. A third member of the triumvirate that had previously kept Bright in check, Alan Clarke, retired in 1999. The other significant executive director, Philip Condon, the Deputy MD, was a close friend of Bright. Garth Ramsay was non-executive chairman of the board and Sir Iain Noble was another non-executive director. KPMG charged £667,000 for their audit, but consultancy and other services produced nearly another million pounds.

Financial problems facing Independent Insurance mounted in the first six months of 2001. A number of reinsurance contracts had been negotiated with GE Capital against the possibility of mounting claims. As the financial situation deteriorated Garth Ramsay, the chairman, replaced Michael Bright. He sought more information on the reinsurance contracts and was horrified to learn that, instead of the substantial cover anticipated, Independent was exposed to a potential liability of many millions. The company had been under-reserving for years. Risks had been insured at cut prices without board approval. There was a major deficit in the company's reserves and, being unable to cap this exposure, further equity could not be raised.

Discussion Questions

1. What went wrong at Independent?

2. How might this have been avoided? Consider board membership, board leadership, and board level information and control systems.

3. Were the auditors at fault?

Then there is a category of company in which the board provide little more than a legalizing rubber stamp for decisions taken elsewhere. As we shall see, there are some situations in which such a situation can be legitimate.

Then there is a fourth category of board which has members representing different interests. A hospital board, with different board members from the hospital administration, the medical team, representing the patients, and possibly the funding bodies, would be an example. In such boards, members tend to take positions that reflect the interests of the groups they represent. Debates can be lively and votes are often called for on issues. The boardroom style, in fact, is more like that of a parliament.

What determines board style? Board style is a function of a number of variables, first and foremost the board leadership, the role adopted by the board chairman. We will study alternative approaches to board leadership in the next section. The size of the board can affect its style: too many members and the opportunity for individuals to contribute become limited and the board may divide into factions; too few and there may be insufficient diversity of views. The balance of the board between executive directors, CNEDs, and INEDs will clearly affect the tenor of board deliberations, also the balance of experience and background among the board members. The actual set of attributes among all the directors—their combined experience, knowledge, and skills—is also a major causal factor in determining board style.

The culture of the board, including its history, its past leadership, and previous events affecting the business, will also influence its style. The following set of criteria lists various attributes affecting board style and shows some of the likely effects. Notice the range of differences that can exist between boards.

Board Traditions
In some boards rituals and customs mean a lot. Corporate stories and traditions are frequently mentioned. Board procedures and precedents are well established. Many members of the board are likely to be long serving. There is probably a formal boardroom and there may be pictures of past chairmen on the wall. At the other extreme are boards with no time for tradition, in which board practices change readily. The average length of directors' service is short. Informality is the keynote of their meetings, which are held wherever it is convenient.

Corporate Vision
This attribute of style indicates the extent to which directors share the same strategic vision about the company's present position and its future direction and prospects. In some companies all of the directors can readily articulate the company's mission and strategic situation: in others directors either do not understand the company's strategic context or, worse, disagree on what it is.

Innovation
Here the issue is the extent to which each director is expected to contribute new ideas. In some boards all ideas are welcomed, even if controversial. In others new thinking is

discouraged, developments are expected to fit established norms, change is resisted, and past successes influence views on the future.

Control

This reflects the way the board accepts responsibility for exerting overall control over the enterprise, if necessary becoming involved in responding to business problems, or delegating that responsibility down to management through the chief executive.

Decision Taking

Decision taking may be strongly influenced by one person or a small group of directors, in which case there may be little analysis and a lot of dogmatic statements; or decisions may be reached after a lot of talking leading to an eventual consensus among all directors.

Leadership

In some boards authority is jealously guarded by one or a few of the directors, with other board members expected to give advice only when called on. In other boards, the leadership style encourages all directors to contribute to board deliberations, with people respected for their experience, knowledge, and wisdom, and encouraged to contribute.

Commitment

At one extreme are those boards whose members show a low commitment to the board, with high levels of self-interest; at the other extreme all directors are highly committed to the company, the board, and their fellow directors.

Adaptability

Some boards are slow to adapt to changing circumstances. Consequently, board meetings tend to be predictable. Whereas other boards are highly adaptive, with flexible responses to changing situations, even though their meetings can sometimes be turbulent.

Collaboration

In some boards the directors support each other, ensuring that everyone is informed, involved, and committed. At the other extreme are boards whose members tend to compete with each other, showing distrust, poor interpersonal relationships, even hostility towards one another.

Conflict

Board level conflict can be either desirable or destructive. Conflict that is creative, with tough-minded but courteous interactions between people who say what they believe but try to understand conflicting points of view is found in some boards. In others overt conflict may be discouraged, but then there may be behind the scenes political activity.

Relationships
In some boards, directors see themselves as part of the board team, and treat each other with frankness, respect, and trust. In others, directors act as individuals, rather than part of the board team. In such cases image building, posturing, and boardroom games may be prevalent.

Communication
Access to information, as we have seen earlier, is a source of potential board level power. Consequently, in some boards directors guard the information they have, protecting their sources, and encouraging secrecy. Gossip and grapevine communication is likely to be prevalent. Other boards, however, seem to encourage open communication with a ready exchange of data, information, and knowledge.

Status
Directors' perceptions of their status can be important, with visible signs of the directors' prestige being important, with formal, even ritual, meetings, and probably with ornate boardrooms and elaborate meals. Conversely, in other boards status is relatively unimportant, with directors seeing each other as equals, and not needing ego-reinforcing signals to be sent to the rest of the organization or the outside world.

Conformity
Some board chairmen, believing that a board has to be united, expect their directors to conform to group norms. Non-conformists are not tolerated, indeed they are unlikely to be appointed in the first place. By contrast other chairmen welcome non-conformists, recognizing that they can bring fresh insights and enliven board thinking.

Trust
As we have seen trust is the underpinning of the concept of the corporation. Typically this refers to the fiduciary duty owed by directors to their shareholders. But the relationship *between* directors also plays an important part. In some boards directors trust each other implicitly. But it has to be noted that in others trust can be low and directors suspicious of each other. As we will see later, much hinges on the ability and leadership style of the board chairman.

Some of these characteristics of board style reflect relationships at board level and the way the board members work together. Others affect how well the board does its work and achieves its goals. The challenge is to balance concern for relationships with

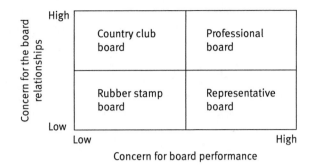

Figure 10.1 Different board styles

concern for achieving board success. The simple matrix in figure 10.1 contrasts a board's concern for the relationships between its members with its concern for getting the job done.

Firms scoring well on both relationships and task can be considered to have a professional style. Those scoring low on each count are rubber stamps, which can be appropriate in subsidiary companies that are managed through a group management structure, or in 'letter-box' companies incorporated to protect a name, limit liability on an exposed risk, or for tax planning purposes. Performing higher on task than on relationships is the representative board that we saw in the hospital board example earlier, whereas high on relationships but poor on task is the hallmark of the country club board style.

The characteristics listed above can be used as the basis for a board level exercise to plot a board's style. Obviously, the results reflect the perceptions of those making assessment on the range between the extremes for each criterion. The exercise can be used in director development or form part of a board performance assessment exercise.

The Significance of the Chairman

The preceding material has highlighted the vital significance of the chairman in creating and managing a successful board. Even though composed of brilliant and highly experienced individuals, a board is not likely to be effective unless it is well led. That's the prime role of the chairman.

Many people speak broadly of the chairman of the company, whereas the role is strictly chairman of the company's board of directors, although he will usually chair the meetings of the members of the organization. As we saw in chapter 3, subject to anything in the company's articles, the directors elect one of their own members to the chairmanship. There are few statutory requirements for the role, so chairmen vary considerably in the way they carry out the responsibilities. At one extreme is the powerful chairman who acts as a figurehead for the company, influences its strategic direction, interacts strongly with the chief executive, and provides wide ranging leadership of the board. At the other extreme the chairman does little more than manage board meetings.

Before proceeding there are some problems of nomenclature to settle. Although the chairman of most major companies are men, many women occupy the position in quangos and not-for-profit organizations. To avoid the use of the inelegant term chairwoman, some boards refer to their board leader as Lady Chairman or Madam Chairman. Others have adopted the genderless title of 'chair', as in 'the chair announced the results'. Here we will avoid confusion and controversy by using the word 'chairman'. Another confusion can arise with the term 'Executive Chairman', which is typically used to indicate either that the holder has a full time commitment to the office, rather than being part time as is frequently the case, or that the chairmanship and chief executive roles are combined, as in the boards of many American companies.

So what should a chairman do? In the opinion of the Cadbury Report:

The chairman's role in securing good corporate governance is crucial. Chairmen are primarily responsible for the working of the board, for its balance of membership subject to board and share-holders' approval, for ensuring that all relevant issues are on the agenda, and for ensuring that all directors, executive and non-executive alike, are enabled and encouraged to play their full part in its activities. (It is important for chairmen to ensure that executive directors look beyond their executive duties and accept their full share of their responsibilities of governance.) Chairmen should be able to stand sufficiently well back from the day-to-day running of the business to ensure that their boards are in full control of the company's affairs and alert to their obligations to shareholders.

The following six functions for a chairman elaborate the above perspective:

Management of the Board

Leadership of the board team is the chairman's primary duty. This provides the foundations of the board's style. The chairman should play a pivotal role in determining the structure and size of the board, along with the nominating committee and subject to the articles. This involves determining the balance between executives, INEDs, and CNEDs, if there are any. The chairman will normally want to be involved, with the nominating committee, in the identification, selection, and nomination of directors. He will want to ensure that they have the necessary qualifications and experience, that they will fit into the existing board culture, that they have the time to devote to board activities and have no conflicting interests. After all these are to be members of the team that he is responsible for leading.

Following appointment, the chairman will often brief a new director on the corporate situation and board practices and will want to ensure that the director's induction programme is adequate. The chairman also has a vital role in reviewing the performance of each director, a responsibility which in the past was often informal and casual but is now formally expected under some of the corporate governance codes. Similarly the chairman needs to ensure that director training, updating, and development, both for individuals and the board as a whole, is appropriate: again an expectation of some governance codes. The duties, membership, and chairmanship of board committees also need to be managed by the chairman. Finally, he needs to initiate the project that evaluates the effectiveness of the board and board committees and follow through on necessary changes within the board and its policies, procedures, and processes.

Management of Meetings

This is the conventional view of the role of chairman and for most directors the most visible. In the management of board meetings the board's style is seen in operation. Prior to the meeting the chairman needs to consider the time, location, duration of the meeting, and who should attend, both as statutory members, but also to provide information or to observe. He has to agree the topics on the agenda, not only the conventional ones but any issue that he feels the board should be aware of and discuss. He should ensure that each director is adequately and appropriately informed, not only through routine board reports but with individual material and briefings if necessary. In conducting the meeting the chairman needs to ensure that each director has the opportunity to contribute, that different points of view are succinctly summarized and that the board, as far as possible is led to a consensus on the outcome. Getting directors involved, restraining the dominant, encouraging the hesitant, whilst focusing attention where needed, and balancing the available time appropriately between topics is the essence of good meeting management. The diffident director may seldom speak but when he does his insights can be worth more than many tedious moments from the garrulous. The chairman should beware of the pitfalls of 'group-think' and game-playing, and encourage independence of thought in his boardroom. We will explore some of these matters further in chapter 12 on board effectiveness.

Strategic Leadership
Some boards delegate a lot of the responsibility for developing the corporate strategy to the CEO and top executive team. We discussed this in chapter 6 on the functions of the board. Nevertheless the board is still responsible overall for setting the direction for the firm. So the chairman needs to ensure that appropriate board attention is given to strategy formulation and policy making, and should stimulate strategic thinking at board level. It is the chairman's duty to ensure that all directors understand the company's mission and its strategic context, and share a common view of the strategic direction being followed.

Linking the Board with Management
Where the chairmanship is separate from the chief executive role (as is recommended or required in all the corporate governance codes, except those reflecting practices in the US), the relationship between the chairman and the CEO is one of the most crucial, the most sensitive, and the most subtle relationships in the organization. The relationship is crucial because these are the two most important roles in the entire organization. It is sensitive because these may be people of significance with high public profiles, and big stakes can be involved. And it is subtle because it involves close liaison between two people who each have the power to affect the other. At its best the CEO perceives his chairman as a wise counsellor, someone with wide and relevant experience, and a person to be trusted implicitly; whilst the chairman sees his CEO as the best and most successful appointment the board has made. Some of the problems with the combined chairman/CEO role become apparent in this analysis. At times, of course, even with split roles the relationship can prove to be difficult. Typical problems arise through a clash of personalities, if the chairman interferes in the executive running of the business, or when events call for the disciplining or ultimately the replacement of the CEO. The 'promotion' of a retiring CEO to the chairmanship (discouraged or prohibited in some governance codes) can also be a recipe for disaster, unless he can adapt to the new responsibilities and leave the running of the business to the new CEO.

Arbitration Between Board Members and Others
An occasional role that some chairmen find themselves called on to play is to arbitrate between feuding members of the board, the shareholders, or other involved parties. In some such cases the best advice may be for the parties to see their lawyers. But a respected chairman can, at times, provide wise counsel and conciliation to the benefit of the parties, the board, and the company.

Being the Public Face of the Company
Finally, we come to a role that chairmen of major corporations are increasingly expected to fulfil, that of being a figurehead for the board and the company. Where the chairman takes on this role, the CEO can focus more specifically on running the business, which can be useful given the current climate of corporate complexity and change.

As a public face for the company the chairman might be called on to interact with shareholders, institutional investors, and financial institutions, to meet with customers or clients for the company's products, and to represent the company in the external world of public inquiries, media investigations, and public relations exercises.

Although, some corporate governance codes now give the role of interacting with institutional investors and financial analysts to the senior independent non-executive director, in other cases this can fall to the chairman. Occasionally, the chairman will represent the company, providing a shareholder perspective to the workforce and management. But treading on the chief executive's legitimate territory needs to be avoided. As the figurehead the chairman could be called on to make public statements, to appear at inquiries, to host representative meetings, as well as meeting in small groups and one on one with significant people.

Case Study 10.2 Iceland

Malcolm Walker was the chairman of Iceland, a UK frozen food firm, and the 5th largest food provider in the UK. In late 2000 he cashed in the bulk of his shares in the company for around £13 million. Five weeks later the company issued a profits warning that sent the share price crashing. Walker avoided the immediate aftermath of his action by going on holiday and on his return announced he was retiring. When castigated in the press for selling his shares, Walker claimed that he had done no wrong: his board of directors had full knowledge of the sale and had sanctioned it.

Discussion Questions

1. What information should the board have had before sanctioning the sale of Walker's shares? Were they told of the daily figures, which were, no doubt, already pointing to the profits warning? Did they question what the impact of the sale might be on investor confidence and the share price?

2. How can directors balance allegiance to their chairman, who probably nominated them to the board and relies on their support, with their primary duty to the company and its shareholder members?

Obviously, each chairman brings a different style to the leadership of the board. Some have a light touch full of humour and charm, others bring a decisive, no-nonsense approach, and a few are downright Napoleonic. Chairmanship of a board or board committee is challenging. Successful chairmen will often claim that the success is due to their team. But that team needed good leadership.

Incidentally, some companies use the title Vice-Chairman to spread the work of the chairman; others use the title to indicate the chairman-elect; and it is used by a few boards to confer prestige without necessarily giving additional responsibilities or powers. As Robert Lacey wrote in *Detroit's Destiny*:

Chairman, Vice-chairman, President—the titles do not always mean quite what they seem. Analysing the hierarchies at the top of American public companies can be a little like working out where real power lies in the Kremlin. The man at the top of the pecking order may, indeed, be the big potato, but it is just as likely that he counts for nothing at all.

Implementing Corporate Governance Below Board Level

Although the need for sound corporate governance is widely accepted in boardrooms around the world, and despite the basics of corporate governance being clearly articulated in principles and codes, many directors and particularly board chairmen still question how it applies in their own case. They ask, for example:

- What is the *real* role of the board?
- How should a board relate to top management?
- How should the board balance collaboration with control?
- What should a board delegate to management?
- How much freedom of action should the CEO have in practice?
- How can a unitary board contribute to performance whilst ensuring conformance?

In an earlier chapter the recommendation was made that boards should establish a policy on decisions that are retained to the board, that is those that cannot be delegated to management. But the above concerns go far beyond the establishment of a formal checklist of retained decisions. They go to the heart of the board's role, the directors' work, and the way corporate governance links with management. In particular the leadership role of the chairman comes under the spotlight.

Surprisingly perhaps, answers to the questions posed above vary significantly between companies and between cultures. Much depends on how corporate governance is perceived and, particularly, on the attitudes and competence of the chairman.

In chapter 8 we reviewed various models of corporate governance around the world and saw how cultural concepts affected practice.

In the UK/Commonwealth model, the principles based comply or explain approach to corporate governance gives boards freedom to interpret the relevant corporate governance code and allows directors considerable freedom to determine their relationship with management. In these circumstances boards face a range of options. These are reinforced by the separation of board chairmanship from the CEO. At one extreme the directors can delegate power over the business of the company to the CEO and his or her management team, in effect discussing and eventually approving strategies, policies, and plans proposed by management, then ensuring that the proposals are followed and the expected results achieved. At the other extreme, the directors can retain power over much of the strategic direction and planning of the business, requiring the CEO and his or her management to carry out those plans and be accountable for results. In between the extremes the delegation of power from the board to management can vary considerably and may change as chairman, directors, senior managers, or business circumstances change.

In the United States model, the rule based approach to corporate governance gives boards fewer degrees of freedom. Combining the roles of board chairman and CEO concentrates power in that person. The top management team, who report to the chairman/CEO, runs the business operations whatever and wherever they are. The chairman/CEO is then accountable to the board, and in effect becomes the lynch-pin between the board and the management. The presence of one or two other executive directors, say the COO and the CFO, on the board typically only serves to reinforce the chairman/CEO's position.

In these circumstances, the board consists predominantly of independent non-executive directors, perceives its role as advising the chairman/CEO perhaps questioning the strategies, risks, and resources, ensuring conformance to plans, and confirming compliance with legal requirements. Though the board is responsible for the CEOs remuneration and contract, disciplining a successful and strong-minded CEO can be difficult. Some critics have suggested that this form of board is closer to the European two-tier supervisory board model than the UK/Commonwealth model, given the abundance of independent directors. The primary differences being, of course, that the American board *does* have some executive directors, probably the CEO and perhaps the COO and CFO, whereas in the European board no common membership is allowed between the supervisory board members and the executive.

The powerful chairman/CEO is at the apex of the American model of corporate governance. This fundamentally differentiates the perception of the board's role and its relationship with management from the UK/Commonwealth model. The American model tends to see the board as a group of independent outside directors, whose experience and knowledge provide advice and oversight. Primarily their power lies in their duty to appoint, assess, and ultimately, if necessary, sack the chairman/CEO. But overall responsibility for the company then lies with the powerful CEO/chairman. Indeed this has caused shareholder activist Bob Monks to question whether boards of some American corporations have ever really understood corporate governance.

In the Continental European model, the two-tier board structure, as we have seen, attempts to overcome the fundamental problem of the unitary board by separating the performance role of the management board from the conformance responsibility of the supervisory board. Thus, unlike the unitary board, no single body is responsible for both performance and conformance. Consequently the relationship between the board and management has quite different dimensions from the unitary board model. In the two-tier model the relationships between the members of the supervisory board and the top executives on the management board is fundamental. Experience shows that, although the separation of performance and conformance functions between the two boards is conceptually appealing, in practice significant problems can arise between the supervisory board and top management.

In the family-centric model of Asian corporate governance, the head of the family is typically the head of management as well as leading the board. In the *keiretsu* and *chaebol* models of Japanese and South Korean corporate governance, power to determine what decisions are delegated from board to management is often heavily centralized. While in the state owned or state dominated models of Asian corporate governance, the state often retains the power to appoint directors and influence the work of the board, which in turn determines what is decided at board level and what is delegated to management.

The implementation of corporate governance below board level goes to the heart of corporate governance: it is about the reality of power. Who wields what power over the corporate entity and in what way? The ultimate challenge is to achieve compliance with competence. Such dilemmas are still unresolved in some companies, and become particularly apparent if the company's activities become international and the directors have to face alternative perspectives.

REFERENCES AND FURTHER READING

Brountas, Paul P. (2004) *Boardroom Excellence: A Commonsense Perspective on Corporate Governance.* San Francisco: Jossey-Bass.

Cornford, F. M. (1908) *Microcosmographia Academia: A Guide to the Young Academic Politician.* London: Bowes and Bowes.

Lipman, Frederick D. and L. Keith Lipman (2006) *Corporate Governance Best Practices: Strategies for Public, Private and Not for Profit Organizations.* Hoboken, NJ: John Wiley.

Law Chee Keong (ed.) (2002) *Corporate Governance: An Asia Pacific Critique.* Hong Kong: Sweet and Maxwell (Asia).

Roe, Mark J. (2003) *Political Determinants of Corporate Governance.* Oxford: Oxford University Press.

Salter, Malcolm (2008) *Innovation Corrupted: The Origins and Legacy of Enron's Collapse.* Cambridge, MA: Harvard University Press.

USEFUL WEBSITES

www.charteredsecretary.net and www.icsa.org.uk
Institute of Chartered Secretaries and Administrators (UK). Best practice guides and other publications.

www.companydirectors.com.au
Australian Institute of Directors.

www.conference-board.org
The Conference Board (USA).

www.hkiod.com
Hong Kong Institute of Directors.

www.iasb.org/Home.htm
International Accounting Standards Board.

www.iod.com
Institute of Directors (UK).

www.iodsa.co.za
The Institute of Directors—South Africa.

www.nacdonline.org
National Association of Corporate Directors (USA).

www.sid.org.sg
The Singapore Institute of Directors. Useful links to other corporate governance sites.

www.tdc.ca/respons.htm
Check list of director responsibilities.

PROJECTS AND EXERCISES

1. Review the section on board level games and meeting manipulation. Develop other examples in each case that might be used to illustrate the idea.

2. Use recent examples of corporate problems, discussed in the financial press, to identify examples of the effect of power on board level situations.

3. Prepare a set of guidelines for chairmen of listed companies, outlining their duties.

4. In groups of eight or ten simulate a board meeting.

SELF-TEST QUESTIONS

To confirm your grasp of the key points in this chapter try answering the following questions. Answers are at the end of the book.

1. What is the fundamental basis of board power?

2. Name some other ways in which a board can find itself influenced.

3. What is the knowledge power that a director might have?

4. Name five other sources of director power.

5. Name four different board styles.

6. What criteria affect board style?

7. What is a chairman's primary duty?

8. Name six functions of a chairman.

9. Explain the chairman's role in strategic leadership.

10. In what ways might a chairman be the public face for the company?

11 Directors' Capabilities and Responsibilities

- In which we consider:
  - desirable attributes in a director
  - the core competencies a director needs
  - roles directors play
  - the legal duties of a director
  - shareholder rights vary between jurisdictions
  - the US Sarbanes-Oxley Act 2002
  - the UK Companies Act 2006

Desirable Attributes in a Director

In the first part of this book, the focus was on corporate governance principles. But behind the corporate constitutions, board structures, and corporate governance codes are people. As we saw in the previous chapter, people can bring a wide range of prejudices, political behaviours, and power plays to board affairs. So what personal attributes are needed in a successful and professional director?

The primary prerequisite for every director is *integrity*. Directors are stewards of the interests of the company (that is of the entire body of shareholders). The enterprise does not belong to the directors. They hold it in trust for the owners to whom they owe a fiduciary duty to act openly and honestly in their interests.

What does integrity mean? It means being able to distinguish right from wrong and judge corporate behaviour accordingly. It means acting in the company interest, not self-interest, resisting the temptation to make a personal gain to the detriment of the company. The case of Lord Black that follows raises some relevant points. Integrity also means being able to recognize and declare a conflict of interest. Essentially, integrity means acting honestly for the benefit of the company. A director with integrity is trusted, which is basic because the very concept of the company is based on trust.

In law, a company is a legal entity and enjoys many of the rights of an individual person. But, unlike a real person, a company does not have a conscience. The board has to act as the corporate conscience. Clearly that means ensuring that the company obeys the laws of the jurisdictions in which it operates. Moreover, it means creating a corporate character which establishes the way the whole organization operates, over and above just staying within the law.

Case Study 11.1 Lord Black

Conrad Black, a Canadian who took British citizenship to enter the British House of Lords, was an international media mogul, famed for his business strategies, his arrogance, and for bringing legal actions against anyone who challenged him. But he eventually appeared in a Chicago court accused of money laundering, racketeering, and obstructing justice.

Black controlled an empire of publications through a chain of companies (see figure 11.1).

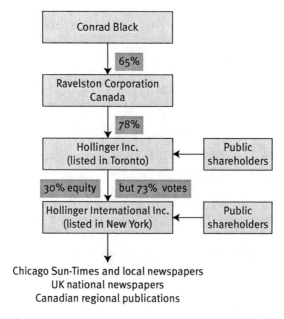

Figure 11.1 Lord Black's chain of companies

Notice two classic corporate governance devices used to leverage Black's control: an ownership chain with outside investors in two listed companies; and dual class shares with voting rights greater than their equity value. In other words, Black was able to control Hollinger International, which owned Canadian, British, and US publications, even though he held less than 16 percent of the chain's equity.

Black was also known for his ostentatious life style, with corporate jets, a fleet of vintage cars, apartments, and domestic staff paid for by the company. His wife memorably commented to *Vogue* that '*I have an extravagance that knows no bounds*', which prompted some institutional investors and the chairman of the audit committee to look more closely at the Black empire.

Like Robert Maxwell, his predecessor in the international media business and other corporate governance case-studies, Black filled his boardroom with prestigious names, including Henry Kissinger, the former US Secretary of State, and Richard Perle, a former Pentagon adviser, plus friends—mainly chairmen of other companies.

Black and some colleagues were charged with diverting over US$80 million from Hollinger International from the sale of newspapers in the US and Canada. It was also alleged that Black's company Ravelston had charged Hollinger International multi-million dollar fees for management and for agreeing not to compete with regional newspapers that had been sold.

Allegedly the directors had approved these payments without question or independent advice. Neither had they queried the personal use of company assets. They allowed Black to treat the company as his private empire. As Black said: '*This is my company and I decide what the board knows, and when they know it.*'

Judge Amy St Eve told Black that she believed he had not accepted his guilt, had abused the trust of shareholders, and had engaged in sophisticated schemes that required more than minimal planning. He was sentenced to six and a half years in prison and fined US$125,000. Protesting his innocence to the end, Black claimed that he was the victim of '*corporate governance zealots*'.

(This case has been prepared from contemporary press reports. The author also acknowledges insights from McNish, Jacquie and Sinclair Stewart, *The Fall of Conrad Black*, Allen Lane, London 2004)

Discussion Questions

1. Black was able to control Hollinger International through an ownership chain with outside investors in two listed companies; and dual class shares with voting rights greater than their equity value, though he held less than 16 percent of the chain's equity. What is your opinion of that situation? Remember that no one forced the outside shareholders to buy into his companies and the ownership structure was in the public domain.

2. Black filled his boardroom with prestigious names, including Henry Kissinger, the former US Secretary of State, and Richard Perle, a former Pentagon adviser, plus friends—mainly chairmen of other companies. What are the pros and cons of such a situation?

3. How can a successful entrepreneurial character, like Lord Black, be controlled to protect outside investors?

In practice, as we have seen, many boards produce a formal statement of their corporate mission and the core values to which they aspire. In some cases these statements are no more than pious aspirations, which do little to affect the way the company is run. In other cases, however, such mission statements can lead to rigorous policies, approved and monitored by the board on, for example, how the company treats its customers, its relations with employees, and its commitment to corporate social responsibility. An example follows:

Box 11.1 Microsoft Corporate Mission and Values

Our Mission

At Microsoft, we work to help people and businesses throughout the world realize their full potential. This is our mission. Everything we do reflects this mission and the values that make it possible.

Our values

As a company, and as individuals, we value:

- Integrity and honesty.
- Passion for customers, for our partners, and for technology.
- Openness and respectfulness.
- Taking on big challenges and seeing them through.
- Constructive self-criticism, self-improvement, and personal excellence.
- Accountability to customers, shareholders, partners, and employees for commitments, results, and quality.

(See www.microsoft.com/enable/microsoft/mission.aspx)

In addition to integrity, a number of other personal qualities are found in high-calibre directors. They can be summarized as intellect, character, and personality.

Intellect is what in Oxford colleges they call having '*a good mind*'. It combines an appropriate level of intelligence, the ability to think at different levels of abstraction, and the imagination to see situations from different perspectives, rather than always seeing things from a fixed viewpoint. A strong intellect is able to see things imaginatively, think originally, and act creatively.

Character traits, what some call 'strength of character', includes being independently minded, objective, and impartial. A director needs to be capable of moving towards consensus. Yet, from time to time a director needs to be tough-minded, tenacious, and resilient, with the courage to make a stand. Further a director needs to be results orientated, with a balanced approach to risk, neither risk-averse nor rash. Finally, some might add wisdom or just plain common sense (even though common sense is not all that common) to useful director character traits.

Desirable *personality* traits in a director include the ability to interact positively with others, which from time to time may call for flexibility, sensitivity, diplomacy, persuasiveness, the ability to motivate, and a sense of humour. Such interpersonal abilities are particularly important in interactions with the chairman and boardroom peers. Other desirable personality traits include being a sound listener and a good communicator, as well as being politically sensitive.

These attributes tend to be inherent in people by the time they are nominated for a board appointment, having been culturally influenced and acquired over a lifetime. By contrast there are certain core competencies that a director needs which can be developed or acquired through director induction programmes, director training, and director development and updating. We will explore these issues in the next chapter.

A successful director looks ahead, anticipates problems, and can articulate possible solutions. He is open, welcomes questioning, and seeks feedback. But he also listens, tries to understand others' points of view, and seeks consensus. Overall he is reliable and trusted by his chairman and peers. On the other hand poor directors tend to adopt a negative attitude, offering platitudes, and fail to face up to serious issues. Strategic thinking is replaced by reliance on past successes and rigorous risk analysis by hope.

Obviously, an INED also needs to be genuinely independent. As the Cadbury Report put it: '. . . *independent of management and free from any business or other relationships which could materially interfere with the exercise of their independent judgement*'. We saw in chapter 7 how subsequent codes of corporate governance principles and stock exchange listing rules have added detail to that definition.

The Core Competencies a Director Needs

Obviously, every corporate entity and every governing body is different, and each director brings a different set of experience, skills, and knowledge to the board. But in the aggregate every board needs to have a mix of capabilities that provide a balanced and well qualified team relevant to that board and that company.

So every director needs to have some basic core competencies appropriate to the type, location, and scale of the enterprise. What experience, skills, and knowledge should a director have?

The *experience* of outside directors should be used to supplement the knowledge available to the board, not to second guess the executives in the company. For example, a director could bring additional experience to the board about corporate governance, board procedures, or strategy formulation and policy making in other (non-competing) companies. Or a director might have experience of overseas markets, frontier technologies, international finance, or other areas that supplement the experience of the existing board.

The essential director-level *skills* include;

• Strategic reasoning, perception, and vision
• A critical faculty capable of quantitative and qualitative analysis and financial interpretation
• Planning and decision making capabilities
• Communication and interpersonal skills
• Networking and political abilities

Directors also need appropriate *knowledge* of the enterprise, its business, and board level activities, as well as relevant information about the company's political, economic, social, and technological contexts.

If directors are to make sense of board information and contribute meaningfully to board discussions, they must have basic knowledge about the company itself, its business, and the company's financials.

Knowledge of the company includes:

- A clear understanding of the basis of power (who the shareholders are and where the power lies to appoint the governing body)
- The basis of law under which the body operates and what the governance rules and regulations are (for a limited company these are company law and the company's memorandum and articles of association)
- The board structure, membership, and personalities
- The board processes, such as the use of board committees and the basis of board information

An awareness of the history of the entity can also be helpful in understanding the board culture, interpreting the current situation, and appreciating the perspectives of the chairman and other board members.

Knowledge of the business embraces an understanding of the basic business activities and processes, its purpose and aims, its strengths and weaknesses and how it measures success, the field of its operations (including markets, competitors, and its current operating context), the strategies being pursued, the structure of the organization, its culture, management, and people, and the form of management control and management control systems. Risk assessment is an important role of a governing body, which we will explore further in chapter 14. Directors need to know where the enterprise is most at risk.

Knowledge of the financials includes knowing how the company is financed, a sound appreciation of its annual accounts and directors' reports, knowledge of developing trends in key financial ratios, the criteria used in investment appraisals, the calibre of financial controls and who the auditors are. It is not necessary to be an accountant to be a good director: indeed, some might argue the reverse! But an ability to appreciate the financial aspects of the company is vital.

Roles Directors Play

Given their various attributes and different competencies, directors inevitably make a variety of contributions to their board and can play a number of roles. Some of these roles contribute to the performance aspects of the board's work (strategy formulation and policy making), others contribute to the conformance aspects (executive supervision and accountability).

The following are examples of some performance-orientated roles that directors can play:

- *Bringing wider business and board experience* to the identification, discussion, and decision making of matters. Identifying issues that the board, not management, should be handling. Directors tend to respect the wisdom of the director who brings accumulated

---

Case Study 11.2 Sunbeam Corporation

In 1996, Sunbeam, a US appliance manufacturer, was in serious financial trouble. Al Dunlap, known as 'Chainsaw Al' for his approach to cutting staff, was appointed to save the company. Over the next two years the business reported dramatically improved results. Investors chased after the shares as the price rocketed. There was talk of a bid, which would make the investors, and particularly Dunlap and his colleagues, a lot of money. But no bid came.

By 1998, some outside directors were uneasy and launched an inquiry. They did not like what they found and Mr Dunlap was fired. The SEC subsequently charged him, other senior executives, and the audit partner at Arthur Andersen, who had approved the accounts, with fraud. The SEC alleged that, on his arrival, Mr Dunlap identified massive previous losses which he wrote off, giving him a 'cookie jar' to dip into to inflate subsequent results.

Then he shipped out more goods through his distribution channels than they could possibly sell, taking credit for the revenues, but pushing forward the problem to the next financial year. Returned goods were overlooked. Other efforts were made to boost sales artificially: a record number of outdoor barbecues were reported sold during the winter months.

In 2001, Andersen agreed to pay US$110 million to the Sunbeam shareholders in settlement of a lawsuit alleging that the auditors had failed to identify the problem.

Discussion Questions

1. Directors have a fiduciary duty to protect the interests of shareholders. In this case they apparently failed. Why?

2. Investors chased after the shares and the price rocketed. There was talk of a bid, which would have made the investors, including Dunlap, a lot of money. But some of the independent outside directors were uneasy and launched an inquiry. Could such a situation have been avoided?

3. Can directors rely on the report of the independent outside auditors?

---

knowledge and experience in business and elsewhere to bear on issues facing the board. As the Cadbury Report put it: '*the board should include non-executive directors of sufficient calibre and number for their views to carry significant weight in the board's decisions*'. Long serving directors may well find themselves cast in this role by newer board colleagues. Accumulated wisdom can, of course, have limitations in rapidly changing situations

- *Adding specialist knowledge, skills, and know-how* to board deliberations. Here a director relies on his or her particular professional training, skills, and knowledge to make a contribution. For example, the specialism might be in the realm of accountancy, banking, engineering, finance, or law; or could stem from specialist knowledge of a particular market, technology, or functional area such as marketing, manufacturing, or personnel. In some newer, growing companies outside directors are appointed to the board specifically to provide such specialist inputs until such time as the company can afford to acquire such skills in-house at the executive level. When a board is relying on such expertise, it is important to ensure that the director remains up to date in the subject, which can sometimes prove difficult for those operating at board level

- *Being the source of external information* for board discussions—a window on the world for other directors. The director is used as a source of information on issues relevant to board discussions. Usually this will be on matters external to the company, such as insights into market opportunities, new technologies, industry developments, financial and economic concerns, or international matters. Obviously, it is essential that the information is relevant, accurate, and current. This is often a role specifically sought from outside directors, who are in a position to obtain such information through their other day-to-day activities. A danger is that directors, chosen because of their access to specific information, lose touch with it

- *Being a figurehead or an ambassador for the company*, being able to represent the company in the outside world. The director represents the company in the external arena; for example, in meetings with fund managers and financial analysts, or in trade and industry gatherings. The chairman of the board often takes on this responsibility, perhaps being invited to join public committees, commissions, and the governing bodies of important public institutions, as well as joining the boards of other, non-competing companies. These days this role can be taken by the director identified as the senior independent non-executive director. For many companies a figurehead is increasingly important in dealing with the media

- *Connecting the board to networks of useful people* not otherwise available to the board. This can be an important role for outside directors, who are able through their personal contacts to connect the board and top management into networks of potentially useful people and organizations. For example, the director might be placed to forge contacts in the world of politics and government; link the company with relevant banking, finance, or stock exchange connections; or make introductions within industry or international trade. Retiring politicians are sometimes offered directorships on the assumption that they have useful contacts and influence in the corridors of power. Such a role may also provide advice on succession in the board and in top management

- *Providing status to the board and the company, adding capability, reputation, and position.* This role is not as significant today as it was a few years ago. In the past eminent public figures were often invited to join boards just to add status, rather than any specific contribution they could make to board deliberations. Past-service as a Senator in the US or a knighthood in the UK almost guaranteed an invitation to join the board of a public company in the past. But these days boards need professionalism ahead of prestige. However, the status role can be useful at times, for example when a listed company faced a financial crisis the market was reassured when a well known financier joined the board. Exposure to litigation may now deter some public figures from accepting directorships. However even today, if a company has been experiencing problems, confidence may be restored if a high profile, well respected figure joins the board

The following are examples of some conformance-orientated roles that directors can play:

- *Providing independent judgement*—the ability to see issues in their totality and from various perspectives, leading to objective judgement: in other words, helicopter vision. This can be a vital contribution of the outside director, who, obviously, has the opportunity to see board matters from an external and independent point of view. As the Cadbury Report suggested: '*non-executive directors should bring an independent judgement to bear on issues of strategy, performance, resources, including key appointments and standards of conduct*'. Such an objective evaluation of top management performance can overcome the tunnel vision sometimes found in those too closely involved with the situation, or the myopia brought on by being personally affected by the outcome. Overall, providing independent judgement brings wise counsel that leads to better decisions

- *Being a catalyst for change*, questioning existing assumptions, introducing new ideas and approaches, and stimulating developments. This role can be played by a director who questions the board's assumptions, and makes others rethink situations. Catalysts point out that what appears to be an incontrovertible truth to some board members is, in fact, rooted in some questionable beliefs about the company, its markets, or its competitors. They highlight inferences that are masquerading as facts. They show when value judgements, rather than rigorous analysis, are being used in board deliberations. Most valuably, catalysts stimulate the board discussions with new, alternative insights and ideas

- *Being a monitor of executive activities*, offering objective criticism and comments on management performance and issues such as the hiring and firing of top management. The entire board is responsible for the monitoring and supervision of executive management. But INEDs, being independent, can bring a particular focus to this role

- *Playing the role of watchdog*, able to provide an independent voice and protect the interests of minority shareholders or lending bankers. Directors cast in this role are seen as protectors of the interests of other parties, such as the shareholders or, more often, a specific interest group. As we commented in chapter 3, nominee directors inevitably find themselves in this position, as they look out for the interests of the party who nominated them to the board. This might be a representative of a major investor in the case of a director on the board of an American or British listed company, a representative of the employees for a director on a German supervisory board, or a representative of the *keiretsu* group interests for a director on the board of a major Japanese company. Every director has a duty to be concerned with the interests of the company as a whole (that is with the interests of *all* the shareholders without discrimination), so the watchdog role has to be applied with care

- *Being a confidante or sounding board for the chairman*, the chief executive, or other directors; a trusted and respected counsellor in times of uncertainty and stress; someone to share concerns about issues (often interpersonal problems) outside the boardroom. Political processes at board level inevitably involve the use, and sometimes abuse, of power, and the confidante can sometimes make a valuable contribution. But it is vital that he or she commands the trust of all the directors, otherwise the problem can be reinforced rather than resolved

- *Acting as a safety valve* able to act in a crisis in order to release the pressure, prevent further damage and save the situation. A classical example would be when a company has run into financial problems, management performance has deteriorated, or the chief executive has to be replaced. Another example might be if the company faced an unexpected catastrophe. The sensible and steadying counsel of a wise member of the board could overcome an otherwise disastrous situation

We move now beyond director attributes, competencies, and roles to the legal responsibilities, duties, and rights of directors.

The Legal Duties of a Director

Although company law varies in detail from jurisdiction to jurisdiction, the essence of directors' duties are common. Directors' responsibilities derive from the nature of the joint stock limited liability company and are enshrined in statute law, case law, and stock exchange and other regulations. Essentially, directors' duties are two-fold:

• A duty of trust—to exercise a fiduciary responsibility to the shareholders
• A duty of care—to exercise reasonable care, diligence, and skill

The duty of trust, or fiduciary duty, requires directors to act with integrity, behaving honestly and fairly for the benefit of the shareholders equally, recognizing the interests of any minority shareholders: also to promote the aims of the company to ensure its success, and to act solely within the powers delegated to them in the company's constitution. Directors of companies incorporated in the United States owe a specific fiduciary duty to any minority shareholders. British Commonwealth based common law (Australia, Canada, Hong Kong, India, New Zealand, Singapore, South Africa, and so on) allows directors to determine the best interests of the whole company, subject to the right of appeal to the courts.

In other words, the primary duty of a director is to act honestly in good faith, giving all shareholders equal, sufficient, and accurate information on all issues affecting their interests. The underlying (and universal) principle is that directors should not treat a company as though it exists for their own personal benefit, unless of course they own all the shares and, even then, they have to recognize the legal rights of creditors and other stakeholders.

In fulfilling their duty of trust, directors should avoid conflicts of interest, declare an interest in any proposed transaction or arrangement, and not make a secret profit or take any unapproved benefit from their position as director.

Box 11.2 Disclosure of Personal Interests

The son of a director of company A had significant personal shareholdings in another company B, which was being considered by company A as an acquisition target. These interests must be disclosed by the director to the board of company A before that director takes part in any board decision making on the matter. The chairman and fellow directors can then decide on the appropriate action, such as asking the director to leave the meeting, to not participate in the discussion, or, having noted the interest, to allow participation in the decision making. Directors should ensure that any interest declared is recorded in the minutes, to provide written evidence in the event of a subsequent legal challenge.

A related party transaction is one between a company and a party closely related to it, such as a director or a major shareholder. For example, the purchase by a company of a property from one of its directors would be a related party transaction and would need to be disclosed by that director to the board. The listing rules of most stock exchanges and securities regulators require related party transactions to be disclosed and, in some cases, to be approved by the shareholders. Related party transactions are frequently found in countries where Chinese family firms operate, where close links exist between assets owned by family members and companies connected with the family. Related party transactions also proved to be a significant problem in the early days of privatization of state companies in both China and Russia.

As we saw in chapter 3, the requirement to treat all shareholders equally can place nominee directors in a potentially difficult position. In board deliberations a director must consider the interests of all shareholders equally and should not represent the interests of the party who nominated him to the board. Moreover, a director should not divulge sensitive board information to the party who nominated him or her.

Insider trading in a listed company's shares on the basis of privileged, share price sensitive insider information is a breach of a director's fiduciary duty: it is also illegal in most countries. Japan, Hong Kong, and Germany were among the last countries to make insider trading a criminal offence. The United States has the most severe penalties for insider dealing. Listed companies are increasingly employing compliance officers to ensure that directors and employees do not trade on privileged insider information.

Insider dealing (or trading) can involve making a secret profit by buying shares in the secret knowledge of events that would drive the price up, or avoiding a loss by selling shares on the basis of privileged intelligence that would cause the price to fall. The argument against the practice is not so much that it is morally wrong or unfair, or because it involves a misuse of information, but because insider dealing destroys the credibility and the

---

Box 11.3 The Seven Principles of Public Life

A committee, chaired by Lord Nolan in the UK, produced a set of principles to guide the holders of public office in the UK. These principles can readily be applied to company directors in fulfilling their fiduciary duty.

Nolan's seven principles were:

1. Selflessness—holders of public office should serve the public interest, and not seek gains for their friends.
2. Integrity—they should not place themselves under financial obligation to outsiders who might influence their duties.
3. Objectivity—they should award public appointments and contracts on merit.
4. Accountability—they should submit themselves to the appropriate scrutiny.
5. Openness—they should give reasons for their decisions.
6. Honesty—they should declare conflicts of interest.
7. Leadership—they should support these principles by personal example.

integrity of the stock market. It can also be difficult to obtain convincing information to support a prosecution. That is why some jurisdictions waited so long to introduce anti-insider legislation.

Directors have to be particularly careful not to trade in their company's shares when they are in possession of inside or privileged information, such as the company results just prior to publication and before the stock market has that information. The company secretary will often inform directors when the window of opportunity for trading in the company's shares is open and, more importantly, when it is closed.

The duty of care requires directors to exercise independent judgement and care, skill, and diligence. In earlier days this duty was not particularly onerous, because courts tended to call for a level of care that could be expected of any reasonable person. In many jurisdictions today, however, courts demand a duty of care that could be expected of a person serving as a director. Moreover, that duty of care should also be relevant to the knowledge, skill, and experience that the director has: if he or she is an accountant, lawyer, or engineer then he or she is expected to bring those skills to bear in his or her work as director. The standard of professionalism now expected of directors around the world is significantly higher than that expected a few years ago.

Broadly, courts recognize that business decisions involve risk and will not second guess board level decisions, taken under normal business circumstances, if they subsequently prove to have been ill judged. This is frequently referred to as the 'business judgement rule'. Courts can act, however, if negligent or fraudulent behaviour is alleged, or where an apparent abuse of power or suppression of minority shareholders' interests has occurred. For example, courts will give a ruling if it is alleged that the directors have negotiated a contract that is detrimental to the interests of minority shareholders.

Every director is a statutory officer of the company and is bound by the requirements of the company law of the state in which the company is incorporated. A company must, of course, also abide by the laws of any other state in which it operates. Directors can face penalties should the company fail in its legal obligations. In some jurisdictions company directors may also find themselves exposed under other legislation, such as health and safety laws, environmental protection law, or anti-monopoly rules. A recent legal development in the UK raises the possibility of directors being charged with corporate manslaughter.

All directors on a unitary board have the same legal duties and potential liabilities. As we saw earlier, in most unitary board jurisdictions company law does not distinguish between executive and non-executive directors. In a two-tier board structure, on the other hand, the responsibilities of the executive board members to run the enterprise are fundamentally different from those of supervisory board members to monitor and supervise the executive.

There is widespread misunderstanding about the liability of directors. In a limited liability company it is the shareholders' liability for the company debts that is limited, not the directors' liability. We discuss directors' and officers' insurance in chapter 12.

Directors are not automatically liable for the debts of their company, provided they have not acted negligently, or made it appear that they accepted personal liability. In some

---

Box 11.4 Lord Caldecote's Advice to Executive Directors

Lord Caldecote, when he was chairman of Delta Metal, called newly appointed executive directors to meet him and reminded them that: *'executive directors have two hats—the hat of the executive and the hat of the director. When you come into my boardroom I want you to be wearing your director's hat. Each director is equally responsible with me for directing the company. You are not there to represent your function or your divisional company. Nor are you there to defend your executive performance or bid for resources for your executive activities. You are there to help me govern the company overall.'*

---

jurisdictions a director can be personally liable for the firm's debts if he or she knew that the company was insolvent and allowed it to continue to trade.

Directors can also be charged if they mislead auditors or fail to file various documents with the companies registry. Most company law jurisdictions provide for the disqualification of directors if they are found unfit to be a director. Causes can include bankruptcy, theft, fraud, and failure to meet the requirements of the companies legislation, or running a company that has traded whilst insolvent and without a reasonable chance of paying its creditors.

Shareholder Rights Differ Between Jurisdictions

In the 19th century model of the joint-stock limited liability, shareholders had the right to nominate and elect the directors for their company. This is still the case in many parts of the world, although the massively increasing scale and diversity of shareholders has meant that company law has had to lay down rules for the election of directors. In the UK, subject to the articles of association, 10 percent of the voting shareholders can call at any time for an extraordinary meeting of shareholder members. A simple majority is all that is needed to remove a director or indeed the entire board.

But shareholders in the UK have substantially more power than their US counterparts.

In America's system for electing directors, the incumbent board sends a list of their preferred candidates to shareholders prior to voting at the shareholders meeting. Shareholders can suggest alternative names but have to bear the cost of distributing the rival nomination form themselves, which can be prohibitively expensive in a large company. Consequently, contested elections are rare. Proposals for companies to cover the costs of dissident shareholders wanting to nominate their own candidates have been around for many years. The Scott Report[1] from the Committee on Capital Markets regulation called for 'majority voting' in which directors are elected with a majority of votes cast and for shareholders to put forward candidates for the board of directors by simply having their names added to the company's nomination proxy form. But the SEC has refused to regulate, most recently in 2007. Pressure to resist change has come from directors, on the grounds that companies are protecting the interests of their shareholders from vested interests such as trade unions, hedge-funds, and single-issue lobbyists wanting to have their representatives on the board. This argument seems flawed since a candidate would need a majority of the votes cast to win. Attempts to force companies to change through class-action law suits on behalf of the shareholders in the US company, notably by Bob Monks, have also failed.

In a response to fears of the growing power of hedge funds, a 2007 Germany law required activist shareholders, who joined together to force changes on a company, to launch a formal takeover bid if their combined holdings exceeded 30 percent. The European Union has tried to rule that companies in all member states should apply the principal of one share, one vote, but has failed to obtain agreement. Opposition came from countries such as Sweden, which permit dual class shares (see the Wallenberg case in chapter 4). Even the United Nations has principles for responsible investment, but some parts of the world have moved a long way away from the original notion of shareholder democracy.

The US Sarbanes-Oxley Act 2002

The Sarbanes-Oxley Act was passed in 2002, as we mentioned in chapter 7, to strengthen corporate governance and restore investor confidence following some major corporate collapses including Enron and WorldCom. US Senator Paul Sarbanes and US Representative Michael Oxley, who sponsored the bill, earned unexpected notoriety around the world from what has become known as SOX or the Sarbox Act.

SOX imposed new accountability standards, with criminal penalties, on directors. For example, CEOs and CFOs must certify under oath that their financial statements neither contain an 'untrue statement' nor omit any 'material fact'. Audit committees must be comprised of totally independent outside directors.

SOX also established new independence standards for external auditors. Areas of lucrative non-audit work by audit firms were prohibited. A Public Company Accounting Oversight Board (PCAOB) was created to oversee public accounting (auditing) firms and to issue accounting standards.

The rules are regulated by the Securities and Exchange Commission and apply to all companies quoted in the United States, including overseas companies listed there. The passing of the Sarbanes-Oxley Act differentiated the United States from many other countries by enshrining corporate governance practice in law. Most other countries still rely on the observance of voluntary codes of principles, with the requirement to report if the code has been followed and if not, why not (the conform or explain approach), as we saw earlier.

---

[1]Chaired by Harvard University Professor Hal S. Scott.

SOX has proved expensive to operate, particularly section 404 (see the ChinaUnicom case) and is seen by some as an expensive over-reaction to the loss of confidence in American audit and corporate governance practices. Some overseas companies have complained about the potential extra-territorial legislation, others have withdrawn from listing in the United States.

Case Study 11.3 ChinaUnicom and SOX

ChinaUnicom is involved in the cellular telephone business in thirty provinces, municipalities, and autonomous regions in China providing nation-wide international and domestic long distance calls, data, and Internet services, and other related telecommunication value-added businesses. It is one of the two major mobile telecommunications operators in the PRC. In 2007 the company had over 140 million subscribers and was the third largest mobile telecommunication operator in the world, and also operated telecommunications businesses in Hong Kong and USA.

The company is listed in New York and Hong Kong. The board of directors has fourteen members—the chairman/CEO, seven executive directors, and six non-executive directors (four of them identified as independent).

The company's corporate governance report notes that:

Internal Control Systems

1. Requirements under Section 404 of the Sarbanes-Oxley Act

It has been strongly emphasized by the Company to comply with the requirements under Section 404 of the Sarbanes-Oxley Act. The relevant section of the Act requires the management of the issuers in other countries with equity securities listing in the US securities market to issue reports and representations as to the internal control system that may affect its financial statements.

The relevant internal control report shall stress the management's responsibility for establishing and maintaining an adequate and effective internal control structure and procedures. The management shall also assess, as of the year end of the financial statements, the effectiveness of the company's internal control structure and procedures for financial reporting. The company's auditor shall also conduct testing and assessment to, and report on the relevant internal control systems.

In order to enhance its corporate governance standards, as well as fulfilling the requirements under the Sarbanes-Oxley Act, a lot of initiatives were taken in 2004 with respect to the establishment of an internal control system. A steering committee led by the Company's management was established, and formulated the proposals for the establishment of the internal control system. Through endeavours in practical work, such as perfecting the internal control over the business processes, identifying risk management checkpoints, finalizing on the accountability system for risk management and building up a complete and accurate filing system, a comprehensive risk management mechanism was established, which served effectively to manage the risks arising from all economic activities of the Company. The accomplishment of the Company's business strategies and improvement in efficiency is thus assured.

(For more information see www.chinaunicom.com.hk)

Discussion Question

1. ChinaUnicom has expressed its commitment to fulfilling the demands of the SOX Act s.404 to report on internal control systems. The details provided above by ChinaUnicom are impressive. But are you satisfied that all companies reporting under s.404 are competent? Should these statements be independently audited?

UK Companies Act 2006

The UK introduced a new Companies Act in 2006, which was the largest UK Act ever, with over 1,300 sections. About a third of this was a straightforward restatement of the previous law in clearer and simpler language.

However, some new measures were included that:

- Clarified directors' duties for the first time in statute law. Previously the role and responsibilities of a director had been determined by case law evolving over the years. The new law made clear that directors have to act in the interests of shareholders. However, significantly, the law also added that in acting in the shareholders' interests, they must pay regard to the longer term interests of employees, suppliers, consumers and the environment

- Encouraged narrative reporting by companies calling for them to be forward-looking, identifying risks as well as opportunities. Quoted companies have to provide information on environmental matters, employees, and social and community issues, including information on any policies relating to these matters and their effectiveness, plus contractual and other relationships essential to the business, as part of their business review and to the extent necessary for an understanding of the business

- Promoted shareholder involvement in governance by enhancing the powers of proxies and making it easier for indirect investors to be informed and exercise governance rights in the company. Shareholders were also able to limit the auditors' liability to the company to what is fair and reasonable. The act also provided powers to require institutional investors to disclose how they used their votes

- Included a new offence for recklessly or knowingly including misleading, false, or deceptive matters in an audit report

- Enabled auditors to agree a limit on their liability with their audit clients, subject to shareholder approval

The act also included measures for private companies such as:

- New model articles dropping the requirement for a company secretary unless the members want one

- Dropping the need for an annual meeting of shareholders unless they want one

Case Study 11.4 Waste Management

In 1992, Arthur Andersen, the auditors of Waste Management, a refuse collection company in the United States, identified some improper accounting practices, which had resulted in an overstatement of reported profits. These misstatements totalled $93.5 million, which was less then 10 percent of reported profit. Also, one-off gains of over US$100 million, which should have been shown separately in the accounts, had been netted against other expenses. A 'clean' audit certificate was signed.

In 1993, the auditors identified further misstatements of US$128 million, which represented 12 percent of reported profit. Andersen again decided that these misstatements were not sufficiently material for the audit report to be qualified. But the auditors did decide to allow the company to write off prior misstatements over a number of years, instead of making immediate disclosure, as required by generally accepted accounting principles. In 1994, the company continued its practice of netting expenses against one-off gains. In fact the SEC claimed that, between 1992 and 1996, Waste Management restated over US$1 billion.

Waste Management was an important and lucrative client for Andersen. Between 1991 and 1997 audit fees totalled US$7.5 million, whilst other fees, such as consulting services, contributed US$11.8 million. In the firm's own words Waste Management was a 'crown jewel' among their clients. Moreover, Waste Management's top finance executives had all previously been Andersen auditors.

In June 2001, the Securities and Exchange Commission (SEC) brought settled enforcement actions against Arthur Andersen LLP and four of its partners in connection with Andersen's audits of the annual financial statements of Waste Management Inc., for the years 1992 through 1996. Those financial statements, on which Andersen issued unqualified or 'clean' opinions, overstated Waste Management's pre-tax income by more than US$1 billion.

The SEC found that Andersen *'knowingly or recklessly issued false and misleading audit reports . . . [which] falsely stated that the financial statements were presented fairly, in all material respects, in conformity with generally accepted accounting principles'*. Without admitting or denying the allegations or findings, Andersen agreed to pay a civil penalty of US$7 million, the largest ever SEC enforcement action against a big five accounting firm.

This case raised the vexed issue of auditor independence (now resolved by the SOX Act). Andersen had a close relationship with a valuable client, which led to creeping year-on-year acceptance of less than acceptable auditing standards. The SEC's Director of Enforcement commented that *'Arthur Andersen and its partners failed to stand up to company management and thereby betrayed their ultimate allegiance to Waste Management's Shareholders and the investing public'*.

As we saw in the earlier case in chapter 3, the Arthur Andersen firm collapsed following the Enron saga, reducing the 'big five' international accounting firms to four.

Discussion Questions

1. The SEC's Director of Enforcement said that *'Arthur Andersen and its partners failed to stand up to company management'*. Does the potential loss of a client

and their audit fee cause a real problem in the conventional relationship between auditor and client?

2. How might it be overcome? Consider regulatory devices such as the Public Company Accounting Oversight Board (PCAOB) introduced by the SOX Act, greater transparency or state involvement.

REFERENCES AND FURTHER READING

Bower, Tom (2006) *Conrad and Lady Black: Dancing on the Edge.* London: Harper Press.

McNish, Jacquie and Sinclair Stewart (2004) *The Fall of Conrad Black.* London: Allen Lane.

USEFUL WEBSITES

www.berr.gov.uk (search the site for 'corporate governance')
UK Department for business, enterprise, and regulatory reform.

www.companieshouse.co.uk
UK Companies Registry.

news.findlaw.com/hdocs/docs/gwbush/sarbanesoxley072302.pdf
US Sarbanes-Oxley Act 2002 in full.

www.opsi.gov.uk/acts/acts2006/ukpga_20060046_en.pdf
UK Companies Act 2006 in full.

PROJECTS AND EXERCISES

1. Design a pro-forma check list for the appointment of a director, identifying the core competencies needed and outlining personal attributes that would be desirable for the appointment.

2. Lord Nolan in the UK produced a set of principles, which are listed in the text, to guide the holders of public office in the UK. Do you believe that these are equally appropriate for directors of a listed public company? If not, why not? Would your answer be different if the company was a private, family firm?

3. Draft a briefing paper for a newly appointed director of a listed company explaining his or her legal duties as a director. Do you think that most directors know this information?

SELF-TEST QUESTIONS

To confirm your grasp of the key points in this chapter try answering the following questions. Answers are at the end of the book.

1. What does integrity mean?
2. Name some of the corporate values declared by Microsoft.
3. In addition to integrity, what other personal qualities are found in high calibre directors?
4. Name some essential director level skills.
5. Name some performance related roles that a director might play.
6. Name some conformance related roles that a director might play.
7. What character traits are desirable in a director?
8. What are the essential legal duties of a director?
9. How does a related party transaction affect a director?
10. What is the PCAOB?

12   Board Effectiveness

- In which we consider some practical matters:
  - managing board committees
  - managing meetings, agenda, and minutes
  - board information
  - the role of the company secretary
  - director induction, training, and development
  - director remuneration
  - director and officer insurance
- Appendix: Director's Induction Checklist

Managing Board Committees

The Audit Committee

As we saw in chapter 3, the essential and original role of the audit committee is to act as a bridge between the independent external auditors and the board, avoiding the possibility of powerful executive directors, such as the CFO or CEO, becoming too close to their auditors and resolving issues before they reach the board. The audit committee is a standing sub-committee of the main board and, these days in most listed companies, is comprised entirely of INEDs, at least one of whom should have current financial expertise.

Over the years the role and responsibilities of the audit committee have expanded. In many cases they now include advising the board on the company's systems of internal management control, oversight of internal audit; liaising with the external auditors, and reporting to the board on the audit process and on any audit issues; reviewing financial information to be provided to shareholders and others, advising the board on matters of board accountability, the oversight of risk management, and corporate governance compliance.

Typically, audit committees meet three or four times a year to discuss the details of the audit, to consider any contentious points that have arisen on the accounts, and to receive the auditor's recommendations on audit related matters such as management controls. Of course the audit committee may meet more frequently if the breadth of their responsibilities requires. The committee will often negotiate the audit fee and make recommendations to the board on auditor appointment.

A board will rely on its audit committee to ensure that a balanced and understandable assessment of the company's position and prospects is presented to shareholders and other legitimate stakeholders, such as the taxation authorities. The board may also expect the audit committee to ensure that the systems of internal control in the organization are sound to safeguard shareholders' investment and the company's assets. Further, the audit committee may be expected to have formal and transparent arrangements applying financial reporting and internal control principles, and for maintaining an appropriate relationship with the company's auditors.

An audit committee needs to have clear terms of reference, which identify its role and responsibilities, define its authority and size; clarify the chairmanship and the independence of members, and the necessary quorum; and specify the frequency of meetings. An audit committee has the power to hold whatever meetings, interviews, or investigations it deems necessary. An audit committee may seek information directly from any company employee, although normally this should be done with the knowledge of the chief executive officer or finance director. The head of the internal audit function often reports directly to the chairman of the audit committee. An audit committee may also obtain independent professional advice in pursuit of its responsibilities.

The chairman of the audit committee is normally appointed by the board. Frequently, the CFO or members of the finance function, the internal auditor, and a representative of the external auditors are invited to attend meetings of the audit committee. Other executive directors or members of management may be asked to attend if necessary. The audit committee may meet separately with the external auditor, the internal auditor, other directors, or members of management, should they have matters they wish to raise privately with the committee. At least once a year, the audit committee should meet with the external auditor without any members of management being present. The external auditors should also meet with the entire board at least once a year and be available to answer questions at meetings of the shareholders.

The specific duties of an audit committee might include:

- Liaising between the external auditor, the internal auditor, and the board as a whole

- Advising the board on the appointment, re-appointment, resignation, or replacement of the external auditor

- Ensuring the independence of the external auditor, reviewing the extent of non-audit work undertaken by the external auditor and the fees involved. In the United States, since the Sarbanes-Oxley (SOX) Act, and elsewhere given the review of many codes of best practice, this is an important responsibility to ensure the external auditor's independence

- Reviewing the audit fees and advising the board accordingly

- Considering the scope and process of the audit by the external auditors

- Agreeing to the scope of the work and plans of the internal audit. Supervising the work of the head of the internal audit function, including the setting of policies, procedures, and plans, the budgeting of resources, the remuneration and performance of staff, the regular monitoring of results, and the overall effectiveness of the function

- Ensuring that the activities of the external and internal auditors are coordinated, avoiding both duplication or incomplete coverage

- Reviewing the appointment, performance, remuneration, and replacement or dismissal of the head of the internal audit function, ensuring continuing independence of the internal audit function from undue managerial influence
- Reviewing with the external and internal auditors and advising the board on the adequacy of the company's internal control systems, security of physical assets, and protection of information.
- Reviewing with the external and internal auditors and advising the board on the conduct of the external audit, particularly on any important findings or matters raised, usually contained in the auditor's 'management letter', with the management's response; and reporting any significant changes to the reporting of financial results or to procedures and management controls that resulted
- Reviewing with the external and internal auditors and advising the board on the company's financial statements (interim and annual) prior to publication, the auditor's report to the shareholders, any changes to accounting policies, material issues arising in or from the financial statements; and compliance with accounting standards, company law, stock exchange reporting requirements, and corporate governance codes of good practice
- Reviewing other published information, such as the directors' report, operating statement, and ensuring that they are consistent with the audited financial statements
- Reviewing the exposure of the company to risk and any issues that might have a material affect on the company's financial position, including any matters raised by company regulators or stock exchange listing committees
- Reviewing annually the charter of the audit committee itself and advising the chairman of the board if changes are necessary

The chairmanship of an audit committee in any company and particularly a listed company can be an onerous responsibility, as the chairman of Enron's audit committee discovered. Indeed, some directors are hesitant to take on the duty (see below for discussion of directors' and officers' liability insurance). Nevertheless, the role of the audit committee and the leadership of its chairman should be a fundamental plank in every company's corporate governance platform.

The Remuneration Committee

The duties of the remuneration committee include establishing a formal and transparent procedure for developing policy on top executive remuneration and for determining the remuneration packages of each director. No director should be involved in fixing his or her own remuneration. Levels of remuneration should be sufficient to attract and retain the directors needed to govern and manage the company successfully. Ideally, the component parts of executive directors' remuneration should be structured to link rewards with both corporate and individual performance, as we will discuss later.

The role of the remuneration committee has become significant and visible. In many jurisdictions, a company's annual report needs to contain a statement of remuneration policy and details of the remuneration of each director. Transparency is vital in corporate governance.

The Nomination Committee

As we saw in chapter 3, the nomination committee is a standing sub-committee of the main board, made up wholly, or mainly, of independent non-executive directors (INEDs), called on to make recommendations on the appointment of new directors to the board. It is an attempt to prevent the board becoming a cosy club, in which the incumbent members appoint like-minded people to join their ranks. It provides a check and balance mechanism that reduces the possibility of a dominant director, including the chairman or CEO, pushing through their own preferred candidates.

Unfortunately, the supposed independence of outside directors on the committee can be illusory. If the members of the nominating committee have themselves been selected by the chairman, and have worked with him for some years, they are likely to feel an allegiance towards the chairman and support his candidates. An alternative view is that newly appointed directors need to work in harmony and trust with the board chairman to be part of an effective board team, so it is just as well that they are acceptable to all.

In the UK, although listed companies have adopted most of the requirements of the combined code, the requirement to have a nominating committee has been resisted by a few. This is not surprising, since the right to influence appointments to the board goes to the very heart of corporate power.

Before leaving the work of the nomination committee, mention should be made of the 'staggered board issue'. In the past, many company's articles of association called for a proportion of the directors to retire each year. Sometimes called a 'classified board', a staggered board is one whose members' terms of appointment are staggered, so that only a part of the board retire each year (often a third, where director appointments are for three years). The argument for this practice is that it provides stability, since there would always be a proportion of directors on the board with experience of the company's business, which enables a longer term strategic perspective to be taken. Critics of staggered boards complain that hostile bidders cannot remove an entire board at a single election. Staggered boards, therefore, could be used as a takeover defence, entrenching underperforming directors. Annual election of all directors allows a change of control through a single successful proxy contest. Consequently resolutions opposing staggered boards and calling for declassification have topped shareholder activists' calls for change in the United States in recent years.

Managing Meetings, Agenda, and Minutes

Meetings need planning as well as running. Meetings also need managing and leading. Meetings of the board and its committees should be learning experiences for all involved. The basic considerations in planning a meeting involve the questions: why, what, when, where, and who? The first question 'Why?' is not often asked by chairmen when calling a meeting. Why is it being called? Clarify its purpose and what it is intended to achieve. Sometimes a meeting may not be necessary at all. At other times consideration of the purpose can avoid repetitious and time wasting issues being brought up and discussed.

The question 'When?' highlights the need to give adequate notice of the meeting. Some meetings, such as the annual general meeting of shareholders, have the minimum period of notice determined by statute, corporate constitution, or standing orders. Notice may also have to be in writing. Whether notice by email will suffice is a matter for the law of the jurisdiction.

The question 'Where?' emphasizes that not all meetings need to be held in the conventional location, typically the boardroom. Holding an occasional company board meeting in one of the other locations of the company, a divisional headquarters or a regional location, can provide an opportunity for directors to learn from first hand experience and meet the personnel, for whom the arrival and interest of the directors can be motivating. Meetings are increasingly held by teleconference. Provided proper attention is given to notice, agenda, and chairmanship, and given the technical facilities are appropriate, such meetings can bring together members from different locations, saving travel time and expense.

Finally, the question 'Who?' makes the point that other people, in addition to the board members, can be invited to attend meetings, either for specific items or for the whole meeting on a non-voting basis. Such people could include those who have relevant information to present to the board and whom directors might question, those who can relay board discussion and decisions to others, and also potential future directors as part of their learning experience and development. In some public organizations, members of the public have the right to attend meetings of the council, governing body, or committee. Of course, subject to the constitution, parts of such meetings may be held in private (in camera).

An agenda lists the items of business to be covered in a meeting. Who decides what matters get on the agenda can be a crucial issue in boards playing political games. So who should decide the agendum (each item on the agenda)? The final decision should rest with the chairman, but in many cases the company secretary and/or the CEO will suggest matters. Professional chairmen give all members of the board the opportunity to ask for matters to be discussed and arrange a periodic review of matters covered.

Box 12.1 Lord Caldecote on Building an Agenda

Lord Caldecote, when Chairman of the Delta Group, wrote to each of his directors periodically to ask whether there were matters they felt that the board should be discussing for the future benefit of the firm. *'In the past year what have we not discussed that we should have discussed?'* he would ask, *'and how could I improve my chairing of our meetings?'*

Three approaches to agenda design can be distinguished:

- The routine approach in which each meeting follows the pattern of the previous (apologies, approval of the minutes of the last meeting, matters arising from those minutes, the usual substantive items—such as the financial and operating reports—and any other business)
- The chairman-led approach, in which the chairman determines the agenda and probably dominates the meeting

• The professional approach in which the chairman seeks advice from relevant people about the agenda and takes great care in balancing the items and ensuring that adequate time is available for a competent discussion and sound resolution of each issue

Another important role for the chairman prior to the meeting is to ensure that all directors have adequate information and are properly briefed, if necessary, on each item on the agenda. Since all directors carry the same director responsibilities, all need to be fully informed so that they can participate on every agenda item. Directors cannot opt out of certain items because they lack appropriate knowledge, although they may rely on information received and the opinions of fellow directors, given in good faith, unless they have any reason to doubt—in which case they must pursue the issue to its root. Similarly a director may rely on information from a board sub-committee, unless unsure, in which case again the director has a duty to pursue the issue until satisfied.

As we saw in chapter 10, taking the chair at meetings typically falls to the chairman, whose leadership style will determine how discussions are handled, how time is allocated and the importance of items balanced, encouraging rational discussion, ensuring that all points of view are raised and that no one is allowed to dominate, calling on members for their opinion if necessary, directing discussions and guiding the meeting towards a consensus and, finally, summarizing, determining the decision and agreeing the output and resources required and establishing who is responsible for taking action and by when. A good chairman may also raise the question: what have we learned from the experience of this meeting?

Box 12.2 An Opinion on Drafting Agenda and Minutes

The head of an Oxford college, after a career in the British civil service, believed that a good chairman, among whom he counted himself, should put much effort into designing agenda. Care should be taken in choosing the items to be discussed; attention given to the time allocated to each, and in their positioning on the agenda. Matters likely to be controversial should come towards the end, he recommended, when members were expecting the meeting to end, or had already left, thus increasing the chairman's chances of getting the decision he wanted. This chairman also drafted the minutes along with the agenda, because he believed that a good chairman always has a preferred outcome. He knew that those who draft the minutes wield the power. His colleagues had to agree.

The minutes are the formal record of a meeting. Although, subject to the articles, there are no specific rules governing the content or format of minutes of board or board sub-committee meetings, they should provide a competent and complete record of what transpired, what was decided, and what actions are to be taken by whom and when. Should there be any future challenge, the minutes, which have been duly approved as a true and fair report at a subsequent meeting, can be used as strong evidence of what was intended.

Companies tend to develop their own style in minute keeping: for example, some boards note the names of the key contributors to the discussion, others do not. In some cases, it has to be admitted, the minutes are no more than a staccato record of who attended and what was decided. At the other extreme, there are minutes that are almost a verbatim report of the proceedings, complete with stage directions. The ideal lies between the two. Minutes should contain sufficient information to capture the key threads of the discussion, any disclosures of personal interest, the alternatives considered, the agreement reached, and plans and responsibilities for action. The person responsible for writing the minutes potentially wields considerable power, although typically minutes of the last meeting are approved and can be challenged at the following meeting.

A few boards record their meetings audio/visually. This can help in writing the minutes, but, if used as a record of proceedings, may inhibit discussion.

In a few companies, minutes are occasionally created for meetings that did not take place, in order to meet statutory requirements. This is bad practice, as is the backdating of minutes, which could be considered fraudulent.

Board Information

As we saw in the last chapter, directors have a right to all the information they feel is necessary to fulfil their obligations. Obviously different directors are likely to have different information needs. Executive directors usually know more about the internal operations of the firm than independent non-executive directors (INEDs): conversely some INEDs are likely to have a wider knowledge of fields such as finance, international development, or the economy than the executive directors. Each may need additional briefing on specific agenda items.

The Cadbury Report suggested that '*it is for chairmen to make certain that their non-executive directors receive timely, relevant information tailored to their needs, that they are properly briefed on the issues arising at board meetings, and that they make an effective contribution as board members in practice*'. The same applies to executive directors.

The information that directors acquire can come from both formal and informal sources on both a routine and non-routine basis. Table 12.1 illustrates this quadrant.

Regular and Routine Sources of Information

Most boards develop a routine set of board papers, which go to all the directors with the agenda for each meeting. These papers might include, for example, the latest financial accounts, cash flow report, report on operations, market report, the CEOs report on significant developments, etc. Some companies have developed computer based systems for producing routine board papers. Proprietary systems are also available, some providing on-line access (see, for example: www.boardbooks.com/diligentbooks/index.shtml and www.icsasoftware.com/boardview).

A good report with high quality information is:

- Understandable—at a level of detail, language, and content appropriate to the likely readers. It would be counter-productive to produce a document assuming technological or financial knowledge that the readers lacked. Conversely, an expert might find a layperson's guide patronizing and irritating

Table 12.1 **How directors get their information: sources and basis of board level information**

	Regular and routine basis	Occasional and non-routine basis
Informal and unofficial sources	Briefings to the board Contacts within the company Questioning in meetings Discussions with staff 'Grapevine' gossip	Contacts outside the company 'off the record' comments Casual reading/TV reports, etc. Unofficial probing and inquiry Visits, presentations, conferences
Formal and official sources	Regular board operating reports Regular board financial reports Statutory and regulatory reports Use of the company seal report Minutes of board committees Presentations to the board	Ad hoc reports and presentations • In-house studies • Consultants reports • Investment proposals • Merger & acquisition proposals • Market reports • Technology reports • Financial studies Details of legal actions

- Reliable—of fundamental importance, the reader must be able to trust that any facts given are accurate and any opinions advanced clearly shown as such
- Relevant—reports need to refer to the matter in hand. However interesting, significant, or worthy the information, unless it refers directly to the issue under consideration the material is not useful
- Comprehensive—half of a story, like half-truths, can mislead. Reports need to be complete and cover all relevant aspects of the situation.
- Concise—directors are inevitably under time constraints. Verbose reports may not be given the attention they deserve, being scanned and some of the salient information missed. Good report writing involves a skill that can be learned and developed with practice
- Timely—directors need reports in sufficient time for them to study the contents, but with material that is up-to-date. The frequency of provision needs to be appropriate to the decisions that are being faced
- Cost-effective—an aspect of report writing that is often overlooked. Report writing involves a cost, sometimes a substantial cost. Chairmen need to ensure that unnecessary expense is not incurred producing reports with little value. With formal board reports there can be a tendency to go on producing standard reports long after the need has disappeared.

Most formal board and board committee reports are still provided on paper, though email attachments are increasingly used in some companies. Access by directors, or their staff, to board files available on the company's intranet, although in its infancy, has considerable potential, particularly where associated with a question facility that enables directors to search for information. The protection of confidentiality and security is of fundamental importance with board level information systems.

The entire board or committee can also be informed by presentations made to them, for example by a senior executive, a consultant, or other expert in a relevant field. Such information may be supplemented by visits made by the board as a whole to various locations.

Box 12.3 Sir Campbell Adamson's Experience of Board Briefing

Sir Campbell Adamson, an INED on a number of British boards, commented that the knowledge and productivity of one board he served on had increased dramatically after the chairman introduced a half-hour briefing from a different outside speaker at the end of each board meeting. Discussion on the topic, of direct relevance to the board's interests, continued over the following lunch, he reported. In that time he often learned more about the company and his fellow directors than he had during the board meetings.

Occasional and Non-routine Sources of Information

Some agenda items may call for special reports with information that is required by all the directors. Ad hoc papers can then be developed for these items. For example, a proposal for a major capital investment, a report on an ongoing project such as a reorganization, or an acquisition proposal would all require one or more specific non-routine reports.

A professional chairman will not assume that the information needs of all directors can be met by a standard set of routine board papers, however comprehensive. Some directors need information that others already have. A good chairman, as the Cadbury Report recommended, should ensure that each director is adequately briefed on every item on the agenda to contribute to the board's deliberations. Such briefings might be with the chairman, the CEO, CFO, or a divisional, regional, or departmental head, the company's auditors, its lawyers, management consultants working with the firm, or other relevant professional advisers. If INEDs are allowed to approach company staff below board level for information a clear policy is needed to ensure that managerial authority is not compromised. Courses, tutorials, and mentoring may also provide sources of information for directors.

Director level information systems, which enable individual directors to access company files from remote locations and seek answers to questions about the business situation, are in the early stages of development. Such facilities go far beyond providing directors with corporate reports on-line. They provide access to the company databases. At issue, however, is how to provide access to the material that the director needs to be appropriately informed whilst preventing the tendency to 'drill-down' into the data to obtain material that is far too detailed and irrelevant to a director's needs.

Again, ensuring that confidentiality is maintained and that security is protected is vital. Such systems have the potential to change the nature of director information. Routine reports, in which management (the company secretary, the CEO, CFO, etc.) decide what directors need to know and produce reports accordingly, are essentially one way—company

Figure 12.1 Framework for analysing board level information

to director. Face-to-face communication provides a two-way link. When directors can search for the information they feel they need, the direction becomes—director to company.

The framework that was introduced in chapter 3 can provide a useful check list for analysing the extent and quality of board information (see figure 12.1).

A board information audit would consider the extent and nature of information made available at board level in each segment of the quadrant. Is it adequate? What is its quality? How might it be improved in content, presentation, availability, and so on?

In strategy formulation, for example, is each director adequately briefed on the firm's strategic context—its markets, distribution, customers, competitors, its suppliers and sources of finance, the labour market, the political, economic, social, and technological environment in all the countries in which the firm operates? Is that knowledge current?

In policy making, is every director familiar with the firm's policies and able to contribute fully to discussions when they are reviewed? Do directors have the background knowledge, for example, about labour relations, product safety, or credit control, to take an informed view of corporate policies?

In many organizations the board level reporting for monitoring and management supervision is developed most fully. Executive management information systems, rooted in the ongoing transactions of the business, report on the performance and the state of internal resources. As we saw in chapter 3, this is also the activity that typically draws the board's attention, because it highlights issues that need immediate board action. However, it is also frequently an area in which improvements can be made to reports.

Accountability, reporting to the outside world, has tended to be the least well developed segment of board level information. Of course, companies must satisfy the minimum disclosure requirements of company laws and stock market listing rules. But for many companies reporting beyond financial matters to include detailed strategic plans and corporate social responsibility and sustainability reporting is in its infancy. (We will discuss corporate social responsibility in chapter 15.)

A survey of board reporting[1] by UK FTSE100 companies comments that many annual reports are *'predictable, indistinguishable compliance statements'*. Few take the opportunity

---

[1] Independent Audit Ltd Board reporting in 2006, a survey of FTSE 100 annual reports. See www.independentaudit.com/us/outrpublications

to communicate with shareholders on real governance issues. The report suggests that companies need to turn their corporate governance statement into a story that investors want to read, emphasizing performance not compliance. It suggests:

- Drop statements of the obvious, such as 'boilerplate' statements that the board supports sound corporate governance
- Separate out the compliance statements, which are necessary but can be put in boxes so that the report flows
- Focus on the changes, referring back to the last report to show changes

However, the study also comments that more audit committees are reporting in detail on the independence and the effectiveness of their external auditor and how the committee makes that assessment.

In Britain, the original intention was to require listed companies to publish a detailed operations and financial review with their annual accounts, including a commentary on company's strategic situation. However, that requirement was dropped from the UK Companies Act 2006 because it was felt that such disclosure and cost might put British firms at a disadvantage against their international competitors.

A danger in director level reporting is that more reports produce more data not more information. In fact what is needed is not more information but better informed directors, who are better able to contribute to the board's activities, producing better quality discussion, and fuller informed and more successful decisions.

The Role of Company Secretary

Some company law jurisdictions require the appointment of a company secretary, an officer of the company with statutory duties. In the UK, until the Companies Act 2006, all companies, however small, had to have a company secretary. That Act required only public companies to have one and gave private companies the option if the members wanted one. In some jurisdictions, the company secretary can be a 'legal person' that is a limited company, and smaller companies often appoint a firm of accountants, lawyers, or a specialist company registrar firm to act as company secretary. In other jurisdiction, including Australia, the company secretary must be an actual person.

In the United States, the role of company secretary, typically known as the corporate secretary, is frequently carried out by the corporate lawyer. The American Society of Corporate Secretaries suggests that their duties and responsibilities include organizing meetings of the board, board committees, and shareholders, maintaining the corporate records and stock (shareholder) records, and liaising with the securities markets. It further states that the corporate secretary should be '*the primary liaison between the corporation's directors and management*'. The company secretary need not be an employee of the company: he or she may work for an outside agency or partnership.

Like directors, the company secretary is an officer of the company and, like them, has a duty to act in good faith in the best interest of the company and to avoid conflicts of interest. Some listing rules, as in Hong Kong, require that '*all directors should have access to the advice and services of the company secretary with a view to ensuring that board procedures, and all applicable rules and regulations, are followed*'.

The Cadbury Report argued that

the company secretary has a key role to play in ensuring that the board procedures are both followed and regularly reviewed. The chairman and the board will look to the company secretary for guidance on what their responsibilities are under the rules and regulations to which they are subject and on how these responsibilities should be discharged. All directors should have access to the advice and services of the company secretary and should recognise that the chairman is entitled to strong support from the company secretary in ensuring the effective functioning of the board.

The UK Combined Code requires that '*the company secretary should be responsible for advising the board through the chairman on all governance matters*', and

under the direction of the chairman, the company secretary's responsibilities include ensuring good information flows within the board and its committees and between senior management and non-executive directors, as well as facilitating induction and assisting with professional development as required. Removal of a company secretary should be a matter for the whole board, the code further adds.

In essence the duties of the company secretary typically include:

- Advising the chairman on legal rules and regulations affecting the enterprise
- Convening board, board committee, and company (shareholder) meetings
- Advising on and guiding board and board committee procedures
- Advising the chairman on agenda and writing the minutes for the chairman's approval
- Maintaining the company's statutory records such as the register of members (shareholders), register of directors and their interests, director's service agreements
- Filing company law returns with the companies registrar or regulatory authority
- Ensuring compliance with companies legislation, including the various filing requirements, the corporate governance codes, and where appropriate the stock exchange listing requirements
- Ensuring compliance with other relevant regulations and laws
- Administering changes to the company constitution (memorandum or articles of association)

In some companies, the company secretary plays a part in shareholder communications; in others, that is the responsibility of the CFO.

Box 12.4 Harvey Jones on the Role of the Company Secretary

Harvey Jones, previously the CEO of British company ICI, wrote

a company secretary should have considerable personal integrity and be seen to stand for probity and right within the company. The secretary should be seen to 'side with the angels' and be prepared to state when the occasion demands that 'I fear that while what we are doing is within the letter of the law we are not within the spirit'. They have to be trusted by everyone. It is a bloody tough job.

The evolution of the company secretary's role highlights its current significance. In Britain in the mid-19th century, when the joint stock limited liability company was developed, directors needed someone to keep their records. This was the job of the secretary to the board. The function was largely clerical with the directors holding the power. The list of duties, above, shows just how far the function has moved, not least in line with the growing complexity of modern organizations, the globalization of business, and the vast array of modern regulation, legislation, and exhortation about company affairs.

Box 12.5 Lord Denning on the Evolution of the Company Secretary's Role

Changing attitudes to company secretaries can be seen in the contrasting comments of two senior British judges. In 1887, Lord Esher, Master of the Rolls (the head of the judiciary), said:

> A secretary is a mere servant. His position is that he is to do what he is told and no person can assume that he has the authority to represent anything at all, nor can anyone assume that statements made by him are necessarily accepted as trustworthy without further enquiry.

A century later things had changed. Corporate life had become complicated. Many companies ran diverse enterprises through complex groups of subsidiary and associated companies. Legislation affecting companies had become substantial. The role of the company secretary called for professional knowledge and skill. In 1971, Lord Denning, Master of the Rolls, said:

> Times have changed. A company secretary is a much more important person nowadays than he was in 1887. He is an officer of the company with extensive duties and responsibilities. This appears not only in modern Companies Acts but also by the role, which he plays in the day-to-day business of companies. He is no longer merely a clerk. He regularly makes representations on behalf of the company and enters into contracts on its behalf. . . . so much so that he may be regarded as [doing] such things on behalf of the company. He is certainly entitled to sign contracts connected with the administrative side of the company's affairs, such as employing staff, ordering cars and so forth. All such matters come within the ostensible authority of a company secretary.

Director Induction, Training, and Development

Director Induction

A newly appointed director needs an induction programme to obtain essential knowledge and training before joining the board. A well planned induction programme can reduce the learning time before a new director begins to contribute to board deliberations. Significantly, new executive directors may have little knowledge and experience of board level work, having been 'promoted' to the board for their successful executive performance.

They need a suitable induction programme, just as new INEDs need to learn about the way the company runs and about its industry. There is an induction checklist for directors at the end of this chapter.

Some companies use a director mentoring programme, in which an experienced member of the board accepts a responsibility, usually quite informally, to induct and guide a new member into the ways of the board and the company. This relationship can help a new director contribute more quickly and effectively.

Director Training and Development

Until quite recently many directors saw no call for director training and development. They felt that the business and management experience that had led them to a board appointment demonstrated their capacity to be a director. Few hold that view today, although no doubt there are still a few of the old school. Many corporate governance codes now call for performance evaluation of directors and director training. A professional approach is needed. With the rapid acceleration of new regulations, codes, and legal requirements, with the ever-changing aspects of global business life, and given the litigious society that exists in many parts of the world, the need for continuous updating and professional education and training for directors has become apparent.

The interest in corporate governance in general, and director training in particular, has increased dramatically in recent years in many parts of the world. The various alternative approaches to director training and development can be classified as:

- *Formal external training courses* on aspects of the director's work. Many organizations around the world—Institutes of Directors; legal, accounting, and managerial professional bodies; and specialist consulting and research organizations—now run programmes for director training and updating. An advantage of such programmes is that they enable directors to be given relevant theoretical frameworks, principles, and practice updates that reflect the latest situation. Such experience can be enhanced by having directors from different types of entity, different industries, and various styles and scales of operation in the programme

- *In-house board development programmes* designed specifically for the entire board. Such activities may involve board level evaluation with discussions that lead to learning in the context of that board. We will discuss director and board evaluation in the next chapter. The problem with such programmes is that by focusing on a specific company and its situation they may lack breadth of insight from other companies, industries, and countries

- *Updating and briefing sessions for the board, or individual directors.* Workshops with experts to lead and provide relevant knowledge, for example on recent developments in relevant company law or employee legislation, new developments in financial instruments, or the implication of private equity funded acquisitions of previously listed companies, can be valuable learning experiences

- *Relevant higher degree courses* in corporate governance, corporate strategy, and other board related topics are now offered by some business schools around the world

- *Experiential sponsorship programmes* can provide individual directors with relevant experience and knowledge. An executive director might be encouraged to become an

INED of a non-competing company to gain experience of board, governance, and managerial topics. Another director might be encouraged to chair an in-house inquiry, join the board of a subsidiary in the group, or lead an in-house project team. Such activities, however, may lack depth and relevance to the needs of the sponsoring company

- *Mentoring* provides another learning opportunity with a one to one personal trainer, as discussed earlier in this chapter. Although, it should be mentioned that such relationships are not value free, particularly if the mentor is a fellow director when hidden agendas may affect the relationship

- *Self-directed learning and continuous self-development* is, probably, the most prevalent learning experience adopted by directors. Participating in conferences, networking with peers, distance learning courses, reading books, journals, and professional articles can all provide learning experiences. As the old saying goes '*if you want a helping hand look at the end of your arm*'.

- *Board experience* itself can be one of the best learning opportunities, provided that the learning experience is recognized. A professional chairman will sometimes raise the question with his board: what have we learned from this experience?

A challenge to every director today is to remain up-to-date. That means continuous learning. Executive directors may need to delegate some day to day managerial work to focus on their director responsibilities. In addition to director evaluation programmes discussed in the next chapter, directors can recognize their own development needs. They can question whether they are sufficiently knowledgeable to contribute fully and responsibly to board level discussions and decision making. Professional directors understand their strengths and their weaknesses, and create an informal self-development plan to remedy the gaps in their knowledge and their competencies. By reinforcing their strengths and remedying weaknesses directors can increase their self-confidence and increase their contributions to their boards.

Director Remuneration

In many countries, directors' rewards have become contentious. Institutional investors in both the United States and the United Kingdom, encouraged by investigative media, have criticized the growing scale of executive directors' and other top managers' rewards, alleging that they are often out of line with the market and unrelated to performance. Although 'golden parachutes'—large benefits paid on a director's retirement—have been seen since the 1970s, large pay-offs are still used, which sometimes seem to be rewarding failure.

We are talking about a director's total pay and benefits, of course—salary, fees, bonuses, share options, pension fund contributions, reimbursement of personal expenses, plus any other benefits. But what is the appropriate level in a given case? Clearly it needs to be sufficient to attract the top executives the company needs, to provide an incentive for better than average performance, to reward success, and to retain the vital executives' involvement in the company. The challenge is to balance the interests of the directors with those of the shareholders.

So, how are the appropriate rewards to be determined? We discussed the work of the remuneration committee in chapter 3 and earlier in this chapter. We noted that it was a sub-committee of the main board, consisting wholly or mainly of independent outside directors, concerned with recommending the remuneration of directors and top management. We recognized the underlying principal that no one should be responsible for determining their own rewards. Of course that left unanswered the question: who should fix the remuneration of the members of the remuneration committee?

Share options have been used as a way of rewarding and motivating top executives for many years. Options give the right to buy shares at a predetermined price sometime in the future, thus enabling the recipient to benefit by exercising the right once the share price has risen. The exercise price is typically that at the time the option is given. Obviously, the belief is that options provide a strong incentive to directors to raise the share price by improving corporate performance.

Some argue that such incentives reward exceptional performance and align directors' interests with those of the shareholders. Unfortunately, that is not always the case. In fact the interests of shareholders are not the same as those of the holders of share options. Shareholders have to invest their funds and run the risk of loss: option holders have no downside, having invested nothing, and are not at risk.

Moreover, on a rising stock market all prices rise, so option holders reap a reward that is not linked to performance. Some schemes attempt to overcome this problem by building in a market index, so that only performance better than the market is rewarded. Such indexation can work on a falling market as well, benefiting executives if their company outperforms the market.

Other disadvantages of options include the possibility of unscrupulous directors attempting to bolster the firm's share price with short term manoeuvres that do not really reflect improved performance—a classical agency dilemma. If a company gives new options, whenever they are exercised (re-loading), executives may be able to play the market, irrespective of their performance. Share options are obviously unattractive on a falling market, so some companies lower the bid price of their directors' options (re-setting). This clearly fails to reward outstanding performance.

In the past, firms were not required to account for share options, merely issuing more shares. Boards tended to act as though they were free of cost to the company. But, obviously, although not a cash charge on the company, when an option is exercised there is a cost as the interests of the other shareholders are diluted. Today accounting standards require options to be valued, at their net present values using appropriate valuation models, and a charge to be shown.

The use of share options tends to be falling and attention has turned to bonuses and other incentive schemes to reward exceptional performance. But unfortunately, unless carefully handled such schemes can also encourage sub-optimization as directors manipulate the target criteria of the incentive scheme.

What are appropriate fees for non-executive directors? In the past these have been relatively low. But it is now widely recognized that sufficient rewards are necessary to persuade people of the required calibre to afford the time and, increasingly important, to shoulder the risk of being an INED. In the US, share options are often issued to outside directors. Hermes, one of the UK's largest fund managers, has suggested that non-executive directors should receive some of their remuneration in shares. But the counter-argument is that share options should be linked to outstanding performance and only given to those top executives whose actions directly determine the results.

As we saw earlier, the focus on board level remuneration has created a market for remuneration consultants to advise remuneration committees. Comparative information about similar companies can clearly be useful, but consultants' recommendations can mislead.

One problem has been called remuneration ratcheting. Various arguments are sometimes advanced to justify high board level rewards, including the following:

- International comparison is essential: '*to ensure that our company attracts and holds executive directors of the calibre we need against international competition, it is essential that we give our directors rewards that are broadly comparable to those they could obtain in the industry anywhere in the world*'. Such an argument may be advanced even if the directors concerned have no prospects of being headhunted and whether or not they have any possibility of working anywhere else in the world

- The headhunter argument: '*we have just recruited a new executive director and the headhunters assured us that he had to receive a package that is 30% more than that of the highest paid director. Of course, we all had to have an increase to maintain differentials.*' This argument conveniently overlooks the fact that the fee of the headhunter is based on 30–35 percent of the first year's salary of the new appointee

- The 'top of the industry' claim: '*our firm prides itself on being one of the leaders in the industry, even though at the moment we are not among the most profitable. We expect to pay our directors in the upper quartile of the industry range as shown by the comparator pay research.*' This argument totally ignores the performance of the firm or its directors

- The fear of loss of people: '*we could lose our directors to the competition unless we pay competitive rates*'. This argument is sometimes advanced even though the directors concerned are within a year or two of retirement and would be of absolutely no interest to competitors

- Doubling up the bonus: '*we believe that it is important for directors' rewards to be performance related. Moreover, we expect excellent performance in both the short and the long term. So we calculate bonuses on the annual profits, then we have a parallel three-year scheme which rewards directors if earnings per share grows by 30% over that period*'. This way directors get rewarded twice for the same performance, inflation is ignored and there is no upside cap should there be exceptional circumstances. Moreover, directors do not get penalized for poor performance.

In the UK, shareholders have had the opportunity to vote on directors' pay since 2002. Admittedly, the result is then only advisory: the board does not have to take any notice, but in practice shareholders' opinions, plus private conversations with institutional investors, resolves most issues avoiding a confrontation. In the United States, SEC rules since 2007 require full disclosure of pay packages of top management remuneration, but shareholders have less opportunity to voice their opinions other than through the annual proxy round.

An interesting initiative of PricewaterhouseCoopers and the UK Institute of Management Accountants produced a model remuneration report which shows the principles of a company's remuneration policy, the link between performance and reward, and the alignment with shareholder interests (see www.reportleadership.com).

Director and Officer Insurance[2]

Around the world, societies are becoming more litigious, with people suing each other over issues that would earlier not have led to legal action. Originating in the United States and spreading around the advanced world, directors and senior executives of companies find themselves in the line of fire. Corporate regulation has increased and the responsibilities of directors are now widely recognized. The expectations of shareholders, customers, employees, and others affected by the company have increased. Most significantly, so has the propensity by such parties to sue the company, its auditors, the board, or specific directors.

Further, the legal context has also changed. Class actions are allowed in more jurisdictions, in which individual actions, from people who might not have mounted a case on their own, are consolidated into a major action on behalf of all those in that class with claims. Contingency fees are also now allowed in some jurisdictions, in which lawyers agree to bring an action for a client on a no-win-no-fee basis, for a share of any damages obtained or for a negotiated fee.

Directors' duties and responsibilities were outlined in the previous chapter. Directors' personal assets can be at risk, which is why some people think twice before accepting a directorship. Directors can be held legally accountable in their personal capacity for actions they are alleged to have taken or failed to take, but also for the actions of other members of the board or top management. Claims can be for unlimited amounts. Suits against directors can be brought by shareholders, employees, creditors, customers, suppliers, government and regulatory bodies, auditors, and liquidators. Even if an action is successfully defended, legal costs can be incurred and directors' personal reputation damaged.

Director and officer insurance, which is almost universally known as D&O insurance, provides some protection to directors, company officers, such as the company secretary, and senior managers if they are sued as the result of decisions taken whilst governing or managing the business. Some investors, such as venture capitalists, insist on D&O insurance before providing funds to a company. D&O insurance should not be confused with E&O (errors and omissions cover), which is concerned with performance failures with respect to products and services.

In a D&O insurance case, directors will first look to their company for indemnification. However, directors cannot be indemnified by their company or by insurance for acts which are shown to be contrary to companies legislation or for other misfeasance. For example, Australian company law prohibits a company from paying the premiums on any policy that insures a director against liability (other than legal costs) arising out of a wilful breach of duty in relation to the company or improper use of corporate information or official position.

D&O insurance pays for actual or alleged wrong decisions, what policies call '*wrongful acts*'. Each insurer defines coverage in its own way, but typically covers '*any actual or alleged act or omission, error, misstatement, misleading statement, neglect or breach of duty by an insured person in the discharge of his/her duties*'. For example, a D&O policy might cover claims of mismanagement of assets, claims by the shareholders of an acquired company that they

---

[2]The author acknowledges helpful advice from the Corporate Governance Practice of Aon Asia.

had been misled by former directors, claims under health and safety legislation (although many D&O policies exclude bodily injury or property damage), actions under employment legislation including harassment, discrimination, and wrongful termination, and environmental legislation (although pollution damage is often excluded in D&O policies).

Each insurance proposal needs to be evaluated on its cover, conditions, and cost/benefit against the perceived risks. Most D&O policies are written on a 'claims-made' basis, which only provides protection for law suits brought during the policy period. 'Occurrence' policies pay from the date of the accident or alleged wrongdoing. In the event that coverage is replaced or cancelled, protection may be desired for events that took place prior to expiration or cancellation but for which no claim has yet been filed. This coverage is called a 'tail' or 'extended reporting period'. 'Run-off cover' can also be important, that is insurance for a director after he/she has left the company until the statute of limitations extinguishes any exposure to risk.

The breadth of the policy is fundamental and needs to cover claims from all possible suitors. Most D&O policies provide cover against the cost of legal fees and civil damages in defending a claim, subject to limits, which need to be carefully reviewed, as do any terms that limit coverage, and 'retroactive date' terms that stipulate the time within which a claim must be made.

Box 12.6 Legal Costs Paid by D&O Insurance

A British company had an air conditioning system in one of their plants which was faulty and became contaminated. Some employees contracted Legionnaires' disease and died. Directors of the company were accused of negligence and corporate manslaughter. The directors' legal costs, which were substantial, were met by the company's D&O insurance. Note, however, that many D&O policies exclude bodily injury.

D&O insurance cover is not available for all who seek it. Successful, long established companies are more likely to be able to obtain cover than companies in riskier situations, such as start-ups or those with financial problems. Some directors expect lower D&O premiums if their company is recognized as having high corporate governance standards. This is seldom the case. Corporate governance standards are difficult to assess, as we will see in the next chapter. What is almost certainly true, however, is that a reputation for poor corporate governance will result in higher premiums, a reduction in cover, or even a failure to find insurance.

The 2003 UK Higgs report (see chapter 7) commented that '*the cost of D&O insurance is increasing and the coverage appears to be getting less*'. A 2004 report from the Australian Corporations and Markets Advisory Committee noted that:

there is an increasing trend to impose personal liability on directors and other officers for the short-comings of companies. In considering the practical consequences of this liability regime, it cannot be assumed that all those exposed to personal liability are able to obtain protection through insurance. The availability of insurance cover reflects the market's appreciation of relevant risks. D&O insurance does not serve as an across-the-board mitigation of the personal financial liabilities to which corporate directors and officers are increasingly exposed. It cannot provide a complete cushion.

Just as all boards need a strategy for assessing and managing risk, they need a strategy for director and officer insurance. The hope that misfortune will be avoided is not a strategy.

Case Study 12.1 The Walt Disney Company

Roy Disney, Walt Disney's nephew, was the last remaining member of the Disney family on the board of the famous Walt Disney Company. He was vice-chairman of the board and an executive director as chairman of the Animated Features Division. He was often paraded as the last survivor of the founder's family serving in the company.

However, in November 2003 he had a shock. The Governance and Nomination Committee of the board lowered the mandatory retirement age for directors to 72. Roy was 73. Moreover, John Bryson, who was chairman and CEO of Edison International, an outside director of the Walt Disney Company, and a member of its nomination and compensation committee, told him that, since he was past mandatory retirement, the committee had decided to make no exceptions and had agreed that he should not run for the Disney board at the next AGM.

Roy's response was that *'you'll regret this . . .'* But he was not really surprised: for a few years relations between him and Michael Eisner, the Chairman and CEO of Disney, had been poor. Indeed, by 2003 they were scarcely speaking.

Michael Eisner, who previously had a highly successful career with ABC and Paramount Pictures, had been appointed to Disney in 1984 by Roy Disney himself. In his early years the company was highly successful in both animated and main films, videos, theme parks, and merchandise. The company's financial performance and its share price had improved significantly. In 1988 Eisner was the highest paid executive in America, with a salary, a bonus on profits, and the exercise of stock options amounting to some US\$40 million. In 1992 he earned over US\$200 million.

But as the 1990s progressed problems arose. Financial performance fell off. Critics complained that Disney had lost its creative energy. The Euro World theme park in Paris faced a massive overspend and below budget revenues: the strategies that had worked in the US did not work in Europe.

Roy Disney was not alone on the board in criticizing Eisner. Stanley Gold, an independent outside director, questioned why, when profits had fallen 25 percent and the Disney share price was low, Eisner had been given a US\$5 million bonus by the Compensation Committee. Gold had been chairman of that committee but had been replaced by Judith Estrin just before this bonus was awarded.

Another outside director, Andrea van der Kamp, was also told in 2003 that she would not be re-appointed to the board. She wrote complaining that:

> I was asked to serve on this board to be an independent director, and now I'm not being re-nominated because that is just what I am—an independent director . . . The performance of this company has not been wonderful. I, along with some employees and shareholders are concerned. Michael Eisner has cost this company a lot of money . . . We have terrible relations with creative people in Hollywood because of Michael Eisner's arrogance. Many of the best executives have left the company. We've just fired all these people and yet Michael Eisner is getting a \$5 million bonus . . .

Other directors on the board of 18 directors supported Eisner, approving the decisions of both the Compensation Committee and the Nomination Committee.

At the September 2002 board meeting, which approved new appointments to the Nominating and Governance Committee, Eisner claimed: '*Today, we furthered our commitment to ensure that Disney remains among the progressive boards in America on governance issues.*'

After John Bryson had told Roy Disney that the governance and nomination committee's decision was final, Roy realized that it would still need board confirmation. But Bryson and Eisner had then contacted the other directors to brief them and confirm they would support the decision.

As James B. Stewart[1] wrote, '*obviously Eisner controlled the Disney executive directors. But he maintained that the rest were independent. But he was defining independence so narrowly as to be meaningless.*' Outside director Irwin Russell, for example, was Eisner's personal lawyer and had negotiated his lucrative contract: an obvious conflict of interest between a lawyer's duty to his client and a director's duty to the shareholders. Robert Stern, another outside director, was Eisner's personal architect whose firm relied on Disney contracts.

In the end Roy Disney decided that he should resign, making public his concerns for the future of the company. He wrote to Eisner:

> It is with deep sadness and regret that I send this letter of resignation from the Walt Disney Company both as Chairman of the Animated Features Division and Vice-Chairman of the Board of Directors.
>
> You know well that you and I have had serious differences of opinion about the direction of the company and style of management . . . you have driven a wedge between me and those I work with, even to the extent of requiring some of my associates to report my conversations and activities back to you. I find this intolerable.
>
> Finally you discussed with the Governance and Nominating Committee its decision to leave my name off the slate of directors to be re-elected.
>
> Michael I believe . . . that after 19 years at the helm you are no longer the best person to run Walt Disney Company . . . It is my sincere belief that it is you who should be leaving and not me . . . The company deserves fresh, energetic leadership . . .
>
> With sincere regret, Roy E Disney

Eisner and his associates felt that Roy's letter raised corporate governance issues. They decided to present his opinions as an attack on the company and the board, with him trying to block needed governance reforms, not as a criticism of Eisner's management.

Over 4,000 present and past members of the staff of Roy's Animation Division wrote to support him. A few weeks later Eisner shut down the Orlando Animation unit.

Then Gold offered his resignation, too, writing:

> I am proud of my more than 15 years of service and my role in reshaping the company . . . I do however, lament that my efforts over the past three years to implement necessary changes has only succeeded in creating an insular board of directors serving as a bulwark to shield management from criticism and accountability . . .

On the decision to oust Roy from the board he commented:

This is yet another attempt by this board to squelch dissent by hiding behind the veil of 'good governance'. What a curious result. The board seems determined to devote its time and energies to adopting policies that . . . only serve to muzzle and isolate those directors who recognize that their role is to be active in shaping the company and planning for executive succession. Further this board isolates those directors who believe that Michael Eisner (when measured by the dismal results of the last seven years) is not up to the challenge.

Institutional investors, such as CalPers, also raised objections to Disney's performance and the lack of succession planning for Eisner. The 2004 annual general meeting of Disney shareholders was going to be crucial.

In February 2004 an influential shareholder advisory firm, Glass Lewis, interviewed Roy Disney and Gold as well as Eisner and his supporters. They asked why the mandatory retirement age had been chosen as 72 and not, say, 75. The subsequent Glass Lewis report to shareholders was unequivocal: '*The Disney Board has been notoriously insular, famously gullible and blindly loyal to Mr. Eisner . . . Given the control Mr. Eisner is accustomed to, we are troubled that he still wields tremendous power over the operation of this board . . . Our concerns are substantial.*'

The report also questioned the independence of Bryson (head of the governance committee), as his wife was a senior executive of a Disney joint venture.

Roy Disney and Gold launched a campaign to undermine and unseat Eisner, with a website—www.SaveDisney.com which claimed that: '*Shareholder democracy, while lauded as the centerpiece of democratic capitalism, has in fact become an oxymoron, with the vast majority of corporations firmly in the grip of their chief executives and acquiescent boards.*'

Other institutional shareholders joined the revolt, citing poor financial performance, loss of creative leadership, and poor board accountability. CalPers announced that it would vote with Gold and Roy Disney against Eisner. The state pension funds in Connecticut, Massachusetts, New Jersey, and New York followed. The T. Rowe Price Mutual Fund, which held 19 million shares, also called for Eisner to go. There were also suggestions that the roles of chairman and CEO should be separated.

ISS, another shareholder advisory group, recommended that shareholders withhold their vote for Eisner to demonstrate their dissatisfaction, although under the US corporate voting system it is almost impossible for shareholders of widely held public companies to evict directors, because of shareholder inertia, problems in identifying owners, and since many mutual funds, brokers, and others automatically support incumbent management.

Just prior to the AGM in March 2004 Gold and Roy held a rally for shareholders opposed to Eisner's leadership, calling for a rediscovery of the original Walt Disney Company values.

The AGM produced a major rebuke from shareholders with 43 percent voting against Eisner's renewal. Subsequently, the board decided to separate the positions of chair and CEO, creating a new role of chairman of the board. George Mitchell, the former senator, was appointed chairman, who assured the Wall Street Journal that corporate governance reforms were already in place. Eisner stayed as CEO.

At the June 2004 board meeting Eisner announced his successor as CEO—Bob Iger—but the choice was not made public. Then at the September 2004 board meeting Eisner announced that he would stand down as CEO in September 2006 when his present contract ended. The board thanked him for his twenty years service and looked forward to his continuing leadership throughout his remaining tenure. Gold and Roy called it window-dressing.

But criticisms of Eisner intensified and in March 2005 he announced that he would step down as CEO a year before the end of his contract, which he did on 30 September 2005. His successor was Bob Iger.

[1]Primary source: Stewart, James B, *Disney War*, Simon and Schuster, New York, 2005. The author also acknowledges insights from various other works on the company

Discussion Questions

1. Identify the issues raised by this case.

2. Andrea van der Kamp, an independent outside director, complained that she was not re-nominated to the board because she had been too independent. What can a director, who has criticized corporate, do if they are then not re-nominated?

3. What is your opinion of the statement made in the case that: '*Shareholder democracy, while lauded as the centerpiece of democratic capitalism, has in fact become an oxymoron, with the vast majority of corporations firmly in the grip of their chief executives and acquiescent boards.*'?

REFERENCES AND FURTHER READING

NACD (2005) 'Board Leadership'. A report of a NACD Blue Ribbon Commission, National Association of Corporate Directors, Washington, DC.

—— (2005) 'CEO Succession'. A report of a NACD Blue Ribbon Commission, National Association of Corporate Directors, Washington, DC.

—— (2005) 'Director Compensation: Purpose, Principles and Best Practices'. A report of a NACD Blue Ribbon Commission, National Association of Corporate Directors, Washington, DC.

—— (2005) 'Executive Compensation and the Role of the Compensation Committee'. A report of a NACD Blue Ribbon Commission, National Association of Corporate Directors, Washington, DC.

Steger, Ulrich and Wolfgang Amann (2008) *Corporate Governance: Cases in Adding Value*. Chichester: Wiley.

Wallace, Peter and John Zinken (2003) *Corporate Governance*, Mastering Business in Asia series. Singapore: John Wiley.

USEFUL WEBSITES

www.boardsource.org
Building effective non-profit boards.

www.ecgtn.org
European Corporate Governance Training Network. Funded by the European Commission under the Marie Curie Research. Coordinated by the Centre for Economic Policy Research (CEPR).

hbswk.hbs.edu/item/4341.html
Robert Kaplan (Harvard Business School)—balanced scorecard for boards.

www.henleymc.ac.uk/henleyres03.nsf/pages/cbe
Centre for Board Effectiveness, Henley College, UK.

www.icsasoftware.com
Corporate governance software from the Institute of Chartered Secretaries UK.

www.independentaudit.com/us/outrpublications
Reports on corporate governance reporting.

www.mentoringcanada.ca/training/Boards
Canadian director mentoring programme.

PROJECTS AND EXERCISES

1. We saw that ensuring the independence of the external auditor was an important role for the audit committee. How can they ensure that this is achieved?

2. Draft a set of briefing notes for directors on the following topics:
   - The role of the company secretary
   - Director induction, training, and development
   - Directors' and officers' insurance

3. You have been asked to advise the board of a listed public company on the use of share options as a way to reward directors. The company has no experience of share options. Prepare a report/ presentation outlining a share option scheme and explaining the pros and cons.

SELF-TEST QUESTIONS

To confirm your grasp of the key points in this chapter try answering the following questions. Answers are at the end of the book.

1. Name ten possible duties of an audit committee.

2. What are the primary duties of a remuneration committee?

3. What is the primary role of the nomination committee and why?

4. What are the key questions that should be posed before calling a meeting?

5. If a director lacks appropriate knowledge on a subject before the board can he or she, legitimately, opt out of discussions on that item?

6. Are there any specific rules governing the content or format of minutes of board or board sub-committee meetings?

7. Name five qualities of a good report with high quality information.

8. Why should companies have a director induction programme?

9. What is D&O?

10. In a limited liability company are the liabilities of the directors limited?

Appendix to Chapter 12
Director's Induction Checklist

Working through the items on this checklist will improve the quality of a director's contribution and reduce the time taken to contribute fully and effectively to the board. Induction exercises for directors ensure that all board members are fully informed about the company, the business, and its financials, which are the three fundamental areas in which directors need to be conversant and competent. Obviously, directors vary in the extent of their knowledge of the company and its business, but the checklist will provide an *aide memoire* for both executive and non-executive directors.

The checklist can be used by chairmen and CEOs to plan an induction programme for their board members and also by newly appointed directors wanting to brief themselves. It has also proved useful for directors of long standing, by highlighting areas of knowledge and work that they might previously have overlooked.

Knowledge of the Company

The first broad focus of the induction programme is on the company and its governance situation. The chairman, other longserving directors, and the company secretary can often be very helpful in this sector. If in any doubt, it is always wise to seek legal opinion.

Ownership Power

In the joint stock, limited liability company ownership is the ultimate basis of governance power. What is the actual balance of the equity shareholding and voting power in this company? Has the balance changed in the past and how have the votes been used? How might it change and the voting strength be used in the future? Consider, in a family company for example, what might happen as shares are transferred on succession. Or, in a widely held public company, consider the potential for a merger or hostile bid. What anti-takeover provisions, if any, are in place? How effective might they be?

In a company limited by guarantee, or any other corporate entity governed by its membership, how active is the membership in governance matters? Could this situation change in the future? Explore the way that the board communicates with the members and whether there have been any attempts by members to influence corporate affairs. Not-for-profit organizations often seem to generate controversial, even adversarial, member activity.

Governance Rules, Regulations, and Company Law

Study the articles of association and memorandum or corporate rule book. These are the formal documents created on incorporation and updated subject to the approval of the members. Within the constraints of the company law and the listing rules (for a quoted public company), they determine the way the company can be governed. The articles, for example, could limit the size of the board, lay down rules for the selection of the board chairman, or define conditions for the meeting and voting of the members. All too often directors are not familiar with the contents of the company's memorandum and articles of association and are surprised to find themselves constrained in some way, for example in the percentage of members' votes needed to change the capital structure or sell off part of the enterprise.

In a listed, public company be familiar with the listing rules of the stock exchanges on which the company's shares are quoted. Some directors feel that this is a matter that can reasonably be left to the company secretary, share registrar, or corporate legal counsel. It is difficult to ask appropriate questions to ensure compliance if one is not familiar with the basic requirements. There is an important distinction between delegation and abdication of responsibility.

Be familiar with the broad scope of the company law of the jurisdiction in which the company is incorporated and operates. Obviously, the detailed requirements of company law vary between Delaware and California, Australia and Canada, or the United Kingdom and France: but there can also be fundamental differences, particularly in the handling of private companies. Companies incorporated in the British Virgin Islands, for example, are not required to have an audit, there is virtually no public filing of documents, and the rights of members can be severely limited if they are not also directors.

It is not necessary for a director to be a lawyer or an accountant to fulfill such responsibilities: but company law around the world typically expects directors to show that degree of knowledge and skill that a reasonable person would associate with company directorship. In the old days this might not have amounted to very much: today expectations run high.

Board Structure, Membership, and Processes

What is the structure of the board—that is, what is the balance between executive and non-executive directors? In your opinion is this appropriate? Are the outside, non-executive directors genuinely independent, or do they have some connection with the company such as being a nominee for a major shareholder or lender, are members of the family of the chairman or CEO, or held an executive position in that company in the past? Such matters could affect your assessment of the position they take on board issues.

Is the board chairmanship separated from the role of chief executive? If not, is there a danger that a single individual dominates the board: are you able to operate in such a climate? What is the style of the chairman of the board: can you work well with him or her? Who are the other board members? Do you know them? If not, some effort to learn about their background, experience, and reputation could reinforce your early contributions to board discussions. Meeting individual directors to discuss corporate matters before your first board meeting might help you to discover whether the chemistry of the board is likely to be appropriate for you. Is there a succession plan for key directors and top management? Is there a strategy for development at board level to ensure that the business does not outgrow the board?

How often does the board meet? Typically how long do the meetings last? What role does the chairman play in board matters? Ask for the agenda and minutes of recent board meetings. Talk to the company secretary about the way the board meetings are run. Does the board operate with committees—an executive committee, audit, remuneration, or nominating committees, for example? Find out what you can about the membership, chairmanship, and style of these committees. Again study their minutes and discuss with their chairman or the company secretary how they operate.

What information do the directors routinely receive? Ask for all the documentation provided for recent meetings: study the reports and consider the scope of the routine performance data provided. Is it adequate? Does the board have briefings and presentations from non-board senior executives or other experts from time to time? Do the directors meet with the auditors periodically?

Knowledge of the Business

The second focus of this induction checklist is on the business itself. Do you know enough about the business to make an effective contribution? Obviously this is a reasonable question to ask an outside director who has little or no experience in this particular industry. Interestingly though, it is also a pertinent question to put to many executive directors. Expertise and success in a particular function (finance and accounting, perhaps) or high managerial performance in running a division or group company, does not necessarily provide a view of the business as a whole. Indeed, it might have created a narrow window of experience through which the entire corporate business is viewed. This part of the checklist is again relevant to *all* directors.

The Basic Business Processes

Can you outline the fundamental steps in the added-value chain or network of the firm? This is as pertinent a question for directors of a bank, a telecommunications company, or an airline, as it is to a manufacturing business (although the basic processes are often more difficult to identify). Where is the business most exposed to risk? What are the core competencies or capabilities of the business? What is the range of products and services provided by the business? Are you familiar with the major sources of the business inputs—where they come from and who provides them?

Which business activities or processes add value and provide competitive advantage? Which business activities or processes drive the costs? Who are the customers? What sectors and markets are served? Pareto's law often applies to products and customers—80 percent of the value comes from 20 percent of the list. Which products and customers form this 20 percent?

Find out all you can from catalogues, trade literature, customer promotions, trade shows, and similar sources of information. Do directors have access to the firm's customer and competitor information systems—capturing and abstracting information, often qualitative, about the activities and plans of customers, competitors, and strategic allies? These systems can be more akin to military or police intelligence systems than typical transaction based systems.

Corporate Strategies

Does the firm have a written mission statement or a set of core values? Is there a shared view of the business direction, clearly articulated in strategies, plans, and projects? Obtain copies; discuss them with the chairman or CEO. If not, what is the broad direction of the business; what strategies are emergent from recent actions, such as strategies of growth through investment in new product development or through acquisition and divestment? Are there any written policies or management manuals? Again study and discuss them. For example, as far as customers are concerned, are there specific pricing policies, credit policies, and returned goods policies?

Who are the principal competitors? What competitive advantages and disadvantages do they have; what strategies are they pursuing? Are there potential new entrants into the market or new technological developments, products, or services that might provide alternative competition? Is the business involved in strategic alliances, for example joint ventures to develop new strategic areas, to supply goods or services, or provide access to distribution channels?

How is strategic change initiated in the firm? Does the board respond to ideas put up by the CEO and top management; or is the board intimately involved in strategy formulation?

Organization, Management, and People

What is the formal organization structure? Discuss with the CEO and other members of top management how the organization works in practice. Form a view of the management culture and style throughout the business: it may differ around the world.

What management control systems are used—budgetary planning and control, profit centres, performance centres, etc.? What management performance measures are used? Are they linked to managerial incentives? Are there employee or top management share option schemes? What is the company's position on monitoring and reporting corporate social responsibility and sustainability?

How many employees in the various parts of the business? What are the characteristics of the work force? Are trades unions important: is there a policy towards them? What are the remuneration and other employment policies?

Overall, how would you assess the current position of the business? What needs to be done to maintain and enhance future performance?

Knowledge of the Financials

Finally, we turn to a sector which inevitably features large in typical board discussions— the financial aspects.

Study the annual accounts and directors' reports for the past few years. What have been the trends? Consider trends in key financial ratios for example: overall performance ratios, such as return on equity and return on investment, inventory turnover rates, liquidity ratios, and debt collection rates. Does the company measure shareholder added-value?

Trends are likely to convey more information than the actual data for the business itself; although financial ratios at a point in time can be useful for cross-industry comparisons. What are the future projections for these financial criteria? How does the financial position of the company compare with that of its key competitors?

Review the financial performance of parts of the business, such as product or geographical divisions or subsidiary companies. Review the criteria used in investment project appraisals.

How is the company financed? What is the financial structure? What implications might the debt/equity ratio have for the future—for example, what might be the effect of a significant change in interest rates given this gearing or leverage?

Who are the auditors? Ask to see any 'management letter' written after the last audit discussing any issues that arose during the audit.

Expectations on Appointment

Every director should discuss with the chairman what is expected of the directorship, before accepting nomination. Consequently, a crucial part of any induction briefing should review the expectations of the chairman and the other directors.

Has the director been proposed to fulfill a specific role; is there a special reason for the nomination to the board? For example, did the nomination reflect particular knowledge in some area, to bring special skills or experience to board discussions, or to provide a channel of communication or networking? Or was the nomination made because of relevant overall experience and potential contribution to all aspects of the board's work? Are you capable of fulfilling these expectations? If not what other information, knowledge, or skills will you need to obtain?

How much time are you expected to give to the board, its committees, and to other aspects of the company's affairs? This should cover not only attendance at regular meetings, but also the time needed for briefings and discussions, visits within the company, and preparation. Outside directors will have to ensure that this is compatible with other demands on their time. Inside, executive directors will need to harmonize these expectations and their director responsibilities with the duties required under their contract of employment with the company.

Although all directors have the right to be informed on all board matters, confirm that you will have appropriate access to the information you require. This should cover not only formal board papers, but also the right to seek additional information if necessary. Are you able to talk with the members of management? If so, under what circumstances?

Last, but not least, review the details of the contractual relationship between you and the company. What are the terms of appointment as a director? Is there a written contract or a formal letter of appointment from the chairman? What is the length of appointment? What are the terms and likelihood of re-appointment? What is the basis of the remuneration package and the manner of review? Does the package include performance related rewards or a pension commitment? What are the terms of director and officer indemnity insurance (particularly important in the increasingly litigious climate facing directors in many parts of the world)?

Finally, a word of encouragement. All directors, without exception, face a challenge as they join a new board. Effective board membership involves a learning experience: it should start well before the director attends that first board meeting and should continue during all the rest. The successful director is the one who says: '*Aha! I hadn't realized that, but now I understand*', not once but continuously, throughout his or her service on the board.

13 Assessment of Directors, Boards, and Companies

- In which we consider:
  - reviewing individual directors' performance
  - reviewing board performance
  - corporate governance rating systems for companies
  - corporate governance assessment systems for countries

Reviewing Individual Directors' Performance

Not many years ago, many directors would have baulked at the idea of reviewing their own performance. Appointment to the board, they argued, proved that a director had the requisite knowledge, experience, and skills. Moreover, how can director level performance be assessed when board room activity is a collective team effort? Inevitably, directors make different contributions, they explained, which have to change as the circumstances facing the company change, so assessment is pointless.

Today, few directors hold such views. Attitudes have changed quickly since many corporate governance codes and stock exchange listing rules now recommend or require an annual assessment of the performance of individual directors. Further, listed companies in many jurisdictions now have to report on their corporate governance practices. Most directors now recognize the importance of an effective director level appraisal programme, just as they accept the need for management level appraisal systems.

How Does One Go About Assessing a Director's Performance?

First, the contribution that is expected of the director needs to be known. Ideally, when a director is nominated to the board the chairman will provide a clear statement of what is expected. A welcome letter from the board chairman can be used to elaborate these expectations. The chairman should explain what time commitment will be needed, what board level skills are required, and why the director has been chosen, including any specific expertise, knowledge, experience, or contacts that the director is expected to bring to the board. Once a director's contribution has been agreed, the foundations for board level performance appraisal have been laid.

As we saw in the previous chapter, an induction briefing can provide an opportunity for the incoming director to explore the way the board and its committees work, to have appropriate briefings, visits, and discussions with key people.

The next stage in director performance evaluation is to determine who is to lead the exercise. Typically, the board chairman will take the initiative, instigating the review but the chairman need not, necessarily, carry it out personally. The chairman of the board nomination committee could be asked to play a significant role. A senior independent non-executive director (INED), a past-chairman, an experienced independent consultant, or a firm specializing in board appraisal could also be considered. Some institutes of directors and company secretary organizations offer professional director and board evaluation services.

The next decision is how the appraisal is to be done. At the moment many director appraisals are conducted in an informal way, with the chairman personally assessing each director's performance and commenting privately to the director involved.

Box 13.1 Director and Self-assessment by Chairman of a UK Company

The chairman of a major UK public company writes a personal letter annually to each of his board colleagues, outlining his view of their contribution and how he thinks it might be strengthened in the future. Interestingly, he also asks each director what the director thinks of *his*, the chairman's, performance. The chairman then invites each director to a private lunch, which gives them both the opportunity to clear the air and determine ways to improve board level effectiveness and the director's input in the future. Plans are made as appropriate for director training, development, or briefing.

But the pressure is on for director appraisals to be more formalized. A board policy decision, with the full support of all the directors, is needed to set up such a process. Given that directors often have considerable experience, strong personalities, and high self-esteem, the need to obtain everyone's support for the process at the outset is vital. Without that support an appraisal exercise can become threatening, adversarial, and dysfunctional.

Next the criteria to be used for the evaluation need to be clarified. The chairman needs to play a key role, outlining the purpose and the process of the assessment, and leading his or her board to recognize the value of a rigorous and regular appraisal system. The director attributes and core competencies discussed in detail in chapter 11 can provide a pro forma for the individual appraisal. The experience, skills, and knowledge expected of the director when he or she first joined the board need to be reviewed in the light of subsequent changes in the company's strategic situation. Directors particularly need to be aware of the critical success factors in the business and where it is significantly exposed to risk.

In a formalized director performance review, the data collection stage follows. Typically, this involves interviewing each director to discuss their experiences both as members of both board and board committees. Information is also obtained by analysing attendance records, and board and board committee minutes, looking for innovative inputs and contributions to discussions and decisions.

Sometimes peer-review techniques are used in board reviews. So-called '360 degree' inputs seek comments from 'above', such as from auditors, institutional investors, and others outside the company dealing with a director; from the 'same level', including the chairman and other board members; and from 'below', involving staff who come in contact with a director.

Typically, following the data gathering, a confidential report to the chairman is drafted. Given the personal nature of the report most chairmen will not table it at a board meeting, but discuss the relevant portion with each director.

During that discussion a strategy for further personal development should be discussed, producing an action plan including any training or development activities such as committee leadership, or service on other boards. The intention, of course, is that each director will be able to make a greater contribution to board effectiveness in the future. Records of the discussion can be used to check progress at the next appraisal.

Box 13.2 Director Development by Chairman of an NYSE Company

Following an appraisal of individual directors' inputs to the board, the chairman of a NYSE listed company found opportunities for accelerating the contribution of various outside directors by asking them to lead various board projects, chair board committees, and lead board discussions on specific topics. He also arranged formal training activities, individual self-development exercises, and informal learning opportunities for everyone, including himself.

Finally, in considering individual director performance appraisal, we come to the ultimate question: who evaluates the chairman? As the Roman general Juvenal asked: '*quis custodes ipsos custodiet?*' Who will guard the guards? (Although, it has to be admitted, he was worried about the guards on his wife when he went off to battle.)

Professor Fred Neubauer at IMD Business School in Lausanne Switzerland recommends that the performance of board chairmen should be evaluated, but that raises the questions: by whom and against what criteria? In a few cases an appraisal of the chairman is carried out by a senior INED, such as the chairman of the audit committee or the nomination committee. But in most cases a chairman's performance is reflected in the performance of the company as a whole. Continued poor performance will bring calls for a change of chairman from major investors, the media, or occasionally from dissatisfied directors.

Reviewing Board Performance

Many corporate governance codes and stock exchange listing rules around the world, in addition to an annual assessment of the performance of individual directors, also expect an annual evaluation of the performance of the main board and its committees. The US National Association of Corporate Directors recommended in 2007 that boards introduce formal procedures to assess both their own collective performance and that of individual directors.

Initially, some boards saw this as an imposition that directors faced with some trepidation. But experience has shown that a board with strong and respected leadership, with directors who trust each other, and which is directing a successful enterprise, find the experience rewarding and the outcomes positive. On the other hand, experience also suggests that a poorly led board, with directors in disagreement, leading an organization that is failing to meet its goals, finds the process antagonistic and the outcome potentially catastrophic. Careful planning and preparation is, therefore, essential before a board review takes place.

Interestingly, research has shown that the typical corporate governance indicators, such as board structure, the independence of directors, and the use of board committees, are not the best predictors of board effectiveness. Rather, less specific indicators, sometimes called 'soft' governance, such as the working relationships between directors, the standard of chairmanship, or directors' knowledge of the company, were found to be more significant.

Why undertake a board review? The worst response is *'because we are required to by the regulations'*. A more positive response is that *'we see the review as a fundamental part of our corporate governance processes. Our corporate governance strategy is a basic part of our overall corporate strategy.'*

Sir Bryan Nicholson, chairman of the UK's Financial Reporting Council usefully commented:

the evaluation process is particularly important. It provides the opportunity for companies to create a virtuous circle of sustained improvement in board effectiveness based on regular objective assessment of past performance and the company's changing needs and circumstances. It introduces a new dynamic which companies can use to improve the quality of their corporate governance and secure competitive advantage.

A competent and regular board performance review can:

- Check whether directors' knowledge of the business and its strategic situation is up to date
- Assess the balance of skills, knowledge, and experience on the board and its committees
- Identify director weaknesses to be remedied by director training and development, or by additional or replacement board members
- Review current board and board committee practices and improve efficiency
- Review the effectiveness of the board's strategic thinking and decision making
- Provide an ongoing challenge to attitudes in boards with long serving directors
- Create the climate if a change of chairmanship is needed
- Provide information for the board's corporate governance report and respond to questions from shareholders and other legitimate stakeholders

A board review should take a strategic perspective. Otherwise the board may not be adapting to the company's changing strategic situation. The board review process to be explored later in this chapter takes just such a strategic perspective. The entire review process is set in the context of the overall corporate strategy and leads to a corporate governance strategy. The outcome can lead to changes in corporate governance policies, and plans for board level development.

Who should initiate the board review? The board as a whole is responsible for ensuring that their company is meeting the corporate governance laws, rules, and regulations, and any other related policies that the board has agreed. The board chairman should ensure that appropriate time and attention is given to such matters, which can easily be overshadowed by other claims on the board's time from pressing business issues, as we have already seen. Detailed work on the board review can be delegated to the company secretary, but the board's overall responsibility and accountability cannot be delegated. A regular corporate governance and board review ensures that all directors periodically pay attention to this area.

Who should carry out the board review? In companies facing a first board review, the chairman often assumes the role. But experience has shown that this approach lacks the independence and objectivity that a serious review really needs. The chairman is effectively marking his own examination paper. An experienced INED, perhaps the senior INED, could be asked to lead the work. Some boards form a special board committee, typically nominating INEDs, to undertake the review; others give the responsibility to the audit committee using the internal audit function. Whilst an executive director such as the CEO or CFO will have appropriate knowledge of the business and the board, his or her perspective is unlikely to be seen as objective by other board members.

However, a thorough board review demands a lot of time and effort, as we will see, in marshalling written material, interviewing directors, and support staff, talking with auditors, institutional investors, and so on. Staff support will be needed if a board member or a committee undertakes the review.

An alternative approach is for the board to seek an independent perspective, inviting someone outside the board to lead the review process and report. A past chairman might be a possibility, who would have knowledge of the business, but possibly lack objectivity on board politics. Another possibility might be a respected chairman or INED from the board of another non-competitor company. Then, of course, there are independent organizations and firms of consultants offering to undertake such a project. Unfortunately, some of those offering such services do not yet have a lot of experience at carrying them out. Management consultancy projects call for a different mind-set to those dealing with board level interactions and political processes.

What does a board review involve? Some boards and their consultants take an external perspective of the corporate governance activities of the company. The review checks whether the accountability reporting demands of company legislation, codes, and stock exchange regulation are being met, and whether the reporting by the company of financial, operational, and corporate social responsibility matters to shareholders and other legitimate stakeholders is appropriate. The opinions of major shareholders, regulators, financial commentators, and others are sought. The resultant report can then be used by the board to confirm that their corporate governance reporting responsibilities are being met. However, such an approach does not address the company's corporate governance process itself.

The more thorough approach described here, in addition to ensuring that appropriate disclosure and accountability is being provided, analyses the board and committee structures, studies the strengths and weaknesses of the board, and reviews the processes of the board and its committee. The resultant report leads to a new strategy for board development and corporate governance improvement. This might include proposals to increase directors' competencies and to improve board level performance.

Just as an enterprise may have longer term strategies for market development, technological development, or management development, the board review project should lead towards an agreed strategy for board and governance development. Because the review will affect all of the members of the board, it is vital for all directors to fully understand the project's objectives,

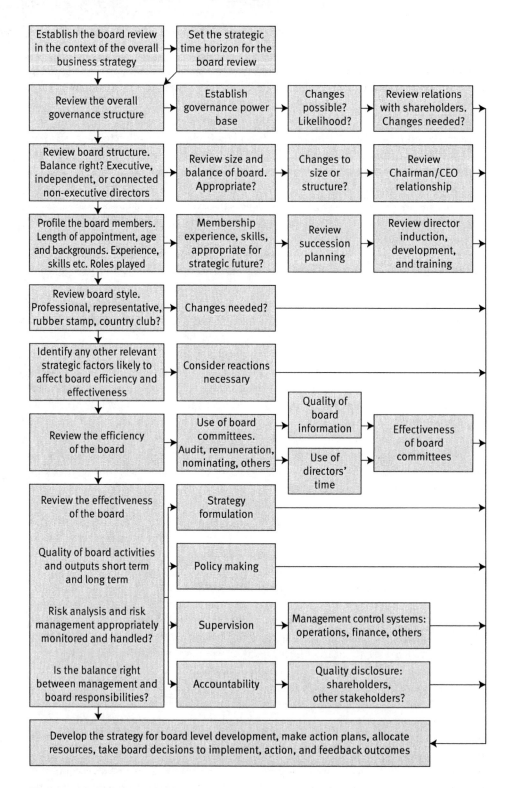

Figure 13.1 The board review process

the processes, and the intended outputs. Moreover, it is essential that every director is committed to the project. Lack of commitment by a director can easily lead to poor cooperation in the project, unwelcome political manoeuvres, and unhelpful criticism of the proposals.

A real danger in long serving boards is that members all grow older together and become increasingly out of touch with the dynamics of the organization and the strategic situation of the underlying business. The more successful the company, the more likely the board is to have longstanding retainers whose focus is on the past. A rigorous board review will avoid any such possibility.

The process now to be described establishes the board review in the context of the overall corporate strategy. Consider the flowchart, figure 13.1, which we will consider section by section.

Figure 13.1 depicts the elements of a board review. We will work through them to see what is involved.

The chairman has an important role in establishing an enthusiastic climate for the study and the report's conclusions. The strategic focus of the study should be emphasized: it is not only reviewing existing corporate governance and board activities, but looking forward to developing strategies and policies for the future. A strategic time horizon should be established, which links the corporate governance and board development strategy with the other elements of the company's overall corporate strategy. In this way the board development strategy will be consistent with the overall corporate strategy. For example, if the corporate strategy calls for strategic developments in new technologies, new markets, new territories, or new forms of finance during the life of that strategy, the board development strategy will ask whether the board's composition and processes will be adequate to these challenges.

Information for a board review is obtained from an analysis of board and board committee agenda, papers, and minutes, from interviews with each director, company secretary, and staff, top executives, group discussions, and director workshops, and from interviews with investors, auditors, analysts, and internal staff.

Review the Overall Governance Structure
The first step in the study is to review the entity's overall governance structure. In essence this establishes the governance power base of the enterprise and determines where ultimate power lies to change the governance structure. Who controls the voting equity? Is there majority control? Do informal power blocks exist? What changes might occur over the strategic time horizon—consider, for example, predator bids, shifts in dominant institutional investor holdings, or changes in family ownership?

In a widely held listed company, establish if there are any blocks of voting shares that do or could influence corporate governance, an association of institutional investors, or a hedge fund acquiring shares, for example. What is the possibility of a merger or acquisition approach within the strategic time horizon? What is preventing such a move? In a public company, with a dominant shareholder, discover that investor's aims. If the dominant shareholder is the founder, what power does he or she exercise over governance matters? If the dominant shareholder is a parent company, what influence does that shareholder exercise over board membership? Within the strategic time horizon what influence could be exercised?

In a subsidiary or associate company establish the expectations of the group parent company. Are there any minority shareholders; how are their rights protected? In a joint venture, what does the joint venture agreement have to say about governance of the enterprise? In a quango, what is the role of the overseeing organization or government department? How does that currently influence governance matters and how could it change? In a closely held family company establish which branches of the family hold the voting shares. Which members of the family are involved in management? Is there a family council or committee concerned with family interests, which could affect governance matters? Could there be shifts in the power base over the time horizon of the study?

Having established the existing governance structure, consider whether the present relationships with the investors, owners, and shareholders are satisfactory. How could they be improved? Moreover, are there are any possible changes in ownership over the strategic time horizon, and what might be the implications?

Review the Board Structure

The next step is to review the board structure. Is the balance between executive directors, independent directors and connected non-executive directors appropriate, now and for the strategic future? Consider the size of the board. The corporate constitution, such as the articles of association, may put limits on board size. Boards tend to grow in size. The case tends to be made for additional people to meet specific needs. One seldom hears the case being argued for a reduction in board size. Yet, as has already been noted, boards with a large number of members tend to inhibit directors' contributions and are in danger of splitting into cliques. Identify any changes necessary. This stage also provides the opportunity to review the relationship between the chairman and the CEO.

Profile Board Members

Now the contributions of each individual director should be reviewed. Profile each director, noting the length of service on the board, the terms of appointment, the age, education, and professional background, relevant experience, and skills, and the roles played and contributions made to the board and board committees including personality characteristics and interpersonal abilities. In the context of the corporate strategy, what experience, skills, and roles will be needed? Identify gaps and develop succession planning for the board.

The profiling and reviewing of the contributions made by individual directors can be linked with each director's performance assessment, discussed earlier in this chapter.

This can then lead directly to a review of director induction, education, and training, whether there is continual development and if this is a learning board. Alternatives and improvements can be identified.

Review Board Style, Efficiency, and Effectiveness

The next stage involves a review of board style. Consider how the board and board committees spend their time, the issues on the agenda, the quality of leadership, and how meetings are planned and run. The board style (see chapter 10) can then be identified and the need for any changes clarified.

Now board efficiency and effectiveness can be considered. It is worthwhile to reflect, at this stage, whether there are any other relevant strategic factors that could affect the governance of the company over the strategic time horizon. For example, are there any changes to company law, corporate regulation, or stock exchange listing requirements on the horizon that would affect corporate governance activities? For companies in a group or network, are there any feasible shifts of power and influence over the strategic time horizon: what might be an appropriate reaction?

Now the review process turns to the efficiency of the board. Does the board have audit, remuneration, and nominating committees? Are there other board standing committees—such as an executive committee, a strategy committee, or a compliance committee? How effective are these committees?

Assess the quality of board information: formal and informal reports, opportunities for directors to obtain information and answers to their questions, access to corporate data, etc. For more information refer back to the previous chapter.

How do directors spend their time, on main board meetings, board committee meetings, and in other board related activities including visits and preparation time? Is this efficient? What improvements might be made?

We next turn to the effectiveness of the board and its committees. Essentially we are concerned with the quality of board processes and outputs, both in the short and the longer term. The four functions of the board—strategy formulation, policy making, executive supervision, and accountability—need to be considered separately.

Strategy formulation, as we have seen, is a prime function for the board. This stage of the review considers the time and effort, the depth, and quality of analysis that goes into the board's strategic thinking. Could a new competitor unexpectedly intervene in the firm's markets? Could a new technology significantly change the cost structure, would a different way of delivering the firm's service dramatically affect the market share, or might an alternative product meet customer needs better? This part of the review also considers whether external risks are adequately recognized. As we saw in chapter 6, the significance of strategy formulation to the board's work might call for a special effort, perhaps a board strategy seminar or workshop to explore the firm's strategic situation and review the overall corporate strategy.

Moving from strategy to policy, the review asks whether the board's policies are still appropriate to the company's situation. This is the place to explore the delegation of board responsibilities to board committees and the work of those committees. Are the terms of reference of the audit committee, the remuneration committee, the nomination committee, and any other board committees still relevant? If not, what changes are needed?

In considering the performance functions—strategy formulation and policy making—is the balance right between those activities delegated to management and those retained by the board. Will this be appropriate through the changing situations envisaged over the company's strategic time horizon?

Reviewing the third function of the board—executive supervision—provides an opportunity to review management controls and management reporting systems. Can the board monitor management in an active, accurate, and timely manner? Enterprise risk assessment and management systems, which are now seen as fundamental to corporate governance, should be reviewed at this stage.

The fourth function of the board—ensuring adequate accountability—has, in recent years, been under the corporate governance spotlight. Is the company compiling with the requirements of the corporate governance codes, company law requirements, and, where appropriate, stock exchange listing requirements? Are the company's public statements to the shareholders, the media, and other legitimate stakeholders meeting the legal requirements and, ideally, projecting the company as the board expect? In addition to the required audited financial statements are operating statements and corporate social responsibility and sustainability reports at the level and in the form that the board want?

Determining a Strategy for Board Development

Finally, after all the data collection and analysis has been done and the results collated, comes report writing and the determination of a strategy for board development, consistent with and part of the overall corporate strategy.

Once the directors have received and accepted the report, the board will want to develop a strategy for board development, and related policies and plans that lead to action. The chairman's leadership role is vital at this stage.

Unlike the directors mentioned earlier in this chapter, who reported that corporate governance was a matter of complying with corporate governance codes, an informed professional director might reply that

in our company we have a set of board level policies which lay down how the board and its committees operate; then a periodic board level review enables us to check on whether these policies are being followed, that we are meeting all the accountability criteria the board has set for the organization, and whether our corporate governance strategy is still appropriate.

The US Conference Board's Corporate Governance Research Centre published *Determining Board Effectiveness* (1999), which offered a set of questions that go to the heart of board assessment:

- How does the board define its role and duties?
- How does the board prioritize its responsibilities?
- How effectively does the board monitor company performance?
- Does the board have sufficient independence to perform its duties properly?
- Does the board have the right mix of skills to achieve its goals?
- Does the board have the right size and structure?
- How does the board oversee auditing functions to minimize risk?
- How does the board best structure and use its nominating committee?
- What is the board's role in determining director and executive compensation?
- How does the board conduct CEO appointment and succession planning?
- Are the board's decision making processes effective?
- Does the board have a process for evaluating whether it is achieving its goals?
- Can the board make course corrections if necessary?
- Does the board communicate effectively to investors?

The 1998 UK Hampel Report called for formal procedures to '*assess both the board's collective performance and that of individual directors*'. But research three years later by PricewaterhouseCoopers showed that only a third of UK companies did so. Today the UK consolidated code requires a board review and an explanation in a company's corporate governance report.

Case 13.1 HIH Insurance

HIH Insurance Group was Australia's largest insurer. When it collapsed in 2001, the £1.9 billion loss left many policyholders and investors bereft. Some lost their homes.

A royal commission questioned the founder and Chief Executive, Ray Williams. Observers commented on a tale of '*spectacular munificence*' and that '*it was like the last days of Pompeii*'. Mr. Williams enjoyed a millionaire's lifestyle. His secretary travelled first class. A corporate adviser was given round-the-world air tickets for himself, his wife, four children, and a nanny to compensate for working over Christmas. A director, Rodney Adler, whose FAI insurance company had been taken over by HIH for more than £200 million, received a £2.3 million termination payment and a £350,000 a year consultancy fee.

Mr Williams, a philanthropist who had donated millions to medical research, claimed that his own life savings were in the company and that he had not sold any shares. The problems, he claimed, were due to errors of judgement, in particular the failure to undertake a due diligence study on FAI, which had gaping holes in its finances.

Discussion Questions

1. What was the board doing whilst this saga was going on? What should they have done?

2. Whose fault was it that FAI had been acquired without a due diligence study and with '*gaping holes in its finances*'?

3. What is your opinion of the reward given to a corporate adviser (round-the-world air tickets for himself, his wife, four children, and a nanny) to compensate for working over Christmas?

Corporate Governance Rating Systems for Companies

The financial climate changed significantly after Enron and the Sarbanes-Oxley Act, not only in the United States but around the world. The quality of a company's corporate governance is now seen as vital. Investors, particularly institutional investors, focus on corporate governance in valuing companies, as we saw in the ABI study described in chapter 9. The standard of corporate governance is an important element in risk evaluation of a company.

Consequently, a way is needed to monitor, measure, and compare standards of corporate governance. A reliable corporate governance rating from an independent and respected organization can reduce a company's cost of capital, reflecting the premium that investors are now prepared to pay for sound governance. A number of rating systems have been developed. However, it is important to recognize that they use different criteria, the scores are not necessarily compatible, and their conclusions sometimes differ. Let us review some of the more popular rating schemes.

Standard and Poor's (S&P), an organization better known for its credit ratings, offers a corporate governance rating service to companies. Unlike some other providers of corporate governance ratings, S&P is independent and does not also offer company advisory or training services. It acts with the cooperation of the company, interviewing senior executives and directors and reviewing information in both the public domain and confidential data. S&P has developed a proprietary methodology to produce its governance scores based on a synthesis of best practices and codes around world. The final score is numeric and based on the following four sectors:

- Ownership structure and external influences, which considers the transparency of ownership structure, the concentration and the influence of ownership, and other external stakeholders
- Shareholder rights and relations, including shareholder meetings and voting procedures, ownership rights, and takeover defences, and other stakeholder relations
- Transparency, disclosure, and audit, such as the content of public disclosure, the timing and access to public disclosure, and the audit process
- Board structure and effectiveness, including director independence, the role and effectiveness of the board, director, and senior executive compensation

The FTSE Group in collaboration with International Shareholder Services (ISS) has produced a worldwide corporate governance rating system (CGI system) which uses the OECD Principles as its benchmark test. ISS methodology, called the corporate governance quotient (CSQ), forms the basis for the CGI ratings. The rating system has been applied to all companies in the FTSE share indices, nearly 2,500 companies in twenty-four developed country markets. Under the CGI methodology some sixty corporate governance variables are monitored in the following five broad categories:

- Compensation schemes for executive and non-executive directors, including the remuneration structure and schemes that are used to reward directors
- Executive and non-executive director stock ownership, such as the alignment of director equity ownership with shareholder interests
- Equity structure, including the protection of shareholder rights and the existence of any anti-takeover devices
- Structure of the board, independence of directors, processes of the board and board committees, and the independence of directors
- Independence and integrity of the audit process, including the audit process, audit fees, and services provided, and members of the audit committee

The performance on the variables in each category is evaluated and then aggregated to form an overall CGI index rating from 5, which indicates a high standard of corporate governance practice, down to 1, reflecting a lower level.

The *GovernanceMetrics International (GMI)* corporate governance ratings cover over 3,200 companies listed on the US S&P 500, S&P midcap, S&P smallcap, Russell 1000, Canada TSX 60, Australian ASX 100, Hang Seng, Nikkei 225, STI, FTSE 350, and all major European markets. The GMI ratings make comparisons within industrial sectors. The GMI methodology is not in the public domain, although the resultant scores have been used in some academic research studies. GKI base their service on the belief that '*companies that emphasize corporate governance and transparency will, over time, generate superior returns and economic performance and lower their cost of capital*'.

Since 2008, GMI has rated companies in emerging markets. The 321 companies rated were found to have governance standards '*below average*', with only two meeting global standards—Goldfields in South Africa and Taiwan Semi-conductor Manufacturing. In Brazil, for example, GMI found a steel company that combined the roles of chairman, CEO, and CFO, and had significant related party transactions; in South Korea a finance company had just one independent director on a board of ten; and in Poland a mining company had had four new CEOs and four different chairmen in the past six years, following intervention by the government, which held a 44 percent ownership stake.

The *Deminor corporate governance ratings* cover the 300 largest European blue chip companies. The organization provides an overall assessment and rating of corporate governance performance for these companies. The results are made available in an annual 'Trends and Ratings' report. In recent years this report has provided country insights noting for example, that:

companies publishing mission statements were up from 53% to 77%, companies publishing ethics codes were up from 44% to 74%, that Switzerland had made a significant leap forward in corporate governance, and that the Netherlands had enacted a new law to require investment managers to publish their voting policies.

The *Thai Rating and Information Service (TRIS)* has developed a corporate governance rating methodology for companies quoted on the Thai Stock Exchange. Whilst reflecting international standards the TRIS system is sensitive to the Thai culture. The Thai Securities and Exchange Commission use TRIS to rate governance practices of listed companies. The TRIS corporate governance rating model uses four sets of criteria:

(1) Shareholder's Rights.

(2) Composition and Roles of the Board of Directors and Management.

(3) Information Disclosure.

(4) Corporate Governance Culture.

'*Shareholders' rights*' consider the equitable treatment of all shareholders. Are all shareholders entitled to attend and vote in the shareholders' meetings and express opinions on and help decide issues of company policy? To rate these criteria, TRIS considers key categories such as the way shareholders gain their full benefits, are able to exercise their voting rights, and whether all shareholders have equal basic rights.

In reviewing the '*composition and roles of the board of directors and management*' TRIS is concerned about the effectiveness of the board and the management. To rate this criterion, TRIS considers the structure and membership of the board, how the board and management exercise their roles and responsibilities to maximize shareholders' benefits, checks and balance mechanisms to avoid abuse of power, and the efficiency and transparency of the board's performance.

On '*information disclosure*', TRIS considers key categories such as the quality of information disclosed in regulatory documents and published annual reports, also the kind of information investors can access, and the ease of access. Finally in assessing the company's '*corporate governance culture*', TRIS considers whether the company's corporate culture promotes an environment within the corporate organization, including among shareholders and other stakeholders, that reinforces corporate governance principles leading to sustainable growth.

In the rating process the company supplies relevant information. Having analysed this material, TRIS makes a site visit and interviews the chairman of the board, the chairman and members of the audit committee, the CEO, and employees as well as suppliers and outside analysts familiar with the company and the industry. A TRIS committee then decides on a rating. The final score is determined by weighting and totalling the scores for the four sets of criteria, and then falls into one of five categories: a score of 9–10 is excellent, 8 very good, 7 good, 5–6 moderate, and with a score of less than 5 improvement is recommended. The company is told the result and has three options, seek further review, accept the rating, or reject it. If the company accepts the rating it has a further option of deciding whether it wants TRIS to publicize it. The rating process is an ongoing process of monitoring and review.

IRRC is a firm providing proxy voting services for institutional investors, which focuses on corporate governance and social responsibility issues. IRRC provides a corporate benchmarker service on governance issues.

The International Finance Corporation (IFC) offers a corporate governance methodology and assessment service to client companies. The IFC methodology uses assessment tools tailored to the different governance priorities of publicly listed companies, founder and family owned firms, financial institutions, newly privatized enterprises, and state owned enterprises. IFC staff review the client's governance practices and use it for risk analysis, investment decision making, and, where necessary, develop a corporate governance improvement programme with the client. Details of the IFC's approach to corporate governance, matrices, check lists, and other tools which are tailored to the client's needs, are available.

DNV, which incorporated *CoreRatings* in 2004, provides companies with an independent evaluation of a company's risk profile, with ratings that benchmarks the standing of their corporate governance and corporate responsibility with comparable companies. The DNV analysis involves an interactive process working with the company on answers to detailed questions derived from the international codes, best practice experience, and the writings of corporate governance experts. The resultant rating assesses the company's risk profile in seven areas:

- Governance policy and business ethics
- Risk management processes
- Ownership structure and control
- Financial reporting, audit, and verification
- Board structure and management
- Board executive compensation
- Investor rights and relations

In effect, the rating measures how well a company is managing corporate governance risks, enabling the board to see whether it is running the company in the interests of its investors and other key stakeholders, and disclosing all the information that is relevant to them.

CRISIL in India provides subscribers with corporate governance ratings for companies in that country, in addition to credit rating services.

In Russia, there are at least five competing corporate governance rating systems, including:

- Brunswick UBS Warburg
- Troika Dialog
- The Institute of Corporate Law and Governance
- Standard and Poor's
- The Russian Institute of Directors and the 'Expert Rating Agency' (A Consortium)

Corporate Governance Assessment Systems for Countries

Attempts have also been made to monitor and assess the calibre of corporate governance country by country. This reflects the growing recognition that corporate governance is important to national financial markets and, ultimately, to national economic success.

The *World Bank* and *International Monetary Fund* launched a joint initiative—the *Reports on the Observance of Standards and Codes (ROSC)* programme—to assess corporate governance country by country. This diagnostic work was intended to strengthen international financial architecture. The ROSC programme considers each country's legal and regulatory framework, as well as the practices and compliance of listed firms, against the OECD Principles of Corporate Governance.

The *European Bank for Reconstruction and Development (EBRD)* launched a twenty-three country corporate governance assessment project in 2003. The study established whether a corporate governance code existed or was being drafted, the degree of compliance with the code, and the legal requirements to disclose financial information.

The output categorized the corporate governance practices of the countries into five groups:

- Group A—very high compliance; none of the countries studied qualified
- Group B—high compliance, nine countries qualified including Hungary, Poland, and Russia
- Group C—medium compliance, ten countries qualified, including Bulgaria, the Czech Republic, and Slovenia
- Group D—low compliance, four countries qualified, including Georgia, Romania, and Turkmenistan
- Group E—very low compliance, four countries identified, including Azerbaijan, Belarus, and the Ukraine

The most comprehensive country level corporate governance rating to date is the FTSE ISS corporate governance index. The methodology involves aggregating the FTSE ISS CGI company ratings, discussed above, country by country. From this, information comparisons can be made across countries, across industrial sectors, and across financial markets.

For example, it was discovered that Canada and the UK have the highest average corporate governance scores by country, that the oil and gas industry scores highest by sector, and that the FTSE 100 has the highest score by stock market sector.

The International Institute for Management Development in Switzerland also produced a country by country ranking in 2004 which ranked corporate governance in sixty economies and the *World Economic Forum* in 2003 ranked forty-nine countries.

Box 13.3 Highest and Lowest Corporate Governance Ratings in Developed Countries

Countries with Highest Rating

UK	average CGI rating	4.75
Canada		4.71
Ireland		4.25

Countries with Lowest Rating

Denmark	1.50
Norway	1.14
Sweden	1.00

(FTSE ISS Corporate Governance Index (CGI) 2004)

REFERENCES AND FURTHER READING

Anand, Sanjay (2007) *Essentials of Corporate Governance*. Hoboken, NJ: Wiley.

NACD (National Association of Corporate Directors) (2005) 'Board Evaluation: Improving Director Effectiveness'. A report of a NACD Blue Ribbon Commission National Association of Corporate Directors, Washington, DC.

Solomon, Jill (2004) *Corporate Governance and Accountability*. Hoboken, NJ: Wiley.

USEFUL WEBSITES

www.acga-asia.org
Asian Corporate Governance Association. Comparative Asian country ratings.

www.clsa.com
Corporate governance research in Asian countries.

www.crisil.com
Ratings, risk and policy advice in India.

www.deminor.org
Annual overall assessment of corporate governance performance of top 300 EU companies publishes 'Trends and ratings' report.

ga.issproxy.com
Institutional Shareholder Services corporate governance quotient.

www.gmiratings.com
GovernanceMetrics International, a New York based private consultant rating the governance of 1750 US companies.

www.icsa.org.uk and **www.icsaboardperformance.co.uk**
Board performance evaluation services.

www.moodys.com
(click on 'corporate governance') Moody's credit and risk ratings service.

www.ifc.org/corporategovernance
IFC corporate governance assessment services.

www.scawards.com
Singapore Corporate Awards for the best annual report.

www.standardandpoors.com
Corporate governance evaluation and rating scores.

www.tris.co.th
Thai corporate governance rating service.

PROJECTS AND EXERCISES

1. Study and compare the corporate governance rating systems noted in the text. Which would you recommend?

2. What problems might be encountered in using the board review process described in the schematic in the text?

3. Draft a note in response to a director who has told you that assessing the performance of individual directors is unnecessary and unrealistic because directors bring different skills, experience, and knowledge to the board table.

SELF-TEST QUESTIONS

To confirm your grasp of the key points in this chapter try answering the following questions. Answers are at the end of the book.

1. How does one go about assessing a director's performance?

2. How are director appraisals done at the moment?

3. Is the pressure on for director appraisals to be more formalized? What is then needed to set up such a process?

4. What is the usual outcome of an individual director performance assessment? How is it used?

5. How is the performance of a chairman assessed?

6. Do many corporate governance codes and stock exchange listing rules now call for an annual assessment of the performance of individual directors and of the performance of the board?

7. Who might be asked to undertake a board review?

8. Describe the stages in a board review project.

9. What are the principal elements in the Standard and Poor's corporate governance ratings?

10. Name some of the systems for evaluating corporate governance at the country level.

14 Corporate Risk Assessment

....

- In which we consider
  - responsibility for risk profiling, risk strategy, risk policy, and risk supervision
  - levels and types of risk
  - risk analysis
  - risk recognition and assessment
  - risk evaluation
  - risk management information systems
  - risk transfer

Responsibility for Risk Profiling, Risk Strategy, Risk Policy, and Risk Supervision

Running a business, indeed running almost every enterprise, involves risk. Risk can only be avoided by choosing to do nothing; and even then unexpected events can occur. In many business situations, as is well known, the greater the risk, the greater the potential return to the enterprise.

The challenge to boards is to balance risk with acceptable reward. In other words to understand the exposure of their company to risk, to determine how those risks are faced, and to ensure that they are handled appropriately. Corporate governance involves creating business value whilst managing risk. Risk management not risk minimization should be the theme.

Every board has a duty to ensure that:

- Significant risks facing their company are recognized
- Risk assessment systems exist and are effective throughout the organization
- Risk evaluation procedures are developed and operational
- Risk monitoring systems are robust, efficient, and effective
- Business continuity strategies and risk management policies exist, are regularly updated, and applied in practice

In chapter 7, we saw that some corporate governance codes and companies laws now call for boards to give assurances that systems are in place to handle corporate risk in their regular corporate governance reports to shareholders. In the United States, the Treadway Commission called for an integrated approach to enterprise risk management in 2004, which was an outgrowth of the 2002 Sarbanes-Oxley Act. In the UK, the 1999 Turnbull Report made similar demands, which are now enshrined in the UK Combined Code. The 2007 Basel II agreement on risk management in the financial world also called for professional risk assessment. This responsibility has been further amplified by the global financial sector crisis in 2007/8. In 2008, the Bank of England Financial Stability Report commented that '*one clear short coming has been banks' over reliance on credit ratings in determining inherent risk*'. A further Bank report on good risk management called for '*effective firm-wide identification and analysis of risk including information sharing across the organization, particularly between senior management and business lines, and firm-wide plans to reduce exposures or hedge risks*'.

Sophisticated investors around the world focus on the nature and extent of risk in the companies and industries in which they invest. Companies that are recognized as having professional enterprise risk management and transparent risk reporting are respected. Their shares can command a premium over competitors, and their overall cost of capital is likely to be lower.

Directors need to understand where value is added within their business, at which points the company is critically exposed to risk, where the most sensitive areas are in which the very survival of the business could be threatened. Boards need to face up to those risks and to develop relevant risk strategies and policies.

Such responsibilities call for a formal system to ensure that risk is properly assessed and considered at board level and then professionally managed throughout the company.

Case Study 14.1 The Sage Group Plc: An Approach to Corporate Risk

The Board is responsible for the operation and effectiveness of the Group's system of internal controls and risk management. There is an ongoing process for identifying, evaluating, and managing the significant risks faced by the Group. It is regularly reviewed by the Board and complies fully with the Turnbull guidance. The internal control systems are designed to meet the Group's particular needs and the risks to which it is exposed and by their nature can only provide reasonable but not absolute assurance against misstatement or loss.

The effectiveness of this process has been reviewed by the Audit Committee, which reports its findings to the Board. The processes used by the Audit Committee to review the effectiveness of the system of internal control include discussions with management on significant risk areas identified and the review of plans for, and results from, internal and external audits.

The Audit Committee reports the results of its review of the risk assessment process to the Board. The Board then draws its collective conclusion as to the effectiveness of the system of internal control.

(Company information, see www.investors.sage.com)

Discussion Question

1. Evaluate the approach to enterprise risk management that the Sage Group has developed.

Some boards include corporate risk assessment in the mandate of the board audit committee. However, audit committees can be orientated towards the past, involved with audit outcomes and approving accountability information for publication. But risk assessment needs a proactive, forward looking orientation. Consequently, other boards have decided to create a risk assessment or risk management committee as a distinct standing committee of the board. Such a committee might have four or five members, wholly or mainly independent non-executive directors (INEDs) with appropriate business experience. Initially, when a company is building its risk management systems, the committee might meet quite frequently, but then two or three times a year, reporting to the board as a whole. Members of senior management and external experts in risk are likely to be invited to attend meetings to advise the committee.

An alternative approach is for the board to form a management based risk management group, perhaps including the CEO, the CFO, profit-responsible division or unit heads, and the responsible risk management executive(s). External experts could also be invited to advise the group. A management based risk management group needs to take a strategic view of corporate risk and avoid adopting a purely financial view. In other words, the group needs to see the enterprise in the context of its overall risk profile, not just from a financial perspective. A management based risk group might typically report to the CEO or CFO, but it is essential that their work is reviewed and approved at board level.

Of course, it is possible that a company might decide to have both a board level risk management committee and a management based group which reports to it.

The issue of risk management is particularly significant in the case of financial institutions. Indeed in essence, their entire business involves the management of risk. This was recently confirmed in a report[1] by the Basel Committee on Banking Supervision, widely known as Basel II—'*The bank's board of directors has a responsibility for setting the board's tolerance for risks*'. Favourable capital adequacy decisions need to demonstrate that the bank's '*board of directors and senior management, as appropriate, are actively involved in the oversight of the operational risk management framework*'. According to the report a risk policy committee to fulfil this requirement should have its own written charter, and board representation with at least three independent directors with the requisite skills and knowledge to oversee risk management, and a chairman appointed by the whole board.

Many major companies now have specialist risk managers to oversee the company-wide risk assessment systems and procedures, who can advise the board on risk issues. The Chief Risk Officer (CRO) is an increasingly important figure in many companies, just as the global head of risk is in international banks. The risk management committee will typically agree the job description, and appoint and monitor the CRO, who is then secretary to that committee.

Unfortunately, in some companies risk management issues seldom reach board level. The management of risk is piecemeal and undertaken at the business unit level—sometimes known as a 'silo' or 'bucket' approach with each part of the organization standing on its own base. Responsibility for risk management is then located in middle management, with managers insuring the business against the classical risks of fire, theft, and accident. This orientation is likely to be operational rather than strategic, and have more to do with cost reduction, searching for the cheapest cover available, than conscientious risk assessment.

[1] *International Convergence of Capital Measurement and Capital Standards: A Revised Framework*. Basel Committee on Banking Supervision, (Basel II) 2007.

Moreover the middle manger can become a bottleneck, even a block, between risk and board responsibility.

Levels and Types of Risk

In every organization risk arises at various levels:

- Strategic risks—exposure to threats from outside the organization
- Management level risks—exposure to risks arising from the firm's activities
- Operational risks—exposure to hazards within the enterprise

One approach to recognizing significant risk is to consider what circumstances or events could affect the key drivers of business value and cause planned performance not to meet expected outcomes. A board needs to recognize potential catastrophic events that could put the very survival of the firm at risk and have a business continuity strategy to respond to such exposure. As an initial brief indicator of the range and implications of possible corporate risk, consider table 14.1 which identifies some causes and consequences of risk recognized in an American manufacturing company.

Box 14.1 is an extract from the risk management policy hand book of a financial institution. The risks recognized at strategic, managerial, and operational levels are shown.

Environmental challenges arising from climate change, rising sea levels, energy shortages, and other global issues are increasingly seen by some companies as being a significant threat and potential risk. We will discuss this further in the next chapter on corporate social responsibilty and sustrainability.

The World Economic Forum, addressing the issue of global business risk in 2007, identified the top ten as:

(1) The business environment.
(2) Competive issues.
(3) Compliance matters.
(4) Employee problems.
(5) Operational factors.
(6) Reputational loss.
(7) Security and fraud.
(8) Strategic failures.
(9) Technological change.
(10) Trade credit and customer insolvency.

Also in 2007 Aon, the international insurance broker, produced another survey of the major risks recognized by directors:

(1) Damage to reputation.
(2) Business interuption.
(3) Third party liability.
(4) Disruption or supply chain failure.

Table 14.1 **US manufacturing company—outline causes and consequences of risk**

Causes	Consequences
Marketing problems:	
Marketing policy mistakes	Revenue loss
Competitive activity	Cash flow difficulties
Changes in consumer behaviour	Market standing and share lost
Customer/client failure	Long term survival threatened
Operational difficulties:	
Product/service faults or failure	Product recall costs
Project failure	Loss of secure information
Failure of joint venture partner	Image damaged
Supplier failure	Reputation loss
Distribution channel problems	Loss of IT service
Expropriation of assets (nationalization)	Additional expenditure
Environmental, pollution issues	Capital losses
IT problems	
Financial difficulties:	
Poor acquisition strategy	Financial loss
Treasury risk	Reduced credit rating
Poor taxation planning policies	Higher cost of capital
Credit assessment policies	Affect on share price
Financial fraud or misfeasance	Cash flow problems
Inappropriate accounting policies	
Personnel problems:	
Loss of key personnel—managerial, technical	Loss of production/service
Labour relations problems	Injury to people
Trades union activities	Tribunals, official investigations
Legal claims	Health and Safety violations
Accidents	
Legal problems:	
Regulatory changes	Legal action and sanctions
Non-compliance issues	Additional costs
Physical asset hazards:	
Fire, flood, weather, earthquake	Costs of recovery; Loss of production/service
Explosion, pollution	Disruption of business
Political/economic situations:	
Actions by other stakeholders—activists, etc.	Bans, limitations, taxes, duties on products/services; Loss of production/service
Global, regional, or local economic problems	Reputational loss

Box 14.1 Risk Management Manual: Contents Page

Levels of Risk Management Policy in a London Finance House

The main board of a significant financial institution has developed risk management strategies and policies that cover all levels of the organization, from externally generated risks to in-house hazards. The board regularly discusses their risk management policies at each level. The following contents page from the risk management manual lists the areas of responsibility recognized by the risk assessment programme:

External Strategic Threats
- Competitors' activities
- Customers' activities
- Stock and finance markets hazards
- Government and regulator activities
- Criminal activity
- Loss of electronic communication channels
- Terrorism or politically activated actions
- Economic, political, or social events
- Suppliers' activities
- Other external events, hazards, or risks

Management Level Risks
- Management weaknesses, inability
- Shortages of skilled, experienced staff
- Management level fraud or misfeasance

Operational risks and hazards (for each risk management department or unit)
- Fire, explosion, flood
- Loss of power (e.g. inability to carry out trades)
- IT systems malfunction
- Shortages of staff (e.g. staff turnover, illness, strike, poaching)
- Errors in trades (unintentional mistakes)
- Deals made by staff beyond their limits, contrary to trading policies
- Fraud and misfeasance (i.e. deliberate actions by traders)
- Theft
- Misuse of company information, equipment, systems, or software
- Other events, risks, or hazards

(5) Market environment.

(6) Regulatory or legislative changes.

(7) Failure to attract or retain staff.

(8) Market risk (financial).

(9) Physical damage.

(10) Merger/acquisition/restructuring failure of the disaster recovery plan.

The Aon survey further found that some respondents, despite identifying risks in the top ten above, had undertaken no reviews of some of them, neither did they have plans in place to address them. Though, predictably, the order differs between the two surveys, notice how many of the items are similar and are at the strategic, not the operational, level.

Yet much of the literature on risk management focuses on risk at the operational level, for example on health and safety hazards to employees, disease risks in hospitals, and waste management hazards in public health. But contemporary thinking about risk recognizes that risk management policies at the operational level are not enough. An enterprise is more likely to fail disastrously from risks at management or strategic levels.

The extracts from the risk assessment system of a global pharmaceutical company in Box 14.2 give an insight into the types of strategic risk that could have catastrophic outcomes.

Box 14.2 Risk Assessment in a Pharmaceutical Company

The main board of an international pharmaceutical group has agreed a set of risk assessment policies, based on information from a comprehensive and continuous risk management system. The detail runs to many pages, but the following extract indicates the type of risk reviewed at the strategic level.

Strategic Level Risks

Marketing Area

1. Competitors

   - New entrants into significant products or markets
   - Change of ownership of competitors (e.g. mergers)
   - Change of competitors' distribution strategy
   - New research breakthroughs
   - Change of pricing/distribution strategies
   - Expansion into new markets (country or type)
   - Competitors change manufacturing technology

2. Customers

   - Cost of product recall (financial and reputational)
   - Adopting substitute products (e.g. generics)
   - Collapse or bankruptcy of major customer
   - Change of ownership of main distributor

- Catastrophic failure of our product in use
- Legal actions for damages
- Alleged patent or copyright infringement

3. Governmental
    - New pharmacological control laws
    - New environmental or hazard limitation laws
    - Constraints on manufacturing or delivery processes
    - Monopoly, anti-trust, or pricing inquiries
    - Cost-cutting by government (e.g. UK NHS)
    - Political threats to operations in overseas countries

Finance Area

1. Predators
    - Hostile take-over approaches
    - Acquisition strategies of private equity firms

3. Sources of finance
    - Recall of debt capital (e.g. bankruptcy of lender)
    - Change of ownership resulting in new policies

4. Shareholders
    - Share price collapse following media revelations
    - Reputational loss following an adverse law case

Information Technology Area

1. e-links with customers, suppliers, and shareholders
    - Hacking of our systems for fraud, spying or mischief

Management and operational level risks are also covered by this risk assessment system.

Risk Analysis

The analysis of risk in an organization involves a number of iterative phases:

- Risk recognition
- Risk assessment
- Risk evaluation
- Risk management policies
- Risk monitoring

The basic elements of the risk analysis process are shown in figure 14.1 overleaf.

Some countries, including Australia, the United States, and the United Kingdom, have created standards for risk management under the auspices of the International Organization for Standardization (ISO). The Business Continuity Institute, which exists to

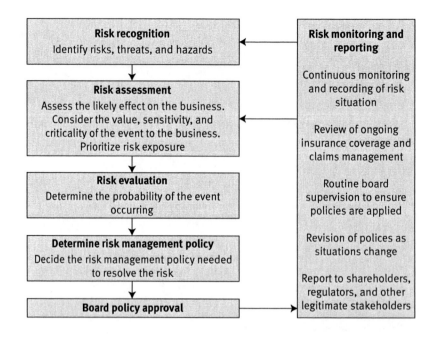

Figure 14.1 The risk analysis and management process

promote business continuity worldwide, offers benchmarks and evaluation criteria (see http://www.thebci.org).

The Institute of Chartered Accountants in England and Wales compiled the following list of benefits from the introduction of sound governance and risk management:

- Greater likelihood of achieving objectives
- Higher share price in the long term
- Greater likelihood of successful change initiatives
- Lower cost of capital
- Early movement into new business areas
- Improved use of insurance
- Reduction in the cost of remedial work and 'fire fighting'
- Achievement of competitive advantage
- Less business interruption
- Achievement of compliance/regulatory targets

Some commentators suggest that good corporate governance with professional risk management can reduce isurance costs. This is not necessarily true, but good corporate governance can protect against excessive penalties and improve the ability to get cover, even against substantial risks.

In chapter 2 we introduced the basic quadrant of board performance and conformance activities (figure 14.2). The components of the risk analysis process, depicted above, can be mapped onto this quadrant (as in figure 14.3).

Figure 14.2 Framework for analysing board activities

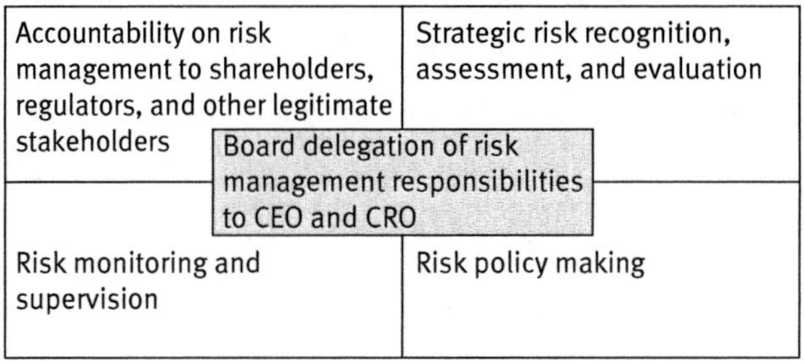

Accountability on risk management to shareholders, regulators, and other legitimate stakeholders	Strategic risk recognition, assessment, and evaluation
Board delegation of risk management responsibilities to CEO and CRO	
Risk monitoring and supervision	Risk policy making

Figure 14.3 Framework showing board risk analysis and management responsibilities

Risk Recognition and Assessment

Identifying threats that could significantly harm a business can be difficult. Although some threats may be obvious and easily guarded against, other risks can be hard to recognize. Unless they have occurred previously there will be no previous experience in the organization. Moreover, other companies tend to hide bad news, thus increaing the under-estimation of potential risks.

Threats, such as those caused by critical changes in competitors' strategies, serious loss of business through criminal activity, disgruntled employees' actions, or terrorist threats, kidnap, or other loss of top executives, or the effects of natural diasaster, for example, may be difficult to imagine, yet could prove to be catastrophic. Major business interruption, even challenges to business continuity, can come from unexpected occurences.

How do firms go about the task of identifying risk at every level? In-house workshops and seminars are used by some to generate insights. External experts may be able to offer experience and an independent view. The advice of independent non-executive directors (INEDs) can also be valuable. Then there are a number of risk assessment and risk management tools available. Many are qualitative in nature, others seek to add an element of quantification, whilst some involve computerized data collection and analysis. The following show the range of options:

A Simple Tabular Approach

The organization is divided into a series of risk analysis centres, which may well reflect the structure of the organization and its management control systems. Executives in each risk analysis centre identify and chart the following:

Table 14.2 **Risk analysis chart**

Nature of risk or hazard	Likely effects and outcome	Likelihood of event occurring	Risk management policy response

The procedures documentation for the risk analysis programme should contain guidance to staff on the range of risks to be covered including likely effects or outcomes of each occurrence. It is important that the risk analysis is conducted in each part of the organization and at every level. Experience shows that the initial risk assessment report will trigger further ideas and insights, which improve the subsequent risk assessment. The simple narrative table can be turned into a matrix by including estimated costs and an estimated probability of the uncertain risk or hazard occurring. A potential drawback of this approach is that a managerial focus might fail to identify strategic risks.

A Questionnaire Designed to Identify Risks and Hazards

If this approach is used throughout the organization, insights into risk can be generated in every part of an organization and at every level. A benefit of this approach is standardization of responses throughout the organization. This format can also be used to document compliance and non-compliance with risk management policies. An elaboration of the questionnaire approach is to include multiple choice responses as well as inviting a narrative description.

Mind Mapping

This involves a visual approach to recognizing risk factors, plotting their interrelationships, and then deriving the possible implications. Users of this method require some training and skill in the methodology. Benefits can include an appreciation of the relationships between risks and the identification of different risk elements from those generated by tabulation or questionnaire.

Risk Benchmarking by Industry, Country, or against Other Companies
This methodology starts with a list of possible risks or hazards as the basis for developing the risk profile of the subject company. The list can identify risks related to the type of company, its industry, and locations of operation.

Software Programs and Systems
IT based solutions to risk analysis and management are used by many organizations These can provide on-line access to the identification and reporting of risks. Proprietary programs and systems are available from software houses, consulting firms, and companies in the insurance industry. Some of these programs provide a risk management information system, which link risk recognition and assessment, risk evaluation, and enterprise risk management policies, and can also be linked to claims management systems.

Information on strategic level risks can be generated as part of an ongoing strategic review, as explored in chapter 6. The firm's strategy formulation process, using tools such as SWOT (strengths, weaknesses, opportunities, and threats) analysis, Porter 'five forces' analysis or some other analytical methodology, can also generate information about potential risk. This can then be used to evaluate possible effects, should they happen, estimate the likelihood that they would occur, and decide the suitable policy response. This information can then be incorporated into the strategic level risk management policies approved by the board.

Experience has shown that a successful risk recognition and assessment programme has a number of critical success factors:

- Sponsorship and oversight at board level
- Top management committment
- Involvement throughout all levels of management and in all parts of the enterprise
- Company-wide definition of procedures, documentation, and reporting
- Identification of risk management centres throughout the organization
- Definition of responsibilities for identifying and recommending risk responses
- Risk management centres are given appropriate responsibility
- Areas of risk are carefully defined and bounded, each one limited in scope
- Involvement of business and technical experts with relevant risk assessment experience
- Document at all stages, regularly updated and building on experience
- Define authentication and approval, confidentiality levels, access control, availability, audit, and overall administration responsibilities
- The creation of a risk awareness, not risk avoidance, attitude throughout the organization
- Ensuring participation by identifying the 'ownership' of risks throughout the organization
- Board level oversight and approval of risk management policies is vital

Introducing a risk assessment programme not only enables firms to recognize risks and develop appropriate risk management policies, but it also supports ongoing business activities by causing staff to recognize risks and thus avoid them, by enabling directors to appreciate the nature and extent of their risk profile and to make appropriate judgements, and finally by enabling the firm to report confidently to shareholders and other stake-holders that corporate risks are being well managed.

Risk Evaluation

The extent of any risk (R) is a function of the magnitude of the potential cost or loss (L) and the probability (p) that the uncertain future event will occur.

Expressed mathmatically:

A specific risk $R_i = L_i p(L)_i$ and the firm's total risk exposure $R_{total} = \Sigma L_i p(L_i)$

Unfortunately, both the cost and the probability of an event can often be difficult to assess. Some costs, such as the loss of customer confidence should a product fail, the loss of reputation following a financial or executive scandal, or the effect on the cost of capital following the lowering of a credit rating, can be difficult to estimate. Reliable and current data often precludes an exact estimate, but broad estimates, within ranges, do need to be made.

Similarly the probability of a risk occurring can be problematical. But a view needs to be taken. The judgement of knowlegeable individuals, including INEDs, can be useful. Careful documentation is important and the resultant policy needs to be well written, so that subsequent action can be taken to ensure that the policy is being followed.

A risk, which would result in a high loss but with a low chance of occurring, may well be treated differently in a firm's risk management policies than one with a lower cost but greater probability. All the more reason, therefore, to identify the existence of a risk or hazard in the first place and for management and, ultimately, the board to face up to the reality of the situation. The risk map in figure 14.4 illustrates the situation.

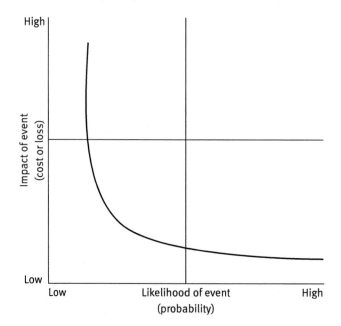

Figure 14.4 Risk mapping

The risk map highlights the importance of board level involvement in enterprise risk management policies:

- In the high impact/high likelihood quadrant the board will want to give a lot of consideration to appropriate policies. For example, the directors may decide to incur considerable expenditure on system redundancy or standby systems, on staff training, on reserves of materials, stock, or finance, or on simulation exercises to test respond time and quality. This is the quadrant in which sharing risk through financial instruments or external insurance cover can be of fudamental importance. The board will also want to ensure that they have information systems that monitor such situations and that the company is able to respond quickly to events

- In the high impact/low likelihood quadrant the board has the option of taking action to mitigate the impact, assume the risk, or insure

- In the low impact/high probability the board can take defensive action to limit the impact but may well decide to carry any further costs themselves. Of course, insurance remains an option but the high probability will produce higher premiums

- In the low impact/low likelihood quadrant the need for board policies varies from low to insignificant. Control systems to reflect the situation, procedures to respond to it, and some staff training to mitigate adverse effects might be all that is needed.

Simple rating schemes can be used to rank the significance of risks and the probability of their occurrence, as in the following case from the UK's University of Sussex.

Case Study 14.2 The University of Sussex (US): Risk Profiling

The tables below demonstrate the rating scheme adopted by the University of Sussex in the UK, to rank the impact and likelihood of uncertain future events, and to produce an overall scale of risk rankings.

Table 14.3 **The potential impact of an uncertain future event**

Estimation	Score	Examples of description
Very Low	1	Financial impact below £50k. No significant adverse publicity for US. Minimal impact on US operations.
Low	2	Financial impact £50k–£250k. Limited unfavourable media coverage.
Medium	3	Financial impact £250k–£1m. Unfavourable local/short-term external media coverage.
High	4	Major financial loss £1m–£5m. Significant public/media concern.
Very High	5	Huge financial loss over £5m. Adverse national/prolonged media coverage. Demand for HEFCE enquiry.

Table 14.4 **The likelihood of an uncertain future event**

Probability	Score	Examples of description
Very Low/Rare	1	May occur only in exceptional circumstances. No previous report of occurrence in US. Maybe once in 10 years.
Low/Unlikely	2	Event not likely to occur inside 4 years. Less than 5% chance of occurrence in US.
Medium/Possible	3	Event could occur at some time during the year.
High/Likely	4	Event will probably occur e.g. every year. History of occurrence at US.
Very High/Probable	5	Event is expected to occur more than once a year. Common or repetitive at US.

By multiplying the impact score with the likelihood score provides an overall risk ranking profile:

Table 14.5 **Overall risk ranking profile**

1–5	6–10	11–15	16–20	21–25
Very low	Low	Medium	High	Very high
Corporate Risk Register normal classification			Corporate Risk Register top risks	

Discussion Questions

1. Evaluate the risk ranking procedures of the University of Sussex.
   - What issues might occur in its application?
   - What benefits might flow from this approach?

Risk Management Information Systems

Currently, in many companies risk management systems are piecemeal, scattered with duplications and errors. Directors in such companies, all too often, learn of risks once they have become problems. Boards should ensure that they are fully appraised of significant risks so that appropriate business continuity strategies and risk management policies can be put in place ahead of time.

Internationally, the trend is towards centralization of information and risk management responsiblity. Such enterprise risk management systems (ERMS) provide information routinely and regularly for management to take executive decisions and for the board to carry out its monitoring and supervisory function. The ERMS should also generate information to enable the company to communicate externally to auditors, regulators, shareholders, and other legitimate stakeholders as well as its insurers and brokers.

A successful enterprise risk management system will provide an information interchange, with links throughout the company to the centre, and also link to brokers and insurers. However, on-line risk management information systems may contain confidential data on strategic issues. Wrongful access could lead to the loss of valuable corporate information. Security and confidentiality are vital. Rights of access need to be controlled. The right to update information also needs to be secure. Such systems are sometimes built in-house, but increasingly packages are available from specialist firms, for example the RiskConsole system from AON Insurance.

A 2007 research report from the Conference Board concluded that, whilst many companies had adopted aspects of enterprise risk management (ERM), improvements could be made by integrating ERM with their operational systems, particularly accounting and budgeting, internal control, and information technology. The report also advocated the public disclosure of long term risk-adjusted strategic goals for the benefit of shareholders and the financial markets.

Risk Transfer

Identifying risk strategies and establishing risk policies are, essentially, board decisions. Board level strategies that recognize strategic threats to the enterprise are vital with policies agreed by the board to determine which risk management decisions are reserved to the board. Every board develops a unique risk profile and establishes that board's risk tolerance, that is the directors' appetite for risks. Detailed work may be delegated to management but the oversight of risk is a basic element in corporate governance and, thus, the responsibility of the board. In developing risk policies, a board has to trade off short term costs with long term benefits.

In establishing the company's risk policies, every board faces four possible responses to risk:

(1) Avoid the risk. Do not commit to the planned action. Abandon the proposed project.

(2) Mitigate the risk by making capital investments or incurring ongoing expenditure, for example, by investing in standby equipment, duplicate/triplicate critical components, staff training, risk policies such as requiring top executives to travel in different cars and planes, or never to build on flood plains or in typhoon/hurricane locations.

(3) Transfer the risk. Spread the exposure with other parties. Insure against the risk, thereby transferring elements of risk to the insurance company, whilst recognizing that some risks may be uninsurable. Create derivative instruments, agreements with financial institutions that transfer risk to third parties.

(4) Retain the risk. In other words, accept the risk. Self-insuring is an approach adopted by many governmental organizations. This risk strategy, what some commentators call the firm's 'risk appetite', needs to be made at board level.

Risk management policies typically involve costs, both capital costs and ongoing expenditure. For example, the cost of building hardware and software systems into a company's customer ordering system to reduce opportunities for a sophisticated hacker to steal information, damage system operations, or perpetrate fraud. Continuing expenditure can include staff and operating expenditure for providing security, ongoing training, and updating routines. In determining the overall risk management policy, the board will need to compare the costs of control with the discounted value of the outcome $[L_i p(L)_i]$ and determine the cost/benefit relationship. We discussed director and officer personal insurance cover in chapter 12.

Not only should directors ensure that the firm's risk management policies are in place, but they should assure themselves that the framework or system for risk management is effective. Induction training and regular updating of directors and senior staff should form part of the firm's risk management programme.

Enterprise risk profiling, risk strategy formulation, and policy making and risk supervision have now become an integral part of the corporate governance portfolio. Every board has a duty to ensure that risk assessment and management systems are functioning at each level and that appropriate risk management policies are in place. Moreover regulators are increasingly requiring firms to report on the quality of their risk management.

Overall, boards which handle risk professionally, as part of their normal corporate governance activities, are able to face increasing risk without making their enterprises more risky.

Case Study 14.3 Northern Rock

A run on a British bank is very rare, but in September 2007 it happened to Northern Rock, the UK's 5th biggest mortgage lender. Northern Rock had around 1.5 million depositors with savings of £28 billion, and some 800,000 home-owner borrowers. The company, formerly a British building society (savings and loan association) was incorporated as a public company in 1997 and floated on the London Stock Exchange. By 2000 it had grown dramatically to join the FTSE 100 index.

In July 2007, Adam J. Applegarth, the Chief Executive wrote:

Operationally Northern Rock had a good first half in 2007. Mortgage lending has been particularly strong with a gross market share of 9.7% and a net market share of 18.9%, helped by improvements in retention of home moving customers, keeping customers coming to the end of their product deals and a strong mortgage market. Credit quality remains robust.

The outlook for the full year is being impacted by sharp increases in money market and swap rates seen in the first half. This has resulted in a negative impact on net interest income as mortgage pricing in the market generally has lagged behind increases in funding costs in the year to date. Action has been taken with changes in our swap transaction policies to minimise exposures in the future to significant changes in interest rates.

The medium term outlook for the Company is very positive.

A warning might have been seen in the second paragraph. Northern Rock was hit by the financial world's reluctance to lend short term, as other institutions hoarded cash to cope with the fallout from defaulting sub-prime mortgage loans in the United States. By mid-September, Northern Rock could not raise enough money to meet its financial obligations.

On Friday 14 September 2007, the Bank of England, acting as 'lender of last resort', provided an emergency facility to prop up Northern Rock. The company urged its savers not to panic, insisting that it was solvent. But they did. Beleaguered savers, many elderly, queued for hours to withdraw all their savings. The Northern Rock Internet access crashed as online customers tried to log on to access their funds.

The panic had some justification. The compensation scheme run by the Financial Services Authority, the UK financial market watchdog, guaranteed repayments on only £2,000 in full and 90 percent on the next £33,000. After that depositors had no recourse to insurance funds. No wonder people queued and withdrew some £3 billion on that day. The British Secretary to the Treasury said that it was not the duty of government to save institutions from the consequences of making risky investments. Northern Rock shares fell by 40 percent.

On the next day, the queues lengthened. The government feared that financial panic could spread to other banks. So, on Monday 17 September, the government took an unprecedented step and gave a cast-iron guarantee to all Northern Rock savers that their savings, £22 billion of personal deposits and £6 billion of business deposits in total, would be underwritten by the government and met in full.

The classical model of mortgage lending is to borrow short from personal savers, who can call on their funds with little or no notice, and lend long to house owners against mortgages on their property. The strategy is based on the assumption that the savers trust the bank.

However, the business model of Northern Rock leveraged this classical model by relying on savers' funds for only part of its mortgage financing. It borrowed additional funds from the money market. Some of its loans were securitized and traded on the swap market. This worked well when interest rates were low and funds readily available. As a result the Northern Rock's business grew and its market share far surpassed its competitors with more traditional and cautious strategies. Then came the funds famine and Northern Rock's crisis.

The Board had twelve members: the chairman, the chief executive, four executive directors, and six non-executive directors. The board had four committees—audit, nominations, remuneration, and risk.

The chief executive was Adam Applegarth, who joined the company in 1980 as a graduate trainee. The company had a reputation for making internal appointments.

The chairman was Dr the Honourable Matthew White Ridley, son of Viscount Ridley. Educated at Eton College and Oxford, his doctorate was in zoology. He was not a financier. He joined the board as an INED in 1994 and became chairman in 2004. He also chaired the nominations committee. His Northern Rock annual fee was £300,000.

The other INEDs were:

• Adam Fenwick, 46, the group managing director of Fenwick Ltd and an INED of John Swire and Sons Ltd. Northern Rock fee £54,000.

- Sir Ian Gibson, 60, the senior INED, who had industrial experience in running Ford Motors and Nissan, and was currently chairman of the publishers of the Daily Mirror and an INED of GKN Plc and Greggs plc. He was previously a member of the Court of the Bank of England. Northern Rock fee £80,000.

- Nichola Pease, 46, chief executive of JO Hambros Capital Management, previously with Barings, famous for its collapse after a Singapore trader was allowed to run excessive risks. Northern Rock fee £65,000.

- Michael Queen, 45, a director of 3i Group plc. Northern Rock fee £54,000.

- Rosemary Radcliffe, 62, a leading chartered accountant and a complaints commissioner for the Financial Services Authority. Northern Rock fee £56,000.

- Sir Derek Wanless, 59, former CEO of NatWest Bank, who steered it through an acquisition strategy that proved disastrous, and left in 1999 with a £3 million pay-off, who was well respected in the City of London, and a member of the actuarial committee of the Financial Reporting Council. He carried out a long term review of the British National Health Service for the Government in 2007. Northern Rock fee £86,000. He was chairman of Northern Rock's audit committee and risk committee.

In February 2008 Northern Rock was nationalized. The Bank came under Government control. A new chief executive was appointed. Shareholders were to be recompensed at a level set by an independent panel. The British Chancellor of the Exchequer insisted that the public ownership was temporary, before 'ultimately trying to return it to the private sector'.

Discussion Questions

1. What role did the board play in this saga?

2. Did the directors understand the underlying business model and how it differed from the classical banking approach to lending? Did they appreciate their company's exposure should the financial markets change? Did they know the extent of their business risk?

3. If the answer to these questions is yes, was the board's business judgement valid? Did the directors accept the risk, deciding that such a level of exposure was reasonable for their company?

Unfortunately, the UK's Northern Rock collapse was just the first of more dramatic collapses around the world. A growing global credit crisis led to bankruptcies, takeovers, and nationalization: in the United States, Bear Stearns was bailed out, Lehman Brothers became bankrupt, AIG, Fannie Mae, Freddie Mac, Merrill Lynch, and Wachovia were all dramatically affected; in Europe, Glitnir, the third largest bank in Iceland, Fortis, the biggest employer in Belgium, Hypo Real Estate in Germany, Dexia Finance in France, and Roskild in Denmark were all supported; whilst in the UK Bradford & Bingley and HBOS needed saving. Governments in the United States and many other countries were forced to pledge massive funds to support their finance markets. But the underlying corporate governance questions remain: who was at fault, did the directors of the failed companies really understand their strategic risk exposure, were any activities illegal, were the banking regulators, the auditors, the credit agencies at fault? Financial markets are based on trust and confidence, which had been lost.

REFERENCES AND FURTHER READING

Barton, Thomas L., William G. Shenkir and Paul L. Walker (2002) *Making Enterprise Risk Management Pay Off: How Leading Companies Implement Risk Management*. Brookfield, CT: Disaster Center Bookstore (Rothstein Associates).

Casualty Actuarial Society (2003) 'Overview of Enterprise Risk Management'. London: Enterprise Risk Management Committee, Casualty Actuarial Society.

Chapman, R. J. (2006) *Simple Tools and Techniques for Enterprise Risk Management*. New Jersey: Wiley.

Conference Board (2005) 'From Risk Management to Risk Strategy', Report no. 1363. New York: Conference Board.

——(2006) 'The Role of US Corporate Boards in Enterprise Risk Management', Report no. 1390. New York: Conference Board.

——(2007) 'Emerging Governance Practices in Enterprise Risk Management', Report no. 1398. New York: Conference Board.

Cornelius, Peter K. and Bruce Kogan (eds.) (2007) *Global Issues in Corporate Governance: Risk and International Investment*. New York: Oxford University Press.

Lam, James (2003) *Enterprise Risk Management: From Incentives to Controls*. New Jersey: Wiley.

Moeller, Robert (2007) *COSO Enterprise Risk Management: Understanding the New Integrated ERM Framework (COSO Committee of Sponsoring Organisations of the Treadway Commission)*. New Jersey: Wiley.

NACD (National Association of Corporate Directors) (2005) *Report of the NACD Blue Ribbon Commission on Director Liability: Myths, Realities and Prevention*. Washington, DC: NACD.

——(2005) *Risk Oversight: Board Lessons for Turbulent Times: A Report of a NACD Blue Ribbon Commission*. Washington, DC: NACD.

Tonello, Matteo (2007) 'Emerging Governance Practices in Enterprise Risk Management', Research report no. R-1398-07. New York: Conference Board.

Treadway Commission (2004) 'Enterprise Risk Management: An Integrated Approach', the Committee of Sponsoring Organizations of the Treadway Commission, New York.

Whitlery, Sherry (2004) 'Leadership Through Progressive Enterprise Risk Management', *Institute of Internal Auditors, FSA Times*, 4th quarter, Vol. 3.

USEFUL WEBSITES

www.aon.com/us/busi/risk_management/risk_consulting/ent_risk_mgmt/default.jsp
Enterprise Risk Management—Aon Insurance Brokers.

www.businesslink.gov.uk
Business information with recommendations on business risk analysis.

www.dnv.com
Mitsui O.S.K. Lines approach to managing risk.

www-306.ibm.com/software/uk/govern
Governance and risk management—IBM (business alignment, visibility, and control).

www.ifpo.org/articlebank/risk_assessment.html
Risk assessment guidelines—International Foundation for Protection Officers.

www.iso.org
International Organization for Standardization—risk management standards.

www.paisleyconsulting.com/Paisley/corporate-governance.html
Software for governance, risk, and compliance—Paisley.

www.qudos-software.co.uk/riskinfo.html
Risk assessor—Avanquest Corporate Solutions.

www.riskassessment101.com
Guide to risk management.

www.riskhive.com
Risk and scenario modelling—RiskHive Risk Management.

www.riskmetrics.com/about/index.html and **www.irrc.org**
Financial risk management expertise.

www.strategicthought.com
Risk management software solutions—Strategic Thought Group.

www.thebci.org
Business continuity management—the Business Continuity Institute.

PROJECTS AND EXERCISES

1. Focus on an organization with which you are familiar (for example, it could be a company, university, or sports club). Identify areas of possible risks (as in tables 14.1, 14.2, and 14.3). Consider strategic, managerial, and operational levels.

2. What consequences might arise should these risks occur?

3. In each situation, make a recommendation to management on what their risk response should be.

SELF-TEST QUESTIONS

To confirm your grasp of the key points in this chapter try answering the following questions. Answers are at the end of the book.

1. Name three regulatory instruments which call for risk management responsibility at board level.

2. Some boards include corporate risk assessment in the mandate of the board audit committee. Why might this have limitations?

3. What alternative do other companies adopt to bring risk issues to the board?

4. Who might be involved in such a risk management sub-committee, and how does it operate?

5. Where else might responsibility for risk assessment and management be placed in a company?

6. Identify the levels of risk in a business.

7. What were the top five issue of global business risk recognized by the World Economic Forum, in 2007?

8. Name the iterative phases involved in the analysis of risk in an organization.

9. Identify some risk assessement and risk management tools that are available.

10. What policy options does a board have when deciding its approach to enterprise risk management?

15 Corporate Social Responsibility and Sustainability

....

- In which we consider
  - new expectations in the governance of organizations
  - corporate social responsibility: strategies and policies
  - corporate social responsibility reporting
  - sustainability reporting
  - balancing corporate responsibilities

New Expectations in the Governance of Organizations

The original corporate governance codes, dating from the early 1990s, were voluntary. At the time they were derided by some company chairmen as being no more than expensive, box-ticking exercises. But since then three significant changes have taken place. Firstly, corporate governance compliance has increasingly become mandatory, enshrined in regulation or in some cases law. Complaints now tend to be about the cost of compliance not about the need for corporate governance codes. Secondly, risk analysis and risk management have become an integral part of the corporate governance process. Thirdly and most recently, corporate social responsibility and sustainability have been added to the corporate governance portfolio.

Questioning the societal legitimacy of corporate entities has a long history. In the original mid-19th century concept of the company, if the liability of the owners for the debts of the entity were to be limited, society demanded that the company's activities should be strictly prescribed. Companies could only carry out those functions described in the memorandum published when they were incorporated. In effect, society gave the entity a licence to operate provided that it limited its activities to a specific set of activities.

Subsequently, lawyers began to draft the constitutional documents, typically the memorandum of association, so widely that the activities of companies were no longer bounded. So the behaviour of corporate entities has had to be constrained by law. The 1884 UK Companies Act had only a few pages: the latest 2006 UK Companies Act was the longest piece of legislation Britain had ever produced. Around the world laws to control monopolies and markets, employee relations, customer protection, health and safety, environmental protection, and much more are now used to regulate and restrain corporate activities.

This raises the vital question, neatly posed by Milton Friedman: '*does a business have responsibilities?*' His view was that the only legitimate purpose for a company was to create wealth, pursuing their business effectively for the benefit of their customers, whilst providing a profitable reward to their investors. It was the role of the state, he believed, to provide the legal framework that regulated companies' behaviour in relation to the rest of the community.

As we saw in the discussion of stakeholder philosophies in chapter 9, the debate continues about companies' responsibilities to shareholders and other stakeholders. On one side are those who argue, like Friedman, that a company has one and only one objective: to make long term sustainable profits by satisfying customers for the benefit of its owners, whilst acting within the law. If society wishes to limit a company's single-minded pursuit of this goal, for example by constraining monopolies, regulating employment, or preventing pollution, it must pass appropriate laws. On the other side are those who believe that, because a company can and does affect the interests and even the lives of people, it should be accountable, and some say responsible, to societal interests over and above those of the owners and beyond the specific limits of the law.

Carroll (1979)[1] attempted to answer Friedman's question by suggesting that corporate responsibility had four levels:

- Economic responsibility—first and foremost the social responsibility to be profit orientated and market driven
- Legal responsibility—to adhere to society's laws and regulations as the price for society's licence to operate
- Ethical responsibilities—to honour society's wider social norms and expectations of behaviour over and above the law in line with the local culture
- Discretionary (or philanthropic) responsibilities—to undertake voluntary activities and expenditures which exceed society's minimum expectations

As we will see in this chapter, many companies in the economically advanced world now accept that their responsibilities go beyond the generation of wealth whilst staying within the laws of the states in which they operate. Such thinking is now widely called corporate social responsibility (CSR) and recognized as part of companies' corporate governance responsibilities. Even in emerging economies such as China, the importance of CSR is recognized. The 10th National Congress of the Chinese People's Political Consultative Conference in 2005[2] recognized that business enterprises were the foundation for building a harmonious society. Enterprises should be required to do three things, it was argued: take a scientific and rational attitude towards development, protect and respect employee rights and benefits, and undertake more social responsibilities.

A distinction needs to be drawn between CSR, business ethics, and corporate philanthropy. CSR raises a strategic concern about the nature and purpose of companies. Socially responsible companies recognize a responsibility for their impact on all stakeholders, communities, and the environment, balancing their interests with the need to make a profit to grow and satisfy their shareholders. CSR goes to the heart of corporate

[1]Carroll (1979) *Academy of Management Review.*
[2]See chapter 8 for more on Chinese state governance.

governance, as we saw in chapter 9 when discussing stakeholder philosophy or, as some call it, stakeholder theory.

Business ethics, on the other hand, concern an organization's behaviour in society and the ethical conduct of those in the organization. Some companies develop policies for the ethical conduct expected of employees and publish codes of ethics. Ethical concerns raise important philosophical, ideological, and moral issues, which are rooted in social, religious, and cultural contexts. Although CSR practices inevitably have an ethical underpinning, the study of ethics is not the focus of this book.

Corporate philanthropy involves charitable giving by a company to support communities that it is concerned about, in money or services such as employees' time. A socially responsible company may include philanthropy as a part of its overall CSR programme. But CSR involves a wider perspective than corporate philanthropy.

Box 15.1 A Comment on CSR from the British Chancellor of the Exchequer (Who later became Britain's Prime Minister)

Today, corporate social responsibility goes far beyond the old philanthropy of the past—donating money to good causes at the end of the year—and is instead an all year round responsibility that companies accept for the environment around them, to the best working practices, for their engagement in the local communities, and for their recognition that brand names depend not only on quality, price, and uniqueness, but on how, cumulatively, they interact with the companies workforce, community, and environment. Now, we need to move forward towards a challenging measure of corporate responsibility, where we judge results not just by input but by its outcomes: the difference we make to the world in which we live, and the contribution we make to poverty reduction.

(The Right Honourable Gordon Brown 2006)

The notion that companies have a responsibility that goes beyond a duty to their shareholders is not, however, universally accepted. Reich,[3] who was previously a CSR advocate, argued that consumers today have a world of choice and businesses face more competition than ever before. In pursuit of corporate performance CEO's incentives become aligned with shareholders' interests as they '*slash payrolls, outsource abroad, and drain our main streets of shops*'. Reich believes that, in fact, better corporate governance makes companies less likely to be socially responsible, concluding that if states want to avoid adverse social consequences they have to pass laws to stop them.

Corporate Social Responsibility: Strategies and Policies

In recent years, a lot has been written about corporate social responsibility (CSR). Around the world, governments, community interest groups, and individuals have been calling for

---

[3]Reich, Robert B. (2006) *Supercapitalism: The Transformation of Business, Democracy and Everyday Life.* London: Borzoi Books/Random House.

business to act in socially responsible ways. The adverse economic effects of companies transgressing acceptable corporate behaviour can be high, not only in direct economic costs (damages, restitution, product recalls, fines, etc.) but in reputation. As we saw earlier, reputational risk should be taken seriously in every risk analysis.

In this chapter we note the growing calls for balanced, objective, and transparent reporting on companies' CSR and ecological impacts and increasing societal pressures for companies to report on the effects they have on the societies in which they operate. We also see that some companies believe that responsible business is good business in the long term, positively affecting customer relations, employee attitudes, and ultimately the share price and cost of capital.

For the first time UK company law, the Companies Act 2006, specifically included CSR responsibilities within the formal duties of company directors:

A director of a company must act in the way he considers, in good faith, would be most likely to promote the success of the company for the benefit of its members as a whole, and in doing so have regard to:

(a) the likely consequences of any decision in the long term

(b) the interests of the company's employees

(c) the need to foster the company's business relations with suppliers, customers and others

(d) the impact of the company's operations on the community and the environment

(e) the desirability of the company maintaining a reputation for high standards of business conduct, and

(f) the need to act fairly as between members of the company

The previous common law in the UK required directors to act in the best interests of the company, which effectively meant in the long term interest of the shareholders, typically maximizing shareholder value. The new law spelt out a statutory duty to recognize the effect of their decisions on a wider public.

Other examples of calls for CSR reports include the European Union's demand for specific CSR policies from companies tendering for contracts (2005), the UK Department of the Environment, Food and Rural Affairs (DEFRA) requirement for occupational pension funds to '*report whether environmental, social and ethical criteria are taken into account in their investment strategy*' (2001), and the Australian Stock Exchange listing rule that requires companies to report their performance against the criteria of environmental legislation (1998).

Investigative media increasingly report cases of firms transgressing accepted behaviour in, for example, the employment of children in manufacturing in third world companies, the alleged ill treatment of animals in pharmaceutical product testing, and pollution in the oil drilling and transport industries, even though such practices may be perfectly legal in the places where they occur.

To be effective, a company's CSR efforts need to be underpinned by a board level CSR policy. Such a policy should include a clear statement about the company's values, what it stands for, and how it engages with its shareholders and other stakeholders, including its employees, customers, and suppliers, the communities in which it operates, and the world at large.

Board approval of CSR policies has led many companies to publish a mission statement that seeks to enshrine that company's values and purpose, as we have seen previously. Made available to all employees, customers, and communities, such mission statements can be valuable in focusing a company's CSR focus. Of course, a mission statement, without the backing of clear board policy commitment, is likely to prove at best a futile public relations exercise and at worst sanctimonious drivel.

But with commitment at board level, a firm's CSR values are likely to influence management decisions, affect employee attitudes, and improve customer relations. CSR activities should penetrate every level and all aspects of a firm's activities. A successful CSR policy will be built into induction programmes at director, manager, and employee levels, as well as being promoted as management and organizational development activities. A clear CSR policy can also influence investment decisions by potential shareholders looking for socially responsible, ethical, or environmentally friendly enterprises in which to invest.

A CSR policy is, basically, a summary of the firm's attitudes to the impact it has on its stakeholders, the communities, and the environment in which it operates. Obviously, every company is different and must develop its own CSR policy and programmes in the context of its own corporate governance methods, including its corporate strategies and policies, and its management supervision and accountability systems.

The following example has been adapted from a manufacturing company's CSR handbook:

Case Study 15.1 A Manufacturing Company's CSR Policy

In addition to the implications for continuing economic success, all company strategies, polices, and management decisions should take account of the following long term effects:

1. *The firm's impact on all its stakeholders including:*

   - customers of the end product or service
   - agents, distributors, and others in the down-stream supply chain
   - original suppliers and others in the up-stream supply chain
   - other creditors
   - bankers and non-equity sources of finance
   - employees including managers
   - self-employed contractors to the company

2. *The firm's impact on all the communities in which it operates:*

   - Consider local, regional and national impacts including:
     - economic effects
     - socially responsible activities
     - philanthropic efforts

3. *The firm's impact on the environment:*

- Consider all the relevant communities, regions and countries affected by our manufacturing and distribution chain, including:
  - the effect of production activities such as

    energy use
    depletion of resources
    exploitation of labour
    pollution

  - the company's products including

    the effect of the product in use
    energy use
    health or other risks
    pollution

  - the end disposal of the product

    energy use
    pollution

Each of these broad policy statements is further amplified in the handbook. For example, the section on the firm's impact on the communities in which it operates is shown below.

Amplification of the Above Manufacturing Company's CSR Policy

Under the section (2) '*The firm's impact on all the communities in which it operates (local, regional and national)*' and its sub-section '*socially responsible activities*' consider the following impacts by the firm:

- the contributions of facilities, staff time to local and other organizations
  - educational and academic contributions
  - support for local and other academic institutions
  - contributions to research and similar activities
- aesthetic and arts contributions
  - expenditure on building and landscape design
  - sponsorship of arts, crafts, and similar activities
- sports and leisure contributions
  - sponsorship and contributions to local and other activities
  - poverty reduction
  - direct cash and indirect support (staff secondment, etc.)

Under the sub-section '*philanthropic efforts*' consider the following impacts by the firm:

- contributions to charities and other causes (including cash, use of facilities, staff time, and indirect support)
- employee giving to charities and other causes

> - director and staff service on charitable and other non-profit boards and management committees
>
> *Discussion Question*
>
> 1. Evaluate the company's CSR policy.
>   - Is there anything missing?
>   - What issues might arise in the application of the policy?
>   - Does the policy provide a sound basis for a CSR report for the company?

To encourage commitment to CSR practices the British Government has created a CSR competency framework; a flexible tool, which is offered as a '*way of thinking*' for companies of all sizes (see websites list at the end of the chapter). The framework has six core characteristics with five levels of attainment for each one.

The core characteristics are:

- Understanding society
  - A knowledge of how the business operates in the broader societal context and a knowledge of the impact that the business has on society; plus a recognition that the business is an important player in society, seeking to make that impact as positive as possible

- Building capacity
  - Working with others to build the capability to manage the business effectively, helping suppliers and employees to understand your environment and apply social and environmental concerns in their day-to-day roles

- Questioning 'business as usual'
  - Constantly questioning your business in relation to a more sustainable future and being open to improving people's quality of life and the environment, acting as an advocate engaging with bodies outside the business who share this concern for the future

- Stakeholder relations
  - Recognizing that stakeholders include all those who have an impact on, or are impacted by, your business, understanding the opportunities and risks they present and working with them through consultation, taking their views into account

- Strategic view
  - Ensuring that social and environmental concerns are included in the overall business strategy so that CSR becomes 'business as usual', with leadership coming from the top and resulting in everyone in the business having an awareness of the social and environmental impacts in their day-to-day roles

- Harnessing diversity
  - Recognizing that people differ and harnessing this diversity, reflected in fair and transparent employment practices, promoting the health, well being, and views of staff with everyone in the business feeling valued.

The five levels of attainment are:

- Awareness
  - The broad application of the core CSR characteristics and how they might impinge on business decisions
- Understanding
  - A basic knowledge of some of the issues, with the competence to apply them to specific activities
- Application
  - The ability to supplement this basic knowledge of the issues with the competence to apply it to specific activities
- Integration
  - An in-depth understanding of the issues and an expertise in embedding CSR into the business decision making process
- Leadership
  - the ability to help managers across the organization in a way that fully integrates CSR in the decision making process.

Overall, the intention of the CSR framework is to change employees' mindsets and to promote an appropriate CSR strategy throughout the organization and between the company and its stakeholders. Introducing such a climate of CSR throughout an organization needs to be part of an ongoing performance assessment of both organizational units and individuals and should not be allowed to become a form-filling exercise.

An organization's response to its social and environmental impacts, recognized through CSR awareness, can provide a cost-effective yet comprehensive way to manage social and environmental risk across the organization. Contrast the CSR policies within different parts of the same organization in the Exxon cases that follow.

Case Study 15.2 Exxon Europe CSR Policy

We take our responsibilities very seriously—for our employees, shareholders, customers, communities, the environment and society at large.

We strongly believe that the way we achieve results is as important as the results themselves. Therefore, we are working hard to embed CSR into the way we do business.

We have integrated CSR policies and practices into our business, which help us to ensure that we meet standards of integrity, safety, health, environment and social responsibility day in and day out and across our worldwide operations. We believe that this approach is essential to achieving superior business results.

Our focus is on helping Europe meet energy demand in an economically, socially and environmentally responsible manner. But we cannot be all things to all people. We must balance the needs of a wide variety of stakeholders. To do so sustainably is what the policies, actions and performance improvements behind CSR are all about.

(See www.exxonmobil.com/Europe-English/Citizen/Eu_VP_responsibility.asp)

Discussion Questions

1. Exxon recognizes that we *'cannot be all things to all people'*. How would you recommend that this dilemma be resolved?

2. What changes would you make to the Exxon CSR statement?

However, despite the clear commitment to CSR in the Exxon Europe policy statement, their holding company in the United States faced a CSR challenge at their 2008 annual shareholders meeting, as described below:

Box 15.2 CSR Resisted in Exxon

John D. Rockefeller founded the Standard Oil Corporation, which became Exxon Mobil, the world's largest publicly owned energy company. At the 2008 AGM some of his descendants brought shareholder motions calling for the company to curb greenhouse gas emissions, to increase renewable energy research, and to develop sources of alternative fuel.

Three resolutions asked Exxon to study the impact of global warming on poor countries, reduce company emissions of greenhouse gases, and do more research on renewable energy sources like wind turbines and solar panels. Neva Rockefeller Goodwin, an economist and great-granddaughter of Rockefeller, told shareholders: *'these increased concentrations of CO_2 in the atmosphere will cause weather disasters that will work against everyone's best hope for robust development in emerging countries, while also increasing the vulnerability of the poor in the rich countries. It will also impact the global economy.'* The proposals were opposed by Exxon Mobil's board.

The family also supported resolutions calling for the company to establish an independent chairman, separating the role from that of the current Chairman and Chief Executive Rex Tillerson. Shell and BP, they noted, had already separated the positions. The motion to split the roles, which had been raised for the last seven years' shareholder meetings, was supported by a significant number of shareholders. But the final poll showed only 39.5 percent of the shares were voted in favour.

Commentators suggested that the US$40 billion profit reported by the company last year may have influenced the rest. *'The past year was an outstanding year and a record for our corporation by nearly every measure'*, Tillerson said, *'millions of people have benefited financially by holding Exxon Mobil shares either directly or indirectly through their pension, insurance, and mutual funds'*, he added.

Mr Tillerson also added that he thought Exxon had to keep focused on its mission of developing more oil and gas reserves, and that oil and gas would remain the primary fuel source for decades to come. Some shareholders disagreed arguing that the company's emphasis on developing oil and gas as energy sources threatened the global environment and ultimately the company's financial health. One shareholder suggested that the company was acting *'like a dinosaur by not adopting to a changing environment'*. Another, a Dominican nun from New Jersey, said *'we're faced with a profound moral and business challenge'*. They were countered by other shareholders who defended the management as a great engine for profits.

Corporate Social Responsibility Reporting

CSR reporting has become an integral and important aspect of corporate governance practices in some companies. These companies typically report their CSR policies and their performance on employee welfare, customer relations, environment, ethical standards, and sustainability in specific reports to shareholders, stakeholders, regulators, the media, and other interest groups. In most cases such information appears both as published reports and on the company's website.

The three case studies that follow are extracts from three quite different companies' corporate governance and CSR reports. Largely self-explanatory, they illustrate and enhance the material in this chapter.

Case Study 15.3 HSBC Holdings Plc: Corporate Responsibility Report

HSBC calls itself the world's local bank. With 312,000 employees in over 10,000 offices, it is listed on five stock exchanges and has 200,000 shareholders spread over 100 countries.

The following extract is taken from the corporate responsibility section of their annual report.

Managing for Long term Success

> How a business like HSBC responds to the challenge of balancing the needs of people, planet and profit is part of our corporate responsibility strategy . . . we want HSBC to be one of the world's leading brands for corporate responsibility.
>
> *Stephen Green, Group Chairman*

At HSBC, we believe that corporate responsibility is critical to our long-term business success. In order to deliver enduring returns to our shareholders, we need to build lasting relationships with our customers that are based on the highest standards of personal integrity, transparency and fair dealing in all our business activities. This is the philosophy that underpins our approach to running our business responsibly.

We are committed to treating all present and future stakeholders in an open and transparent way. This commitment to openness is vital, whether in relation to the products and services we provide to our 125 million customers, in the way we manage our global workforce of 312,000 employees, or in the assessment of sustainability risks in our lending and investment activities, which range from commercial banking loans to multi-million dollar infrastructure projects.

Companies like ours must also share responsibility for addressing some of the formidable challenges currently facing societies across the globe, including the impact of climate change. We also provide support for educational and environmental projects worldwide through our charitable donations which totalled US$86.3 million in 2006.

Managing for sustainable growth

We aspire to be one of the world's leading brands in corporate responsibility. An example of our strategy here is microfinance, which demonstrates the growing alignment between business and community investment. Our new microfinance strategy is based on commercial viability albeit with high social impact . . . small-scale financial services for those without banking relationships largely in the developing world.

In pursuit of our goal to attract, develop and motivate our staff, we continue to shape our human resource strategy to take advantage of the diversity within our global network. . . . By embracing and managing diversity within our organisation we gain the best from our people while providing the best service to our customers.

We believe that a key component of career development at HSBC should be working internationally because it allows our employees to gain the experience of another country and culture.

HSBC continues to develop and implement sector risk policies that reinforce our commitment to social and environmental sustainability. (The Group has published guidelines for the energy, forest, freshwater and chemicals industry sectors)

HSBC and climate change

We believe financial institutions will be critical in minimising the impacts of climate change, playing a key role in financing the shift to cleaner energy and more efficient transport. HSBC itself aspires to be among the leading financial institutions in a low-carbon economy. . . . HSBC is supporting its clients to run environmentally responsible businesses. . . . As part of our long-standing commitment to the environment we have since 2003 measured energy usage and CO_2 emissions from our offices around the world, along with waste production and water usage. . . . In addition, since we became the world's first carbon neutral bank in 2005, we have purchased carbon dioxide 'offsets' . . . thereby bringing our own net impact to zero.

Investing in communities

Education and environment continue to be HSBC's key priorities for community involvement. [The report describes the work of the HSBC Global Education Trust, the 'Investing in Nature' eco-partnership, and involvement in other environmental conservation projects.]

Measuring our success

. . . HSBC was named overall winner in the first *Financial Times* Sustainable Banking Awards.

[HSBC was also a winner in the 2007 Hong Kong Institute of CPA's Best Annual Report Competition.]

(HSBC Holdings Plc 2006 Annual Review and www.hsbc.com/1/2/sustainability)

Discussion Questions

1. How might the HSBC statements on corporate responsibility and sustainability be improved?

2. Research the websites of other international banks. What do they have to say about CSR and sustainability? Why should HSBC have won the *Financial Times* Sustainable Banking award?

Case Study 15.4 Li & Fung Ltd

Li & Fung is incorporated in Bermuda and listed in Hong Kong. Its 2006 turnover was around US$8.5 billion, principally in the United States and Europe. The company is the parent of a group of companies in the export trading and importing businesses. Its supply chain embraces identifying consumer needs, product design, product development, raw material sourcing, factory sourcing, manufacturing control, shipping control, forward consolidation, customs clearance, local forwarding consolidation, wholesaler, to satisfied customer.

The corporate social responsibility and sustainability section of their 2006 annual report states:

Li & Fung has developed a supplier Code of Conduct to be observed by its approved suppliers around the globe. The code is a set of standards based on local and national laws and regulations and the International Labor Organisation code conventions. These standards include underage labor, force/prison labor, wages and compensation, working hours, discrimination, disciplinary practices, freedom of association, health and safety, environment, and the right of access. A copy of the code is available at our corporate website (www.lifung.com).

In 2006, the Group employed more than 100 dedicated in-house compliance staff worldwide to conduct supplier evaluations and monitor compliance to the code among the suppliers that produce our customer's merchandise. The vendor compliance division is organized independently of our sourcing/merchandising divisions and focuses on improving our suppliers' labor conditions and working standards.

. . . Li & Fung also provides systematic training to its suppliers to equip them with awareness, knowledge and the necessary skills and tools they need to meet compliance requirements.

Li & Fung is a member of Business for Social Responsibility (BSR), an international US-based non-profit organization whose mission is to promote socially responsible business practices, innovation and collaboration that demonstrate respect for ethical values, people, community and the environment . . .

Li & Fung also enforces its customers environmental purchasing policies with respect to re-cycling, package waste minimization, and sustainable development initiatives. By adopting environmental considerations as an integral part of our business activities, the Group equates the environment to our other critical business considerations such as compliance, quality and value.

Li & Fung is also a partner in the United Nations Global Compact Initiative, which embraces and supports a set of core values in human rights, labor standards, the environment and anti-corruption. The initiative achieves this through the dissemination of good practices based on certain universal principles derived from international conventions and declarations—the Ten Principles. These cover the respect of and support for the protection of human rights, abstinence from human rights abuses, freedom of association, elimination of all forms of forced and child labor, elimination of discrimination in employment, promotion of environmental responsibility, and the elimination of corruption.

Since 2001, Li & Fung has been included as a component of the Dow Jones Sustainability World Indexes, the world's first global indexes tracking the performance of companies worldwide in the three main dimensions of corporate sustainability: social, economic and environmental responsibilities. Li & Fung has also been included as a constituent member in the FTSE4Good Index Series from FTSE Group (UK) recognizing Li & Fung's commitment to high corporate social responsibility standards.

In 2007 they were awarded a prize in the Hong Kong Institute of CPA's annual corporate governance report competition.

The company won the Corporate Governance Asia Recognition Awards 2006 and the Best Corporate Governance Disclosure Awards 2006 (Gold Award since 2002).

(Li & Fung 2006 annual report and www.lifung.com/eng/ir/governance.php)

Discussion Questions

1. Li and Fung is a trading company that applies its Code of Conduct to the activities of its suppliers. Is this a sound business practice?

2. Study the code on the company's website. How might it be improved?

Case Study 15.5 CLP Group: Social and Environmental Report

CLP is a major generator and supplier of electricity in Australia, China, Hong Kong, India, and Taiwan. In their 2006 Social and Environmental Report, CLP summarizes their approach to governance and ethics with the diagram in figure 15.1.

Vision	→ What do we want to be?
Mission	→ What benefits will we bring to our stakeholders?
Strategy	→ How will we achieve this?
Values	→ What guides the pursuit of our strategy?
Commitments	→ What must we do to uphold our values?
Policies and Codes	→ What must we do to meet our commitments?

Figure 15.1 CLP Group's approach to governance and ethics

We regard good ethics, embodied in the CLP Value Framework and our corporate governance structure, as fundamental to the achievement of our business goals. We set up the Social, Environmental and Ethics (SEE) Committee of the Board and put in place policies, processes and reporting structures to ensure ethical behaviour throughout the Group.

Corporate Citizenship

CLP Group has set high standards of corporate citizenship. We believe that wherever we operate we have a role to play in contributing to the social, economic and environmental well being of the local community.

Our actions must be aligned with our aspirations and standards and contribute to the economic and social progress of the communities in which we operate. We maintain these standards by:

- Actively and consistently supporting programmes in the local communities in which we operate. These are specifically targeted towards the areas of community care, youth and education, and arts and culture.

- Engaging stakeholders substantively to provide timely and open communication and to take into account public views on our infrastructure development projects, as well as to participate in public policy debates on matters of public interest. We provide regular briefings and other 2-way communication for our stakeholders, including our customers, employees, shareholders, suppliers, the financial community, other businesses, government, the community and the media.

- An explicit commitment to corporate social responsibility.

- Commitment to managing the impact of all our operations on the environment. It is our policy to use our resources responsibly while complying with all the applicable laws and regulations. We educate our people about environmental concern and responsibility as we continuously monitor, report and improve the environmental performance of our business. CLP is an active participant in air quality and climate change discussions.

- Maintenance of supply reliability. CLP takes pride in its world-class performance of supply reliability and excellent customer services. Comprehensive and effective risk management and asset management systems safeguard the reliability and robustness of our power systems.

(CLP 2006 Social and Environmental Report and www.clpgroup.com)

Discussion Questions

1. Compare the social and environmental report of CLP with the social and environmental activities of Hong Kong Electric Ltd, the other major electricity generator in Hong Kong (see www.hec.com.hk).

2. CLP has made a major commitment to corporate social responsibility. If you were a shareholder of CLP would you be satisfied?

As we saw in the earlier discussion of stakeholder philosophies, many stakeholders are potentially in competition for corporate resources: for example, customers wanting lower retail prices, employees demanding higher wages, and environmental protection costs are potentially in conflict. The challenge to the board in pursuing its CSR strategies and policies is to strike a suitable and sustainable balance.

A crucial question is whether there is a link between CSR and economic performance. Although research studies have been conducted, a basic problem has been how to measure CSR. Some studies have also been marred by an ideological bias or limited methodology. Although a few studies have shown some correlation between firms' CSR and their financial performance, current research does not point to a decisive link. However, the longer term effects of a sound CSR reputation in both the consumer market and the stock market may well persuade boards of the importance of CSR efforts.

Some firms have claimed that their CSR policies and reports have:

- Improved brand recognition and reputation
- Made the firm more attractive to existing and potential employees
- Improved top management and board level strategic thinking and decisions
- Produced innovations in the way the firm operates
- Responded to customers' demands
- Met stakeholders' and society's changing expectations

For such reasons, many firms approach CSR as enlightened self-interest. But few claim a demonstrable positive correlation between good CSR practices and corporate financial performance. That is why some companies talk about a 'triple bottom line', measuring and reporting on organizational performance in economic, social, and environmental terms. Some have called this a 'profits, people, and planet' approach. This approach has been adopted in public sector organizations as well as profit orientated firms. The growing number of investment funds now focusing on 'socially responsible investing' also suggests that there may be a share price premium in due course.

Nevertheless, CSR reports can build new links between companies and their stakeholders. Relationships between companies and their contractual partners in the added value chain, such as suppliers, distributors, and customers, can be enhanced. Employees and their trades unions are provided with an additional focus in their relations with the employer. Indeed, a standard (SA8000), rooted in norms developed by the International Labour Organisation (ILO) and the UN's Universal Declaration of Human Rights, is used by some companies as a basis for reporting on their employee relations. Further, the standing of the company in society, at the local, national, and even international level can be increased.

Sustainability Reporting

In recent years the impact of global business activities has added a further dimension to CSR. Many countries have perceived threats to their environment and, ultimately, to their societies. Calls have been made for sustainable development, which the United Nations' Brundtland Report defined as *development that meets the needs of the present without compromising the ability of future generations to meet their own needs* (1987).

Or to quote the Institute for Research and Innovation in Sustainability in Canada:

sustainability is about living and working in ways that meet and integrate existing environmental, economic and social needs without compromising the well-being of future generations. The transition to sustainable development benefits today's society and builds a more secure future for our children.

Some examples of states' recognition of the need for sustainable development include:

- The European Union established fishing quotas and other fishing limits to sustain fish stocks

- China's Guangdong Province required companies that pollute the ground water table in that region to clear up or close down
- South American and European Union control forestry products to protect the rain forest and to ensure that woodland is sustained by replanting
- One hundred and ninety nations, representing the producers of around half the world's greenhouse gas emissions, ratified the Kyoto Protocol, which commits them to reduce the world's greenhouse gases below 1990 levels by 2012 and ultimately to reverse the greenhouse effect

The General Motors (GM) case, which follows, provides a working example of a recent environmental and sustainability report. For nearly a century, GM has affected the lives of countless people around the world. Today, against an ever more competitive and challenging backdrop, GM remains committed to leading not only from a business standpoint, but economically, socially, and environmentally as well.

GM's Key Performance Indicators (KPIs) for environmental, economic, product, and social criteria are reported in a performance scorecard. The information covers four areas of GM activities—economic, product, environmental, and social. GM policy is to improve their environmental, social, and economic performance continuously. GM's intention is to increase the number of KPIs published each year. The information below is extracted from tables published by GM for their worldwide operations.

Case Study 15.6 General Motors: CSR Key Performance Indicators

Table 15.1 **General Motors: CSR key performance indicators**

Economic Indicators	Quantitative measure	Comment on annual performance
Net sales and revenue	US$	Up 4.3%
Net income	US$	Down 3.4%
Earnings per share	US$ per share	Down 30.1%
Vehicles sales	Number cars and trucks	Up 1.8%
Market share vehicle market	%	Down 0.7%
Product indicators		
Fuel economy (in US) – cars and light trucks	Miles per US gallon	2% and 1% increase
CO_2 emissions (in US) – cars and light trucks	CO_2 per mile by model year	2% and 1% reduction
Quality (in US) GM and industry average	Initial quality problems	7.7/10.5% improvement

Table 15.1 *Continued*

Economic Indicators	Quantitative measure	Comment on annual performance
Environmental indicators		
Energy use	GWh	Reduced 13.6%
CO_2 emissions	Mil. metric tons	Reduced 12.5%
Waste	Mil. metric tons	Reduced 11.5%
Recycling rate	percentage	Increased 4.4%
Water use	mil. cubic meters	Reduced 23.3%
Sites certifies to ISO14001	percentage	117 of 118 facilities have implemented
Social indicators		
Community donations/sponsors	$million	Reduced 6.3%
Employees	number	Reduced 0.6%
Diversity (US)	% female empl'ees	Reduced 1.5%
Diversity (US)	% minority empl'ees	Increased 2.6%
Discrimination charges	number	Reduced 16.7%
Employee satisfaction	% satisfied empl'ees	10% increase in satisfaction
Injury rate	% per 100 empl'ees	Reduced 14.6%
Lost time accident rate	% per 100 empl'ees	Reduced 6.9%

(See www.gm.com/corporate/responsibility/
reports/01/sustainability_and_gm)

Discussion Questions

Consider the KPIs in each of the four areas used by General Motors:

- economic
- product
- environment
- social

1. Are these indicators appropriate?

2. Would you add any others?

3. Are the measures used appropriate? Is the use of percentage changes sound?

An interesting example of one company's commitment to sustainability and the basis of their sustainability development policy follows.

Case Study 15.7 Swire Pacific's Sustainable Development Policy

Swire Pacific Ltd (www.swirepacific.com) is publicly quoted in London and Hong Kong. It operates a diverse range of businesses including Cathay Pacific Airways, property, beverages and Coca-Cola bottling, marine services, trading, retail, and support services for the offshore oil and gas industry worldwide. Consequently, the group adopts a decentralized approach to management.

The board of Swire Pacific accepted the October 2007 UN Environment Agency Report on the Global Environmental Outlook:

> We appear to be living in an era in which the severity of environmental problems are increasing faster than our policy responses. To avoid the threat of catastrophic consequences in the future, we need new policy approaches to change the direction and magnitude of drivers of environmental change and shift environmental policy making to the core of decision making.

The directors believed that the significant problems included global warming, pollution, loss of biodiversity, non-sustainable fishing, non-sustainable use of ground water, depletion of non-renewable resources such as oil, and the risk of population growth outpacing food production. Recognition of the magnitude of the global warming problem and that these increasingly severe environmental problems would undoubtedly impact on the development of their businesses, the company appointed their first Director of Sustainable Development, Robert Gibson, in 2007. The board also endorsed a Sustainable Development programme to be implemented throughout the group (see www.swirepacific.com/eng/global/home.htm).

The chairman of the company, Christopher Pratt, outlined the company's approach to the management of sustainable development as follows:

Swire Pacific Sustainable Development Policy

We adopt this policy because:

- Long term value creation for our shareholders depends on the sustainable development of our businesses and the communities in which we operate.
- We wish to excel as corporate citizens.

Our policy:

- *Industry leadership*: We will work with others to promote sustainable development in the industries in which we operate.
- *In our operations*: We will meet or exceed all legal requirements and:
  - Be a good steward of the natural resources and biodiversity under our influence and ensure that all potential adverse impacts of our operations on the environment are identified and appropriately managed.
  - Operate as far as is reasonably practicable in a manner which safeguards the health and safety of all our stakeholders.
  - Strive to be an employer of choice by providing an environment in which all employees are treated fairly and with respect and can realise their full potential.

- Favour suppliers and contractors who promote sustainable development and encourage the responsible use of our products and services by our customers and consumers.
- Promote good relationships with the communities of which we are a part and enhance their capabilities while respecting people's culture and heritage

Making it happen:

- All companies in which Swire Pacific has a controlling interest will have action plans for applying this policy in a way which is relevant to their business. We will encourage other companies in which we have an interest as a shareholder or through our supply chain to implement similar policies.
- We will encourage and empower our staff to be proactive on sustainable development matters both at work and in the community.
- We will monitor our performance and report regularly.
- We will review this policy periodically, having regard, in particular, to stakeholder dialogues.

The role of each group company:

Management of Sustainable Development includes protecting against risks and taking advantage of opportunities. Responsibility for doing this rests with the line management of operating companies. They are recommended to use the following tools:

For strategy setting:

1. Best in Class (see note below) to set aspirations
2. Enterprise Risk Management to identify business risks
3. Stakeholder Engagement to identify stakeholder issues which may impact the business.

For control:

1. Self Assessment Questionnaires to confirm risk management procedures are being followed.

For reporting:

1. Global Reporting Initiative's framework to report in a consistent manner to stakeholders.

Note: The reporting should be the end result of a comprehensive approach to managing sustainable development. Care should be taken to avoid 'reporting for reporting's sake'. GRI is adopted as it is widely used and provides:

i. A consistent framework for thinking about sustainable development issues enabling all companies to use the same data definitions and terminology.

ii. A checklist to assist companies ensure they cover all important issues.

iii. Flexibility to only report on what is important to a business. For the basic level of GRI reporting it is only necessary to report 10 out the possible 72 performance indicators. This minimises the waste of 'reporting for reporting's sake.'

iv. Material to educate staff on the reporting process.

v. Reports which are more useful to stakeholders because they are based on common definitions and process.

Swire Pacific's oversight role

Swire Pacific provides support in terms of group direction, policies and risk management culture. It requires operating companies to report on their activity so that risks can be monitored and overall risk exposure managed at group level.

Note: The 'Best in Class' process was started in 2007 for climate change issues. (https://webmail.pp.jsshk.com:8001/jrg/Drafts/RE:%20Swire.EML?Cmd= reply&Create=0#_ftn1)

Companies are encouraged to extend it to other environmental stewardship issues which are relevant to their business. The process involves answering the following questions for each issue under consideration.

1. What industry is your company in and which leading companies in that industry can you take as a 'Peer Group'?

2. What, from examining your 'Peer Group', is best in class behaviour for your industry?

3. For important items where your Peer Group is doing better than you what do you need to do to catch up and how much is this going to cost?

The process should identify differences between current business operations and the 'best' possible way of meeting customer demand. This can clarify risks the business is exposed to and set aspirations for improvement. Best in Class performance will improve as technology advances and other changes affect the world. The speed with which a company moves towards its 'best in class' aspirations should be decided by its board and management taking into account commercial considerations. If a company owns long-life assets which are not 'best in class' then there may be strong commercial reasons for retaining these assets rather than investing in new 'best in class' assets. A key element of defining 'best in class' on climate change issues is to define green house gas emission and energy intensity metrics appropriate to gauging progress in each industry.

(See www.swirepacific.com and www.swire.com)

Discussion Questions

1. Where is the boundary between 'Enterprise Risk Management' and 'Managing for Sustainable Development'?

2. The board of Swire Pacific made the 2007 UN Environment Agency Report on the Global Environmental Outlook the basis for their sustainable development strategy. Are the policies that flow from this view consistent with maximizing shareholder value?

3. The Swire Pacific group operates in a diverse range of industries from airlines to Coca Cola bottling. Is the pursuit of a group wide sustainable development programme realistic?

The Global Reporting Initiative (GRI)

The Global Reporting Initiative (GRI), which was sparked by the UN work mentioned earlier, is a worldwide, multi-stakeholder network to create and develop a sustainability reporting framework, in which business, civil society, labour, investors, accountants, and others collaborate. The GRI is based on the underlying belief that reporting on economic, environmental, and social performance by all organizations should be as routine and comparable as financial reporting. The GRI facilitates transparency and accountability by organizations of all sizes and sectors, across the world—companies, governmental and other public agencies, and non-profit entities.

The sustainability reporting guidelines provide the cornerstone for the sustainability reporting framework, which provides organizations with the basis for disclosure about sustainability performance, and stakeholders with a universally recognized comparable framework to assess such information. The guidelines consist of reporting principles and guidance, with standard disclosures and performance indicators.

Figure 15.2 provides an outline of the sustainability reporting guidelines.

The principles and guidance section of the framework defines the sustainability report's content, which helps to determine where its boundaries should be drawn. The content principles cover materiality, stakeholder inclusiveness, sustainability context, and completeness, along with a brief set of tests for each principle. The quality principles cover balance, comparability, accuracy, timeliness, reliability, and clarity, along with tests that can be used to help achieve the appropriate quality of the reported information.

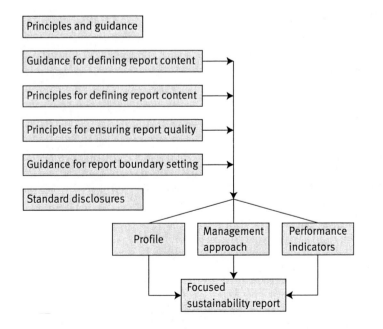

Figure 15.2 Outline of the sustainability reporting guidelines

The standard disclosures section of the framework has guidelines that identify the information that is relevant and material to most organizations and of interest to most stakeholders.

Three types of standard disclosure are included:

- The organization's profile—information that sets the overall context for understanding the organization's performance including its strategy, profile, and governance
- The organization's management approach—information about the organization that provides the context for understanding its performance
- Performance indicators—which provide information on the economic, environmental, and social performance of the organization

The GRI is being adopted by many organizations around the world: hundreds of companies based in many countries disclosed sustainability reports last year using the GRI framework. In addition many other companies, particularly those operating globally, have developed their own approaches to environmental and sustainability reporting.

As corporate sustainability becomes increasingly important, systems are being developed to manage the masses of data involved to produce regular CSR and sustainability reports. Software has been developed to use a company's existing intranet facilities to collect and collate the necessary information.

Balancing Corporate Responsibilities

Every board has to balance its overall responsibility to investors with obligations to employees, suppliers, distributors, customers, non-equity sources of finance, local communities affected by their decisions, and for environmental impacts their company might have, as well as with broader societal expectations, whilst staying within the laws of the countries in which they operate. But the challenge to corporate directors, to establish CSR strategies and policies, and to balance competing claims on resources, is significant.

Microsoft provides a useful example. Most people would agree that this company has been superbly successful and made a significant impact in the world of information technology. Its software drives countless business and personal computers in every country in the world. We have studied its corporate values and mission statement earlier. Its founder, Bill Gates, continues to donate massive sums of his wealth derived from the company, through the Bill and Melinda Gates Foundation, to enhance health-care and reduce extreme poverty around the world, and, in the United States, to expand educational opportunities and access to information technology. Yet the European Union and the United States government both continue to challenge the company with massive legal battles claiming monopolistic practices, and attempting to reduce Microsoft's domination of the marketplace.

In non-profit entities the governing bodies' primary duty is to its members, but broader societal responsibilities have also to be balanced. Boards need to make choices. Inertia inevitably leads to unresolved dilemmas.

Each board has to be the conscience of its company. Directors need to provide the company with its moral compass. In fulfilling its role the board is responsible for considering the potential effect of the strategies it formulates, for identifying the likely impact of policies it approves, both short and long term, for recognizing possible outcomes on people, and for accepting its duty to be accountable. As we have already seen every board has a duty to formulate the company's strategy, recognizing the risks involved. Part of that process involves determining how the company will behave; in other words establishing how social responsibility will be exercised throughout the enterprise. A company does not have morals: directors do.

REFERENCES AND FURTHER READING

Banks, Erik (2004) *Corporate Governance: Financial Responsibility, Controls and Ethics.* New York: Palgrave Macmillan.

Chandler, David and William B. Werther Jr. (2005) *Corporate Social Responsibility: Stakeholders in a Global Environment.* London: Sage.

Cramer, Jacqueline (2006) *Corporate Social Responsibility and Globalisation: An Action Plan for Business.* Sheffield: Greenleaf Publishing.

Crowther, David and Lez Rayman-Bacchus (eds.) (2004) *Perspectives on Corporate Social Responsibility.* London: Ashgate Publishing.

Grayson, David and Adrian Hodges (2004) *Corporate Social Opportunity: 7 Steps to Make Corporate Social Responsibility Work for Your Business.* Sheffield: Greenleaf Publishing.

Habisch, André et al. (eds.) (2005) *Corporate Social Responsibility across Europe.* London: Springer.

Hamschmidt, Jost (2007) *Cases in Sustainability Management and Strategy: The Oikos Collection.* Sheffield: Greenleaf Publishing.

Hancock, John (2004) *Investing in Corporate Social Responsibility: A Guide to Best Practice, Business Planning and the UK's Leading Companies.* London: FTSE.

Kotler, Philip and Nancy Lee (2004) *Corporate Social Responsibility: Doing the Most Good for your Company and your Cause.* New Jersey: John Wiley and Sons.

Raynard, Peter (ed.) (2006) *Tomorrow's History: An Anthology of Simon Zadek's Work.* Sheffield: Greenleaf Publishing. (Academy of Management's 2006 SIM book prize.)

Sims, Ronald R. (2003) *Ethics and Corporate Social Responsibility: Why Giants Fall.* Westport, CT: Praeger/Greenwood.

Stationery Office (UK) (2006) 'How to Use the CSR Competency Framework'. A resource pack for using the CSR Competency Framework. Available at: www.tso.co.uk

Reich, Robert B. (2006) *Supercapitalism: The Transformation of Business, Democracy and Everyday Life.* Londong: Borzoi Books/Random House.

Rezaee, Zabihollah, Lynn Turner and Diane L. Swanson (2008) *Corporate Governance and Ethics.* Chichester: Wiley.

Schaltegger, Stephan and Marcus Wagner (eds.) (2006) *Managing the Business Case for Sustainability: The Integration of Social, Environmental and Economic Performance.* Sheffield: Greenleaf Publishing.

Waddock, Sandra and Charles Bodwell (2007) *Total Responsibility Management: The Manual.* Sheffield: Greenleaf Publishing.

Zadek, Simon and Malcolm McIntosh (2000) 'Accountability and Governance', *Journal of Corporate Citizenship*, Winter, No. 8.

Zerk, Jennifer A. (2006) *Multinationals and Corporate Social Responsibility: Limitations and Opportunities in International Law*. Cambridge: Cambridge University Press.

USEFUL WEBSITES

www.article13.com
Advisor on CSR policy and strategy.

www.business-ethics.com
Business Ethics—the journal for corporate responsibility.

www.ceres.org/sustreporting
Sustainability reporting.

www.complianceweek.com
Newsletter on corporate governance, risk, and compliance.

www.csracademy.org.uk/managermindsets.htm
Business in the Community—CSR Academy.

www.csr.gov.uk
UK Government gateway to corporate social responsibility.

www.csrwire.com
News items on CSR.

www.esp-net.com
Software for tracking and reporting on CSR and sustainability.

www.gm.com
(follow link through 'investors' and 'corporate information') General Motors corporate governance and corporate responsibility reports.

www.sustainability-reports.com
Portal for sustainability reports of multinational companies all over the world.

www.sustreport.org
Canadian Institute for Research and Innovation in Sustainability. The Sustainability Report.

PROJECTS AND EXERCISES

1. Develop a CSR policy statement for any organization with which you are familiar. It could be, for example, for a profit orientated company, an academic institution, or some other 'not-for-profit' enterprise. Develop a set of performance indicators to monitor and measure the organization's achievements.

2. Use the Internet to find and compare the CSR statements of a variety of companies around the world. Prepare a report/presentation with your findings.

3. Develop a sustainability report for an organization with which you are familiar.

SELF-TEST QUESTIONS

To confirm your grasp of the key points in this chapter try answering the following questions. Answers are at the end of the book.

1. Name six types of stakeholder that a company might have.

2. What might a firm's socially responsible activities include?

3. Is there a link between CSR and economic performance?

4. What is the Global Reporting Initiative and who is involved?

5. How does the Brundtland Report define sustainable development?

6. What is the underlying belief of the Global Reporting Initiative (GRI)?

7. What is GRI?

8. What does GRI facilitate?

9. What do the principles and guidance section of the GRI framework provide?

10. What do the content principles of the GRI framework cover?

16   The Future of Corporate Governance

....

- In which we consider:
  - some remaining questions
  - driving forces for change
  - what might the future look like?

So we come to the final chapter of this text book, but not to the end of the story of corporate governance. The 19th century saw the foundations laid for modern corporations: that was the century of the entrepreneur. The 20th century became the century of management, with new management theories, management gurus, and management consultants. But the 21st century promises to be the century of corporate governance.

Around the world, in large and small enterprises, in the public and the private sectors, governance has become the focus of attention. The exercise of power over corporate entities, the legitimacy of companies and their directors, the effectiveness of governing bodies, and their accountability in society have become crucial topics. The field of corporate governance is expanding and changing dramatically and fast. Twenty-five years ago the phrase 'corporate governance' was not used: at the time of writing googling the phrase provided 18,500,000 entries.

Some Remaining Questions

Of course, some of the issues that we have discussed remain unresolved. Let us review some of the more important ones before concluding with a look to the future.

Should Corporate Governance Practices be Based on Rules or Principles?

This is a fundamental issue that goes to the heart of the way corporate governance is practised. We saw earlier how companies listed in the United States are required to abide by the corporate governance rules enshrined in SEC and stock exchanges' regulations, and in the law under the Sarbanes-Oxley (SOX) Act. Similarly, financial accounts filed in the United States need to abide by US accounting standards, which are also rule based, although recently the SEC has moved towards accepting accounts framed under international accounting standards.

By contrast, companies listed in the United Kingdom, the Commonwealth, and 'OECD-code' countries are expected to comply with the principles of their country's code, unless the circumstances are such that the board concludes that the principles do not fit the company's situation, in which case they need to report that they have not followed the code and explain why: the classical 'comply or explain' approach to corporate governance. Similarly international accounting standards are principles based, not rule based.

Both rule based and principles based corporate governance have their proponents. The convergence/differentiation debate has a long way to go.

Should the Chairman also be the Chief Executive Officer?

Most codes of good corporate governance practice recommend that the roles of chairman of the board and CEO should be held by different people, thus providing checks and balances against the domination of decision making and over-enthusiastic risk-taking by a single all-powerful individual. A few codes, however, do recognize that in some circumstances a single leader may be appropriate, but in that case a strong group of non-executives is needed with their own appointed leader.

However, in the United States the roles of chairman and CEO of listed companies are frequently combined in a single, powerful individual, who leads the company in both managerial and governance matters. The independent outside directors provide a check and balance mechanism, supported by independent external auditors and the requirements of the SOX Act, SEC regulations, and the stock exchanges rules.

The question is which is preferable: a dominant leader, who can provide single-minded leadership and enhance performance, or shared responsibility, which reduces risk? This duality question remains unanswered.

A related matter concerns board size and structure. In the United States companies take credit for the large proportion of independent non-executive directors (INEDs) compared with executive directors. The chairman/CEO may be supported by no more than one or two top executives, perhaps the COO and the CFO. A similar trend has occurred in the United Kingdom, although the chairman and CEO roles are separated. In recent years the boards of many listed companies have fewer executive directors and more INEDs. But some chairmen, in the UK, argue that board discussions benefit from having a larger group of top management on the board. Of course, these executives could be invited to attend board meetings without being appointed directors. Concern has also been expressed that fewer executive directors makes the chairman's task of keeping the INEDs well informed more difficult.

Should a Retiring CEO Ever Become Chairman of the Board?

Some corporate governance codes recommend or require that retiring CEOs do not move into the chairmanship of the same company. This issue has been hotly debated in principle. It has also raised practical difficulties in some companies.

Arguments in favour of allowing the retiring CEO to become chairman recognize that a retiring CEO has accumulated experience of the company, the business, and the board, which it would be a pity to lose. The retiring CEO is known by fellow directors and senior managers. His or her personal qualities—integrity, leadership, and communication skills—are also well known and appreciated. So risks associated with introducing a new chairman are reduced. Moreover, the retiring CEO is known and trusted by investors, customers, employees, and all those dealing with the company. Quite a strong case, it would appear.

Yet, the arguments against allowing a retiring CEO to become chairman are also formidable. Chairmanship of the board, it is argued, is a quite different role from that of CEO: strong performance at one does not guarantee success at the other. Past experience, moreover, quickly decays in a rapidly changing world. Finally, and probably most significantly, a retiring CEO on becoming chairman needs to pass on the powers and duties of top management to his or her successor. The outgoing CEO may find handing over these reins difficult, and the successor may have problems with establishing appropriate relations with the chairman. As we have seen, the relationship between CEO and chairman is one of the most subtle yet vital in corporate governance.

The question of whether the retiring CEO should become chairman of the board remains unanswered around the world.

Can Outside Independent Directors be Genuinely Independent?

A basic tenet of corporate governance codes for unitary boards rests on the use of outside, non-executive directors who are independent of management. Independence broadly means having no interest in the enterprise, which could affect the exercise of objective judgement. Although many codes and stock exchange regulations, as we have seen, now define 'independence' in considerable detail.

But can any director be genuinely independent, and be seen by the outside world to be independent, when his or her nomination to the board came from existing members of that board, including the chairman and the CEO? Surely, there is a danger that such INEDs will feel a sense of commitment and loyalty to him or her, which could affect the exercising of objective judgement.

As members of a unitary board, INEDs have to work closely with the CEO and the other executive directors, so it is important that they form an effective team. But, can INEDs be really independent when they are part of the board team, working closely with the executive directors on strategic and other matters? How can independence be shown if they are personally involved with determining the issues they are supposed to be monitoring?

Another dilemma is that the longer an independent director serves, the more his independence is likely to be compromised as he becomes enmeshed in board culture. Conversely, the more an INED knows about the company and its business, the greater his potential contribution. The paradox is that the greater the director's independence the less he knows about the company. How long does it take from an INED to become so much a part of the board that he is no longer independent? Some codes now suggest a period of service after which an outside director will no longer be considered independent. Some companies also limit the terms of INEDs to not more than two or three appointments of three years each.

As we have seen, a different approach is adopted in Continental Europe, in the two-tier board. The upper supervisory board consists entirely of outside directors, who monitor and control the work of the lower, executive board, who run the enterprise. Here the independence issue arises in a different form. Since members of a supervisory board are appointed to represent the interests of various stakeholder groups—capital, labour, and, in some countries, society—their ability to apply objective, independent judgement may be distorted by their allegiance to the interests of the groups they represent. Indeed, as a result, relationships within a supervisory board can become adversarial.

For example, in the German company Volkswagen, half of the supervisory board members represented employee interests. All were German. Could they be independent when the company proposed shifting production to Brazil? The other half of the board included representatives of major banks, who were also major creditors of the company. Could they be independent when considering strategic exposure to risk?

Proponents of the unitary board emphasize the value of having executive and non-executive directors working together, drawing on outside experience and perspective to identify key issues and formulate strategy. But independence can lead to remoteness. The more remote outside directors are from the workings of the company the lower their contribution to board strategy formulation and executive supervision may be. Many of the vignette cases in this book have shown problems arising from independent, but out-of-touch, non-executive directors.

What is the answer? Independence in directors is a matter of character, personal ability, and independence of mind, not of precise definitions. Codes establish boundaries, but only practice can determine the real contribution that an independent non-executive director makes.

Should Shareholders be Able to Nominate Directors?

In the original 19th century model of the corporation, directors were nominated and elected by the shareholders of the company and reported to them on their stewardship of the shareholders' funds. But the quantity, dispersion, and variety of shareholders now means that this is no longer possible, except in small and medium-sized companies, subsidiary companies, and family firms. In large listed companies it is usual for the board, on the advice of their nominating committee, to propose the names of directors for shareholders' approval at the AGM. No vehicle exists in many listed companies for shareholders to propose an alternative slate of names. Proposals have recently been heard in both the US and the UK for shareholders to be given better opportunities to propose candidates. Predictably, this suggestion has not been welcomed in many board rooms, where the opportunity to determine who joins them at the table is jealously guarded. The right to influence the membership of a board is powerful.

An alternative approach, advocated by Shann Turnbull in Australia, is for a separate forum of shareholder representatives. Modelled on the successful Spanish Mondragon worker cooperatives, he has applied the concept to public companies that he has formed. His 'corporate senate' has three members, elected by the shareholders on the basis of one vote per shareholder, not one vote per share as in the traditional model. The senate, although it is a form of dual board structure, has no proactive power except the right to veto where it feels the board has a conflict of interest. Turnbull's rationale is that '*most corporations in the English speaking world are essentially corrupt because their unitary board structures create conflicts of interest and concentrate corporate power*'.

Should Institutional Investors Exercise More Power Over Listed Companies?

Many commentators have called for institutional investors to '*exercise their power*' and vote the shares they hold at company meetings. But despite these calls, many fund managers show relatively little interest in the governance of companies in which they invest, preferring to 'do the Wall Street walk' or 'vote with their feet' by trading their shares rather than incurring the costs of involvement in governance, and risk getting locked in with a falling share price.

The primary responsibility of institutional investors, such as investment trusts, mutual funds, unit trusts, life assurance companies, and banks running portfolios for clients is to their members or investors. If they do vote their shares, it must be in the interests of those beneficial owners, whose objectives may well differ from each other. Some regulations now require institutional investors to declare whether and how they have voted their shares. A related question, of growing importance when a stock price falls, is how institutional investors, themselves, are held accountable if they had become proactive in governance?

Are External Auditors Really Independent?

Independent external auditors play a fundamental role in corporate governance systems throughout the world. Their principle role is to reassure the investors and others by reporting that the reports and financial accounts, produced by the directors, truly and fairly reflect the state of the company's affairs. Clearly, to fulfil this role objectively, they need to be independent of the company and its directors. But if the company appoints the auditors, pays them for their services, and is one of their clients, can the auditor then be seen as truly independent? Does not this economic dependency infringe their independence?

In the 19th century concept of the company the importance of an audit of the managers' reports to the members was recognized and provided by an audit committee drawn from among the shareholders. The increasing sophistication of accounting and financial reporting, during the second half of the 19th century, saw the arrival of professional auditors, the establishment of small audit firms, and formation of accounting professional bodies: the first being in Scotland in 1855. Today the auditing and accounting profession is global and vast, with hundreds of thousands of firms providing services to millions of companies and other enterprises.

There is a dilemma. In effect, auditors serve two masters—the shareholders and the company. There is a potential conflict of interest between satisfying the interests of the shareholders, for whom they provide an independent external check on the directors, and the company and its directors, with whom they must work closely and who determine their fees.

Moreover, the audit of large companies around the world today is dominated by just four firms. There were five but the Enron collapse led to the demise of Andersen and reduced the number by a 5th overnight (see the Arthur Andersen case for more information). These four firms, though closely involved with the accounting professional bodies and the accounting regulators around the world, are larger and more economically powerful than any of them.

In no other profession have legislatures allowed such market domination. An unresolved question is how the audit profession will evolve in the years ahead. Some believe that the second tier of smaller accounting firms will grow to be capable of auditing large global companies. Others point out that audit by one of the 'big four' bestows legitimacy on the accounts of companies, adding that the 'big four' are also unlikely to give up market share easily. A further potential problem is what would happen if the big four were reduced to the 'big three' by another Arthur Andersen style debacle.

The audit process necessarily involves a close and continuing relationship between auditor and company. The lead auditor from the audit firm is likely to spend a lot of time with his client's finance director and other senior executives; his more junior colleagues will become familiar with all aspects of the enterprise. Obviously, this familiarity with the company and knowledge of its business, and a close relationship between auditor and client is valuable.

But the formal audit can also provide a platform for the audit firm to offer non-audit work to their client, such as tax consulting, management consulting, or information technology services. Prior to the Enron debacle, many of the global accounting firms were earning more in non-audit work from their clients than the audit fee. Some even suggested that firms used the audit fee as a 'loss-leader' to attract other more profitable consulting work. Under these circumstances could an auditor still be, and be seen to be, independent of the client?

Post Enron, the SOX Act created a new regulatory regime for auditors in the US. Other corporate governance codes and stock exchange regulations also tackled the auditor independence issue. In many jurisdictions today the type of additional services that an audit firm can offer to its audit client are strictly limited. Essentially, an auditor should not undertake any advisory or consulting work that would subsequently be audited by the same firm. As a result many audit firms hived off their consulting work.

Various other proposals have been suggested to resolve the auditor independence dilemma, including the periodic rotation of audit partners, which is now required by SOX and some codes, and a mandatory change of auditors every few years, which has been strenuously resisted by the auditing profession. Senior auditors are also now not allowed to join the finance staff of their client firm, by SOX and some codes, until an appropriate passage of time had elapsed, reducing the immediacy of their connections but possibly also lowering their immediate value to the client firm.

Another possibility, which we will consider when we look to the future, is that states become proactive in the governance of large companies operating in their territories including an involvement in the audit process.

How Should Directors' Remuneration be Determined?

In the 1980s a major concern in corporate governance was the ways directors protected themselves from hostile takeover (see Box 16.1). More recently, the interest has focused on director remuneration, particularly the remuneration of executive directors. The top management of large listed corporations wield enormous power. Claiming to reflect owners' interests, directors are seen by some to be pursuing their own agendas and extracting huge rewards—privileges reserved in earlier generations for aristocrats and kings.

Institutional investors in both the US and the UK have challenged the levels of director rewards and, prompted by an investigative media, the issue has attracted the attention of the general public. Although, given the work done and the risks involved, it is a legitimate question in some companies whether director remuneration is sufficient. But the real concern is about directors' rewards that appear excessive, or even directors who are apparently rewarded for failure.

Box 16.1 Classical Phraseology of Corporate Governance

- Fat cats—a media term to describe directors with allegedly excessive remuneration packages
- Golden handcuffs—a term in a director's remuneration contract granting significant rewards provided he or she remains with the company for a given period
- Golden hello—a large one-off payment made to an incoming executive director to persuade him or her to join the company
- Golden parachutes—large severance payments given to directors on leaving a company, often offered in connection with a takeover bid
- Golden share—a single share in a company with special rights which grant overall voting control in the event of a specific event, usually a takeover bid
- Green mail—buying shares in the anticipation of a takeover bid with the intention of forcing one side to buy them at a premium to retain or gain control
- Poison pills—devices introduced by a board to deter potential predators. Examples include giving existing shareholders, other than the bidder, the right to acquire shares on beneficial terms in the event of a bid, thus increasing the cost of buying control
- White knight—a company that rides to the rescue of a company threatened by a hostile takeover bid, usually by buying shares

---

Although the justification for most director remuneration schemes is the maximization of long term shareholder value, the bias of power on many boards in favour of incumbent executive directors can mean that remuneration schemes are structured to benefit top executives at the expense of the shareholders. The practical question is: how should directors' remuneration be determined?

The preferred solution in the corporate governance literature, as we saw, is for a board remuneration committee, comprised entirely of independent outside directors, to determine executive director remuneration. The problem with this, again as we saw, is whether such directors can be seen to be genuinely independent or are really members of the 'directors club'. Other proposals for monitoring directors' rewards have included mandatory shareholder voting on director rewards or legislation that would impose statutory duties and rewards. The issue remains largely unresolved.

What is the Future for the Corporation?

For this book, this has to be the ultimate question. The mid-19th century gave us the public company, designed to incorporate corporate entities that can attract funds from outside investors without making them personally liable for that company's debts. The early 20th century brought the private company, which was not set up to attract outside funds, but to enable traders, family firms, and other owner-managed businesses to limit the liability of their owners for the company's debts. The later years of the 20th century saw a bludgeoning of diversity using the corporate form for vast group pyramids, geared ownership chains, complex corporate networks, joint ventures, and many different types of ownership. Whether boards should be responsible to other stakeholders as well as shareholders remains an open question.

What might future social and economic historians report for the 21st century? Let us look to the future. What forces are driving changes in corporate governance thinking and practice? How might societies' expectations change? What might corporate governance look like in a decade or two? By considering such questions we can prepare ourselves and our companies, and better make positive contributions to developments.

Driving Forces for Change

Sources of Change

The driving forces in corporate governance thinking and practice have often come from the United States. Federal protection for investors and the regulation of listed companies dates back to the 1930s, with the creation of the SEC. America's current pre-eminence in corporate governance reflects the vast amounts of capital provided through reliable and liquid markets, the availability of sophisticated legal and accountancy services, the existence of well developed investor information systems, with strong and trusted regulation, backed up by a massive and successful economy, challenged, admittedly, by the 2008 crisis.

American institutional investors, such as CalPers, have influenced corporate governance practices in the overseas countries in which they invest, by demanding US governance norms. On a theoretical level, more academic research and publications on corporate governance have come from American scholars than the rest of the world combined.

But the passing of the SOX Act in 2002 added a new dimension and increased the influence of US governance practices on governance thinking worldwide. Most significantly, it reinforced and emphasized the rule based underpinning of American corporate governance a mandatory and legal 'obey or face the consequences' regime.

But the focus is changing. In recent years corporate governance initiatives have originated in other countries, starting with the influential 1992 Cadbury Report on the financial aspects of corporate governance from the UK. As we have seen, many other countries then produced their own governance codes, followed by international codes from organizations such as the OECD and the World Bank. As we have seen the underpinning philosophy of these codes has been principles based, not rule based, a voluntary and judgemental 'conform or explain' regime.

International access to US funds is becoming less important as other economies, including the Middle East and China, generate surpluses on the back of oil prices and economic growth. Emerging economies, such as China and India may need less inward investment. Other finance markets are growing in scale, sophistication, and reputation. Therefore, the pressure to adopt American corporate governance processes is less marked and corporate governance initiatives from other financial markets and company law jurisdictions may become more significant.

Moreover, the expensive regulatory demands and, as some perceive them, challenging attitudes of SOX, SEC regulation, and US listing rules could be a disincentive for non-US companies to list in the United States. The lighter regulatory touch of other jurisdictions and financial markets are seen as more attractive, with their call to comply with corporate governance principles (or explain why not), rather than strictly adhere to legally binding rules risking litigation or even prosecution. The costs of compliance in some of these markets may also be lower. Successful capital markets will inevitably be those that are judged effective by their users—both those investing and those raising capital.

International Drivers for Change

Elements of the OECD Corporate Governance Principles and the Commonwealth Corporate Governance Code have been reflected in the codes of other countries, and principles based corporate governance is now commonplace. As we discussed in chapter 8, some significant forces around the world are tending to keep corporate governance practices differentiated (culture, legal systems, and economic development, for example).

But some international developments continue to contribute to convergence. Significant international forces for change include:

- The application of International Accounting Standards (IAS), which have already been adopted within the European Union and many other countries. The Generally Accepted Accounting Principles (GAAP) of the United States are slowly converging and the SEC now allows companies to use IAS

- The regulation of financial markets under the influence of the International Organisation of Securities Commissions (IOSCO)

- The development of electronic trading in stocks, which promotes international securities trading

- Cross-border mergers of stock markets, which is changing country-centric investment dealing

- The impact of institutional investors, hedge funds, and other sources of funds for international investment

- The effect of private equity funding, which is changing the investment scene. Owners of significant private companies may decide not to list in the first place. Major investors in public companies may find an incentive to privatize. Overall the existence of private equity funds challenges boards of listed companies by sharpening the market for corporate control. As the power of private equity grows expect calls for more transparency, accountability and control

Looking further ahead, the rapidly growing and massive economic potential of China, followed by India, and subsequently an energy-led Russia are likely to have effects on corporate governance practices. No doubt economic downturns, political interference, corporate collapses, top management domination, fraud, misfeasance, and other problems will emerge en route, but the future of corporate governance is unlikely to look like its past.

The Development of New Organizational Forms

Another significant driving force is likely to be the emergence of new organizational forms. The original corporate concept did not envisage the complexity of today's organizational structures. As we saw in chapter 4, international business these days often involves complex networks of subsidiary and associated companies, companies with off-balance sheet vehicles, chains of companies giving leveraged power to companies at the top of the chain, limited partnerships controlling listed companies, groups with cross-holdings of shares and cross-directorships, and other networks with joint ventures and strategic alliances. Frequently, these networks of corporate interest operate in multiple jurisdictions, cultures, and currencies. They may have voracious appetites for growth, with the attendant risks.

Such entities raise significant questions for corporate governance and financial reporting—as the employees, creditors, and shareholders of Enron discovered. Moreover, these organizational forms can be dynamic and evolve rapidly. Corporate regulation and financial disclosure rules are struggling to keep pace. Corporate governance processes have to respond, and directors must be sensitive to the implications of operating with complex, dynamic organizational and financial forms. How complex, dynamic, and often global corporate entities are governed provides a major challenge for the future.

Society's Changing Expectations

Just as economic and political forces around the world are driving change in corporate governance, society's changing expectations, particularly in the developed world, are also prompting change. As we saw in chapter 15, society's expectations of corporate entities operating in their midst are broadening. Norms for corporate social responsibility and sustainability are becoming commonplace in the advanced world. Eventually, they are likely to be written into regulations and law. Current initiatives in this area by the United Nations are diffuse, but may well be taken up at national level. Corporate governance rating criteria are likely to consolidate and standards emerge. The inevitable differences between cultures, jurisdictions, and stages of economic development could be recognized more specifically in defining governance requirements, and appropriate risk profiles could be created, avoiding the process of merely adopting advanced country norms.

Just as society's expectations of corporate entities are changing, so are its expectations of the performance and behaviour of individual directors. The concept of good governance is founded on trust. If a corporate entity is to be trusted, its governing body must be trusted, and that means that individual directors must be trusted, too. Honesty, integrity, openness, putting the needs of the members ahead of personal interest are inherent in the idea of good governance. This perspective is likely to be reinforced in the years ahead as the pressures on corporate entities and the challenges facing directors expand.

New Theoretical Drivers of Change

At the moment there is no universally accepted theory of corporate governance, as we saw in chapter 9. The relationships between corporate governance practices and corporate, board, or individual director performance are unclear. Potentially research developments can improve this situation. Fundamental rethinking may follow the recognition that agency theoretical insights, whilst producing statistically significant conclusions, are strictly bounded by a limited and questionable model of reality.

New fields for research into corporate governance may include academic perspectives other than those of financial economics, including interpersonal, behavioural, or political concepts. New models, frameworks, and concepts are needed and are likely to emerge. Systems theory offers the potential of a better understanding of boundaries, levels, and input/output relationships. Corporate governance could be studied as an information process. Other insights could come from studies of the socio-politics of boards, seeing board and board committees as teams, as networks of interactions.

The concept of power applied to owners, governing bodies, and other power brokers might repay further exploration. The psychology of boards and the individual motivations of key players could also offer other insights. New thinking and better understanding might emerge on board leadership and the style of the chairman. The culture of the board or the study of interactions and perceptions all offer potential research avenues. A real problem with corporate governance research is getting access to the boardroom. But that is being overcome and further rigorous studies are likely to be reported.

Of singular importance might be the development of an accepted taxonomy of corporate entities. The current simple distinction between public companies, which permit the raising of outside investment, and private companies, which do not, is naive. The new taxonomy would enable all types of entity to be distinguished and classified—including entities in the public sector, and the not-for-profit sector as well as private sector profit generating entities. It would, therefore, need to extend beyond the classical model where ownership is the basis of power over the entity.

Clearly, investment is not the only basis for the exercise of power over a corporate entity. In the future it may be seen that this is not even the best way. There are many alternative bases. Some of them have already been tried. But a brief review may provide some pointers for the future:

• The monarch or the church

This is the ancient way that power was wielded over valuable resources.

• The federal state

This is power exercised by government or a ruling elite, and was typically rooted in political dogma, even though sometimes euphemistically referred to as governance by 'the people'. The mid-20th century structures in China and Russia provide salutary warnings of the effect of centralized state planning and control. The privatization of many state run enterprises, which were seen in the later years of the 20th century, such as the de-nationalization of British railways, power utilities, and water enterprises, reflected a shift towards the investor-power model. Although, in most cases, the state retained influence, sometimes through a shareholding, or formally through regulators and informally through political processes.

• Communities at the state, regional, or local level

Many community organizations have been created over the years to manage resources, provide local facilities, and run utilities. The 2008 global financial crisis forced some states to take over significant financial institutions.

- Customers, consumers, or clients

  The late 19th century saw the establishment of consumer cooperatives, savings and loan associations (building societies), mutual insurance associations, and self-help societies, in which the ultimate arbiters of governance were governing bodies elected by the registered member organizations.

- Members

  Many organizations, including some charitable bodies, trades unions, professions such as accountancy, law, and medicine, and academic institutions are governed by a council or other governing body, appointed by the members.

- Suppliers

  Some organizations have been formed to provide services to suppliers in an industry or market, for example farmers and growers cooperatives in Canada and Australia. Governance is provided by a governing body elected by the members of the organization.

- Employees

  Governance by the employees of an enterprise have been arranged by the employees holding shares in companies, as in United Airlines in the United States and the John Lewis partnership in the UK, or through worker cooperatives as in the Mondragon worker cooperative in Spain.

- Listed companies with no dominant individual or block holders
- Listed companies with a dominant investor, including government or a parent company
- Wholly or partly owned subsidiary or associated companies
- Not-for-profit companies with guarantors not shareholders
- Corporate entities mandated by government
- Non-government organizations (NGOs)
- Self-governing social organizations
- The management of an enterprise
- The partners in a professional or other partnership
- The partners in a joint venture
- Family firms and private companies
- Sole traders

Each of these arrangements can provide the base for wielding power over corporate resources, in other words for corporate governance. So far a great deal of corporate governance thinking has been focused on the governance of listed companies. The list above suggests that there is considerable scope for further work.

The Rate of Change

Of course, the pace of change will not be steady. In some cases, as following the collapse of Enron and the 2008 crisis, catastrophic events will drive rapid change. In other cases, change may be glacially slow. Vested interests, faith in traditional approaches, and basic human resistance to change will, inevitably, slow the rate of change. (See the University of Oxford case below.) Past experience of corporate governance enables one prediction to be made with certainty: corporate governance has not reached a steady state, so change will continue. New ways of governing, breakthroughs in information technology, imaginative ideas, and findings from research could all stimulate change. But it does look, as we have said before, that the 21st century will be seen as the century of corporate governance.

Case Study 16.1 The Governance of the University of Oxford

Oxford is a collegiate university, each college having its own constitution, finances, and governance. The University awards degrees and provides facilities for scientific research, libraries, museums, and other central facilities, and is the recipient of UK government funds, some of which are passed to the colleges.

Not surprisingly change tends to come slowly in an ancient institution. It took many years in the late 19th century for the study of science to be accepted and nearly as long for management studies to be recognized in the late 20th. Predictably, the governing bodies of each college guard their independence jealously.

Governance of the University is in the hands of the members of Congregation (over 4,000)—self-rule by the dons—which elects members to a Council composed largely of dons, which oversees the running of the University's finances and administration.

A review of corporate governance, starting in 2000, led to a proposal for a governing body composed half of dons and half of independent outside members, which would approve budgets and oversee the University's affairs. The Vice Chancellor, Dr John Hood argued that only thus could Oxford retain its international pre-eminence. The proposals had the backing of the UK Government's Higher Education Funding Council and the University's Chancellor Lord Patten.

However, Congregation had other ideas and voted convincingly against the proposals.

Discussion Questions

1. What do you think of the new form of governance proposed by the Vice-Chancellor and widely supported outside Oxford?

2. Would you have recommended introducing the new form of governance in a different way? How pertinent were the objections?

3. How are other universities governed?

What Might the Future Look Like?

Some things are relatively easy to predict, being rather obvious developments of current situations. Let us review some of these first.

The Choice of Directors

New ways are likely to be developed to identify and select suitable directors, particularly independent directors. The new approaches will avoid domination by existing directors or major shareholders. In listed companies, shareholders may be invited to nominate directors. Institutional investors may play a specific role. Some form of proportional representation, such as cumulative voting could be used to give shareholders a greater influence.

Shann Turnbull (2006) made an important submission to the Australian authorities when he proposed that

instead of the Australian Stock Exchange Principles specifying the appointment of independent directors, and the conditions of what might make them independent, it would be much simpler to invite companies to report the arrangements they have in place to achieve (what) independent directors (are now) expected to achieve: protect minority investors from dominant shareholders and directors, protect the company from unfair related party transactions, protect the rights of employees, protect the rights of other stakeholders, and protect the company from breaching the law or regulations.

Turnbull also called for a shift of power from boards to shareholder elected committees, or senates as he calls them, thus reducing the need for regulation by law or code.

Director Information

As we have seen, all directors have the right and the duty to be fully informed on matters affecting the company. Relevant information is vital for effective board deliberations and decisions. We also recognized some of the problems in keeping directors, particularly outside directors, fully abreast of developments in the company and its business environment. New ways will undoubtedly be developed to enable directors and their staff to acquire relevant knowledge, rather than just receiving standard reports of historical data.

Technology will allow directors to access information, wherever they are and whenever they want. Such access will enable them to be updated immediately on relevant aspects of the company, to be kept informed about the financial situation, on the competitive market position, and with relevant information about the firm's political, economic, societal, and technological context. But these board level information systems will also enable directors to search for the information they feel they want, perhaps applying simulations to explore possible outcomes, whilst communicating their ideas to other board colleagues online.

Director Rewards

More consistent, multi-factor measures of director, board, and company performance will be developed and linked to director remuneration. The emerging reward systems will reward long term success, whilst avoiding the distortions and short-termism that can arise with complex incentive schemes. The rewards will be sufficiently generous to attract and hold people of high calibre, but end the transfer of shareholder wealth to those directors whose overriding motivation is personal greed.

Corporate Governance Reporting

Codes of good practice are likely, in due course, to be replaced with quantifiable corporate governance norms, ratings, and rankings. This information will be available to investors, fund managers, and analysts, regulating authorities (who can apply sanctions), and to all stakeholders affected by corporate activities.

The current rating schemes around the world are likely to consolidate. The current box ticking approach to simple structural questions will be replaced by performance measures against corporate governance criteria. The reports will also provide independent and objective opinions on the calibre of directors and boards, and on the quality of corporate governance, in the same way that auditors now report on corporate finances.

An Informed Society

The overall information needs of investors, regulators, and all legitimate stakeholders will also be met in innovative new ways. For example, systems may be developed that allow them to access material to answer questions they have, rather than merely receiving public relations reports that the company wants them to have. The presentation of financial reports, produced to meet prescriptive accounting rules, will improve. Though the auditors confirm that such reports are 'true and fair', they often contain masses of obscure data and footnotes that are impenetrable to all but financial analysts and experienced accountants (and sometimes not even them!). Reports which trace historical trends, chart directors' perceptions of the likelihood of uncertain future events, and provide explanatory strategic and operational commentary that carries a higher information content than many contemporary accounts. Predictably, greater transparency may lead to calls for wider accountability and control. Better protection for investors and other legitimate stakeholders, related to the degree of risk they face, or have chosen to take, could result.

Governance of All Corporate Entities

The predominant focus of corporate governance, as we have seen, has been on public, quoted companies. This has been extended in some places to government trading entities and not-for-profit entities with corporate governance codes and calls for good governance. In the future the expectation of sound governance will be extended to small and medium enterprises, partnerships, joint ventures, private equity firms, hedge funds, cooperatives, not-for-profit charitable, cultural, sports, health, housing associations—indeed to all corporate entities where power has been delegated from members to a governing body. Corporate governance will be seen to be concerned with the long term integrity not only of listed companies and financial markets, but of all corporate entities and their impact on the societies in which they operate.

Responsibilities to Society

In the past, the duty of directors, and the boards on which they served, was to their members. Company law to date has required directors to recognize a primary responsibility to the company, which really means to all the shareholders. But that perspective is changing, as we have seen. Society will expect more of the corporate concerns it licenses to operate in its midst. The demand will be to recognize their responsibilities to the society they affect and serve. The UK 2006 Companies Act, as we saw, specifically calls on directors to recognize such a broader responsibility. Balancing conflicting interests and competing expectations between different stakeholders will inevitably become a challenge for governing bodies.

The developments that have just been mentioned are all fairly predictable outcomes of current trends. There are other possible developments, which would be evolutionary changes to the concept of the corporation itself. To speculate on such developments we need to remind ourselves on the original thinking behind the corporate concept.

The Evolution of an Idea

The limited liability company was a child of mid-19th century Victorian England, as we have already seen. This was an era of institutional invention. Britain was at the height of empire led self-confidence. Trades unions, building societies (savings and loan associations), cooperative societies, missionary societies, professional bodies including law societies and accountants' associations, were all formed in the later half of the 19th century. Religion, individualism, and self-help, associated with societal duty, flourished. This was a society in which the concepts of duty, trust, and self-reliance were basic.

These qualities were reflected in the brilliant idea of the joint stock company. The state passed legislation that permitted the incorporation of corporate entities separate from those managing and investing in them, whilst limiting the liability of the shareholders for companies' debts. In effect the state licensed corporate entities, and regulated their behaviour, but the directors, appointed by the investors, were trusted to act on their behalf.

As Daniel Bell[1] commented, capitalism developed and drew its strength from an ethic of sobriety, saving, and deferred gratification. Although, he also noted that free-market capitalism actually worked to undermine these qualities, stimulating hedonism and instant gratification.

Every subsequent development—the formation of millions of private companies, the separation between owners and top management with power shifting to directors, the creation of regulatory bodies, the formation of complex corporate groups with pyramids, chains, and networks, the corporate governance codes, the SOX Act, calls for corporate social responsibility and sustainability, indeed, everything that has happened since to limited liability companies, is rooted in that 19th century creation: the virtual reality of an autonomous corporate entity.

But a company is a concept. It is a fiction, albeit a legal one. The directors and officers, managers and employees, individual shareholders, customers, and suppliers, competitors, government, and tax authorities, auditors, and regulators are the reality. All corporate governance to date has been based on the old legal-entity paradigm. The corporate governance literature has uncritically embraced this virtual reality.

---

[1] Bell, Daniel (1976) *The Cultural Contradictions of Capitalism.* New York: Basic Books.

As we have seen throughout this book, the corporate form has its limitations—corporate collapses, environmental hazards, corruption, and abuse of power, with personal greed rather than a fiduciary concern for members' interests being the driving force.

The Need for a New Paradigm

The corporation is at once a legal entity, an economic artefact, and a social organization. It can be studied as each of them. As a legal entity the company is an artificial being created, bounded, and controlled by the laws of the land in which it was incorporated. As an economic artefact the company strives to respond to market forces and meet the goals of its owners and directors. As a social organization it works through people, operationally, managerially, and, most significantly, strategically through its directors. Each viewpoint adds important elements to our understanding of its governance. None provides a total perspective.

A new paradigm is needed, one that adequately categorizes and reflects the reality of corporate entities and their activities in the world today. It would need to embrace all types and size of corporate entity, whatever their purpose, membership, or funding, and capture the basis of power over the entity, society's evolving expectations, new organizational forms, and new theoretical developments. It would need to rethink the relationship between individual, enterprise, and state in a way appropriate to the 21st century instead of the 19th.

Alternative forms of governance structure might reflect the interests of all the principal stakeholders in the prosperity of the enterprise, effectively linking all the sources of power, not just those of the investors or the members of an organization.

Currently, networks of corporate entities are defined by the boundaries of legal incorporation. Control over meetings of shareholders and the appointment and activities of directors are based on ownership. This is not the only way. Moreover, given dynamically evolving groupings and relationships rather than static structures, it may not be the best way.

Instead of legal entities, corporate bodies could be seen as self-governing social institutions. Their boundaries, connections, and functions, could be defined by cybernetic communication and control linkages with the nodes defined with requisite variety, rather than legal rules and governance regulations. Organizations could be defined by the ability of external parties to exercise power over the entity. Information boundaries and data linkages to participating and affected stakeholders, rather than ownership boundaries, could be used to define an entity. Dynamic and rapidly evolving groupings of networked or chained entities could be represented as organic systems rather than through the legal, mechanistic model. New forms of networked organizations could emerge that link entities created as classical joint stock limited liability companies with government and non-government organizations and community groupings.

Some commentators, looking at companies operating globally, have commented that such entities are now often larger than the states in which they operate. The profits of a company such as Microsoft or Exxon, they point out, are greater than the GDP of many of the countries in which they operate. The inference is that, therefore, they wield more power. But companies have to act under the legal, economic, and cultural shadow of the countries in which they operate. Not since the days of the East India Company can they operate their own armies. States give corporate entities the licence to operate in their territories. Companies do not acquire power from their global scale. What states give, they can take away. Governance power could be redefined by the state.

States could become more proactive in the governance of large companies operating in their territories that affect the lives and well being of their people. States could be involved in the audit process, for example. They could contract with the external auditors, who could be paid for by the enterprise as now, but who would report through the state to all the stakeholders involved. The auditors' confirmation that corporate entities' reports show a true and fair representation of the business would then be made, not just to the financial markets, but to all stakeholders and from every perspective.

Undoubtedly, corporate governance thinking and practices will continue to evolve. As new organizational forms emerge their governance arrangements may also have to be more participative, less secretive, and far more transparent.

Some Drivers of Change

Finally, there are a number of ongoing issues that may well affect the future direction of corporate governance principles, policies, and practices. These include:

- The 2008 financial crisis forced the takeover, liquidation, or nationalization of financial institutions around the world, as we saw in chapter 14. Despite the 2007 Basel II agreement, which called for professional risk assessment in the financial world, boards failed in their responsibilities. The Bank of England criticized over-reliance on credit ratings. Excessive risk taking, encouraged by over-generous incentives, was another suggestion. Inquiries, litigation, and changes to the regulations and regulatory authorities will follow. Enron brought down one of the big five accounting firms, as we have seen: failure of another would be catastrophic. The messages for corporate governance are legion including the need to match directors' rewards with performance, to improve strategic risk assessment at board level, and to rebuild confidence and trust through professional corporate governance

- The growing importance and wealth generating capacities of the emerging economies, particularly China and India, which are likely to give them power to influence international corporate governance and accounting standards

- The acquisition by overseas interests of major companies where the economic performance of a country could be affected. Expect calls for new corporate governance standards and controls in response

- The effects of globabalization as international companies apply common governance and accounting standards across their groups. The integration of both financial and product/service markets around the world will accelerate this trend. But countering this movement nationalism and economic patriotism will attempt to protect domestic consumption, employment, or capital formation

- The potential of companies in China, India, and other emerging economies to become global through cross-border acquisitions

- The trans-national membership of boards of companies operating globally. Though developments are likely to be slow, ultimately a class of directors of global companies may emerge who transcend national boundaries, economic interests, and political barriers

- The governance of sovereign wealth funds whose ownership power and responsibilities are often unclear. These issues will have to be addressed at an international level. The outcome could be a code of conduct for sovereign funds requiring more transparency and a statement of the strategic aims of the fund and details of its main holdings, perhaps regulated by an international body such as the International Monetary Fund

- The supplanting of the classical audited annual accounts by more frequent financial reviews, strategic reports, risk analyses, corporate resource reviews, operating statements, and corporate governance reports. The use of probabilities, directors' expectations of the likelihood of future events, may become more acceptable than strategic statements in corporate reports. Websites and real-time Internet corporate commentary have the potential to supplant some periodic published company information

- The structure of public company boards. The need to balance the skills, experience, network connections, and other attributes of directors to produce an effective team will become more apparent. Also expect more discussion on board diversity (gender, age, nationality, ethnic background, shareholder representation, stakeholder interests, etc.) and further definitions of independence

- The qualifications and characteristics of directors. As the challenges and risks of taking on a directorship in major entities grow, more clarification and better definition of the skills, knowledge, and experience needed to be capable of meeting the challenges will occur

- The vital importance of the leadership role of the chairman will be recognized. Going beyond the structures and strictures of the compliance codes, more attention is likely to be paid to board dynamics and the chairman's leadership role to achieve corporate success

Better Corporate Governance

It is clear that there is no one ideal structure for corporate governance. Many alternative structures can work well in the appropriate context. In fact, despite all the commentary on governance structures—unitary and two-tier boards, the proportion of INEDs, the separation of chairman and CEO, board committees and the rest—the issue of effective governance is not really about structure but about process.

Governance involves a political process. Governing bodies need to ensure that the entity fulfils its mission, meets its aims, whether these are providing goods or services to satisfy markets, offering a social service to meet society's needs, or fulfilling some other purpose. In the process the entity may create wealth, provide employment, facilitate innovation, and contribute to society at the local and national levels.

A successful governing body needs a cadre of the competent. Respected leadership is a crucial driving force. Professionalism, with continuous personal development and learning, is fundamental. In future, governing bodies may have to be less rigid, less bounded, and more adaptable. That might mean board styles that are transient, more flexible, and certainly less formal.

The original concept of the corporation was founded on trust. Trust was at the heart of the capitalist system. Agreements were sealed with a hand shake. Directors were recognized as reliable stewards of the interests of others.

Unfortunately, in recent years it has been corruption, crisis, and corporate collapse that have driven changes in corporate governance practice. Greed seems to have replaced trust as capitalism's driving force. Indeed, the dominant paradigm of corporate governance, agency theory, is rooted in the belief that people are utility maximizers who need to be controlled because they cannot be trusted. Certainly, too often a directorship seems to have been used as a means of self-aggrandisement, a basis for power, or a path to personal gain.

The overall challenge in developing corporate governance is to balance conformance with performance: to encourage entrepreneurial risk-taking, whilst appropriately rewarding investors, and adequately protecting other stakeholders who may be affected by corporate activities, in both the short and the long term. The place of corporate entities within society needs to be rethought. Above all, governing bodies need people who can be trusted, people who understand their fiduciary responsibilities, people who put the rights and needs of others ahead of their own.

Some might retort that the socialist experiment clearly showed, on a global scale, that it is impossible to build organizations run by people who are not primarily acting in their own best interests. But the best interests of people need not be solely power, personal aggrandisement, or greed. In the not-for-profit sector, and indeed in the corporate sector too, people do act responsibly in the interests of others, showing integrity, treating employees and other stakeholders fairly, and contributing to their community's and society's needs, being reliable stewards for others' interests.

The concept of trust in corporate governance needs to be rediscovered. As T. S. Elliott wrote:

> We shall not cease from explorations
> And the end of all our exploring
> Will be to arrive where we started
> And know the place for the first time

REFERENCES AND FURTHER READING

Carter C. B and J. W. Lorsch (2004) *Back to the Drawing Board*. Boston, MA: Harvard Business School Press.

Chew, Donald H. and Stuart L. Gillan (2005) *Corporate Governance at the Crossroads: A Book of Readings*. Boston: McGraw Hill,

Lipton M. (2007) *Some Thoughts for Boards of Directors*. New York: Watchell, Lipton, Rosen and Katz.

Lowery Kellan V. (2008) *Corporate Governance in the 21st Century*. New York: Nova Science Publishers.

MacAvoy, P. W. and I. M. Millstein (2003) *The Recurrent Crisis in Corporate Governance*. Basingstoke: Palgrave Macmillan.

Monks, Robert A. G. (2008) *Corpocracy: How CEOs and the Business Roundtable Hijacked the World's Greatest Wealth Machine, And How to Get it Back*. Chichester: Wiley.

USEFUL WEB SITES

www.blackwellpublishing.com/corg
Corporate Governance: An International Review. The first academic corporate governance journal.

www.corpgov.net/links/links.html
The original corporate governance website. Links to almost everything connected with the subject.

www.ecgi.org
European Corporate Governance Institute.

www.emeraldinsight.com/1472-0701.htm
Academic journal—Corporate Governance.

www.encycogov.com/WhatIsGorpGov.asp
Web encyclopaedia of corporate governance.

www.forbes.com/leadership/governance
Web news sheet on corporate governance.

http://papers.ssrn.com/abstract_id=1008453
Shann Turnbull's paper on corporate senates.

rru.worldbank.org/Themes/CorporateGovernance
The World Bank corporate governance.

site.www.wcfcg.net
World Council for Corporate Governance—an international network to galvanize good governance practices worldwide.

Finally, some examples of companies' corporate governance concerns and commitment:

www.asx.com.au/supervision/governance
Corporate governance of the Australian Securities Exchange.

www.boeing.com/corp_gov
The Boeing company's corporate governance site.

www.infosys.com/investors/corporate-governance/default.asp
The corporate governance policies of Infosys (a pioneer in benchmarking corporate governance practices).

www.novell.com/company/ir/cg
Corporate governance at Novell, home of Linux operating systems.

www.unilever.com/ourcompany/investorcentre/corp_governance
Unilever's corporate governance arrangements.

PROJECTS AND EXERCISES

Around the world, in large and small enterprises, in the public and the private sectors, governance has become the focus of attention. The exercise of power over corporate entities, the legitimacy of companies and their directors, the effectiveness of governing bodies and their accountability in society, have become crucial topics. The field of corporate governance is expanding and changing dramatically and fast.

1. Consider a corporate entity with which you are familiar.
    In the next ten or twenty years, what forces for change could occur that would cause the organization to change its approach to governance?

2. What will corporate governance look like in ten or twenty years' time? Prepare a report/presentation outlining your expectations.

3. In 2008 all public companies in Norway were obliged by law to ensure that at least 40 percent of their board directors were women. Advance the arguments for and against such legislation in your country.

The merger of Houston Natural Gas and Inter-North in 1985 created a new Texas energy company called Enron. In 1989 Enron began trading in commodities—buying and selling wholesale contracts in energy. By 2000 turnover was growing at a fantastic rate, from US$40 billion in 1999 to US$101 billion in 2000, with the increased revenues coming from the broking of energy commodities. The rapid rate of growth suggested a dynamic company and Enron's share price rocketed. Top executives reaped large rewards from their share options. The company's bankers, who received substantial fees from the company, also employed the analysts who encouraged others to invest in Enron. But the cash flow statement included an unusual item: 'other operating activities $1.1 bn'. The accounts for 2000 were the last Enron was to publish.

The chief executive of Enron, Joseph Skilling, believed that old asset based businesses would be dominated by trading enterprises such as Enron making markets for their output. Enron was credited with 'aggressive earnings management'. To support its growth hundreds of Special Purpose Entities (SPEs) were created. These were separate partnerships that traded with Enron, with names such as Cayman, Condor and Raptor, Jedi and Chewco, often based in tax havens. Enron marked long term energy supply contracts with these SPEs at market prices, taking the profit in its own accounts immediately. The SPEs also provided lucrative fees for Enron top executives. Further, they gave the appearance that Enron had hedged its financial exposures with third parties, whereas the third parties were, in fact, contingent liabilities on Enron. The contemporary American accounting standards (GAAP) did not require such SPEs to be consolidated with partners' group accounts, so billions of dollars were kept off Enron's balance sheet.

Enron in 2000 had US$100 billion in annual revenues and was valued by the stock market at nearly US$80 billion. It was ranked 7th in Fortune's list of the largest US firms. Enron then had three principal divisions, with over 3,500 subsidiaries: Enron Global Services, owning physical assets such as power stations and pipelines, Enron Energy Services, providing management and outsourcing services, and Enron Wholesale Services, the commodities and trading business. Enron was the largest trader in the energy market created by the deregulation of energy in the US.

The company had many admirers. As the authors of the book The War for Talent (Harvard Business School Press, 2001) wrote: 'few companies will be able to achieve the excitement extravaganza that Enron has in its remarkable business transformation, but many could apply some of the principles'.

Enron's auditor was Arthur Andersen, whose audit and consultancy fees from Enron were running at about US$52 million a year. Enron also employed several former Andersen partners as senior financial executives. In February 2001 partners of Andersen discussed dropping their client because of Enron's accounting policies, including accounting for the SPEs and the apparent conflicts of interest by Enron's chief financial officer, Andrew Fastow, who had set up and was benefiting from the SPEs. In August 2001 Skilling resigned 'for personal reasons'. Kenneth Lay, the chairman took over executive control. Lay was a close friend of the US President George W. Bush and was his adviser on energy matters. His name had been mentioned as a future US Energy Secretary. In 2000 Lay made £123m from the exercise of share options in Enron.

A week after Skilling resigned, Chung Wu, a broker with UBS Paine Webber US (a subsidiary of Swiss bank UBS), emailed his clients advising them to sell Enron. He was sacked and escorted out of his office. The same day Lay sold US$4 million of his own Enron shares, while telling employees of his high priority to restore investor confidence, which 'should result in a higher share *price'*. Other UBS analysts were still recommending a '*strong buy*' on Enron. UBS Paine Webber received substantial brokerage fees from administering the Enron employee stock option programme. Lord Wakeham, a former UK cabinet minister, was a director of Enron and chairman of its nominating committee. Wakeham, who was also a chartered accountant and Chairman of the British Press Complaints Council, was paid an annual consultancy fee of US$50,000 by Enron, plus a US$4,600 month retainer and US$1,250 attendance fee each meeting.

A warning about the company's accounting techniques was given to Lay in mid-2001 by Sherron Watkins, an Enron executive, who wrote, '*I am nervous that we will implode in a wave of accounting scandals*'. She also advised Andersen about potential problems. In October 2001 a crisis developed, when the company revised its earlier financial statements revealing massive losses due to hedging risks taken as energy prices fell, which had wiped out US$600 million of profits. An SEC investigation into this restatement of profits for the past five years, revealed massive, complex derivative positions and the transactions between Enron and the SPEs. Debts were understated by US$2.6 billion. Fastow was alleged to have received more than US$30 million for his management of the partnerships. Eventually he was indicted with seventy-eight counts involving the complex financial schemes that produced phantom profits, enriched him, and doomed the company. He claimed that he did not believe he committed any crimes.

The FBI began an investigation into possible fraud at Enron three months later, by which time files had been shredded. In a subsequent criminal trial Andersen was found guilty of destroying key documents, as part of an effort to impede an official inquiry into the energy company's collapse. Lawsuits against Andersen followed. The Enron employees' pension fund sued for US$1 billion, plus return of US$1 million per week fees, seeing the firm as their best chance of recovering some of the US$80 billion lost in the Enron debacle. Many Enron employees held their retirement plans in Enron stock: some had lost their entire retirement savings. The Labour Department alleged that Enron illegally prohibited employees from selling company stock in their '401k' retirement plans as the share price fell. Andersen

subsequently collapsed, with partnerships around the world joining other 'big four' firms.

In November 2001 Fastow was fired. Standard and Poor's, the credit rating agency, downgraded Enron stock to junk bond status, triggering interest rate penalties and other clauses. Merger negotiations with Dynergy that might have save Enron failed.

Enron filed for chapter 11 bankruptcy in December 2001. This was the largest corporate collapse in US history to that time: Worldcom was to surpass it. The New York Stock Exchange (NYSE) suspended Enron shares. John Clifford Baxter, a vice chairman of Enron until his resignation in May 2001, was found shot dead. He had been one of the first to see the problems at Enron and had heated arguments about the accounting for off-balance sheet financing, which he found unacceptable. Two outside directors, Herbert Weinokur and Robert Jaedicke, members of the Enron audit committee, claimed that the board was either not informed or was deceived about deals involving the SPEs.

Early in 2002 Duncan, the former lead partner on Enron's audit, who had allegedly shredded Enron files and been fired by Andersen, cooperated with the Justice Department's criminal indictment, becoming whistle blower and pleading guilty to charges that he did '*knowingly, intentionally and corruptly persuade and attempt to persuade Andersen partners and employees to shred documents*'.

Why did it happen? Three fundamental reasons can be suggested: Enron switched strategy from energy supplier to energy trader, effectively becoming a financial institution with an increased risk profile, Enron's financial strategy hid corporate debt and exaggerated performance, and US accounting standards permitted the off-balance sheet treatment of the SPEs.

What are the implications of the Enron case? Firstly, important questions are raised about corporate governance in the United States including the roles of the CEO and board of directors, and the issue of duality; the independence of outside, non-executive directors; the functions and membership of the audit committee; and the oversight role of institutional shareholders. Secondly, issues of regulation in American financial markets arise, including the regulation of industrial companies with financial trading arms like Enron, the responsibilities of the independent credit rating agencies, the regulation of US pension funds and the effect on capital markets worldwide. Thirdly, there are implications for accounting standards, particularly the accounting for off-balance sheet SPEs, the regulation of the US accounting profession, and the convergence of American GAAPs with international accounting standards. Finally, auditing issues include auditor independence, auditors right to undertake non-audit work for audit clients, the rotation of audit partners, audit firms or government involvement in audit, and the need for a cooling off period before an auditor joins the staff of a client company.

Some British banks were caught in the Enron net. Andrew Fastow, the former CFO, produced an insider account of how the banks had helped to prop up the house of cards. Three British bankers were extradited to the United States to stand trial, under legislation designed to repatriate terrorists. These banks could be liable for US$30 billion losses.

Jeffrey Skilling, the former CEO was sentenced to twenty-four years prison and to pay US$45 million restitution in October 2006. Claiming innocence he appealed. Kenneth Lay (64) was also found guilty but died of a heart attack in July 2006, protesting his innocence and believing he would be exonerated.

Although Enron collapsed with such dramatic results, international corporate governance guidelines had in fact been followed, with a separate chairman and CEO, an audit committee chaired by a leading independent accounting academic, and a raft of eminent INEDs. However, the subsequent collapse owes more to abuse of their power by top management and their ambivalent attitudes towards honest and balanced corporate governance.

New York Stock Exchange: Corporate
Governance Rules

What follows are the final corporate governance rules of the New York Stock Exchange approved by the SEC on November 4, 2003.

General Application

Companies listed on the Exchange must comply with certain standards regarding corporate governance as codified in this Section 303A. Consistent with the NYSE's traditional approach, as well as the requirements of the Sarbanes-Oxley Act of 2002, certain provisions of Section 303A are applicable to some listed companies but not to others.

Equity Listings

Section 303A applies in full to all companies listing common equity securities, with the following exceptions:

Controlled Companies

A company of which more than 50% of the voting power is held by an individual, a group or another company need not comply with the requirements of Sections 303A.01, .04 or .05. A controlled company that chooses to take advantage of any or all of these exemptions must disclose that choice, that it is a controlled company and the basis for the determination in its annual proxy statement or, if the company does not file an annual proxy statement, in the company's annual report on Form 10-K filed with the SEC. Controlled companies must comply with the remaining provisions of Section 303A.

Limited Partnerships and Companies in Bankruptcy

Due to their unique attributes, limited partnerships and companies in bankruptcy proceedings need not comply with the requirements of Sections 303A.01, .04 or .05. However, all limited partnerships (at the general partner level) and companies in bankruptcy proceedings must comply with the remaining provisions of Section 303A.

Closed-End and Open-End Funds

The Exchange considers the significantly expanded standards and requirements provided for in Section 303A to be unnecessary for closed-end and open-end management investment companies that are registered under the Investment Company Act of 1940, given the pervasive federal regulation applicable to them. However, closed-end funds must comply with the requirements of Sections 303A.06, .07(a) and (c), and .12. Note, however, that in view of the common practice to utilize the same directors for boards in the same fund complex, closed-end funds will not be required to comply with the disclosure requirement in the second paragraph of the Commentary to 303A.07(a), which calls for disclosure of a board's determination with respect to simultaneous service on more than three public company audit committees. However, the other provisions of that paragraph will apply.

Business development companies, which are a type of closed-end management investment company defined in Section 2(a)(48) of the Investment Company Act of 1940 that are not registered under that Act, are required to comply with all of the provisions of Section 303A applicable to domestic issuers other than Sections 303A.02 and .07(b). For purposes of Sections 303A.01, .03, .04, .05, and .09, a director of a business development company shall be considered to be independent if he or she is not an 'interested person' of the company, as defined in Section 2(a)(19) of the Investment Company Act of 1940.

As required by Rule 10A-3 under the Exchange Act, open-end funds (which can be listed as Investment Company Units, more commonly known as Exchange Traded Funds or ETFs) are required to comply with the requirements of Sections 303A.06 and .12(b). Rule 10A-3(b)(3)(ii) under the Exchange Act requires that each audit committee must establish procedures for the confidential, anonymous submission by employees of the listed issuer of concerns regarding questionable accounting or auditing matters. In view of the external management structure often employed by closed-end and open-end funds, the Exchange also requires the audit committees of such companies to establish such procedures for the confidential, anonymous submission by employees of the investment adviser, administrator, principal underwriter, or any other provider of accounting related services for the management company, as well as employees of the management company. This responsibility must be addressed in the audit committee charter.

Other Entities

Except as otherwise required by Rule 10A-3 under the Exchange Act (for example, with respect to open-end funds), Section 303A does not apply to passive business organizations in the form of trusts (such as royalty trusts) or to derivatives and special purpose securities (such as those described in Sections 703.16, 703.19, 703.20 and 703.21). To the extent that Rule 10A-3 applies to a passive business organization, listed derivative or special purpose security, such entities are required to comply with Sections 303A.06 and .12(b).

Foreign Private Issuers

Listed companies that are foreign private issuers (as such term is defined in Rule 3b-4 under the Exchange Act) are permitted to follow home country practice in lieu of the provisions of this Section 303A, except that such companies are required to comply with the requirements of Sections 303A.06, .11 and .12(b).3.

Preferred and Debt Listings

Section 303A does not generally apply to companies listing only preferred or debt securities on the Exchange. To the extent required by Rule 10A-3 under the Exchange Act, all companies listing only preferred or debt securities on the NYSE are required to comply with the requirements of Sections 303A.06 and .12(b).

Effective Dates/Transition Periods

Except for Section 303A.08, which became effective June 30, 2003, listed companies will have until the earlier of their first annual meeting after January 15, 2004, or October 31, 2004, to comply with the new standards contained in Section 303A, although if a company with a classified board would be required (other than by virtue of a requirement under Section 303A.06) to change a director who would not normally stand for election in such annual meeting, the company may continue such director in office until the second annual meeting after such date, but no later than December 31, 2005. In addition, foreign private issuers will have until July 31, 2005, to comply with the new audit committee standards set out in Section 303A.06. As a general matter, the existing audit committee requirements provided for in Section 303 continue to apply to listed companies pending the transition to the new rules.

Companies listing in conjunction with their initial public offering will be permitted to phase in their independent nomination and compensation committees on the same schedule as is permitted pursuant to Rule 10A-3 under the Exchange Act for audit committees, that is, one independent member at the time of listing, a majority of independent members within 90 days of listing and fully independent committees within one year. Such companies will be required to meet the majority independent board requirement within 12 months of listing. For purposes of Section 303A other than Sections 303A.06 and .12(b), a company will be considered to be listing in conjunction with an initial public offering if, immediately prior to listing, it does not have a class of common stock registered under the Exchange Act. The Exchange will also permit companies that are emerging from bankruptcy or have ceased to be controlled companies within the meaning of Section 303A to phase in independent nomination and compensation committees and majority independent boards on the same schedule as companies listing in conjunction with an initial public offering. However, for purposes of Sections 303A.06 and .12(b), a company will be considered to be listing in conjunction with an initial public offering only if it meets the conditions of Rule 10A-3(b)(1)(iv)(A) under the Exchange Act, namely, that the company was not, immediately prior to the effective date of a registration statement, required to file reports with the SEC pursuant to Section 13(a) or 15(d) of the Exchange Act.

Companies listing upon transfer from another market have 12 months from the date of transfer in which to comply with any requirement to the extent the market on which they were listed did not have the same requirement. To the extent the other market has a substantially similar requirement but also had a transition period from the effective date of that market's rule, which period had not yet expired, the company will have the same transition period as would have been available to it on the other market. This transition period for companies transferring from another market will not apply to the requirements of Section 303A.06 unless a transition period is available pursuant to Rule 10A-3 under the Exchange Act.

References to Form 10-K

There are provisions in this Section 303A that call for disclosure in a company's Form 10-K under certain circumstances. If a company subject to such a provision is not a company required to file a Form 10-K, then the provision shall be interpreted to mean the annual periodic disclosure form that the company does file with the SEC. For example, for a closed-end fund, the appropriate form would be the annual Form N-CSR. If a company is not required to file either an annual proxy statement or an annual periodic report with the SEC, the disclosure shall be made in the annual report required under Section 203.01 of the NYSE Listed Company Manual.

1. **Listed companies must have a majority of independent directors.**

Commentary: Effective boards of directors exercise independent judgment in carrying out their responsibilities. Requiring a majority of independent directors will increase the quality of board oversight and lessen the possibility of damaging conflicts of interest.

2. **In order to tighten the definition of 'independent director' for purposes of these standards:**
   (a) **No director qualifies as 'independent' unless the board of directors affirmatively determines that the director has no material relationship with the listed company (either directly or as a partner, shareholder or officer of an organization that has a relationship with the company). Companies must disclose these determinations.**

Commentary: It is not possible to anticipate, or explicitly to provide for, all circumstances that might signal potential conflicts of interest, or that might bear on the materiality of a director's relationship to a listed company (references to 'company' would include any parent or subsidiary in a consolidated group with the company). Accordingly, it is best that boards making 'independence' determinations broadly consider all relevant facts and circumstances. In particular, when assessing the materiality of a director's relationship with the company, the board should consider the issue not merely from the standpoint of the director, but also from that of persons or organizations with which the director has an affiliation. Material relationships can include commercial, industrial, banking, consulting, legal, accounting, charitable and familial relationships, among others. However, as the concern is independence from management, the Exchange does not view ownership of even a significant amount of stock, by itself, as a bar to an independence finding.

The basis for a board determination that a relationship is not material must be disclosed in the company's annual proxy statement or, if the company does not file an annual proxy statement, in the company's annual report on Form 10-K filed with the SEC. In this regard, a board may adopt and disclose categorical standards to assist it in making determinations of independence and may make a general disclosure if a director meets these standards. Any determination of independence for a director who does not meet these standards must be specifically explained. A company must disclose any standard it adopts. It may then make the general statement that the independent directors meet the standards set by the board without detailing particular aspects of the immaterial relationships between individual directors and the company. In the event that a director with a business or other relationship that does not fit within the disclosed standards is determined to be independent, a board must disclose the basis for its determination in the manner described above. This approach provides investors with an adequate means of assessing the quality of a board's independence and its independence determinations while avoiding excessive disclosure of immaterial relationships.

    (b) **In addition:**

        (i) **A director who is an employee, or whose immediate family member is an executive officer, of the company is not independent until three years after the end of such employment relationship.**

Commentary: Employment as an interim Chairman or CEO shall not disqualify a director from being considered independent following that employment.

        (ii) **A director who receives, or whose immediate family member receives, more than $100,000 per year in direct compensation from the listed company, other than director and committee fees and pension or other forms of deferred compensation for prior service (provided such compensation is not contingent in any way on continued service), is not independent until three years after he or she ceases to receive more than $100,000 per year in such compensation.**

Commentary: Compensation received by a director for former service as an interim Chairman or CEO need not be considered in determining independence under this test. Compensation received by an immediate family member for service as a non-executive employee of the listed company need not be considered in determining independence under this test.

        (iii) **A director who is affiliated with or employed by, or whose immediate family member is affiliated with or employed in a professional capacity by, a present or former internal or external auditor of the company is not 'independent' until three years after the end of the affiliation or the employment or auditing relationship.**

        (iv) **A director who is employed, or whose immediate family member is employed, as an executive officer of another company where any of the listed company's present executives serve on that company's compensation committee is not 'independent' until three years after the end of such service or the employment relationship.**

        (v) **A director who is an executive officer or an employee, or whose immediate family member is an executive officer, of a company that makes payments to, or receives payments from, the listed company for property or services in an amount which, in any single fiscal year, exceeds the greater of $1 million, or 2% of such other company's consolidated gross revenues, is not 'independent' until three years after falling below such threshold.**

Commentary: In applying the test in Section 303A.02(b)(v), both the payments and the consolidated gross revenues to be measured shall be those reported in the last completed fiscal year. The look-back provision for this test applies solely to the financial relationship between the listed company and the director or immediate family member's current employer; a listed company need not consider former employment of the director or immediate family member. Charitable organizations shall not be considered 'companies' for purposes of Section 303A.02(b)(v), provided however that a listed company shall disclose in its annual proxy statement, or if the listed company does not file an annual proxy statement, in the company's annual report on Form 10-K filed with the SEC, any charitable contributions made by the listed company to any charitable organization in which a director serves as an executive officer if, within the preceding three years, contributions in any single fiscal year exceeded the greater of $1 million, or 2% of such charitable organization's consolidated gross revenues. Listed company boards are reminded of their obligations to consider the materiality of any such relationship in accordance with Section 303A.02(a) above.

General Commentary to Section 303A.02(b): An 'immediate family member' includes a person's spouse, parents, children, siblings, mothers and fathers-in-law, sons and daughters-in-law, brothers and sisters-in-law, and anyone (other than domestic employees) who shares such person's home. When applying the lookback provisions in Section 303A.02(b), listed companies need not consider individuals who are no longer immediate family members as a result of legal separation or divorce, or those who have died or become incapacitated. In addition, references to the 'company' would include any parent or subsidiary in a consolidated group with the company.

3. **To empower non-management directors to serve as a more effective check on management, the non-management directors of each company must meet at regularly scheduled executive sessions without management.**

Commentary: To promote open discussion among the non-management directors, companies must schedule regular executive sessions in which those directors meet without management participation. 'Non-management' directors are all those who are not company officers (as that term is defined in Rule 16a-1(f) under the Securities Act of 1933), and includes such directors who are not independent by virtue of a material relationship, former status or family membership, or for any other reason.

Regular scheduling of such meetings is important not only to foster better communication among non-management directors, but also to prevent any negative inference from attaching to the calling of executive sessions. There need not be a single presiding director at all executive sessions of the non-management directors. If one director is chosen to preside at these meetings, his or her name must be disclosed in the company's annual proxy statement or, if the company does not file an annual proxy statement, in the company's annual report on Form 10-K filed with the SEC. Alternatively, a company may disclose the procedure by which a presiding

director is selected for each executive session. For example, a company may wish to rotate the presiding position among the chairs of board committees.

In order that interested parties may be able to make their concerns known to the non-management directors, a company must disclose a method for such parties to communicate directly with the presiding director or with the non-management directors as a group. Companies may, if they wish, utilize for this purpose the same procedures they have established to comply with the requirement of Rule 10A-3 (b)(3) under the Exchange Act, as applied to listed companies through Section 303A.06.

While this Section 303A.03 refers to meetings of non-management directors, if that group includes directors who are not independent under this Section 303A, listed companies should at least once a year schedule an executive session including only independent directors.

4. (a) **Listed companies must have a nominating/corporate governance committee composed entirely of independent directors.**

   (b) **The nominating/corporate governance committee must have a written charter that addresses:**

      (i) **the committee's purpose and responsibilities—which, at minimum, must be to: identify individuals qualified to become board members, consistent with criteria approved by the board, and to select, or to recommend that the board select, the director nominees for the next annual meeting of shareholders; develop and recommend to the board a set of corporate governance principles applicable to the corporation; and oversee the evaluation of the board and management; and (ii) an annual performance evaluation of the committee.**

Commentary: A nominating/corporate governance committee is central to the effective functioning of the board. New director and board committee nominations are among a board's most important functions. Placing this responsibility in the hands of an independent nominating/corporate governance committee can enhance the independence and quality of nominees. The committee is also responsible for taking a leadership role in shaping the corporate governance of a corporation.

If a company is legally required by contract or otherwise to provide third parties with the ability to nominate directors (for example, preferred stock rights to elect directors upon a dividend default, shareholder agreements, and management agreements), the selection and nomination of such directors need not be subject to the nominating committee process.

The nominating/corporate governance committee charter should also address the following items: committee member qualifications; committee member appointment and removal; committee structure and operations (including authority to delegate to subcommittees); and committee reporting to the board. In addition, the charter should give the nominating/corporate governance committee sole authority to retain and terminate any search firm to be used to identify director candidates, including sole authority to approve the search firm's fees and other retention terms.

Boards may allocate the responsibilities of the nominating/corporate governance committee to committees of their own denomination, provided that the committees are composed entirely of independent directors. Any such committee must have a published committee charter.

5. (a) **Listed companies must have a compensation committee composed entirely of independent directors.**

   (b) **The compensation committee must have a written charter that addresses:**

      (i) **the committee's purpose and responsibilities—which, at minimum, must be to have direct responsibility to:**

         (A) **review and approve corporate goals and objectives relevant to CEO compensation, evaluate the CEO's performance in light of those goals and objectives, and, either as a committee or together with the other independent**

directors (as directed by the board), determine and approve the CEO's compensation level based on this evaluation; and

   (B) **make recommendations to the board with respect to non-CEO compensation, incentive-compensation plans and equity-based plans; and**

   (C) **produce a compensation committee report on executive compensation as required by the SEC to be included in the company's annual proxy statement or annual report on Form 10-K filed with the SEC;**

(ii) **an annual performance evaluation of the compensation committee.**

Commentary: In determining the long-term incentive component of CEO compensation, the committee should consider the company's performance and relative shareholder return, the value of similar incentive awards to CEOs at comparable companies, and the awards given to the listed company's CEO in past years. To avoid confusion, note that the compensation committee is not precluded from approving awards (with or without ratification of the board) as may be required to comply with applicable tax laws (i.e., Rule 162(m)).

The compensation committee charter should also address the following items: committee member qualifications; committee member appointment and removal; committee structure and operations (including authority to delegate to subcommittees); and committee reporting to the board.

Additionally, if a compensation consultant is to assist in the evaluation of director, CEO or senior executive compensation, the compensation committee charter should give that committee sole authority to retain and terminate the consulting firm, including sole authority to approve the firm's fees and other retention terms. Boards may allocate the responsibilities of the compensation committee to committees of their own denomination, provided that the committees are composed entirely of independent directors. Any such committee must have a published committee charter.

Nothing in this provision should be construed as precluding discussion of CEO compensation with the board generally, as it is not the intent of this standard to impair communication among members of the board.

6. Listed companies must have an audit committee that satisfies the requirements of Rule 10A-3 under the Exchange Act.

Commentary: The Exchange will apply the requirements of Rule 10A-3 in a manner consistent with the guidance provided by the Securities and Exchange Commission in SEC Release No. 34-47654 (April 1, 2003). Without limiting the generality of the foregoing, the Exchange will provide companies the opportunity to cure defects provided in Rule 10A-3(a)(3) under the Exchange Act.

7. (a) The audit committee must have a minimum of three members.

Commentary: Each member of the audit committee must be financially literate, as such qualification is interpreted by the company's board in its business judgment, or must become financially literate within a reasonable period of time after his or her appointment to the audit committee. In addition, at least one member of the audit committee must have accounting or related financial management expertise, as the company's board interprets such qualification in its business judgment. While the Exchange does not require that a listed company's audit committee include a person who satisfies the definition of audit committee financial expert set out in Item 401(e) of Regulation S-K, a board may presume that such a person has accounting or related financial management expertise. Because of the audit committee's demanding role and responsibilities, and the time commitment attendant to committee membership, each prospective audit committee member should evaluate carefully the existing demands on his or her time before accepting this important assignment. Additionally, if an audit committee member simultaneously serves on the audit committees of more than three public companies, and the listed company does not limit the number of audit committees on which its audit committee members serve, then in each case, the board must determine that such simultaneous service would not impair the ability of such member to effectively serve on the listed company's

audit committee and disclose such determination in the company's annual proxy statement or, if the company does not file an annual proxy statement, in the company's annual report on Form 10-K filed with the SEC.

(b) In addition to any requirement of Rule 10A-3(b)(1), all audit committee members must satisfy the requirements for independence set out in Section 303A.02.

(c) The audit committee must have a written charter that addresses:

(i) the committee's purpose—which, at minimum, must be to:

(A) assist board oversight of

(1) the integrity of the company's financial statements,

(2) the company's compliance with legal and regulatory requirements,

(3) the independent auditor's qualifications and independence, and

(4) the performance of the company's internal audit function and independent auditors;

(B) prepare an audit committee report as required by the SEC to be

(i) included in the company's annual proxy statement;

(ii) an annual performance evaluation of the audit committee; and

(iii) the duties and responsibilities of the audit committee—which, at a minimum, must include those set out in Rule 10A-3(b)(2), (3), (4) and (5) of the Exchange Act, as well as to:

– at least annually, obtain and review a report by the independent auditor describing: the firm's internal quality-control procedures; any material issues raised by the most recent internal quality-control review, or peer review, of the firm, or by any inquiry or investigation by governmental or professional authorities, within the preceding five years, respecting one or more independent audits carried out by the firm, and any steps taken to deal with any such issues; and (to assess the auditor's independence) all relationships between the independent auditor and the company;

Commentary: After reviewing the foregoing report and the independent auditor's work throughout the year, the audit committee will be in a position to evaluate the auditor's qualifications, performance and independence. This evaluation should include the review and evaluation of the lead partner of the independent auditor. In making its evaluation, the audit committee should take into account the opinions of management and the company's internal auditors (or other personnel responsible for the internal audit function). In addition to assuring the regular rotation of the lead audit partner as required by law, the audit committee should further consider whether, in order to assure continuing auditor independence, there should be regular rotation of the audit firm itself. The audit committee should present its conclusions with respect to the independent auditor to the full board.

(B) discuss the company's annual audited financial statements and quarterly financial statements with management and the independent auditor, including the company's disclosures under 'Management's Discussion and Analysis of Financial Condition and Results of Operations';

(C) discuss the company's earnings press releases, as well as financial information and earnings guidance provided to analysts and rating agencies;

Commentary: The audit committee's responsibility to discuss earnings releases, as well as financial information and earnings guidance, may be done generally (i.e., discussion of the types of

information to be disclosed and the type of presentation to be made). The audit committee need not discuss in advance each earnings release or each instance in which a company may provide earnings guidance.

(D) discuss policies with respect to risk assessment and risk management;

Commentary: While it is the job of the CEO and senior management to assess and manage the company's exposure to risk, the audit committee must discuss guidelines and policies to govern the process by which this is handled. The audit committee should discuss the company's major financial risk exposures and the steps management has taken to monitor and control such exposures. The audit committee is not required to be the sole body responsible for risk assessment and management, but, as stated above, the committee must discuss guidelines and policies to govern the process by which risk assessment and management is undertaken. Many companies, particularly financial companies, manage and assess their risk through mechanisms other than the audit committee. The processes these companies have in place should be reviewed in a general manner by the audit committee, but they need not be replaced by the audit committee.

(E) meet separately, periodically, with management, with internal auditors (or other personnel responsible for the internal audit function) and with independent auditors;

Commentary: To perform its oversight functions most effectively, the audit committee must have the benefit of separate sessions with management, the independent auditors and those responsible for the internal audit function. As noted herein, all listed companies must have an internal audit function. These separate sessions may be more productive than joint sessions in surfacing issues warranting committee attention.

(F) review with the independent auditor any audit problems or difficulties and management's response;

Commentary: The audit committee must regularly review with the independent auditor any difficulties the auditor encountered in the course of the audit work, including any restrictions on the scope of the independent auditor's activities or on access to requested information, and any significant disagreements with management. Among the items the audit committee may want to review with the auditor are: any accounting adjustments that were noted or proposed by the auditor but were 'passed' (as immaterial or otherwise); any communications between the audit team and the audit firm's national office respecting auditing or accounting issues presented by the engagement; and any 'management' or 'internal control' letter issued, or proposed to be issued, by the audit firm to the company. The review should also include discussion of the responsibilities, budget and staffing of the company's internal audit function.

(G) set clear hiring policies for employees or former employees of the independent auditors; and

Commentary: Employees or former employees of the independent auditor are often valuable additions to corporate management. Such individuals' familiarity with the business, and personal rapport with the employees, may be attractive qualities when filling a key opening. However, the audit committee should set hiring policies taking into account the pressures that may exist for auditors consciously or subconsciously seeking a job with the company they audit.

(H) report regularly to the board of directors.

Commentary: The audit committee should review with the full board any issues that arise with respect to the quality or integrity of the company's financial statements, the company's compliance with legal or regulatory requirements, the performance and independence of the company's independent auditors, or the performance of the internal audit function.

General Commentary to Section 303A.07(c): While the fundamental responsibility for the company's financial statements and disclosures rests with management and the independent auditor, the audit committee must review: (A) major issues regarding accounting principles and financial statement presentations, including any significant changes in the company's selection or application of accounting principles, and major issues as to the adequacy of the company's internal controls and any special audit steps adopted in light of material control deficiencies; (B) analyses prepared by management and/or the independent auditor setting forth significant financial reporting issues and judgments made in connection with the preparation of the financial statements, including analyses of the effects of alternative GAAP methods on the financial statements; (C) the effect of regulatory and accounting initiatives, as well as off-balance sheet structures, on the financial statements of the company; and (D) the type and presentation of information to be included in earnings press releases (paying particular attention to any use of 'pro forma,' or 'adjusted' non-GAAP, information), as well as review any financial information and earnings guidance provided to analysts and rating agencies.

(d) Each listed company must have an internal audit function.

Commentary: Listed companies must maintain an internal audit function to provide management and the audit committee with ongoing assessments of the company's risk management processes and system of internal control. A company may choose to outsource this function to a third party service provider other than its independent auditor.

General Commentary to Section 303A.07: To avoid any confusion, note that the audit committee functions specified in Section 303A.07 are the sole responsibility of the audit committee and may not be allocated to a different committee.

8. Reserved.

9. Listed companies must adopt and disclose corporate governance guidelines.

Commentary: No single set of guidelines would be appropriate for every company, but certain key areas of universal importance include director qualifications and responsibilities, responsibilities of key board committees, and director compensation. Given the importance of corporate governance, each listed company's website must include its corporate governance guidelines and the charters of its most important committees (including at least the audit, and if applicable, compensation and nominating committees). Each company's annual report on Form 10-K filed with the SEC must state that the foregoing information is available on its website, and that the information is available in print to any shareholder who requests it. Making this information publicly available should promote better investor understanding of the company's policies and procedures, as well as more conscientious adherence to them by directors and management. The following subjects must be addressed in the corporate governance guidelines:

- **Director qualification standards.** These standards should, at minimum, reflect the independence requirements set forth in Sections 303A.01 and .02. Companies may also address other substantive qualification requirements, including policies limiting the number of boards on which a director may sit, and director tenure, retirement and succession.
- **Director responsibilities.** These responsibilities should clearly articulate what is expected from a director, including basic duties and responsibilities with respect to attendance at board meetings and advance review of meeting materials.
- **Director access to management and, as necessary and appropriate, independent advisors.**
- **Director compensation.** Director compensation guidelines should include general principles for determining the form and amount of director compensation (and for reviewing those principles, as appropriate). The board should be aware that questions as to directors' independence may be raised when directors' fees and emoluments exceed what is customary. Similar concerns may be raised when the company makes substantial charitable contributions to organizations in which a director is affiliated, or enters into consulting contracts with (or provides other indirect forms of compensation to) a director. The board should critically evaluate each of these matters when determining the form and amount of director compensation, and the independence of a director.
- **Director orientation and continuing education.**
- **Management succession.** Succession planning should include policies and principles for CEO selection and performance review, as well as

policies regarding succession in the event of an emergency or the retirement of the CEO.
- **Annual performance evaluation of the board.** The board should conduct a self-evaluation at least annually to determine whether it and its committees are functioning effectively.

10. **Listed companies must adopt and disclose a code of business conduct and ethics for directors, officers and employees, and promptly disclose any waivers of the code for directors or executive officers.**

Commentary: No code of business conduct and ethics can replace the thoughtful behaviour of an ethical director, officer or employee. However, such a code can focus the board and management on areas of ethical risk, provide guidance to personnel to help them recognize and deal with ethical issues, provide mechanisms to report unethical conduct, and help to foster a culture of honesty and accountability.

Each code of business conduct and ethics must require that any waiver of the code for executive officers or directors may be made only by the board or a board committee and must be promptly disclosed to shareholders. This disclosure requirement should inhibit casual and perhaps questionable waivers, and should help assure that, when warranted, a waiver is accompanied by appropriate controls designed to protect the company. It will also give shareholders the opportunity to evaluate the board's performance in granting waivers. Each code of business conduct and ethics must also contain compliance standards and procedures that will facilitate the effective operation of the code. These standards should ensure the prompt and consistent action against violations of the code. Each listed company's website must include its code of business conduct and ethics. Each company's annual report on Form 10-K filed with the SEC must state that the foregoing information is available on its website and that the information is available in print to any shareholder who requests it. Each company may determine its own policies, but all listed companies should address the most important topics, including the following:

- **Conflicts of interest.** A 'conflict of interest' occurs when an individual's private interest interferes in any way—or even appears to interfere—with the interests of the corporation as a whole. A conflict situation can arise when an employee, officer or director takes actions or has interests that may make it difficult to perform his or her company work objectively and effectively. Conflicts of interest also arise when an employee, officer or director, or a member of his or her family, receives improper personal benefits as a result of his or her position in the company. Loans to, or guarantees of obligations of, such persons are of special concern. The company should have a policy prohibiting such conflicts of interest, and providing a means for employees, officers and directors to communicate potential conflicts to the company.

• **Corporate opportunities.** Employees, officers and directors should be prohibited from (a) taking for themselves personally opportunities that are discovered through the use of corporate property, information or position; (b) using corporate property, information, or position for personal gain; and (c) competing with the company. Employees, officers and directors owe a duty to the company to advance its legitimate interests when the opportunity to do so arises.

• **Confidentiality.** Employees, officers and directors should maintain the confidentiality of information entrusted to them by the company or its customers, except when disclosure is authorized or legally mandated. Confidential information includes all non-public information that might be of use to competitors, or harmful to the company or its customers, if disclosed.

• **Fair dealing.** Each employee, officer and director should endeavour to deal fairly with the company's customers, suppliers, competitors and employees. None should take unfair advantage of anyone through manipulation, concealment, abuse of privileged information, misrepresentation of material facts, or any other unfair dealing practice. Companies may write their codes in a manner that does not alter existing legal rights and obligations of companies and their employees, such as 'at will' employment arrangements.

• **Protection and proper use of company assets.** All employees, officers and directors should protect the company's assets and ensure their efficient use. Theft, carelessness and waste have a direct impact on the company's profitability. All company assets should be used for legitimate business purposes.

• **Compliance with laws, rules and regulations (including insider trading laws).** The company should proactively promote compliance with laws, rules and regulations, including insider trading laws. Insider trading is both unethical and illegal, and should be dealt with decisively.

• **Encouraging the reporting of any illegal or unethical behaviour.** The company should proactively promote ethical behaviour. The company should encourage employees to talk to supervisors, managers or other appropriate personnel when in doubt about the best course of action in a particular situation. Additionally, employees should report violations of laws, rules, regulations or the code of business conduct to appropriate personnel. To encourage employees to report such violations, the company must ensure that employees know that the company will not allow retaliation for reports made in good faith.

11. **Listed foreign private issuers must disclose any significant ways in which their corporate governance practices differ from those followed by domestic companies under NYSE listing standards.**

Commentary: Foreign private issuers must make their U.S. investors aware of the significant ways in which their home-country practices differ from those followed by domestic companies under NYSE listing standards. However, foreign private issuers are not required to present a detailed, item-by-item analysis of these differences. Such a disclosure would be long and unnecessarily complicated. Moreover, this requirement is not intended to suggest that one country's corporate governance practices are better or more effective than another. The Exchange believes that U.S. shareholders should be aware of the significant ways that the governance of a listed foreign private issuer differs from that of a U.S. listed company. The Exchange underscores that what is required is a brief, general summary of the significant differences, not a cumbersome analysis. Listed foreign private issuers may provide this disclosure either on their web site (provided it is in the English language and accessible from the

United States) and/or in their annual report as distributed to shareholders in the United States in accordance with Sections 103.00 and 203.01 of the Listed Company Manual (again, in the English language). If the disclosure is only made available on the web site, the annual report shall so state and provide the web address at which the information may be obtained.

12. (a) **Each listed company CEO must certify to the NYSE each year that he or she is not aware of any violation by the company of NYSE corporate governance listing standards.**

Commentary: The CEO's annual certification to the NYSE that, as of the date of certification, he or she is unaware of any violation by the company of the NYSE's corporate governance listing standards will focus the CEO and senior management on the company's compliance with the listing standards. Both this certification to the NYSE, and any CEO/CFO certifications required to be filed with the SEC regarding the quality of the company's public disclosure, must be disclosed in the company's annual report to shareholders or, if the company does not prepare an annual report to shareholders, in the companies annual report on Form 10-K filed with the SEC.

   (b) **Each listed company CEO must promptly notify the NYSE in writing after any executive officer of the listed company becomes aware of any material non-compliance with any applicable provisions of this Section 303A.**

13. **The NYSE may issue a public reprimand letter to any listed company that violates a NYSE listing standard.**

Commentary: Suspending trading in or delisting a company can be harmful to the very shareholders that the NYSE listing standards seek to protect; the NYSE must therefore use these measures sparingly and judiciously. For this reason it is appropriate for the NYSE to have the ability to apply a lesser sanction to deter companies from violating its corporate governance (or other) listing standards. Accordingly, the NYSE may issue a public reprimand letter to any listed company, regardless of type of security listed or country of incorporation, that it determines has violated a NYSE listing standard. For companies that repeatedly or flagrantly violate NYSE listing standards, suspension and delisting remain the ultimate penalties. For clarification, this lesser sanction is not intended for use in the case of companies that fall below the financial and other continued listing standards provided in Chapter 8 of the Listed Company Manual or that fail to comply with the audit committee standards set out in Section 303A.06. The processes and procedures provided for in Chapter 8 govern the treatment of companies falling below those standards.

Chapter 1

1. Corporate governance is about the exercise of power over corporate entities.

2. The key concept of the joint stock, limited liability company is that, separate from the owners, it has many of the legal property rights of a real person—to contract, to sue and be sued, to own property, and to employ. The company has a life of its own, giving continuity beyond the life of its founders, who could transfer their shares in the company. Crucially, the owners' liability for the company's debts is limited to their equity investment.

3. Ownership is the basis of power over the joint stock limited liability company.

4. Berle and Means (1932) drew attention to the growing separation of power between the executive management of major public companies and their increasingly diverse and remote shareholders.

5. The Bullock Report—*The Report of the Committee of Inquiry on Industrial Democracy* (1977) proposed a continuation of the unitary board, but with worker representative directors.

6. *The Corporate Report* (1975) called for all economic entities to report publicly and accept accountability to all those whose interests were affected by the directors' decisions.

7. In Australia, Alan Bond, Laurie Connell of Rothwells, and the Girvan Corporation; in Japan, Nomura Securities and The Recruit Corporation; in the United States, Ivan Boesky, Michael Levine, and Michael Milken of Drexel Burnham Lambert; in the UK, Guinness case and Robert Maxwell's companies.

8. The first report on corporate governance in 1992 came from Sir Adrian Cadbury in the UK and was on the financial aspects of corporate governance. The committee he chaired was set up in response to various company collapses.

9. The report called for
   - Wider use of independent outside, non-executive directors
   - Audit committees as a bridge between board and external auditor
   - Separation of the roles of chairman of the board and chief executive

10. The Hilmer report argued that governance is about performance as well as conformance, *'the board's key role is to ensure that corporate management is continuously and effectively striving for above-average performance, taking account of risk . . . (although) this is not to deny the board's additional role with respect to shareholder protection'.*

Chapter 2

1. To define the rights and duties of members, and lay down the rules about the way it is to be governed.

2. A private company may not offer its shares for sale to the general public: a public company can.

3. Refer to detailed explanations in the text and the 'governance circle and management triangle' model.

4. Performance (strategy formulation and policy making) and conformance (supervising executive activities and accountability).

5. See figure 2.8 and related text in the chapter.

6. Companies House, see www.companieshouse.co.uk

7. The great 1929 financial crash in the United States.

8. The mission of the US Securities and Exchange Commission is to protect investors, maintain fair, orderly, and efficient markets, and to facilitate capital formation.

9. Among the key participants in the securities world that the SEC oversees are securities

exchanges, securities brokers and dealers, investment advisors, and mutual funds.

10. Corporate Social Responsibility. CSR is now routinely seen as an important component of a company's corporate governance responsibilities.

Chapter 3

1. An independent non-executive director (INED) is a director with no affiliation or other relationship with the company, other than the directorship, that could affect, or be seen to affect, the exercise of objective, independent judgement. A connected non-executive director (CNED) is a director who does have some relationship with the company.

2. An outside director is another word for non-executive director. Mainly used in the United States, it is often taken to refer to an independent director.

3. A shadow director is a person who, though not formally a member of a board, is able to exert pressure on the decisions of that board.

4. Yes. They are sometimes referred to as associate directors.

5. Chairman of the board of directors.

6. There are different perspectives. Those in favour point out the years of experience, knowledge, and connections that the retiring top executive could bring to the board as its chairman, experience that would otherwise be lost. Those questioning the move point out potential difficulties for the new CEO. It is a rare person, having been a successful CEO, who can pass on the managerial reins to a new CEO without interfering in the day to day running of the business. Some codes of good practice in corporate governance oppose the appointment of a retiring CEO to the chairman of that company's board.

7. No. In most jurisdictions and consistent with most constitutions, the roles and responsibilities of all directors are the same.

8. To provide a bridge between the external auditor and the board, thus avoiding domina-

tion of the audit process by the finance director or other senior staff.

9. The remuneration committee is a sub-committee of the main board, consisting wholly or mainly of independent outside directors, which is set up with responsibility for overseeing the remuneration packages of board members, particularly the executive directors and, possibly, members of senior management.

10. The nominating committee is a sub-committee of the main board, made up wholly, or mainly, of independent outside directors, to make recommendations on replacement or additional members of the board and attempt to prevent the board becoming a cosy club, in which the incumbent members appoint like-minded people to join their ranks. In effect it offers a check and balance mechanism designed to reduce the possibility of a dominant director, such as the chairman or CEO, pushing through their own candidates.

Chapter 4

1. A *holding company* is a company which holds all or a dominant share of the voting rights in another company. A *subsidiary company* is a company in which another company (its holding company) holds all of its voting shares (a *wholly owned subsidiary*) or a majority of its voting shares (a *partially owned subsidiary*). An *associate company* is a company over which another company exercises dominant power, even though it does not hold a majority of the voting rights in that company, for example where the other shareholdings are widely spread.

2. The primary reason is, typically, low taxation possibly with some businesses exempt, and no capital gains tax or wealth tax. Additionally an off-shore jurisdiction might have good communications, political and economic stability, no exchange controls, and offer companies registered there flexibility, corporate privacy, and confidentiality, a pool of professional service providers, sound company law, and regulation that is reasonable but not bureaucratic.

3. In most jurisdictions company law shrouds each separate company with a veil that protects

its owners from liability for its debts. Corporate groups are able to protect themselves from the failure of one member of the group. Piercing this corporate veil is not allowed in these jurisdictions, although in a few places group companies may not protect themselves in this way and creditors can pursue their debts throughout the group.

4. Principally to leverage financial power gained from the gearing. By investing in a chain, the head of the chain is able to exercise more influence over the companies in the chain than would be available by investing in individual companies in the chain.

5. Traditionally, in *keiretsu* companies the board plays a formal, even ritualistic role. Boards are large and almost entirely executive. In effect, the board is the top four or five layers of the management organization. Promotion to the board, as in the West, is a mark of distinction; but, unlike the West, interpersonal competition, which has been a feature of life throughout the organization, continues on the board for promotion to the next 'level' up to the top management ranks. Non-executive directors, in the Western sense, are not typical. Although, under recent poor economic conditions, pressure has grown to introduce INEDs not least to protect outside investors interests. The *'ringi'* approach to communication within Japanese companies provides dialogue up and down the management hierarchy, leading over time to an agreed position which makes decision making easy. Nevertheless, power lies in the group of senior managers, including the president and chief executive.

6. *Chaebols* are South Korean groups of companies, formed with close government involvement and financial support, but dominated by a few families after the Second World War. Member companies in a *chaebol*, which often includes a bank, use cross-ownership of their shares.

7. A dual listed company is a group structure in which two listed companies merge but both companies continue to exist and share ownership of a single, operational business. The group then has two stock exchange listings, with different bodies of shareholders, usually in different countries.

8. Many companies use joint ventures with another company to enter markets, transfer technology, procure supplies, obtain finance, share management skills, manufacture products around the world, or share risk on an international scale.

9. Many companies use joint ventures with another company to enter markets, transfer technology, procure supplies, obtain finance, share management skills, manufacture products around the world, or share risk on an international scale.

10. Only in some company law jurisdictions. Jardine Matheson Holdings and the Sincere Group. In other jurisdictions companies are prohibited from investing in themselves through group networks.

Chapter 5

1. If disagreements arise that were not envisaged in the initial joint venture agreement, directors of the JV company can face conflicts between their responsibilities to the joint venture company and to the JV partner company that employs them. Although many joint venture companies do appoint the managing director or CEO of the joint venture to the board, others now appoint only representative directors from the partner companies and have the joint venture managing director attend meetings in a non-voting, non-partisan way.

2. Basically, in a partnership the partners are responsible for governing the firm. In a firm with few partners governance is by meeting of all the partners. In larger firms the partnership may decide to appoint a managing partner and a governing body, perhaps called an executive or management committee, which meets regularly to manage partnership affairs, with a periodic, perhaps annual, meeting of the entire partnership to accept the accounts, to transact business reserved to the meeting, and to appoint members to the governing body.

3. Some countries have a form of limited liability partnerships (LLP). This governance vehicle gives the benefits of limited liability to the members but allows the flexibility of

organizing as a traditional partnership. The governance of an LLP is similar to that of a partnership: members provide the capital, contribute personally, and share profits and losses. To give some protection to those dealing with a limited partnership, however, the disclosure requirements tend to be more stringent than for a traditional partnership, and similar to those of a company.

4. A holding company is the company at the head of the group pyramid. Its board of directors is often called the 'main board'. A subsidiary company is one in which the holding or parent company holds all or a majority of the voting shares in that company. An associated company is one in which the holding company, though not holding a majority of the shares, has sufficient interests to control it and determine its actions.

5. • Group-company self-governance, allowing each company in the group to govern itself and manage its own affairs, subject to overall group-wide policies and resource allocation

   • Group-wide governance, treating the group companies as divisions or departments of the holding company

6. The opportunity for cross-group coordination, the sharing of expertise, training, and development of future main board directors, management development, and the building of group norms and culture.

7. A family council, consisting of all the family members who own shares (management and non-management), meets prior to meetings of the shareholders and the directors to identify issues that affect family members and to resolve them in the best interest of the family.

8. An investment fund that invests a country's financial surpluses in the shares of companies in other countries. Arab and Asian countries' state-owned funds have been used to invest in the United States and Europe.

9. Sovereign-wealth funds have invested in telecoms, technology, real estate, ports, and transport operations, and in the financial sectors.

10. The distinguishing features include:

    • They are working for the public good (not the benefit of shareholders)

    • Their aims reflect community objectives (not bottom-line profit)

    • Their legal status is rooted in the law of trusts, charities, cooperatives, or other legal acts (not company law)

    • Their form can take various legal structures (not a limited company)

    • Their underpinning constitution determines their form and purpose

    • Governance is provided by a governing body, which can be known variously as a council, board of trustees, management committee, etc.

    • Their performance is measured by the achievement of multiple goals and is often difficult to measure

    • Their governing body is often large and drawn entirely from outside, non-executive members

    • Their objectives can conflict

    • Nomination to the governing body may come from the members, funding bodies, representative bodies (staff, beneficiaries, funding bodies, the local community, etc.), subject to the constitution

    • The top executive and the top management team are typically invited to attend meetings of the governing body, make reports, and answer questions, but are seldom voting members of it

    • Membership of the governing body is usually voluntary and unpaid, with no fees, remuneration, or capital gains, subject perhaps to reasonable expenses

    • Trustees are the guardian angels of a voluntary organization, watching over its activities, and need to be competent, informed, but personally disinterested

Chapter 6

1. Strategy formulation is the process of generating and reviewing alternative longer term directions for the firm that lead towards the achievement of its purpose.

2. A mission statement is a concrete statement of the company's purpose, aims, and direction, which can inspire employees and inform customers and other stakeholders.

3. In long range planning the planner is, conceptually, inside the organization looking out. The approach fails to take a strategic perspective, perpetuating the existing business, rather than recognizing strategic changes in technology, markets, and competition, and ignoring the economic and social context.

4. • Who is currently competing in our market?
   • What strategic powers do our upstream suppliers of goods and services have?
   • What strategic powers do our downstream distributors and ultimate customers have?
   • Could our customers needs be met in other ways—with substitute goods or services?
   • Could other firms enter the market?

5. Resource based strategic theory sees a firm as a collection of resources and capabilities that need to be utilized to create a winning strategy. The resources could include access to capital, employee skills, unique products or services, managerial talent and experience, equipment and buildings, or goodwill. This resource based perspective seeks to find a fit between a firm's internal capabilities and its external market situation that will produce a competitive advantage.

6. Corporate policies can be thought of as the rules, systems, and procedures that are laid down by the board to guide and constrain executive management.

7. • Financial accounts
   • Profit and loss account and balance sheet
   • Budgetary control with cost centres
   • Profit performance with profit or profitability centres
   • Multiple performance measures control systems

8. In designing a management control system, in which units of the organization are to be held responsible for various performance criteria, in seeking to meet their required performance each unit will tend to take action which is beneficial to achieving its own objectives but potentially detrimental to the organization as a whole.

9. Universally, the answer is: the members. In the case of a joint stock, limited liability company, the members are those shareholders with voting rights. In a cooperative society the members are those with voting rights under the constitution. In a professional body the members are those paid-up and qualified to vote under the rules of that association.

10. To reduce the reports presented to directors some firms rely on exception reporting in which only significant variations from planned performance have occurred and board level action required.

Chapter 7

1. The Cadbury Report called for:
   • The wider use of independent non-executive directors
   • The introduction of an audit committee of the board with a minimum of three non-executive directors with a majority of them independent
   • The division of responsibilities between the chairman of the board and the chief executive. But, should the roles be combined, the board should have a strong independent element
   • The use of a remuneration committee of the board to oversee executive rewards
   • The introduction of a nomination committee with independent directors to propose new board members and
   • Adherence to a detailed code of best practice

2. (a) On professional development
   • All directors should receive induction training
   • All directors should have regular updates on relevant skills, knowledge, and familiarity with the company

   (b) On boards performance evaluation
   • Boards should undertake an annual evaluation of their own performance
   • There should also be an annual assessment of the performance of individual directors and of the main board committees

3. The OECD has produced sets of principles that are intended to assist governments in their efforts to evaluate and improve the legal, international, and regulatory framework for corporate governance in their countries, and to provide guidance and suggestions to stock exchanges, investors, corporations, and others that have a role in the process of developing good corporate governance.

4. Companies should manage effectively relationships with their employees, suppliers, and customers and with others who have a legitimate interest in the company's activities. Companies should behave ethically and have regard for the environment and society as a whole (Principle 9).

5. Section 404 of the Act requires management to produce an 'internal control report' as part of each annual Exchange Act report. The report is required to affirm *'the responsibility of management for establishing and maintaining an adequate internal control structure and procedures for financial reporting'*.

6. • Principle 7: Companies should have and continue to develop coherent strategies for each business unit. These should ideally be expressed in terms of market prospects and of the competitive advantage the business has in exploiting these prospects. The company should understand the factors which drive market growth, and the particular strengths which underpin the competitive position

   • Principle 8: Companies should be able to explain why they are the best 'parent' of the businesses they run. Where they are not best parent they should be developing plans to resolve the issue

7. No director qualifies as 'independent' unless the board of directors affirmatively determines that the director has no material relationship with the listed company (either directly or as a partner, shareholder, or officer of an organization that has a relationship with the company).

8. The audit committee must have a minimum of three members. Each member of the audit committee must be financially literate, as such qualification is interpreted by the company's board in its business judgement, or must become financially literate within a reasonable period of time after his or her appointment to the audit committee. In addition, at least one member of the audit committee must have accounting or related financial management expertise, as the company's board interprets such qualification in its business judgement.

9. Listed companies must adopt and disclose a code of business conduct and ethics for directors, officers, and employees, and promptly disclose any waivers of the code for directors or executive officers.

10. The responsibilities of the board include the strategic guidance of the company, the effective monitoring of management by the board, and the board's accountability to the company and the shareholders.

Chapter 8

1. Refer to the text.

2. Table 8.5 Proportion of individual, as against institutional, investors in the UK and USA

Country	Individuals	Institutional investors
UK	19%	58%
USA	51%	41%

3. Refer to the text.

4. Studies suggest that overseas Chinese firms are:
   • Family-centric with close family control
   • In listed companies the public are in a minority with a controlling equity stake kept within the family, sometimes causing problems of family related transactions
   • Entrepreneurial often with a dominant entrepreneur, centralized decision making, with close personal links emphasizing trust and control
   • Paternalistic management style, in a social fabric dependent on relationships and social harmony, avoiding confrontation and the risk of loss of 'face'

- Intuitive strategy formulation in which business is seen as more of a succession of contracts or ventures, relying on intuition, superstition, and tough-minded bargaining rather than quantitative analysis

5. Listing 'through the back door' involves the acquisition of a Hong Kong listed company and backing a China business into this shell.

6. Refer to the text.

7. • A reliable legal system
   - A stock market with liquidity
   - Financial institutions
   - Regulatory authorities
   - A companies registry
   - Accounting and legal professions
   - Auditing firms that are professional
   - Professional organizations
   - Educational institutions
   - Consulting organizations
   - Financial and corporate governance training, continuous professional development
   - Corporate governance research with academic and professional publications

8. • Corporate governance codes of good practice
   - Securities regulations
   - International accounting standards
   - Global concentration of audit practices
   - Raising capital on overseas stock exchanges
   - International institutional investors
   - Research publications, international conferences, and professional journals

9. • Legal differences
   - Standards in the legal process
   - Stock market differences
   - Ownership structures
   - Historical, cultural, and ethnic differences

10. Trust.

Chapter 9

1. Agency theory is based on the premise that a director will maximize his or her own personal utility and cannot be expected to act in the best interests of the shareholder. Stewardship theory follows the legal perspective that directors can be trusted to fulfil their fiduciary duty to shareholders.

2. Stewardship theory follows the legal requirement for directors to act solely in the interests of the shareholders. Stakeholder philosophy believes that companies should be accountable to a wide range of stakeholders affected by its activities.

Chapter 10

1. The fundamental power of the board is derived from the shareholders who have delegated the running of the company to the directors. This power is reinforced by authority derived from the company's constitution backed up by company law.

2. • By a majority or dominant shareholder putting pressure on the board
   - From the threat of a potential takeover
   - By the prospect of litigation
   - Through the influence of the auditors
   - From the effects of legislation and regulation
   - From media pressure and other external exhortation
   - By a dominant or charismatic leader and
   - Obviously, through the changing of business circumstances

3. Knowledge power is power derived from access to information, skills, or experiences not available to the other directors (e.g. the influence on board discussions about international currency rates by the INED who is also a director of an international bank).

4. • Personality power
   - Knowledge power
   - Sanction power
   - Interpersonal power
   - Networking power
   - Ownership power
   - Representative power

5. Professional, representative, rubber-stamp, and country club.

6. See the text.

7. To manage the board.

8. • Management of the board
   • Management of meetings
   • Strategic leadership
   • Linking the board with management
   • Arbitration
   • Figurehead or public face of the company

9. See the text.

10. See the text.

Chapter 11

1. Integrity means being able to distinguish right from wrong and judge corporate behaviour accordingly. It means being able to recognize and declare a conflict of interest. It means acting in the company interest, not self interest, resisting the temptation to make an unacceptable personal gain. Essentially integrity means acting honestly.

2. • Integrity and honesty
   • Passion for customers, for our partners, and for technology
   • Openness and respectfulness
   • Taking on big challenges and seeing them through
   • Constructive self-criticism, self-improvement, and personal excellence
   • Accountability to customers, shareholders, partners, and employees for commitments, results, and quality

3. They can be summarized as intellect, character, and personality.

4. The essential director level skills include:
   • Strategic reasoning, perception, and vision
   • A critical faculty capable of quantitative and qualitative analysis and financial interpretation
   • Planning and decision making capabilities
   • Communication and interpersonal skills
   • Networking and political abilities

5. See the text.

6. See the text.

7. Character traits, what some call 'strength of character', includes being independently minded, objective, and impartial. A director needs to be capable of moving towards consensus. Yet, from time to time a director needs to be tough-minded, tenacious, and resilient, with the courage to make a stand. Further a director needs to have a balanced approach to risk, be results orientated—neither risk-averse nor rash.

8. • A duty of trust—to exercise a fiduciary responsibility to the shareholders
   • A duty of care—to exercise reasonable care, diligence, and skill

9. Related party transactions provide a good example of the requirement to disclose personal interests. The listing rules of most stock exchanges and securities regulators require related party transactions to be disclosed and, often, approved by the other shareholders.

10. A Public Company Accounting Oversight Board (PCAOB) was created under the SOX Act to oversee public accounting (auditing) firms and to issue accounting standards.

Chapter 12

1. Fourteen possible duties are listed in the text.

2. The duties of the remuneration committee include the duty to establish a formal and transparent procedure for developing policy on top executive remuneration and for determining the remuneration packages of each director.

3. The primary role of the nomination committee is to make recommendations on new appointments to the board. It is an attempt to prevent the board becoming a cosy club, in which the incumbent members appoint like-minded people to join their ranks.

4. Why, what, when, where, and who.

5. A director cannot opt out of certain items because he or she lacks appropriate knowledge, although they may rely on information received and the opinions of fellow directors, given in good faith, unless they have any reason to doubt—in which case they must pursue the issue to its root.

6. Although, subject to the articles, there are no specific rules governing the content or format of minutes of board or board subcommittee

meetings, they should provide a competent and complete record of what transpired, what was decided, what actions are to be taken, by whom, and when.

7. A good report with high quality information is
   • Understandable
   • Reliable
   • Relevant
   • Comprehensive
   • Concise
   • Timely
   • Cost-effective

8. A newly appointed director needs a proper induction programme to reduce the learning time taken before beginning to make significant contributions to board deliberations.

9. Director and officer insurance.

10. No. Actions can be brought against the company, the board, and/or individual directors. Claims for unlimited amounts can make directors' personal assets at risk.

Chapter 13

1. See text.

2. In many cases at the moment, director appraisals are being conducted in an informal way, with the chairman personally assessing the performance and commenting privately to the director involved.

3. Yes, the pressure is on for director appraisals to be more formalized. To set up such a process needs a board policy decision, with the full support of all the directors.

4. Typically, the output of an individual director performance assessment will be a confidential report to the chairman and, possibly, the chairman of the board's nomination committee, if involved in the review process. Given the personal nature of the report most chairmen will not table it at a board meeting, but discuss the relevant portion with each director.

5. In most cases the chairman's performance is reflected in the performance of the company

as a whole. Continued poor performance will bring calls for a change of chairman from major investors, the media, or occasionally from fellow directors who are dissatisfied.

6. Yes and yes.

7. • The chairman often assumes the role
   • An experienced INED, perhaps the senior INED
   • An executive director, such as the CEO or the CFO
   • The internal auditor
   • The audit committee
   • A past chairman
   • A respected chairman or INED from the board of another company not in competition
   • An independent organization or firms of consultants

8. Refer to the text.

9. • Ownership structure and external influences
   • Shareholder rights and relations
   • Transparency, disclosure, and audit
   • Board structure and effectiveness

10. • The World Bank and International Monetary Fund—Reports on the Observance of Standards and Codes (ROSC) programme
    • The European Bank for Reconstruction and Development (EBRD) corporate governance assessment project (2003)
    • The FTSE ISS CGI company ratings

Chapter 14

1. The UK Combined Code. The Sarbanes-Oxley Act. The Basel II agreement.

2. Audit committees tend to be orientated towards the past, involved with audit outcomes and approving accountability information for publication—whilst risk assessment needs a proactive, forward-looking orientation.

3. Form a risk assessment or risk management committee as a distinct standing committee of the board.

4. Such a risk management committee might have four or five members, wholly or mainly INEDs, with appropriate business experience, meeting perhaps four times a year, and reporting to the board as a whole. Members of senior management and external experts in risk might be invited to attend meetings to advise.

5. In a management based risk management committee, which might include the CEO, the CFO, profit-responsible division or unit heads, and the CRO, with external experts invited to attend to advise.

6. See the details in the text.

7. • The business environment
   • Competitive issues
   • Compliance matters
   • Employee problems
   • Operational factors

8. • Risk recognition
   • Risk assessment
   • Risk evaluation
   • Risk management policies
   • Risk monitoring
   • Risk transfer (buying insurance, creating a derivative, or just self-insuring).

9. • A simple tabular approach
   • A questionnaire designed to identify risks and hazards
   • Mind mapping
   • Risk benchmarking by industry, country, or other company
   • Software programs and systems

10. • Avoid the risk. Do not commit to the planned action. Abandon the project
    • Mitigate the risk by making capital investment or incurring ongoing expenditure
    • Transfer the risk. Enter derivative agreements. Insure against the risk
    • Risk retention. Accept the risk. Self-insure

Chapter 15

1. The stakeholders of a company could include:
   • Customers of the end product or service

   • Agents, distributors, and others in the downstream supply chain
   • Original suppliers and others in the upstream supply chain
   • Other creditors
   • Bankers and non-equity sources of finance
   • Employees including managers
   • Self-employed contractors to the company

2. A firm's 'socially responsible activities' might include:
   • The contributions of facilities or staff time to local and other organizations
   • Educational and academic contributions
   • Support for local and other academic institutions
   • Contributions to research and similar activities
   • Aesthetic and arts contributions
   • Expenditure on building and landscape design
   • Sponsorship of arts, crafts, and similar activities
   • Sports and leisure contributions

3. Although many research studies have been conducted, a basic problem has been how to measure CSR. Some studies have also been marred by an ideological bias or limited methodology. Although some studies have shown a limited correlation between firms' CSR and their financial performance, the present view is that linkages are indecisive.

4. The Global Reporting Initiative (GRI) is a worldwide, multi-stakeholder network to create and develop the Sustainability Reporting Framework, in which business, civil society, labour, investors, accountants, and others collaborate.

5. The United Nations Brundtland Report defines sustainable development as '*development that meets the needs of the present without compromising the ability of future generations to meet their own needs*'.

6. The Global Reporting Initiative (GRI) is based on the underlying belief that reporting on economic, environmental, and social performance by all organizations should be as routine and comparable as financial reporting.

7. GRI is a worldwide, multi-stakeholder network, in which business, civil society, labour, investors, accountants, and others collaborate to create and develop the Sustainability Reporting Framework.

8. GRI facilitates transparency and accountability by organizations of all sizes and sectors, across the world—companies, governmental and other public agencies, and non-profit entities.

9. The principles and guidance section of the GRI framework provides guidance and principles for defining the report content, which helps to determine what should be covered by the sustainability report and where its boundaries should be drawn.

10. The content principles of the GRI framework cover materiality, stakeholder inclusiveness, sustainability context, and completeness, along with a brief set of tests for each principle.

Index

Accountability
board function, 131–132
board reviews, 316
delegation of board functions, 134–138
seven principles of public life, 274
Adaptability, 253
Agency theory
criticisms of, 222–223
fundamental challenge, 218–219
general principles, 219–220
links with performance, 220–222
Agendas
drafting points, 287
importance, 285–287
Lord Caldicote's approach, 286
Alliances
power and politics, 244
Alternative stock markets, 94
Appointment of directors
general principles, 55–57
likely future changes, 387
NGOs, 114
nomination committees, 71–72, 285, 319
Articles of association
contents, 28–31
dual class shares, 94, 95
Asia
complex corporate structures
chain structures, 84
cross shareholdings, 90
network structures, 87
family controlled companies, 101
implementation of governance below board
level, 261
international listed regulatory codes, 170–172
model of corporate governance, 189–190
Assessment. *see* **Performance assessment**
Associate companies
defined, 98
governance pyramids, 76–77
methods of governance
family controlled companies, 101–103
group wide governance, 100–101
overview, 98–99
self-governance, 99–100
Associate directors, 55

Audit requirements
audit committees, 67–70, 282–284, 319
Enron case history, 395–397
partnerships, 118
remaining questions, 378–379
Australia
development of regulation, 151–153
international listed regulatory codes, 170
ownership of listed countries, 182

Block shareholders, 91–92
Boards of directors
case studies
Arcelor Mittal, 63
Arthur Andersen, 69
BP, 71
Marks and Spencer, 58–59
performance assessment, 321
Sir Campbell Adamson, 290
Vodaphone, 60, 66
Volkswagen, 65
chairmen
combined chairman and CEO, 57–60
regulatory codes, 58–60
chairman's role
conflict resolution, 258
link between board and management, 257
management of board, 256
management of meetings, 256–257
public relations, 258–259
significance, 255–256
strategic leadership, 257
changing expectations, 17–18
chief executives
combined chairman and CEO, 57–60
regulatory codes, 58–60
committees
audit committees, 68–70
nominating committees, 71–72
overview, 67
remuneration committees, 70–71
corporate vision, 252
D&O insurance, 299–304
effectiveness of directors
induction, 294–295

Boards of directors (*continued*)
    remuneration, 296–298
    training and development, 295–296
  executive and non executive structures, 61–67
  functions
    accountability, 131–138
    balancing performance and
      conformance, 139
    monitoring and supervision, 129–131
    overview, 120–121
    policy making, 126–131
    strategy formulation, 121–129
  groups of companies, 99–100
  independence, 150
  information
    importance, 288
    occasional and non-routine sources, 290–292
    regular and routine sources, 288–290
  joint ventures, 113
  managing board committees
    audit committees, 282–284
    nomination committees, 285
    remuneration committees, 284
  meetings
    agendas, 285–287
    minutes, 287–288
  OECD principles of governance, 159
  organizational theories, 228–229
  performance assessment
    board reviews, 313–317
    company ratings, 321–325
    procedure, 317–320
    strategy formulation, 320–321
  power and politics, 241–250
  private and foreign-invested companies in
    China, 198
  risk transfer and avoidance, 343–346
  role of secretary, 292–294
  styles
    diversity, 250–255

Cadbury Report (1992), 146–150
Case studies
  board committees
    Arthur Andersen, 69
    BP, 71
  board structures
    Arcelor Mittal, 63
    Vodaphone, 66
    Volkswagen, 65
  boards of directors
    performance assessment, 321
    power and politics, 241–250
    Sir Campbell Adamson, 290

  chairmen and CEOs
    combined chairman and CEO at
      M&S, 58–59
    conflict at Vodaphone, 60
  chairman's role, 258–259
  company secretaries, 293
  complex corporate structures
    Agnelli chain structure, 85
    ARE group, 78
    General Electric, 83
    Hutchison Whampoa Ltd, 81
    tax havens, 79
    Union Carbide, 80
  corporate social responsibility
    CLP Group, 361–362
    HSBC Holdings Plc, 358–359
    Li & Fung Ltd, 360–361
    manufacturing company, 353–355
    resisting Exxon, 357
  D&O insurance, 299–304
  directors' attributes
    core competencies, 267–268
    Lord Black, 264–265
  dual class shares, 94, 95
  dual listed companies, 93
  forces for change, 386
  hedge funds
    LTCM, 104
    Man Group, 105–106
  Hermes Principles, 162–163
  incorporation
    American Red Cross, 33
    Network Rail, 34–35
  joint ventures, 112
  Maxwell affair, 16
  models of corporate governance
    China Sinopec, 199–200
    Gazprom, 202
    Siemens, 187
    TYCO, 185
    Yukos, 203–204
  network structures
    Elders IXL, 89
    Jardine Matheson Group, 87–88
    Overseas Trust Bank, 86
  NGO, 116
  partnerships, 117
  policy making, 127–129
  private equity firms, 108–109
  regulatory codes
    General Electric, 157
    Marconi, 154–155
  removal of directors, 57
  risk
    Northern Rock, 344–346
    pharmaceutical company, 334–335

risk profiling, 341–342
Sage Group Plc, 329
self-governance, 99–100
strategy formulation
  IBM/Microsoft, 125
  mission statements, 122
  SWOT analysis, 123
sustainability reporting
  General Motors, 364–365
  Swire Pacific, 366–368
theories of governance, 235–236
types of director
  cross-directorships, 55, 56
  independent directors, 50–53
  nominee directors, 53, 54
Wallenberg Group, 95
Chain structures, 82–85
Chairmen
assessment of individual directors, 312
board reviews, 316
code of practice, 58–60
combined chairman and CEO, 57–60
financial reporting, 132
private and foreign-invested companies in
  China, 198
remaining questions
  combined chairmen and CEOs, 375
  retiring CEOs becoming chairmen,
    375–376
role
  conflict resolution, 258
  link between board and management, 257
  management of board, 256
  management of meetings, 256–257
  public relations, 258–259
  significance, 255–256
  strategic leadership, 257
Character traits, 266
Chief executives
board reviews, 315, 318
code of practice, 58–60
combined chairman and CEO, 57–60
implementation of governance below board
  level, 260
joint ventures, 113
NGOs, 114
private and foreign-invested companies in
  China, 198
remaining questions
  combined chairmen and CEOs, 375
  retiring CEOs becoming chairmen,
    375–376
China
alternative stock markets, 95–96
board characteristic of listed companies, 68
cultural considerations, 21

models of governance in mainland China
  contemporary governance, 194–196
  emergence of company law, 192–194
  future proposals, 199
  private and foreign-invested companies, 198
  state control, 196–198
models of governance in overseas China,
  190–191
rule or principles based governance, 19–20
sovereign wealth funds, 111
Coalitions and cabals
power and politics, 244
Codes of practice. *see* **Regulatory codes**
Collaboration
corporate vision, 253
Combined Code
board and committee independence, 150
diligence, 150
origins and development, 146–150
performance assessment, 151
professional development, 150
Commitment
corporate vision, 253
Committees
audit committees, 67–70
board reviews, 316, 319
managing board committees
  audit committees, 282–284
  nomination committees, 285
  remuneration committees, 284
nominating committees, 71–72
overview, 67
remuneration committees, 70–71
**Commonwealth Association for Corporate
  Governance,** 160–161
Communication skills
core competency of director, 267
corporate visions, 254
power and politics, 244, 250
Companies. *see* **Corporate entities**
Company secretaries
case study, 293
Lord Denning on evolution of role, 294
role, 292–294
Complex corporate structures
agency theory, 218–219
alternative stock markets, 95
block shareholders, 91–92
case studies
  Agnelli chain structure, 85
  ARE group, 78
  General Electric, 83
  Hutchison Whampoa Ltd, 81
  tax havens, 79
  Union Carbide, 80
chain structures, 82–85

Complex corporate structures (*continued*)
 cross shareholdings, 90–91
 dual class shares, 94, 95
 dual listed companies, 92–93
 governance pyramids
  overview, 76–77
  principal organizational form, 77–83
 group company governance
  family controlled companies, 101–103
  group-wide governance, 99–101
  overview, 98–99
  self-governance, 99
 network structures, 85–90
 ownership patterns, 75–76
Compliance
 Chinese model, 199
 overview, 166
 principles or prescription, 158
Conflict
 chairman's role, 258
 corporate visions, 254
Conformance
 balancing performance and conformance, 139
 corporate visions, 254
Connected non-executive directors
 board styles, 252
 role, 51
Constitutions
 articles of association, 28–31
 dual class shares, 94
 limited liability companies, 27–28
 memorandum of association, 28–31
 necessity, 25–26
 NGOs, 113
 other forms of incorporation, 32–34
Corporate entities
 evolution of corporate governance in 21stC, 17
 forces for change
  international drivers, 382
  new organizational forms, 383
  overview, 380–381
  rate of change, 385–386
  societal expectations, 383
  theoretical drivers, 383–385
  United States of America, 381–382
 incorporation, 27–28
 likely future changes, 389–390
 need for new paradigm, 390–391
 regulatory policies from major companies, 163–165
Corporate governance. *see also* **Regulatory codes**
 alternative structures leading to improvement,
  392–393
 classical phraseology, 380
 evolution
  developments in 1980s, 12–13
  developments in 1990s, 13–15
  early practices, 8–9

 listed companies, 15–17
 new concepts, 22
 other corporate entities, 17
 overview, 7–8
 separation of management and ownership, 9–10
 significant developments, 10–12
 introduction, 1–2
 likely future changes
  choice of directors, 387
  information, 387, 388
  remuneration, 387
  reporting, 388
  scope of governance, 388
  social responsibility, 388–389
 new frontiers
  changing expectations, 17–18
  changing ownership, 18
  continuity and risk, 19
  cultural considerations, 21
  growing complexity, 18–19
  performance assessment, 20
  social responsibility, 22
  sustainability, 22
 ongoing issues, 391–392
 rationale for book, 2–4
 remaining questions
  combined chairmen and CEOs, 375
  external auditors, 378–379
  independent directors, 376–377
  institutional investors, 377
  listed companies, 377
  remuneration, 379–380
  retiring CEOs becoming chairmen, 375–376
  rules or principles, 374–375
  shareholders' rights, 377
 sources and layout of material, 4
Corporate social responsibility
 balancing responsibilities, 370–371
 case studies
  CLP Group, 361–362
  HSBC Holdings Plc, 358–359
  Li & Fung Ltd, 360–361
  manufacturing company, 353–355
  resisting Exxon, 357
 likely future changes, 388–389
 new expectations, 349–351
 reporting, 358–363
 strategies and policies, 351–357
Cronyism
 power and politics, 245
Cross-directorships, 55, 56
Cross shareholdings, 90–91
Cultural influences, 183

D&O insurance
 case studies, 301–304
 meaning and scope, 299–304

Deal making
 power and politics, 245
Decision taking
 core competency of director, 267
 corporate visions, 253
Definitions
 associate companies, 98
 holding companies, 98
 independent directors, 50–53
 subsidiary companies, 98
Delegation of functions
 implementation of governance below board
  level, 259–261
 management, 134–138
 NGO trustees, 115
Directors
 absence of single accepted theory, 233–236
 agency theory
  criticisms of, 222–223
  general principles, 219–220
 appointment, 55–57
 balancing performance and conformance, 139
 board functions
  accountability, 131–138
  balancing performance and
   conformance, 139
  monitoring and supervision, 129–131
  overview, 120–121
  policy making, 126–131
  strategy formulation, 121–129
 case studies
  core competencies, 267–268
  cross-directorships, 55, 56
  independent directors, 50–53
  Lord Black, 264–265
  Microsoft, 266
  nominee directors, 53
 changing expectations, 17–18
 complex corporate obligations
  chain structures, 84
  subsidiaries and associate companies, 82
 core competencies, 267–268
 desirable attributes, 263–267
 effectiveness
  induction, 294–295
  remuneration, 296–298
  training and development, 295–296
 independence, 150
 individual codes of conduct, 166
 induction
  checklist, 306–310
  importance, 294–295
 joint ventures, 113
 legal duties
  care, 274–275
  trust, 272–274
 likely future changes, 387

 managerial and class hegemony, 226–227
 OECD principles of governance, 159
 performance assessment
  changing attitudes, 311
  formal appraisals, 311–313
  new frontiers, 20
 private and foreign-invested companies in China, 198
 profiling, 318
 psychological theories, 227–228
 resource dependency theory, 226
 roles, 268–72
 seven principles of public life, 273
 shareholders' rights
  overview, 275–276
  United Kingdom, 278
  United States of America, 276–278
 stewardship theory
  criticisms of, 225–226
  general principles, 223–225
 types, 50–55
Disclosure of personal interests, 272
Divide and rule
 power and politics, 245
Dual class shares, 94, 95
Dual listed companies
 case study, 93
 complex corporate structures, 92–93

Empire building
 power and politics, 245
Enterprise risk management systems, 342–343
Equity finance, 182–183
Europe
 board characteristics of listed companies, 68
 chain structures, 84–85
 family controlled companies, 101
 implementation of governance below board level,
  260–261
 international listed regulatory codes, 172–179
 ownership of listed countries, 182
 significant developments in corporate
  governance, 11
 two-tier model of governance, 186–187
Evaluation. *see* **Performance assessment**
Executive directors
 board structure, 61–67
 board styles, 250–255
 family controlled companies, 102
 role, 50

Family controlled companies, 101–103
Financial reporting
 convergence or differentiation, 208
 stewardship theory
  criticisms of, 225–226
  general principles, 223–225
 transparency, 132–134

Game theory, 229
Global reporting initiative, 369–370
Governing directors, 54
Greenbury Report (1995), 146–150
Groups of companies
  agency theory, 218–219
  chain structures, 82–85
  cross shareholdings, 90–91
  governance pyramids
    overview, 76–77
    principal organizational form, 77–83
  methods of governance
    family controlled companies, 101–103
    group-wide governance, 99–101
    overview, 98–99
    self-governance, 99
  network structures, 85–90

Half truths
  power and politics, 246
Hedge funds
  activities, 103
  agency theory, 218
  case studies
    LTCM, 104
    Man Group, 105–106
Hegemony theory, 226–227
Hempel Report (1998), 146–150
Hermes Principles, 162–163
Hidden agendas
  power and politics, 246
Higgs Report (2003), 148–149
Holding companies
  defined, 98
  governance pyramids, 76–77
  methods of governance
    family controlled companies, 101–103
    group-wide governance, 99–101
    overview, 98–99
    self-governance, 99
  principal organizational form, 77–78

Incorporation
  case studies
    American Red Cross, 33
    Network Rail, 34–35
  constitutions
    articles of association, 28–31
    limited liability companies, 27–28
    memorandum of association, 28–31
    necessity, 25–26
    other forms of incorporation, 32–34
Independent directors
  board styles, 250–255
  defined, 50–53
  remaining questions, 376–377

Independent non-executive directors
  board reviews, 315
  board styles, 252
  essential attributes, 267
  role, 50–51
  subsidiaries and associate company obligations, 82
India
  family controlled companies, 101
  models of corporate governance, 205–207
  rule or principle based governance, 20
Induction of directors
  checklist, 306–310
  importance, 294–295
Information. *see also*
    Financial reporting; Transparency
  importance, 288
  likely future changes, 387, 388
  occasional and non-routine sources, 290–292
  regular and routine sources, 288–290
  risk information systems, 342–343
Innovation
  corporate visions, 253
Institutional investors
  regulatory codes, 161–163
  remaining questions, 377
Insurance. *see* D&O insurance
Integrity
  directors' attributes, 263–266
  seven principles of public life, 273
Intellect, 266
International Corporate Governance Network (ICGN), 160
International investors
  external effects on regulation, 183
  requirement for specific regulation, 209

Japan
  board characteristic of listed companies, 68
  complex corporate structures
    cross shareholdings, 90–91
    network structures, 87
  cultural considerations, 21
  implementation of governance below board level, 261
  international listed regulatory codes, 171
  model of corporate governance, 187–189
  ownership of listed countries, 182
Joint ventures
  agency theory, 218
  strategic alliances, 111–113

Leadership
  corporate vision, 252
Legal duties
  care, 274–275
  trust, 272–274

'Letter-box' companies, 81
Limited liability companies
    benefits of complex structure, 79–80
Limited liability partnerships, 118
Listed companies
    agency theory, 218
    balance of ownership in various countries, 182
    board characteristics, 68
    compliance regime, 158
    dual listed companies, 92–93
    evolution of corporate governance, 15–17
    NYSE Corporate Governance Rules, 398–409
    ownership of complex corporate structures, 75–76
    private equity firms, 107
    remaining questions, 377
    state control in China, 196–198
Lobbying
    power and politics, 246
Log rolling
    power and politics, 246

Management
    board committees
        audit committees, 282–284
        nomination committees, 285
        remuneration committees, 284
    chairman's role
        link between board and management, 257
        management of board, 256
        management of meetings, 256–257
    constitutions
        articles of association, 28–31
        limited liability companies, 27–28
        memorandum of association, 28–31
        necessity, 25–26
        other forms of incorporation, 32–33
    delegation of board functions, 134–138
    dual listed companies, 92–93
    groups of companies
        family controlled companies, 101–103
        group-wide governance, 99–101
        overview, 98–99
        self-governance, 99
    joint ventures, 113
    managerial and class hegemony, 226–227
    NGOs, 113
    risk
        management information systems, 342–343
        transfer and avoidance, 343–346
    risk levels, 331, 333
    separation from ownership, 9–10
Manipulation of meetings
    power and politics, 248–250
Meetings
    agendas, 285–287
    minutes, 287–288
    power and politics, 248–251

Memorandum of association
    contents, 28–31
    dual class shares, 94, 95
Mergers and acquisitions
    creation of complex structures, 81
    effect on models of corporate governance, 182–183
    network structures, 90
    private equity firms, 107
Minutes
    drafting points, 287
    importance, 287–288
Mission statements
    directors' attributes, 266
    strategy formulation, 122
Models of corporate governance. *see also*
        Regulatory codes
    Asia, 189–190
    case studies
        China Sinopec, 199–200
        Gazprom, 202
        Siemens, 187
        TYCO, 185
        Yukos, 203–204
    China
        mainland China, 192–200
        overseas China, 190–191
    convergence or differentiation, 208–210
    essential institutions, 210–211
    European two-tier model, 186–187
    evolution of corporate governance, 19–20
    external effects on
        culture, 183
        equity finance, 183
        mergers and acquisitions, 182–183
        patterns of ownership, 181–182
    India, 205–207
    Japan, 187–189
    Middle East, 207–208
    Russia, 200–205
    UK principles based model, 184–186
    US rule based system, 183–184
Monitoring and supervision
    accountability, 131–132
    board reviews, 316
    delegation of board functions, 134–138
    overview, 120–121
    transparency, 132–134

Network structures
    case studies
        Elders IXL, 89
        Jardine Matheson Group, 87–88
        Overseas Trust Bank, 86
Nominated Advisers, 94–95
Nomination committees, 71–72
Nominee directors, 53

Non-executive directors
  board structure, 61–67
  board styles, 252
  essential attributes, 267
  independence, 150
  individual codes of conduct, 166
  joint ventures, 113
  NGOs, 114
  role, 50–51
Non-government organizations
  board leadership, 114–116
  case study, 116
  distinguishing features, 113–114
  evolution of corporate governance in 21stC, 17
Non-profit corporate entities
  agency theory, 219
  evolution of corporate governance in 21stC, 17
  incorporation, 28–31

**Organization for Economic Development and
    Co-operation (OECD)**, 159
Organizational theories, 228–229
Outside directors, 53
Ownership
  absence of single accepted theory, 233–236
  agency theory
    criticisms of, 222–223
    general principles, 219–220
  complex corporate structures, 75–76
  effect on models of corporate
    governance, 181–182
  evolution of corporate governance
    changing patterns, 18
    separation from management, 9–10
  stakeholder philosophies
    general principles, 229–231
    OECD principles of governance, 159
    public service regulation, 165
  stewardship theory
    criticisms of, 225–226
    general principles, 223–225

Partnerships
  audit requirements, 118
  case study, 117
  defined, 116–117
  limited liability partnerships, 118
  regulation and constraints, 117
Performance assessment
  balancing performance and conformance, 139
  boards of directors
    board reviews, 313–317
    company ratings, 321–325
    procedure, 317–320
    strategy formulation, 320–321
  Enron case history, 395–397

individual directors
  changing attitudes, 311
  formal appraisals, 311–313
international approach to governance, 325–326
links with agency theory, 220–222
new frontiers
  countries, 20–21
  directors, 20
NGOs, 113
Personality traits, 266–267
Philosophies. *see* **Theories of governance**
Policies. *see* **Regulatory codes**
Policy making
  board function, 126–131
  board reviews, 316, 319
  case study, 127–129
  corporate social responsibility, 351–357
  delegation of board functions, 134–138
  overview, 120–121
  risk transfer and avoidance, 343–346
Political skills
  core competency of director, 267
  meaning and scope, 241–250
Private companies
  agency theory, 218
  evolution of corporate governance in 21stC, 17
  family controlled companies, 101–103
  private equity acquisitions, 108
Private equity firms, 106–110
  case study, 108–109
  regulatory codes, 109–110
Propaganda
  power and politics, 246
Psychological theories, 227–228
Public companies. *see* **Listed companies**
Public relations
  chairman's role, 258–259
  director's role, 270
Public service regulation, 165

Rating systems, 321–325
Regulatory codes. *see also* **Corporate governance;
    Models of corporate governance**
  case studies
    General Electric, 157
    Marconi, 154–155
  combined chairman and CEO, 57–60
  Combined Code
    board and committee independence, 150
    diligence, 150
    origins and development, 146–150
    performance assessment, 151
    professional development, 150
  compliance, 166
  convergence or differentiation, 208–210
  hedge funds, 105

implementation below board level, 259–261

individual directors, 166

institutional investors, 161–163

international agencies

    Commonwealth Association for Corporate Governance, 160–161

    International Corporate Governance Network, 160

    OECD, 159

international listed codes

    Africa, 169

    Asia, 170–172

    Australia and New Zealand, 170

    Europe, 172–179

    India, 171

    Japan, 171

    North America, 179

    South America, 180

    United States of America, 179–180

    West Indies, 180

NGOs, 114

NYSE Corporate Governance Rules, 398–409

other countries

    Australia, 151–153

    Canada, 154

    South Africa, 153–154

    United States of America, 155–158

overview, 145–146

policies from major companies, 163–165

private equity firms, 109–110

public services, 165

simplification by group structure, 78

Relationships

corporate vision, 254

Removal of directors, 57

Remuneration

board reviews, 319

committees, 70–71, 284

likely future changes, 387

overview, 296–298

remaining questions, 379–380

Reporting

financial reporting

    convergence or differentiation, 208

    stewardship theory, 225–226

    transparency, 132–134

global reporting initiative, 369–370

social responsibility, 358–363

sustainability, 363–368

Resource dependency theory, 226

Responsibility. *see* **Social responsibility**

Risk

alternative stock markets, 94–96

analysis, 335–337

board reviews, 316

case studies

    Northern Rock, 344–346

pharmaceutical company, 334–335

    risk profiling, 341–342

    Sage Group Plc, 329

Enron case history, 395–397

evaluation, 340–342

hedge funds, 104

levels and types, 331–335

management information systems, 342–343

management manual, 333

network structures, 90

overall responsibility, 328–331

recognition and assessment

    benchmarking, 339

    mind mapping, 338

    overview, 337–338

    questionnaires, 338

    software programs and systems, 339–340

    tabular approach, 338

transfer and avoidance, 343–346

Rival camps

power and politics, 247

'Safe harbour' provisions, 133

Scaremongering

power and politics, 247

Secretaries. *see* **Company secretaries**

Shadow directors, 53

Shareholders, 159

absence of single accepted theory, 233–236

accountability of board, 131–132

agency theory

    criticisms of, 222–223

    general principles, 219–220

complex corporate structures

    block shareholders, 91–92

    chain structures, 82–85

    dual class shares, 94, 95

    dual listed companies, 92–93

    governance pyramids, 76–83

    network structures, 85–90

    overview, 75–76

dual class shares, 94, 95

family controlled companies, 101–103

NGOs, 113

regulatory codes from institutional investors, 161–163

remaining questions, 377

rights

    overview, 275–276

    United Kingdom, 278

    United States of America, 276–278

stewardship theory

    criticisms of, 225–226

    general principles, 223–225

Snowing

power and politics, 247

Social network theory, 226
Social responsibility
  balancing responsibilities, 370–371
  likely future changes, 388–389
  new expectations, 22, 349–351
  reporting, 358–363
  strategies and policies, 351–357
Sovereign wealth funds
  criticisms, 111
  evolution and scale, 110–111
Spinning
  power and politics, 247
Sponsorship
  power and politics, 247
Stakeholder philosophies
  corporate social responsibility, 355
  general principles, 229–231
  OECD principles of governance, 159
  public service regulation, 165
Status
  corporate visions, 254
Stewardship theory
  criticisms of, 225–226
  general principles, 223–225
Strategy formulation
  alliances, 112–113
  board function, 121–126
  board reviews, 316
  case studies
    IBM/Microsoft, 125
    mission statements, 122
    SWOT analysis, 123
  chairman's role, 257
  core competency of director, 267
  corporate social responsibility, 351–357, 355
  delegation of board functions, 134–138
  Enron case history, 395–397
  overview, 120–121
  risk transfer and avoidance, 343–346
Sub-optimization
  power and politics, 248
Subsidiaries
Subsidiary companies
  defined, 98
  governance pyramids, 76–77
  methods of governance
    family controlled companies, 101–103
    group-wide governance, 99–101
    overview, 98–99
    self-governance, 99
  principal organizational form, 76–77
Supervision. see Monitoring and supervision
Sustainability
  case studies
    General Motors, 364–365
    Swire Pacific, 366–368

global reporting initiative, 369–370
new expectations, 22
reporting, 363–368
SWOT analysis, 123
Systems theory, 231–233

Taxation
  benefits of complex structure, 78–79
  dual listed companies, 92–93
  group-wide governance, 99–101
  network structures, 90
  private equity firms, 109
Theories of governance
  absence of single accepted basis, 233–236
  agency theory
    criticisms of, 222–223
    fundamental challenge, 218–219
    general principles, 219–220
    links with performance, 220–222
  case study, 235–236
  forces for change, 383–385
  managerial and class hegemony, 226–227
  organizational theories, 228–229
  principles or prescription in regulatory codes, 158
  psychological theories, 227–228
  remaining questions, 374–375
  resource dependency theory, 226
  stakeholder philosophies, 229–231
  stewardship theory
    criticisms of, 225–226
    general principles, 223–225
  systems theory, 231–233
  transaction cost economics, 223
Transaction cost economics, 223
Transparency
  board function, 132–134
  hedge funds, 105
  NGOs, 115
  OECD principles of governance, 159
  private equity firms, 107
  seven principles of public life, 273
  sovereign wealth funds, 111
Trust
  corporate visions, 254–255
  legal duties, 272–274
Trustees
  NGOs
    appointment, 114
    board leadership, 114–116
  voluntary sector regulation, 165

United Kingdom
  board characteristic of listed companies, 68
  Combined Code
    board and committee independence, 150
    diligence, 150

origins and development, 146–150
performance assessment, 151
principles or prescription, 158
professional development, 150
evolution of corporate governance
continuity and risk, 19
developments in 1980s, 12–13
developments in 1990s, 13–15
listed companies, 15–17
rule or principles based governance, 19–20
significant developments, 11–12
ownership of listed countries, 182
principles based model, 184–186
shareholders' rights, 278
United States of America
board characteristic of listed companies, 68
evolution of corporate governance
continuity and risk, 19
developments in 1980s, 12
developments in 1990s, 13–15
listed companies, 15–17
rule or principles based governance, 19–20

separation of management and ownership,
9–10
significant developments, 10–12
forces for change, 381–382
implementation of governance below board
level, 260
international listed regulatory codes, 179–180
NYSE Corporate Governance Rules, 398–409
objections to sovereign wealth funds, 111
ownership of listed countries, 182
regulatory codes
origins and development of SOX Act, 155–158
principles or prescription, 158
rule based model, 183–184
shareholders' rights, 276–278
Universal ownership, 91–92

Voluntary sector regulation, 165

Window dressing
power and politics, 248